CAMBRIDG

Boo.

MW01169617

Linguistics

From the earliest surviving glossaries and translations to nineteenth century academic philology and the growth of linguistics during the twentieth century, language has been the subject both of scholarly investigation and of practical handbooks produced for the upwardly mobile, as well as for travellers, traders, soldiers, missionaries and explorers. This collection will reissue a wide range of texts pertaining to language, including the work of Latin grammarians, groundbreaking early publications in Indo-European studies, accounts of indigenous languages, many of them now extinct, and texts by pioneering figures such as Jacob Grimm, Wilhelm von Humboldt and Ferdinand de Saussure.

Language and the Study of Language

William Dwight Whitney (1827–94) was the foremost American philologist and Sanskrit scholar of the nineteenth century. After studying in Germany, then at the forefront of linguistic scholarship, he assumed the chair of Sanskrit at Yale in 1854, with comparative philology added to his professorship in 1869. As well as teaching modern languages, Whitney published over 300 scholarly papers and books, acted as chief editor of the ten-volume *Century Dictionary*, and co-founded the American Philological Association. This 1867 work is an expanded version of lectures he had given at the Smithsonian Institution and in Boston, rewritten for a wider audience and emphasising the importance of recent German philological scholarship. The first five lectures concentrate mostly on the English language and the study of languages in general, including discussion of regional dialects and American English. The lectures then go on to look at the Indo-European language family as well as methods of linguistic research.

Cambridge University Press has long been a pioneer in the reissuing of out-of-print titles from its own backlist, producing digital reprints of books that are still sought after by scholars and students but could not be reprinted economically using traditional technology. The Cambridge Library Collection extends this activity to a wider range of books which are still of importance to researchers and professionals, either for the source material they contain, or as landmarks in the history of their academic discipline.

Drawing from the world-renowned collections in the Cambridge University Library and other partner libraries, and guided by the advice of experts in each subject area, Cambridge University Press is using state-of-the-art scanning machines in its own Printing House to capture the content of each book selected for inclusion. The files are processed to give a consistently clear, crisp image, and the books finished to the high quality standard for which the Press is recognised around the world. The latest print-on-demand technology ensures that the books will remain available indefinitely, and that orders for single or multiple copies can quickly be supplied.

The Cambridge Library Collection brings back to life books of enduring scholarly value (including out-of-copyright works originally issued by other publishers) across a wide range of disciplines in the humanities and social sciences and in science and technology.

Language
and
the Study of Language

Twelve Lectures on the Principles
of Linguistic Science

WILLIAM DWIGHT WHITNEY

CAMBRIDGE
UNIVERSITY PRESS

CAMBRIDGE
UNIVERSITY PRESS

University Printing House, Cambridge, CB2 8BS, United Kingdom

Published in the United States of America by Cambridge University Press, New York

Cambridge University Press is part of the University of Cambridge.

It furthers the University's mission by disseminating knowledge in the pursuit of education, learning and research at the highest international levels of excellence.

www.cambridge.org
Information on this title: www.cambridge.org/9781108062770

© in this compilation Cambridge University Press 2013

This edition first published 1867
This digitally printed version 2013

ISBN 978-1-108-06277-0 Paperback

LANGUAGE

AND

THE STUDY OF LANGUAGE.

LANGUAGE

AND

THE STUDY OF LANGUAGE:

TWELVE LECTURES

ON THE

PRINCIPLES OF LINGUISTIC SCIENCE.

BY

WILLIAM DWIGHT WHITNEY,

PROFESSOR OF SANSKRIT AND INSTRUCTOR IN MODERN LANGUAGES
IN YALE COLLEGE.

LONDON:

N. TRÜBNER & CO., 60, PATERNOSTER ROW.

1867.

JOHN CHILDS AND SON, PRINTERS.

TO

JAMES HADLEY,

PROFESSOR OF GREEK IN YALE COLLEGE,

THIS FRUIT OF STUDIES WHICH HE HAS DONE MORE

THAN ANY ONE ELSE TO ENCOURAGE AND AID

IS AFFECTIONATELY INSCRIBED.

PREFACE.

THE main argument of the following work was first drawn out in the form of six lectures " On the Principles of Linguistic Science," delivered at the Smithsonian Institution, in Washington, during the month of March, 1864. Of these, a brief abstract was printed in the Annual Report of the Institution published in the same year.* In the following winter (December, 1864, and January, 1865) they were again delivered as one of the regular courses before the Lowell Institute, in Boston, having been expanded into a series of twelve lectures. They are now laid before a wider public, essentially in their form as there presented. But they have been in the mean time carefully rewritten, and have suffered a not inconsiderable further expansion, as the removal of the enforced Procrustean limit, of sixty minutes to a lecture, has given opportunity to discuss with greater fulness important points in the general argument which had before come off with insufficient treatment. The chief matter of theory upon which my opinion has undergone any noteworthy modification is the part to be attributed to the onomatopoetic principle in the first steps of language-making (see the eleventh lecture). To this principle, at each revision

* Report for 1863, pp. 95 –116.

of my views, I have been led to assign a higher and
higher efficiency, partly by the natural effect of a deeper
study and clearer appreciation of the necessary conditions
of the case, partly under the influence of valuable works
upon the subject, recently issued.* In the general style
of presentation I have not thought it worth while to make
any change—not even to cast out those recapitulations
and repetitions which are well-nigh indispensable in a
course of lectures meant for oral delivery, though they
may and should be avoided in a work intended from the
outset for continuous reading and study.

More than one of the topics here treated have been
from time to time worked up separately, as communica-
tions to the American Oriental Society, and are concisely
reported in its Proceedings; also, within no long time
past, I have furnished, by request, to one or two of our
leading literary periodicals, papers upon special themes
in linguistic science which were, to no small extent,
virtual extracts from this work.

The principal facts upon which my reasonings are
founded have been for some time past the commonplaces
of comparative philology, and it was needless to refer for
them to any particular authorities : where I have consciously taken results recently won by an individual, and to
be regarded as his property, I have been careful to
acknowledge it. It is, however, my duty and my pleasure
here to confess my special obligations to those eminent
masters in linguistic science, Professors Heinrich Steinthal
of Berlin and August Schleicher of Jena, whose works †

* I will refer only to Mr Farrar's "Chapters on Language" (London,
1865), and to Professor Wedgwood's little book, "On the Origin of Language" (London, 1866).

† As chief among them, I would mention Steinthal's "Charakteristik der

I have had constantly upon my table, and have freely consulted, deriving from them great instruction and enlightenment, even when I have been obliged to differ most strongly from some of their theoretical views. Upon them I have been dependent, above all, in preparing my eighth and ninth lectures ;* my independent acquaintance with the languages of various type throughout the world being far from sufficient to enable me to describe them at first hand. I have also borrowed here and there an illustration from the "Lectures on the Science of Language" of Professor Max Müller, which are especially rich in such material.

To my friend Professor Fitz-Edward Hall, Librarian of the East India Office in London, I have to return my thanks for his kindness in undertaking the burdensome task of reading the revise of the sheets, as they went through the press.

It can hardly admit of question that at least so much knowledge of the nature, history, and classifications of language as is here presented ought to be included in every scheme of higher education, even for those who do not intend to become special students in comparative philology. Much more necessary, of course, is it to those who cherish such an intention. It is, I am convinced, a mistake to commence at once upon a course of detailed comparative philology with pupils who have only enjoyed the ordinary training in the classical or the modern languages,

Hauptsachlichsten Typen des Sprachbaues" (Berlin, 1860), and Schleicher's "Compendium der Vergleichenden Grammatik der Indogermanischen Sprachen" (Weimar, 1861 ; a new edition has appeared this year): other writings of both authors, of less extent and importance, are referred to by name in the marginal notes upon the text.

* I should mention also my indebtedness, as regards the Semitic languages, to the admirable work of M. Ernest Renan, the "Histoire Générale des Langues Sémitiques" (seconde édition, Paris, 1858).

or in both. They are liable either to fail of apprehending the value and interest of the infinity of particulars into which they are plunged, or else to become wholly absorbed in them, losing sight of the grand truths and principles which underlie and give significance to their work, and the recognition of which ought to govern its course throughout: perhaps even coming to combine with acuteness and erudition in etymological investigation views respecting the nature of language and the relations of languages of a wholly crude or fantastic character. I am not without hope that this book may be found a convenient and serviceable manual for use in our higher institutions of learning. I have made its substance the basis of my own instruction in the science of language, in Yale College, for some years past; and, as it appears to me, with gratifying success. In order to adapt it to such a purpose, I have endeavoured to combine a strictly logical and scientific plan with a popular mode of handling, and with such illustration of the topics treated as should be easily and universally apprehensible. If, however, the lecture style should be found too discursive and argumentative for a text-book of instruction, I may perhaps be led hereafter to prepare another work for that special use.

YALE COLLEGE,
New Haven, Conn., U. S. A.
August, 1867.

CONTENTS.

LECT.   PAGE
  I. Introductory : history, material, objects of linguistic science ;
     plan of these lectures. Fundamental inquiry. How we
     acquired our speech, and what it was ; differences of indi-
     vidual speech. What is the English language ; how kept
     in existence; its changes. Modes and causes of linguistic
     change.   1

 II. Nature of the force which produces the changes of language ;
     its modes of action. Language an institution, of his-
     torical growth; its study a moral science. Analogies of
     linguistic science with the physical science. Its methods
     historical. Etymology its foundation. Analysis of com-
     pound words. Genesis of affixes. Nature of all words as
     produced by actual composition.   34

III. Phonetic change ; its ground, action on compound words,
     part in word-making, and destructive effects. Replace-
     ment of one mode of formal distinction by another.
     Extension of analogies. Abolition of valuable distinc-
     tions. Conversion of sounds into one another. Physical
     characters of alphabetic sounds ; physical scheme of the
     English alphabet. Obsolescence and loss of words.
     Changes of meaning; their ground and methods. Variety
     of meanings of one word. Synonyms. Conversions of
     physical into spiritual meaning. Attenuation of mean-
     ing ; production of form-words. Variety of derivatives
     from one root. Unreflectiveness of the process of making
     names and forms. Conceptions antedate their names.
     Reason of a name historical, and founded in convenience,
     not necessity. Insignificance of derivation in practical
     use of language.   68

 IV. Varying rate and kind of linguistic growth, and causes affect-
     ing it. Modes of growth of the English language. In-

LECT.   PAGE

fluences conservative of linguistic identity.   Causes producing dialects; causes maintaining, producing, or extending homogeneity of speech.   Illustrations: history
of the German language; of the Latin ; of the English.
The English language in America.   136

V. Erroneous views of the relations of dialects.   Dialectic
variety implies original unity.   Effect of cultivation on a
language.   Grouping of languages by relationship.   Nearer
and remoter relations of the English.   Constitution of the
Indo-European family.   Proof of its unity.   Impossibility
of determining the place and time of its founders; their
culture and customs, inferred from their restored vocabulary.   176

VI. Languages and literatures of the Germanic, Slavonic, Lithuanic, Celtic, Italic, Greek, Iranian, and Indian branches
of Indo-European speech.   Interest of the family and its
study ; historical importance of the Indo-European races ;
their languages the basis of linguistic science.   Method
of linguistic research.   Comparative philology.   Errors
of linguistic method or its application.   209

VII. Beginnings of Indo-European language.   Actuality of linguistic analysis.   Roots, pronominal and verbal ;   their
character as the historical germs of our language ; development of inflective speech from them.   Production of
declensional, conjugational, and derivative apparatus,
and of the parts of speech.   Relation of synthetic and
analytic forms.   General character and course of inflective
development.   249

VIII. Families of languages, how established.   Characteristic
features of Indo-European language.   Semitic family : its
constitution, historic value, literatures, and linguistic
character.   Relation of Semitic to Indo-European language.   Scythian or Altaic family : its five branches :
their history, literatures, and character.   Unity of the
family somewhat doubtful.   288

IX. Uncertainties of genetic classification of languages.   " Turanian" family.   Dravidian group.   North-eastern Asiatic.
Monosyllabic tongues : Chinese, Farther Indian, Tibetan,
etc.   Malay-Polynesian and Melanesian families.   Egyptian
language and its asserted kindred : Hamitic family.   Languages of southern and central Africa.   Languages of
America : problem of derivation of American races.
Isolated tongues : Basque, Caucasian, etc.   322

CONTENTS.

LECT.   PAGE
X. Classification of languages. Morphological classifications;
their defects. Schleicher's morphological notation.
Classification by general rank. Superior value of genetic
division. Bearing of linguistic science on ethnology.
Comparative advantages and disadvantages of linguistic
and physical evidence of race. Indo-European language
and race mainly coincident. Difficulty of the ethnological problem. Inability of language to prove either unity
or variety of human species. Accidental correspondences:
futility of root comparisons.   356

XI. Origin of language. Conditions of the problem. In what
sense language is of divine origin. Desire of communication the immediate impulse to its production. Language and thought not identical. Thought possible
without language. Difference of mental action in man
and lower animals. Language the result and means of
analytic thought, the aid of higher thought. The voice
as instrument of expression. Acts and qualities the first
things named. The 'bow-wow,' 'pooh-pooh,' and 'ding-
dong' theories. Onomatopœia the true source of first
utterances. Its various modes and limitations. Its traces
mainly obliterated. Remaining obscurities of the problem. 395

XII. Why men alone can speak. Value of speech to man. Training involved in the acquisition of language. Reflex influence of language on mind and history. Writing the
natural aid and complement of speech. Fundamental
idea of written speech. Its development. Symbolic and
mnemonic objects. Picture writing. Egyptian hieroglyphs.
Chinese writing. Cuneiform characters. Syllabic modes
of writing. The Phenician alphabet and its descendants.
Greek and Latin alphabets. English alphabet. English
orthography. Rank of the English among languages. .. 436

LANGUAGE

AND

THE STUDY OF LANGUAGE.

LECTURE I.

Introductory : history, material, objects of linguistic science ; plan of
these lectures. Fundamental inquiry. How we acquired our speech,
and what it was; differences of individual speech. What is the English
language ; how kept in existence ; its changes. Modes and causes of
linguistic change.

THOSE who are engaged in the investigation of language
have but recently begun to claim for their study the rank
and title of a science. Its development as such has been
wholly the work of the present century, although its germs
go back to a much more ancient date. It has had a history,
in fact, not unlike that of the other sciences of observation
and induction—for example, geology, chemistry, astronomy,
physics—which the intellectual activity of modern times has
built up upon the scanty observations and crude inductions
of other days. Men have always been learning languages,
in greater or less measure ; adding to their own mother-
tongues the idioms of the races about them, for the practical
end of communication with those races, of access to their
thought and knowledge. There has, too, hardly been a time
when some have not been led on from the acquisition of
languages to the study of language. The interest of this
precious and wonderful possession of man, at once the sign
and the means of his superiority to the rest of the animal

1

creation, has in all ages strongly impressed the reflecting and philosophical, and impelled them to speculate respecting its nature, its history, and its origin. Researches into the genealogies and affinities of words have exercised the ingenuity of numberless generations of acute and inquiring minds. Moreover, the historical results attainable by such researches, the light cast by them upon the derivation and connection of races, have never wholly escaped recognition. The general objects and methods of linguistic study are far too obviously suggested, and of far too engaging interest, not to have won a certain share of regard, from the time when men first began to inquire into things and their causes.

Nothing, however, that deserved the name of a science was the result of these older investigations in the domain of language, any more than in those of chemistry and astronomy. Hasty generalizations, baseless hypotheses, inconclusive deductions, were as rife in the former department of study as they were in the two latter while yet passing through the preliminary stages of alchemy and astrology. The difficulty was in all the cases nearly the same; it lay in the paucity of observed facts, and in the faulty position which the inquirer assumed toward them. There had been no sufficient collection and classification of phenomena, to serve as the basis of inductive reasoning, for the establishment of sound methods and the elaboration of true results; and along with this, and partly in consequence of it, prejudice and assumption had usurped the place of induction. National self-sufficiency and inherited prepossession long helped to narrow the limits imposed by unfavourable circumstances upon the extent of linguistic knowledge, restraining that liberality of inquiry which is indispensable to the growth of a science. Ancient peoples were accustomed to think each its own dialect the only true language; other tongues were to them mere barbarous jargons, unworthy of study. Modern nations, in virtue of their history, their higher culture, and their Christianity, have been much less uncharitably exclusive; and their reverence for the two classical idioms, the Greek and Latin, and for the language of the Old Testament, the He-

brew, so widened their linguistic horizon as gradually to prepare the way for juster and more comprehensive views of
the character and history of human speech. The restless
and penetrating spirit of investigation, finally, of the nineteenth century, with its insatiable appetite for facts, its
tendency to induction, and its practical recognition of the
unity of human interests, and of the absolute value of all
means of knowledge respecting human conditions and history, has brought about as rapid a development in linguistic
study as in the kindred branches of physical study to which
we have already referred. The truth being once recognized
that no dialect, however rude and humble, is without worth,
or without a bearing upon the understanding of even the
most polished and cultivated tongues, all that followed was a
matter of course. Linguistic material was gathered in from
every quarter, literary, commercial, and philanthropic activity
combining to facilitate its collection and thorough examination. Ancient records were brought to light and deci-
phered ; new languages were dragged from obscurity and
made accessible to study.

The recognition, not long to be deferred when once attention was turned in the right direction, of the special relationship of the principal languages of Europe with one
another and with the languages of south-western Asia—the
establishment of the Indo-European family of languages—
was the turning-point in this history, the true beginning of
linguistic science. The great mass of dialects of the family,
descendants of a common parent, covering a period of four
thousand years with their converging lines of development,
supplied just the ground which the science needed to grow
up upon, working out its methods, getting fully into view
its ends, and devising the means of their attainment. The
true mode of fruitful investigation was discovered ; it appeared that a wide and searching comparison of kindred
idioms was the way in which to trace out their history, and
arrive at a real comprehension of the life and growth of language. Comparative philology, then, became the handmaid
of ethnology and history, the forerunner and founder of the
science of human speech.

1 *

No single circumstance more powerfully aided the onward
movement than the introduction to Western scholars of the
Sanskrit, the ancient and sacred dialect of India. Its exceeding age, its remarkable conservation of primitive
material and forms, its unequalled transparency of structure,
give it an indisputable right to the first place among the
tongues of the Indo-European family. Upon their comparison, already fruitfully begun, it cast a new and welcome
light, displaying clearly their hitherto obscure relations,
rectifying their doubtful etymologies, illustrating the laws
of research which must be followed in their study, and
in that of all other languages. What linguistic science
might have become without such a basis as was afforded it
in the Indo-European dialects, what Indo-European philology
might have become without the help of the Sanskrit, it were
idle to speculate : certain it is that they could not have
grown so rapidly, or reached for a long time to come the
state of advancement in which we now already behold them.
As a historical fact, the scientific study of human speech is
founded upon the comparative philology of the Indo-European languages, and this acknowledges the Sanskrit as its
most valuable means and aid.

But to draw out in detail the history of growth of linguistic science down to the present time, with particular notice
of its successive stages, and with due mention of the scholars
who have helped it on, does not lie within the plan of these
lectures. Interesting as the task might be found, its execution would require more time than we can spare from topics
of more essential consequence.* A brief word or two is all
we can afford to the subject. Germany is, far more than
any other country, the birthplace and home of the study of
language. There was produced, at the beginning of this
century, the most extensive and important of the preliminary collections of material, specimens of dialects with rude
attempt at their classification — the "Mithridates" of
Adelung and Vater. There Jacob Grimm gave the first
exemplification on a grand scale of the value and power of

* For many interesting details, see Professor Max Müller's Lectures on
the Science of Language, first series, third and fourth lectures.

the comparative method of investigation in language, in his grammar of the Germanic dialects, a work of gigantic labour, in which each dialect was made to explain the history and character of all, and all of each. There—what was of yet greater consequence—Bopp laid, in 1816, the foundation of Indo-European comparative philology, by his " Conjugation-system of the Sanskrit Language, as compared with the Greek, Latin, Persian, and German; " following it later with his Comparative Grammar of all the principal languages of the Indo-European family—a work which, more than any other, gave shape and substance to the science. There, too, the labours of such men as the Schlegels, Pott, and Wilhelm von Humboldt, especially of the last-named, extended its view and generalized its principles, making it no longer an investigation of the history of a single department of human speech, but a systematic and philosophical treatment of the phenomena of universal language and their causes. The names of Rask, too, the Danish scholar and traveller, and of Burnouf, the eminent French *savant*, must not be passed unnoticed among those of the founders of linguistic science. Indeed, how ripe the age was for the birth of this new branch of human knowledge, how natural an outgrowth it was of the circumstances amid which it arose, is shown by the fact that its most important methods were worked out and applied, more or less fully, at nearly the same time, by several independent scholars, of different countries—by Rask, Bopp, Grimm, Pott, Burnouf.

A host of worthy rivals and followers of the men whose names we have noted have arisen in all parts of Europe, and even in America, to continue the work which these had begun ; and by their aid the science has already attained a degree of advancement that is truly astonishing, considering its so recent origin. Though still in its young and rapidly growing stage, with its domain but just surveyed and only partially occupied, its basis is yet laid broadly and deeply enough, its methods and laws are sure enough, the objects it aims at and the results it is yielding are sufficiently important, in themselves and in their bearing upon other branches of human knowledge, to warrant it in challenging a place among the sciences, as not the least worthy, though one of the youngest, of their sisterhood, and to give it a claim which may not be disregarded to the attention of every scholar, and of every well-educated person.

The material and subject of linguistic science is language, in its entirety; all the accessible forms of human speech, in their infinite variety, whether still living in the minds and mouths of men, or preserved only in written documents, or carved on the scantier but more imperishable records of brass and stone. It has a field and scope limited to no age, and to no portion of mankind. The dialects of the obscurest and most humbly endowed races are its care, as well as those of the leaders in the world's history. Whenever and wherever a sound has dropped from the lips of a human being, to signalize to others the movements of his spirit, this science would fain take it up and study it, as having a character and office worthy of attentive examination. Every fact of every language, in the view of the linguistic student, calls for his investigation, since only in the light of all can any be completely understood. To assemble, arrange, and explain the whole body of linguistic phenomena, so as thoroughly to comprehend them, in each separate part and under all aspects, is his endeavour. His province, while touching, on the one hand, upon that of the philologist, or student of human thought and knowledge as deposited in literary records, and, on the other hand, upon that of the mere linguist, or learner of languages for their practical use, and while exchanging friendly aid with both of these, is yet distinct from either. He deals with language as the instrument of thought, its means of expression, not its record; he deals with simple words and phrases, not with sentences and texts. He aims to trace out the inner life of language, to discover its origin, to follow its successive steps of growth, and to deduce the laws that govern its mutations, the recognition of which shall account to him for both the unity and the variety of its present manifested phases; and, along with this, to apprehend the nature of language as a human endowment, its relation to thought, its influence upon the development of in-

tellect and the growth of knowledge, and the history of mind
and of knowledge as reflected in it.

The exceeding interest of this whole class of inquiries is
at first sight manifest, but it grows to our sense in measure
as we reflect upon it. We are apt to take language, like so
many other things of familiar daily use, as a thing of course,
without appreciating the mystery and deep significance
which belong to it. We clothe our thoughts without effort
or reflection in words and phrases, having regard only to the
practical ends of expression and communication, and the
power conferred by them : we do not think of the long history, of changes of form and changes of signification, through
which each individual vocable employed by us has passed, of
the labour which its origination and gradual elaboration has
cost to successive generations of thinkers and speakers. We
do not meditate upon the importance to us of this capacity
of expression, nor consider how entirely the history of man
would have been changed had he possessed no such faculty ;
how little of that enlightenment which we boast would have
been ours, if our ancestors had left no spoken memorial of
their mental and spiritual acquisitions ; how, in short, without speech, the noble endowments of our nature would have
remained almost wholly undeveloped and useless. It is, indeed, neither to be expected nor desired that our minds
should be continually penetrated with a realizing sense of
the marvellous character of language ; but we should be in-
excusable if we neglected altogether to submit it to such an
examination as should make us understand its nature and
history, and should prepare our minds to grasp by reflection
its whole significance.

These and such as these are the objects most directly
aimed at by the scientific student of language. But there
are others, of a different character, to which his investigations conduct him hardly less immediately, and which constitute an essential part of the interest which invests them.
It is a truth now almost as familiar as, fifty years ago, it
would have been deemed new and startling, that language
furnishes the principal means of fruitful inquiry into the

deeds and fates of mankind during the ages which precede direct historical record.   It enables us to determine, in the main, both the fact and the degree of relationship subsisting among the different divisions of mankind, and thus to group them together into families, the members of which must have once set forth from a common home, with a common character and a common culture, however widely separated, and however unlike in manners and institutions, we may find them to be, when they first come forth into the light of written history.   Upon the study of language is mainly founded the science of ethnology, the science which investigates the genealogy of nations.   I say, mainly founded, without wishing to depreciate the claims of physical science in this regard : the relation between linguistic and physical science, and their joint and respective value to ethnology, will be made the subject of discussion at a point further on in our inquiries.   But language is also pregnant with information respecting races which lies quite beyond the reach of physical science : it bears within itself plain evidences of mental and moral character and capacity, of degree of culture attained, of the history of knowledge, philosophy, and religious opinion, of intercourse among peoples, and even of the physical circumstances by which those who speak it have been surrounded.   It is, in brief, a volume of the most varied historical information to those who know how to read it and to derive the lessons it teaches.

To survey the whole vast field of linguistic science, taking even a rapid view of all the facts it embraces and the results derived from their examination, is obviously beyond our power in a brief series of lectures like the present.   I shall not, accordingly, attempt a formally systematic presentation of the subject, laying out its different departments and defining their limits and mutual relations.   It will, I am persuaded, be more for our profit to discuss in a somewhat general and familiar way the fundamental facts in the life of language, those which exhibit most clearly its character, and determine the method of its study.   We shall thus gain an insight into the nature of linguistic evidence, see how it is elicited from the material containing it, and what and how

it has force to prove. We shall, in short, endeavour to
arrive at an apprehension of the fundamental principles of
the science.   But we shall also find occasion to glance at
the main results accomplished by its means, seeking to understand what language is and what is its value to man, and
to recognize the great truths in human history which it has
been instrumental in establishing.

In order to these ends, we shall first take up one or two
preliminary questions, the discussion of which will show us
how language lives and grows, and how it is to be investigated, and will guide us to an understanding of the place
which its study occupies among the sciences.   We shall
then go on to a more detailed examination and illustration
of the processes of linguistic growth, and of the manner in
which they produce the incessant changes of form and content which language is everywhere and always undergoing.
We shall note, further, the various causes which affect the
kind and rate of linguistic change.   The result of these
processes of growth, in bringing about the separation of
languages into dialects, will next engage our attention.
This will prepare us for a construction of the group of
dialects, and the family of more distantly related languages,
of which our own English speech is a member, and for an
examination and estimate of the evidence which proves them
related.   The extent and importance, historical and linguistic, of this family will be set forth, and its course of development briefly sketched.   We shall next pass in review
the other great families into which the known forms of
human speech are divided, noticing their most striking
characteristics.   Then will be taken up certain general
questions, of prime interest and importance, suggested by
such a review—as the relative value and authority of linguistic and of physical evidence of race, and the bearing of language upon the ultimate question of the unity or variety of
the human species.   Finally, we shall consider the origin of
language, its relation to thought, and its value as an element
in human progress.   And a recognition of the aid which it
receives in this last respect from written and recorded
speech will lead us, by way of appendix, to take a cursory

view of the historical development of the art of writing.
The method which we shall follow will be, as much as
possible, the analytic rather than the synthetic, the inquiring rather than the dogmatic. We shall strive, above
all things, after clearness, and shall proceed always from
that which is well-known or obvious to that which is more
recondite and obscure, establishing principles by induction
from facts which lie within the cognizance of every well-
educated person. For this reason, our examples, whether
typical or illustrative, will be especially sought among the
phenomena of our own familiar idiom; since every living
and growing language has that within it which exemplifies
the essential facts and principles belonging to all human
speech. We shall also avoid, as far as is practicable, the
use of figurative, metaphysical, or technical phraseology,
endeavouring to talk the language of plain and homely fact.
Not a little of the mystery and obscurity which, in the
minds of many, invest the whole subject of language, is due
to the common employment respecting it of terms founded
on analogies instead of facts, and calling up the things they
represent surrounded and dimmed by a halo of fancy, instead of presenting sharply cut outlines and distinct lineaments.

The whole subject of linguistic investigation may be conveniently summed up in the single inquiry, "Why do we
speak as we do?" The essential character of the study of
language, as distinguished from the study of languages, lies
in this, that it seeks everywhere, not the facts, but the reasons of them; it asks, not how we speak, or should speak,
but for what reason; pursuing its search for reasons back to
the very ultimate facts of human history, and down into the
very depths of human nature. To cover the whole ground
of investigation by this inquiry, it needs to be proposed in
more than one sense; as the most fitting introduction to
our whole discussion, let us put it first in its plainest and
most restricted meaning: namely, why do we ourselves
speak the English as our mother-tongue, or native language,
instead of any other of the thousand varying forms of speech
current among men? It is indeed a simple question, but to

answer it distinctly and truly will lay the best possible foundation for our further progress, clearing our way of more than one of the imperfect apprehensions, or the misapprehensions, which are apt to encumber the steps of students of language.

The general answer is so obvious as hardly to require to be pointed out : we speak English because we were taught it by those who surrounded us in our infancy and growing age. It is our mother-tongue, because we got it from the lips of our mothers ; it is our native language, inasmuch as we were born, not indeed into the possession of it, but into the company of those who already spoke it, having learned it in the same way before us. We were not left to our own devices, to work out for ourselves the great problem of how to talk. In our case, there was no development of language out of our own internal resources, by the reflection of phenomena in consciousness, or however else we may choose to describe it ; by the action of a natural impulse, shaping ideas, and creating suitable expression for them. No sooner were our minds so far matured as to be capable of intelligently associating an idea and its sign, than we learned, first to recognize the persons and things about us, the most familiar acts and phenomena of our little world, by the names which others applied to them, and then to apply to them the same names ourselves. Thus, most of us learned first of all to stammer the childish words for ' father ' and ' mother,' put, for our convenience, in the accents easiest for unpractised lips to frame. Then, as we grew on, we acquired daily more and more, partly by direct instruction, partly by imitation : those who had the care of us contracted their ideas and simplified their speech to suit our weak capacities ; they watched with interest every new vocable which we mastered, corrected our numberless errors, explained what we but half understood, checked us when we used longer words and more ambitious phrases than we could employ correctly or wield adroitly, and drilled us in the utterance of sounds which come hard to the beginner. The kind and degree of the training thus given, indeed, varied greatly in different cases, as did the provision made for the necessary wants of childhood in respect to other matters ; as, for instance, the food, the dress, the moral nurture. Just as some have to rough their way by the hardest through the scenes of early life, beaten, half-starved, clad in scanty rags, while yet some care and provision were wholly indispensable, and no child could have lived through infancy without them—so, as concerns language, some get but the coarsest and most meagre instruction, and yet instruction enough to help them through the first stages of learning how to speak. In the least favourable circumstances, there must have been constantly about every one of us in our earliest years an amount and style of speech surpassing our acquirements and beyond our reach, and our acquisition of language consisted in our appropriating more and more of this, as we were able. In proportion as our minds grew in activity and power of comprehension, and our knowledge increased, our notions and conceptions were brought into shapes mainly agreeing with those which they wore in the minds of those around us, and received in our usage the appellations to which the latter were accustomed. On making acquaintance with certain liquids, colourless or white, we had not to go through a process of observation and study of their properties, in order to devise suitable titles for them ; we were taught that these were *water* and *milk*. The one of them, when standing stagnant in patches, or rippling between green banks, we learned to call, according to circumstances and the preference of our instructors, *pool* or *puddle*, and *brook* or *river*. An elevation rising blue in the distance, or towering nearer above us, attracted our attention, and drew from us the staple inquiry " What is that ? "—the answer, " A mountain," or " A hill," brought to our vocabulary one of the innumerable additions which it gained in a like way. Along with the names of external sensible objects, we thus learned also that practical classification of them which our language recognizes : we learned to distinguish *brook* and *river ; hill* and *mountain ; tree, bush, vine, shrub,* and *plant ;* and so on, in cases without number. In like manner, among the various acts which we were capable of performing, we were taught to designate certain ones by specific titles : much reproof, for instance, doubtless made us early understand what was meant by *cry, strike, push, kick, bite*, and other names for misdeeds incident to even the best-regulated childhood. How long our own mental states might have remained a confused and indistinct chaos to our unassisted reflection, we do not know; but we were soon helped to single out and recognize by appropriate appellations certain ones among them : for example, a warm feeling of gratification and attachment we were made to signify by the expression *love;* an inferior degree of the same feeling by *like;* and their opposite by *hate.* Long before any process of analysis and combination carried on within ourselves would have given us the distinct conceptions of *true* and *false*, of *good* and *naughty*, they were carefully set before us, and their due apprehension was enforced by faithful admonition, or by something yet more serious. And not only were we thus assisted to an intelligent recognition of ourselves and the world immediately about us, but knowledge began at once to be communicated to us respecting things beyond our reach. The appellations of hosts of objects, of places, of beings, which we had not seen, and perhaps have not even yet seen, we learned by hearing or by reading, and direct instruction enabled us to attach to them some characteristic idea, more or less complete and adequate. Thus, we had not to cross the ocean, and to coast about and traverse a certain island beyond it, in order to know that there is a country *England*, and to hold it apart, by specific attributes, from other countries of which we obtained like knowledge by like means.

But enough of this illustration. It is already sufficiently clear that the acquisition of language was one of the steps of our earliest education. We did not make our own tongue, or any part of it; we neither selected the objects, acts, mental states, relations, which should be separately designated, nor devised their distinctive designations. We simply received and appropriated, as well as we could, whatever our instructors were pleased to set before us. Independence of the general usages of speech was neither encouraged nor tolerated in us; nor did we feel tempted toward independence. Our object was to communicate with those among whom our lot was cast, to understand them and be understood by them, to learn what their greater wisdom and experience could impart to us. In order to this, we had to think and talk as they did, and we were content to do so. Why such and such a combination of sounds was applied to designate such and such an idea was to us a matter of utter indifference ; all we knew or cared to know was that others so applied it. Questions of etymology, of fitness of appellation, concerned us not. What was it to us, for instance, when the answer came back to one of our childish inquiries after names, that the word *mountain* was imported into our tongue out of the Latin, through the Norman French, and was originally an adjective, meaning 'hilly, mountainous,' while *hill* had once a *g* in it, indicating its relationship with the adjective *high ?* We recognized no tie between any word and the idea represented by it excepting a mental association which we had ourselves formed, under the guidance, and in obedience to the example, of those about us. We do, indeed, when a little older, perhaps, begin to amuse ourselves with inquiring into the reasons why this word means that thing, and not otherwise : but it is only for the satisfaction of our curiosity ; if we fail to find a reason, or if the reason be found trivial and insufficient, we do not on that account reject the word. Thus every vocable was to us an arbitrary and conventional sign : arbitrary, because any one of a thousand other vocables could have been just as easily learned by us and associated with the same idea ; conventional, because the one we acquired had its sole ground and sanction in the consenting usage of the community of which we formed a part.

Race and blood, it is equally evident, had nothing to do directly with determining our language. English descent would never have made us talk English. No matter who were our ancestors ; if those about us had said *wasser* and *milch*, or *eau* and *lait*, or *hüdōr* and *gala*, instead of *water* and *milk*, we should have done the same. We could just as readily have accustomed ourselves to say *lieben* or *aimer* or *philein*, as *love*, *wahrheit* or *vérité* or *alētheia*, as *truth*. And so in every other case. An American or English mother, anxious that her child should grow up duly accomplished, gives it a French nurse, and takes care that no English be spoken in its presence; and not all the blood of all the Joneses can save it from talking French first, as if this were indeed its own mother-tongue. An infant is taken alive from the arms of its drowned mother, the only waif cast upon the shore from the wreck of a strange vessel; and it learns the tongue of its foster-parents; no outbreak of natural and hereditary speech ever betrays from what land it derived its birth. The child of a father and mother of different race and speech learns the tongue of either, as circumstances and their choice may determine; or it learns both, and is equally at home in them, hardly knowing which to call its native language. The bands of Africans, stolen from their homes and imported into America, lost in a generation their Congo or Mendi, and acquired from their fellow-slaves a rude jargon in which they could communicate with one another and with their masters. The Babel of dialects brought every year to our shores by the thousands of foreigners who come to seek a new home among us, disappear in as brief a 'time, or are kept up only where those who speak them herd together in separate communities. The Irish peasantry, mingled with and domineered over by English colonists, governed under English institutions, feeling the whole weight, for good and for evil, of a superior English civilization, incapacitated from rising above a condition of poverty and ignorance without command of English speech, unlearn by degrees their native Celtic tongue, and adopt the dialect of the ruling and cultivated class.

No one, I am confident, can fail to allow that this is a true account of the process by which we acquire our "mother-tongue." Every one recognizes, as the grand advantage connected with the use of language, the fact that in it and by it whatever of truth and knowledge each generation has learned or worked out can be made over into the possession of the generation following. It is not necessary that each of us study the world for himself, in order to apprehend and classify the varied objects it contains, with their qualities and relations, and invent designations for them. This has been done by those who came before us, and we enter into the fruits of their labours. It is only the first man, before whom every beast of the field and every fowl of the air must present itself, to see what he will call it ; whatever he calls any living creature, that is the name thereof, not to himself alone, but to his family and descendants, who are content to style each as their father had done before them.

Our acquisition of English, however, has as yet been but partially and imperfectly described.

In the first place, the English which we thus learn is of that peculiar form or local variety which is talked by our instructors and models. It is, indeed, possible that one may have been surrounded from birth by those, and those only, whose speech is wholly conformed to perfect standards ; then it will have been, at least, his own fault if he has learned aught but the purest and most universally accepted English. But such cases cannot be otherwise than rare. For, setting aside the fact that all are not agreed as to whose usage forms the unexceptionable standard, nothing can be more certain than that few, on either side of the ocean, know and follow it accurately. Not many of us can escape acquiring in our youth some tinge of local dialect, of slang characteristic of grade or occupation, of personal peculiarities, even, belonging to our initiators into the mysteries of speech. These may be mere inelegancies of pronunciation, appearing in individual words or in the general tone of utterance, like the nasal twang, and the flattening of *ou* into *ău*, which common fame injuriously ascribes to the Yankee ; or they may be ungrammatical modes of expression, or uncouth turns and forms of construction ; or favourite recurrent phrases, such as *I guess, I calculate, I reckon, I expect, you know*, each of which has its own region of prevalence ; or colloquialisms and vulgarisms, which ought to hide their heads in good English society ; or words of only dialectic currency, which the general language does not recognize. Any or all of these or of their like we innocently learn along with the rest of our speech, not knowing how to distinguish the evil from the good. And often, as some of us know to our cost, errors and infelicities are thus so thoroughly

wrought into our minds, as parts of our habitual modes of
expression, that not all the care and instruction of after life
can rid us of them. How many men of culture and
eminent ability do we meet with, who exhibit through life
the marks of a defective or vicious early training in their
native tongue! The dominion of habit is not less powerful
in language than in anything else that we acquire and prac-
tise. It is not alone true that he who has once thoroughly
learned English is thereby almost disqualified from ever
attaining a native facility, correctness, and elegance in any
foreign tongue; one may also so thoroughly learn a bad
style of English as never to be able to ennoble it into the
best and most approved form of his native speech. Yet,
with us, the influences which tend to repress and eradicate
local peculiarities and individual errors are numerous and
powerful. One of the most effective among them is school
instruction. It is made an important part of our education
to learn to speak and write correctly. The pupil of a faithful and competent instructor is taught to read and pronounce, to frame sentences with the mouth and with the
pen, in a manner accordant with that which is accepted
among the well-educated everywhere. Social intercourse is
a cultivating agency hardly less important, and more enduring in its action; as long as we live, by associating with
those who speak correctly, we are shown our own faults, and
at the same time prompted and taught to correct them.
Reading—which is but another form of such intercourse—
consultation of authorities, self-impelled study in various
forms, help the work. Our speech is improved and perfected, as it was first acquired, by putting ourselves in the
position of learners, by following the example of those who
speak better than we do. He who is really in earnest to
complete his mastery of his mother-tongue may hope for
final success, whatever have been his early disadvantages ;
just as one may acquire a foreign tongue, like German or
French, with a degree of perfection depending only on his
opportunities, his capacity, his industry, and the length of time
he devotes to the study.

Again, even when the process of training which we have

2

described gives general correctness and facility, it is far from conferring universal command of the resources of the English tongue. This is no grand indivisible unity, whereof the learner acquires all or none ; it is an aggregation of particulars, and each one appropriates more or less of them, according to his means and ability. The vocabulary which the young child has acquired the power to use is a very scanty one ; it includes only the most indispensable part of speech, names for the commonest objects, the most ordinary and familiar conceptions, the simplest relations. You can talk with a child only on a certain limited range of subjects ; a book not written especially for his benefit is in great part unintelligible to him : he has not yet learned its signs for thought, and they must be translated into others with which he is acquainted ; or the thought itself is beyond the reach of his apprehension, the statement is outside the sphere of his knowledge. But in this regard we are all of us more or less children. Who ever yet got through learning his mother-tongue, and could say, " The work is done ? " The encyclopedic English language, as we may term it, the English of the great dictionaries, contains more than a hundred thousand words. And these are only a selection out of a greater mass. If all the signs for thought employed for purposes of communication by those who have spoken and who speak no other tongue than ours were brought together, if all obselete, technical, and dialectic words were gathered in, which, if they are not English, are of no assignable spoken tongue, the number mentioned would be vastly augmented. Out of this immense mass, it has been reckoned by careful observers that from three to five thousand answer all the ordinary ends of familiar intercourse, even among the cultivated ; and a considerable portion of the English-speaking community, including the lowest and most ignorant class, never learn to use even so many as three thousand : what they do acquire, of course, being, like the child's vocabulary, the most necessary part of the language, signs for the commonest and simplest ideas. To a nucleus of this character, every artisan, though otherwise uninstructed, must add the technical language of his own craft—names for tools, and processes, and products which his every-day experience makes familiar to him, but of which the vast majority, perhaps, of those outside his own line of life know nothing. Ignorant as he may be, he will talk to you of a host of matters which you shall not understand. No insignificant part of the hundred-thousand-word list is made up of selections from such technical vocabularies. Each department of labour, of art, of science, has its special dialect, fully known only to those who have made themselves masters in that department. The world requires of every well-informed and educated person a certain amount of knowledge in many special departments, along with a corresponding portion of the language belonging to each : but he would be indeed a marvel of many-sided learning who had mastered them all. Who is there among us that will not find, on every page of the comprehensive dictionaries now in vogue, words which are strange to him, which need defining to his apprehension, which he could not be sure of employing in the right place and connection ? And this, not in the technical portions only of our vocabulary. There are words, or meanings of words, no longer in familiar use, antiquated or obsolescent, which yet may not be denied a place in the present English tongue. There are objects which almost never fall under the notice of great numbers of people, or of whole classes of the community, and to whose names, accordingly, when met with, these are unable to attach any definite idea. There are cognitions, conceptions, feelings, which have not come up in the minds of all, which all have not had occasion and acquired power to express. There are distinctions, in every department of thought, which all have not learned to draw and designate. Moreover, there are various styles of expression for the same thing, which are not at every one's command. One writer or speaker has great ease and copiousness of diction ; for all his thoughts he has a variety of phrases to choose among ; he lays them out before us in beautiful elaboration, in clear and elegant style, so that to follow and understand him is like floating with the current. Another, with not less wealth of knowledge and clearness of judgment, is cramped and awkward in his use of language;

2 *

he puts his ideas before us in a rough and fragmentary way ;
he carries our understandings with him, but only at the cost
of labour and pains on our part. And though he may be able
to comprehend all that is said by the other, he has not in the
same sense made the language his own, any more than the
student of a foreign tongue who can translate from it with
facility, but can express himself in it only lamely. Thus the
infinite variety of the native and acquired capacity of different
individuals comes to light in their idiom. It would be as
hard to find two persons with precisely the same limits to
their speech, as with precisely the same lineaments of countenance.

Once more, not all who speak the same tongue attach the
same meaning to the words they utter. We learn what
words signify either by direct definition or by inference
from the circumstances in which they are used. But no
definition is or can be exact and complete ; and we are
always liable to draw wrong inferences. Children, as
every one knows, are constantly misapprehending the extent
of meaning and application of the signs they acquire. Until it learns better, a child calls every man *papa ;* having
been taught the word *sky*, it calls the ceiling of a room the
sky ; it calls a donkey or a mule a *horse*—and naturally
enough, since it has had to apply the name *dog* to creatures
differing far more than these from one another. And so
long as the learning of language lasts, does the liability to
such error continue. It is a necessity of the case, arising
out of the essential nature of language. Words are not
exact models of ideas ; they are merely signs for ideas, at
whose significance we arrive as well as we can ; and no
mind can put itself into such immediate and intimate com-
munion with another mind as to think and feel precisely
with it. Sentences are not images of thoughts, reflected in
a faultless mirror ; nor even photographs, needing only to
have the colour added : they are but imperfect and fragmentary sketches, giving just outlines enough to enable the
sense before which they are set up to seize the view intended,
and to fill it out to a complete picture ; while yet, as regards
the completeness of the filling out, the details of the work,

and the finer shades of colouring, no two minds will produce
pictures perfectly accordant with one another, nor will any
precisely reproduce the original. The limits of variation of meaning are, of course, very
different in different classes of words. So far as these are
designations of definite objects, cognizable by the senses,
there is little danger of our seriously misapprehending one
another when we utter them. Yet, even here, there is
room for no trifling discordance, as the superior knowledge
or more vivid imagination of one person gives to the idea
called up by a name a far richer content than another can
put into it. Two men speak of the *sun*, with mutual intelligence : but to the one he is a mere ball of light and heat,
which rises in the sky every morning, and goes down again at
night ; to the other, all that science has taught us respecting
the nature of the great luminary, and its influence upon our
little planet, is more or less distinctly present every time he
utters its name. The word *Pekin* is spoken before a number of persons, and is understood by them all : but some
among them know only that it is the name of an immense
city in Asia, the capital of the Chinese empire ; others have
studied Chinese manners and customs, have seen pictures of
Chinese scenery, architecture, dress, occupation, and are able
to tinge the conception which the word evokes with some
fair share of a local colouring ; another, perhaps, has visited
the place, and its name touches a store of memories, and
brings up before his mind's eye a picture vivid with the
hues of truth. I feel a tolerable degree of confidence that
the impressions of colour made on my sense are the same
with those made upon my friend's sense, so that, when we
use the words *red* or *blue*, we do not mean different things :
and yet, even here, it is possible that one of us may be
afflicted with some degree of colour-blindness, so that we do
not apprehend the same shades precisely alike. But just so
is every part of language liable to be affected by the personality of the speaker ; and most of all, where matters of
more subjective apprehension are concerned. The volup-
tuary, the passionate and brutal, the philosophic, and the
sentimental, for instance, when they speak of *love* or of *hate*,

mean by no means the same feelings. How pregnant with
sacred meaning are *home, patriotism, faith* to some, while
others utter or hear them with cool indifference! It is needless, however, to multiply examples. Not half the words in our
familiar speech would be identically defined by any considerable number of those who employ them every day. Nay,
who knows not that verbal disputes, discussions turning on
the meaning of words, are the most frequent, bitter, and interminable of controversies?

Clearly, therefore, we are guilty of no paradox in maintaining that, while we all speak the English language, the
English of no two individuals among us is precisely the
same: it is not the same in form; it is not the same in
extent; it is not the same in meaning.

But what, then, is the English language? We answer:
It is the immense aggregate of the articulated signs for
thought accepted by, and current among, a certain vast
community which we call the English-speaking people, embracing the principal portion of the inhabitants of our own
country and of Great Britain, with all those who elsewhere
in the world talk like them. It is the sum of the separate
languages of all the members of this community. Or—since
each one says some things, or says them in a way, not to be
accepted as in the highest sense English—it is their average
rather than their sum; it is that part of the aggregate which
is supported by the usage of the majority; but of a majority
made in great part by culture and education, not by numbers alone. It is a mighty region of speech, of somewhat
fluctuating and uncertain boundaries, whereof each speaker
occupies a portion, and a certain central tract is included in
the portion of all: there they meet on common ground; off it,
they are strangers to one another. Although one language, it
includes numerous varieties, of greatly differing kind and
degree: individual varieties, class varieties, local varieties.
Almost any two persons who speak it may talk so as to be
unintelligible to each other. The one fact which gives it
unity is, that all who speak it may, to a considerable extent,
and on subjects of the most general and pressing interest,
talk so as to understand one another.

How this language is kept in existence is clearly shown by the foregoing exposition. It is preserved by an uninterrupted tradition. Each generation hands it down to the generation following. Every one is an actor in the process; in each individual speaker the language has, as we may say, a separate and independent existence, as has an animal species in each of its members; and each does what in him lies to propagate it—that is to say, his own part of it, as determined in extent and character by the inherent and acquired peculiarities of his nature. And, small as may be the share of the work which falls to any one of us, the sum of all the shares constitutes the force which effects the transmission of the whole language. In the case of a tongue like ours, too, these private labours are powerfully aided and supplemented by the influence of a literature. Each book is, as it were, an undying individual, with whom, often, much larger numbers hold intercourse than any living person can reach, and who teaches them to speak as he speaks. A great body of literary works of acknowledged merit and authority, in the midst of a people proud and fond of it, is an agent in the preservation and transmission of any tongue, the importance of which cannot easily be over-estimated: we shall have to take it constantly into account in the course of our further inquiries into the history of language. But each work is, after all, only a single person, with his limitations and deficiencies, and with his restricted influence. Even Shakspeare, with his unrivalled wealth and variety of expression, uses but about fifteen thousand words, and Milton little more than half so many—mere fragments of the encyclopedic English tongue. The language would soon be shorn of no small part of its strength, if placed exclusively in the hands of any individual, or of any class. Nothing less than the combined effort of a whole community, with all its classes and orders, in all its variety of characters, circumstances, and necessities, is capable of keeping in life a whole language.

But, while our English speech is thus passed onward from generation to generation of those who learn to speak it, and, having learned themselves, teach others, it does not remain

precisely the same ; on the contrary, it is undergoing all the
time a slow process of modification, which is capable of rendering it at length another language, unintelligible to those
who now employ it. In order to be convinced of this, we
have only to cast an eye backward over its past history, during the period for which we have its progress recorded in
contemporary documents. How much is there in our present familiar speech which would be strange and meaningless
to one of Elizabeth's court! How much, again, do we find
in any of the writers of that period—in Shakspeare, for instance—which is no longer good current English! phrases
and forms of construction which never fall from our lips
now save as we quote them ; scores of words which we have
lost out of memory, or do not employ in the sense which
they then bore. Go back yet farther, from half-century to
half-century, and the case grows rapidly worse ; and when
we arrive at Chaucer and Gower, who are separated from us
by a paltry interval of five hundred years, only fifteen or
twenty descents from father to son, we meet with a dialect
which has a half-foreign look, and can only be read by careful study, with the aid of a glossary. Another like interval
of five hundred years brings us to the Anglo-Saxon of King
Alfred, which is absolutely a strange tongue to us, not less
unintelligible than the German of the present day, and nearly
as hard to learn. And yet, we have no reason to believe
that any one of those thirty or forty generations of Englishmen through whom we are descended from the contemporaries of King Alfred was less simply and single-mindedly
engaged to transmit to its children the same language which
it had received from its ancestors than is the generation of
which we ourselves form a part. It may well be that circumstances were less favourable to some of them than to us,
and that our common speech stands in no danger of suffering in the next thousand years a tithe of the change which
it has suffered in the past thousand. But the forces which
are at work in it are the same now that they have always
been, and the effects they are producing are of the same
essential character : both are inherent in the nature of lan-

guage, and inseparable from its use. This will be made
plain to us by a brief inquiry.

The most rapid and noticeable mode of change in our
language is that which is all the time varying the extent and
meaning of its vocabulary. English speech exists in order
that we may communicate with one another respecting those
things which we know. As the stock of words at the command of each individual is an approximate measure of the
sum of his knowledge, so the stock of words composing a
language corresponds to what is known in the community ;
the objects it is familiar with, the distinctions it has drawn,
all its cognitions and reasonings, in the world of matter and
of mind, must have their appropriate expression. That
speech should signify more than is in the minds of its speakers
is obviously impossible ; but neither must it fall short of indicating what they think. Now the sum of knowledge in
every community varies not a little from generation to
generation. Every trade and handicraft, every art, every
science, is constantly changing its materials, its processes,
and its products ; and its technical dialect is modified accordingly, while so much of the results of this change as affects
or interests the general public finds its way into the familiar
speech of everybody. As our material condition varies, as
our ways of life, our institutions, private and public, become
other than they have been, all is necessarily reflected in our
language. In these days of railroads, steamboats, and telegraphs, of sun-pictures, of chemistry and geology, of improved
wearing stuffs, furniture, styles of building, articles of food
and luxury of every description, how many words and phrases
are in every one's mouth which would be utterly unintelligible
to the most learned man of a century ago, were he to rise
from his grave and walk our streets ! It is, of course, in its
stores of expression for these more material objects and relations, and for the details of technical knowledge, that language changes most notably, because it is with reference to
these that the necessity for change especially arises. The
central and most indispensable substance of every language
is made up of designations for things, properties, acts, the

apprehension of which is nearly as old as humanity itself, which men learned to name as soon as they learned to talk at all, and whose names are not liable to pass away or become superseded. The words *red, green, blue, yellow,* or their equivalents, go back to the earliest period of human speech; it is when some new and delicate shades of colour, like the aniline dyes, are invented, that appellations must be sought for them, and may be found even among names of localities, as Magenta, Solferino, to which the circumstances of the time have given a sudden notoriety. Any two rustics, from the time of Adam to the present, could talk with one another, with all the particularity which their practical ends required, of earth and rock, of pebbles and stones, of sand and gravel, of loam and clay: but, since the beginning of the present century, the mineralogist and geologist have elicited a host of new facts touching the history and constitution of the earth's crust and the materials of which this is made up, have arranged and classified its strata and their contents, have brought to light numberless relations, of cause and effect, of succession, of origin, date, and value, which had hitherto lain hidden in it; and, to express these, they have introduced into English speech a whole technical vocabulary, and one which is still every year extending and changing. So it is with botany; so with metaphysics; so with every other branch of science and art. And though the greater part of the technical vocabularies remains merely technical, understood and employed only by special students in each branch, yet the common speech is not entirely unaffected by them. Some portion of the results of the advancement in knowledge made by the wise and learned reaches even the lowest, or all but the very lowest, and is expressed in their language; and it thus becomes a part of the fundamental stock of ideas which constitute the heritage of each generation, which every child is taught to form and use. Language, in short, is expanded and contracted in precise adaptation to the circumstances and needs of those who use it; it is enriched or impoverished, in every part, along with the enrichment or impoverishment of their minds. This is, as I have said, the most noticeable mode of change

in language, and also the most natural, inevitable, and legitimate. Even the bigoted purist cannot object to it, or wish
it otherwise: conservatism here would be the conservatism
of ignorance, opposing itself to the progress of civilization
and enlightenment. Along with it, too, comes its natural
counterpart, the dropping out of use and out of memory of
words and meanings of words and phrases which circumstances have made it no longer desirable to maintain in
existence; which denote the things of a by-gone time, or, by
the substitution of more acceptable expressions, have become
unnecessary and otiose.

But there are also all the time going on in our language
changes of another and a more questionable character,
changes which affect the form rather than the content of
speech, and are in a sense unnecessary, and therefore stoutly
opposed by the authority of exact tradition; yet which have
hitherto shown themselves not less inevitable than the others.
We have seen that the transmission of language is by tradition. But traditional transmission is by its inherent nature
defective. If a story cannot pass a few times from mouth
to mouth and maintain its integrity, neither can a word pass
from generation to generation and keep its original form.
Very young children, as every one knows, so mutilate their
words and phrases that only those who are most familiar
with them can understand what they say. But even an
older child, who has learned to speak in general with tolerable correctness, has a special inaptness to utter a particular
sound, and either drops it altogether or puts another and
nearly related one in its place. There are certain combinations of consonants which it cannot manage, and has to
mouth over into more pronounceable shape. It drops a
syllable or two from a long and cumbrous word. It omits
endings and confounds forms together: *me*, for instance, has
to do duty in its usage for *me, my,* and *I;* and *eat,* to stand
for all persons, tenses, and numbers of the verb. Or, again,
having learned by prevailing experience that the past sense
in a verb is signified by the addition of a *d,* it imagines that,
because it says *I loved,* it must also say *I bringed;* or else,
perhaps, remembering *I sang* from *I sing,* it says *I brang.*

It says *foots* and *mouses* ; it says *gooder* and *goodest ;* it confounds *sit* and *set, lie* and *lay* (in which last blunders, unfortunately, it is supported by the example of too many among
the grown-up and educated). Care, on its own part and on
that of its instructors, corrects by degrees such childish
errors ; but this care is often wanting or insufficient, and it
grows up continuing still to speak bad English. Moreover,
as we have already seen, not each child only, but each man,
to his dying day, is a learner of his native tongue ; nor is
there any one who is not liable, from carelessness or defective
instruction, to learn a word or phrase incorrectly, or to reproduce it inaccurately. For these reasons there always lies,
in full vigour and currency, in the lower strata of language-
users, as we may term them—among the uneducated or half-
educated—a great host of deviations from the best usage,
offences against the propriety of speech, kept down in the
main by the controlling influence of good speakers, yet
all the time threatening to rise to the surface, and now
and then succeeding in forcing their way up, and compelling recognition and acceptance from even the best authorities.

Of this origin are the class of changes in language which
we are at present considering. They are, in their inception,
inaccuracies of speech. They attest the influence of that
immense numerical majority among the speakers of English
who do not take sufficient pains to speak correctly, but whose
blunders become finally the norm of the language. They
are mainly the results of two tendencies, already illustrated
in the instances we have given : first, to make things easy
to our organs of speech, to economize time and effort in the
work of expression ; second, to get rid of irregular and exceptional forms, by extending the prevailing analogies of the
language. Let us look at a few examples.

Our written words are thickly sown with silent letters,
which, as every one knows, are relics of former modes of
pronunciation, once necessary constituents of spoken language, but gradually dropped, because it was easier to do
without them. Instances are *knight, calm, psalm, would,
doubt, plough, thought, sword, chestnut.* If we will but carry

our investigations further back, beyond the present written form of our words, we shall light upon much more extraordinary cases of mutilation and abbreviation. Thus, to take but a single, though rather striking, example, our *alms* is the scanty relic of the long Greek vocable *eleëmosunē*. All the monosyllables, in fact, of which especially the Anglo-Saxon portion of our daily speech is in so great measure composed, are relics of long polysyllabic forms, usual at an earlier stage of the language. Some words are but just through, or even now passing through, a like process. In *often* and *soften*, good usage has taken sides with the corruption which has ejected the *t*, and accuses of being old-fashioned or affectedly precise the large and respectable class who still pronounce that letter; while, on the other hand, it clings to the *t* of *captain*, and stigmatizes as vulgar those who presume to say *cap'n*.

Again, it is the prevailing English custom to accent a noun of two syllables on its first syllable; hosts of nouns of French origin have had their native accent altered, in order to conform them to this analogy. Such changes have been going on at every period in the history of our tongue : in Pope, in Milton, in Shakspeare, in Chaucer, you will find examples of their action, in ever increasing numbers as you go backward from the present time. Nor are they yet over : there is *ally*, which all the authorities agree in pronouncing *allý*, while prevailing popular usage, on both sides of the Atlantic, persists in favouring *álly*; and it is not unlikely that, in the end, the people will prove too strong for the orthoëpists, as they have done so many times before.

When our Bible translation was made, the verb *speak* had a proper imperfect form, *spake* : a well-educated Englishman would no more have written *he spoke* than *he come and done it*. But, just as the ill-instructed and the careless now-a-days are often guilty of these last two blunders, so then, undoubtedly, large numbers habitually said *spoke* for *spake;* until, at last, the struggle against it was given up as hopeless ; and no one now says *I spake* save in conscious imitation of Biblical style.

At the same period, but two centuries and a half ago, the

English language contained no such word as *its*. *His* had been, in the old Anglo-Saxon and ever since, the common possessive of *he* and *it* (A.-S., *hit*) ; it belonged to the latter no less than to the former. But almost all the possessive cases in the language were formed by adding *s* to the nominative, and *his* wore the aspect of being so formed from *he*, and of having nothing to do with *it*. Why not, then, form a new possessive in like manner for *it* itself ? This was a question which very probably suggested itself to a great many minds about the same time, and the word *its* may have sprung up in a hundred places at once, and propagated itself, under the ban of the purists of the day, who frowned upon it, pronounced it "as bad as *she's*, for *her*, would be," and carefully avoided its use ; until at last its popularity and evident desirableness caused it to be universally adopted and recognized as proper. And, at the present time, few of us read our Bibles so curiously as to have discovered that they contain no such word as *its*, from Genesis to Revelation.

The Anglo-Saxon employed *ye* (*ge*) as subject of a verb, and *you* (*eow*) as object, and the early English was careful to make the same distinction. Nor is it yet entirely lost ; but the use of *ye* now belongs to a solemn style only, and *you* has been set up as subject not less than object. There was a time when *you are* for *ye are*, and yet more for *thou art*, would have been as offensive to the ear of a correct English speaker as is now the *thee is* of the Quaker.

Not a few of the irregular verbs which our language formerly contained have been in later usage assimilated to the more numerous class, and conjugated regularly. Take as examples *help*, of which the ancient participle *holpen*, instead of *helped*, is found still in our Bibles ; and *work*, which has gained a modern preterit and participle, *worked*, although the older form, *wrought*, is also retained in use, with a somewhat altered and specialized signification.

Here are changes of various kind and value, though all tracing their origin to the same tendencies. Words change their shape without losing their identity ; old forms, old marks of distinction, are neglected and lost: some of these could well be spared, but others were valuable, and their relinquishment has impaired the power of expression of the language ; while new forms are created, and new marks of distinction are adopted into general use, and made part and parcel of English speech.

So full and abundant illustration of this department of change in language as might be desired cannot be drawn from facts with which we are all familiar, because, for some time past, the conservative forces have been so powerful in our mother-tongue, and the accuracy of historical trans-mission so strict, that what is now good English has, in the main, long been such, and is likely long to continue such. Its alteration goes on so slowly that we hardly perceive it in progress, and it is only as we compare the condition of the language at a given time with that which it shows at the distance of a considerable interval, earlier or later, that they come clearly to light. The English is, indeed, among all cultivated tongues, the one which has suffered, under the influences which we have been describing, the most thorough and pervading change of its grammar and vocabulary ; but the greater part of this change occurred at a certain definite period, and from the effect of circumstances which are well known. Our English ancestors, between the time of Alfred and that of Chaucer, endured the irruption and conquest of a French-speaking people, the Normans—just as did the Irish, at a later day, that of the English. That the Saxons did not, like the Irish, gradually relinquish their own tongue, and learn to talk French altogether, was owing to their ad-vanced culture and superior independence of character : after a long time of confusion and mutual unintelligibility, as every one knows, the Saxons gave up a part of their vocabulary for that of the Normans, and the Normans a part of theirs, with nearly all their grammar, for those of the Saxons, and our present composite dialect, with its mea-gre system of grammatical inflections, was the result. The example is an extreme one of the transformation which a language may be made to undergo in the lapse of a few

generations, at the bidding of imperious circumstances; as
the present stability of the same language is an extreme
example of what favouring circumstances can do to prevent
change, and maintain the integrity of speech.

The facts and conditions which we have been considering
are of no exceptional character: on the contrary, they are
common to all the forms of speech current among the sons
of men. Throughout the world, the same description, in its
essential features, will be found to hold good. Every
spoken language is a congeries of individual signs, called
words; and each word (with the rare exception of the actual
additions made by individuals to language, of which we shall
take account later) was learned by every person who employs it from some other person who had employed it before
him. He adopted it as the sign of a certain idea, because
it was already in use by others as such. Inner and essential connection between idea and word, whereby the mind
which conceives the one at once apprehends and produces
the other, there is none, in any language upon earth. Every
existing form of human speech is a body of arbitrary and
conventional signs for thought, handed down by tradition
from one generation to another, no individual in any generation receiving or transmitting the whole body, but the sum
of the separate givings and takings being effective to keep
it in existence without essential loss. Yet the process of
traditional transmission always has been, is now, and will
ever continue to be, in all parts of the world, an imperfect
one: no language remains, or can remain, the same during
a long period of time. Growth and change make the life of
language, as they are everywhere else the inseparable accompaniment and sign of life. A language is living, when it is
the instrument of thought of a whole people, the wonted
means of expression of all their feelings, experiences, opinions, reasonings; when the connection between it and their
mental activity is so close that the one reflects the other,
and that the two grow together, the instrument ever adapting itself to the uses which it is to subserve. The ways in
which this adaptation takes place, and the causes which

accelerate or retard the inevitable change of language, have been already in part glanced at, and will come up for more detailed examination hereafter; it is sufficient at present that we fully recognize the fact of change. It is the fundamental fact upon which rests the whole method of linguistic study.

LECTURE II.

Nature of the force which produces the changes of language; its modes of action. Language an institution, of historical growth ; its study a moral sciences. Analogies of linguistic science with the physical science Its methods historical. Etymology its foundation. Analysis of compound words. Genesis of affixes. Nature of all words as produced by actual composition.

IN the preceding lecture, after a very brief survey of the history and objects of linguistic science, we entered upon an inquiry into the means by which we had become possessed of our mother-tongue, an inquiry intended to bring out to our view the mode of transmission and preservation of language in general. And we saw that it is the work of tradition ; that each generation passes along to the generation succeeding, with such faithfulness as the nature of the case permits, the store of words, phrases, and constructions which constitute the substance of a spoken tongue. But we also saw that the process of transmission is uniformly an imperfect one ; that it never succeeds in keeping any language entirely pure and unaltered : on the contrary, language appeared to us as undergoing, everywhere and always, a slow process of modification, which in course of time effects a considerable change in its constitution, rendering it to all intents and purposes a new tongue. This was illustrated from the history of our English speech, which, by gradual and accumulated alterations made in it, during the past thousand years, by the thirty or forty generations through whose mouths it has passed, has grown from the Anglo-Saxon of King Alfred, through a succession of inter-

mediate phases, into what it is at present. Before, now, we
go on to examine in detail the processes of linguistic change,
setting forth more fully their causes and modes of action,
and exhibiting their results upon a more extended scale, we
have to draw from what has been already said one or two
important conclusions, touching the nature of the force by
which those processes are carried on, and the character, and
place among the sciences, of the study which undertakes
their investigation.

And, in the first place, we see, I think, from our examination of the manner in which language is learned and taught,
in which its life is kept up, what is meant when we speak
and write of it as having an independent or objective existence,
as being an organism or possessing an organic structure,
as having laws of growth, as feeling tendencies, as developing, as adapting itself to our needs, and so on. All these
are figurative expressions, the language of trope and metaphor,
not of plain fact ; they are wholly unobjectionable when consciously employed in their proper character, for the sake of
brevity or liveliness of delineation ; they are only harmful
when we allow them to blind us to the real nature of
the truths they represent. Language has, in fact, no existence save in the minds and mouths of those who use it ; it
is made up of separate articulated signs of thought, each of
which is attached by a mental association to the idea it
represents, is uttered by voluntary effort, and has its value
and currency only by the agreement of speakers and hearers.
It is in their power, subject to their will ; as it is kept up,
so is it modified and altered, so may it be abandoned, by
their joint and consenting action, and in no other way whatsoever.

This truth is not only often lost from view by those who
think and reason respecting language, but it is also sometimes explicitly denied, and the opposite doctrine is set up,
that language has a life and growth independent of its
speakers, with which men cannot interfere. A recent
popular writer * asserts that, " although there is a continu-

* Professor Max Muller, in his Lectures on the Science of Language,
first series, second lecture.

ous change in language, it is not in the power of man
either to produce or to prevent it : we might think as well
of changing the laws which control the circulation of our
blood, or of adding an inch to our height, as of altering the
laws of speech, or inventing new words according to our
own pleasure." Then, in order to establish the truth of this
opinion, he goes on to cite a couple of historical instances,
in which two famous emperors, Tiberius of Rome and Sigismund of Germany, committed blunders in their Latin, and
were taken to task and corrected by humble grammarians,
who informed their imperial majesties that, however great
and absolute their power might be, it was not competent to
make an alteration in the Latin language.   The argument
and conclusion we may take to be of this character : If so
high and mighty a personage as an emperor could not do so
small a thing as alter the gender and termination of a single
word—not even, as Sigismund attempted, in a language
which was dead, and might therefore be supposed incapable
of making resistance to the indignity—much less can any
one of inferior consideration hope to accomplish such a
change, or any other of the changes, of greater or less
account, which make up the history of, speech : therefore,
language is incapable of alteration by its speakers.

The utter futility of deriving such a doctrine from such a
pair of incidents, or from a score, a hundred, or a thousand
like them, is almost too obvious to be worth the trouble of
pointing out.   Against what authority more mighty than
their own did these two emperors offend ? Simply against
the immemorial and well-defined usage of all who wrote
and had ever written Latin—nothing more and nothing
less.   High political station does not confer the right
to make and unmake language ; a sovereign's grammatical
blunders do not become the law of speech to his subjects,
any more than do those of the private man.   Each individual is, in a way, constantly trying experiments of modification upon his mother-tongue, from the time when, as
a child, he drops sounds and syllables which it does not suit
his convenience to pronounce, and frames inflections upon
mistaken analogies, to that when, as a man, he is guilty of

slang, vulgarisms, and bad grammar, or indulges in mannerisms and artificial conceits, or twists words out of their true
uses, from ignorance or caprice.   But his individual influence is too weak to make head against the consenting usage
of the community; his proposals, unless for special reasons,
are passed over unnoticed, and he is forced to conform his
speech to that of the rest; or, if he insist upon his independence, he is contemned as a blunderer, or laughed at
as a humourist.

That an alteration should have been made at the time of
Sigismund in any item of Latin grammar, either by the emperor himself, or by all the potentates and learned men
of Christendom, was an impossibility.   For the language
was a dead one; its proprieties of speech were no longer
dependent upon the sanction of present usage, but upon
the authority of unchanging models.   Much that we say is
good English, though Shakspeare and Milton knew it not;
nothing can be good Latin, unless it be found in Cicero and
Virgil, or their compeers.   And even under Tiberius, the
case was nearly the same: the great authors whose example
makes the law of Latin speech had already lived and written;
and any deviation from their usage would have been recognized by all coming time as a later corruption.   Hence,
even had that emperor's blunder been accepted and slavishly
imitated by his courtiers, his army, and his subjects at
large, their consent could have made it good second-rate
Latin only; it might have become the very best usage in
the later Italian, French, and Spanish, but it would always
have been rejected and avoided by the strict classicists.
And all this, not for the reason that man has no power over
language, but precisely for the contrary reason, that he has
all power over it—that men's usage makes language.   He,
accordingly, who can direct usage can make or alter language.
In this way only can exalted rank confer authority over
speech: it can give a more powerful impulse toward that
general acceptance and currency which anything must win
in order to be language.   There are instances on record in
which the pun of a monarch has changed for all time the
form of a word.   Ethnologists well know that the name of

the so-called " Tartar " race is properly *Tatar*, and they are
now endeavouring to restore this, its correct orthography.
The intrusion of the *r* is accounted for in the following manner. When, in the reign of St Louis of France, the
hordes of this savage race were devastating eastern Europe,
the tale of their ravages was brought to the pious king, who
exclaimed with horror : " Well may they be called *Tartars*,
for their deeds are those of fiends from *Tartarus*." The
appositeness of the metamorphosed appellation made it take,
and from that time French authors—and, after their example, the rest of Europe—have called the *Tatars* " Tartars."
Whether the story is incontestably authentic or not is
of small consequence : any one can see that it might be true,
and that such causes may have produced such effects times
innumerable.

The speakers of language thus constitute a republic, or
rather, a democracy, in which authority is conferred only
by general suffrage and for due cause, and is exercised
under constant supervision and control. Individuals are
abundantly permitted to make additions to the common
speech, if there be reason for it, and if, in their work, they
respect the sense of the community. When the first
schooner ever built, on the coast of Massachusetts, slid
from her stocks and floated gracefully upon the water, the
chance exclamation of an admiring by-stander, " Oh, how
she *scoons !*" drew from her contriver and builder the answer, " A *scooner* let her be, then," and made a new English
word. The community ratified his act, and accepted the
word he proposed, because the new thing wanted a new
name, and there was no one else so well entitled as he to
name it ; if, on the other hand, he had assumed to christen
a man-of-war a *scooner*, no one but his nearest neighbours
would ever have heard of the attempt. The discoverer of a
new asteroid, again, is allowed to select its title, provided
he choose the name of some classical goddess, as is the
established precedent for such cases—although, even then,
he is liable to have the motives of his choice somewhat
sharply looked into. The English astronomer who sought,
a few years since, with covert loyalty, to call his planetling

"Victoria," was compelled to retract the appellation and offer another. An acute and learned Italian physician, some time in the last century, discovered a new physical force, and some one called it *galvanism*, after his name. Many of us well remember how, not long ago, a French *savant* devised a novel and universally interesting application of certain chemical processes; and here, again, by some person to whose act the community gave its assent, the product was named for its inventor a *daguerreotype* : and *galvanism* and *daguerreotype*, with their derivatives, are now as genuine and well established parts of the English language as are *sun* and *moon*, or *father* and *mother*. If Galvani had denominated his new principle *abracadabra*, or if Daguerre had styled his sun-pictures *aldiborontiphoscophornios*, these names would, indeed, have been not less inherently suitable than the ones actually chosen, in the view of the great majority of those who have since learned to use the latter ; for comparatively few have ever heard of the two eminent discoverers, or learned enough of Greek to be able to perceive the etymological aptness of *type ;* yet those who are accustomed to direct public opinion upon such subjects would have revolted, and insisted upon the substitution of other titles, which should seem to them to possess an obvious reason and applicability. The public has looked on quietly, during the last half-century, while the geologists have been bringing into our English speech their flood of new words, nouns, adjectives, and verbs, of various origin and not seldom of uncouth and barbarous aspect, wherewith to signify the new knowledge added by them to the common stock that we all draw from : these gentlemen know best; if they agree among themselves that necessity and propriety require us to say *Silurian, palæontological, oölite, post-pleiocene*, and the like, we are ready to do so, whether our acquaintance with ancient and modern geography and with the classical tongues be or be not sufficient to enable us to discover or appreciate the reason of each term.

But even in respect to the more intimate and sacred part of language, the words and phrases of universal and every-day use, the community confers some measure of authority upon

those who have a just title to it, upon great masters in the
art of speech, upon speakers whose eloquence carries captive all hearts, upon writers whose power in wielding the
common instrument of thought is felt and acknowledged
through all ranks. Such a one may now and then coin a
new word, if he follow established analogies ; he may revive
and bring again into currency one which had fallen into
desuetude ; he may confer on an old word a new value,
not too far differing from that already belonging to it—and
the license shall be ratified by general acceptance. A great
author may, by his single authority, turn the trembling scale
in favour of the admission to good usage of some popular
word or phrase, born of an original corruption or blunder,
which had hitherto been frowned upon and banned ; nay,
even his mannerisms and conceits may perhaps become the
law of the language. The maxim *usus norma loquendi*,
' usage is the rule of speech,' is of supreme and uncontrolled
validity in every part and parcel of every human tongue,
and each individual can make his fellows talk and write as
he does just in proportion to the influence which they are
disposed to concede to him.

In a language circumstanced like ours, a conscious and
detailed discussion sometimes arises on the question of admitting some new word into its recognized vocabulary. We
all remember the newspaper controversy, not long ago, as to
whether we ought to call a message sent by telegraph a
telegraph or a *telegram ;* and many of us, doubtless, are yet
waiting to see how the authorities settle it, that we may
govern our own usage accordingly. We have a suffix *able*,
which, like a few others that we possess, we use pretty freely
in forming new words. Within no very long time past, some
writers and speakers have added it to the verb *rely*, forming
the adjective *reliable*. The same thing must have been done
at nearly the same time to other verbs, awakening neither
question nor objection ; while, nevertheless, *reliable* is still
shut out from the best—or, at least, from the most exclusive
—society in English speech. And why ? Because, in the
first place, say the objectors, the word is unnecessary ; we
have already *trustworthy*, which means the same thing : fur-

ther, it is improperly and falsely formed ; as we say " to
rely *on* " anything, our derivative adjective, if we make one,
should be *relionable*, not *reliable :* finally, it is low-caste ; A,
B, and C, those prime authorities in English style, are careful never to let it slip from their pens. The other side,
however, are obstinate, and do not yield the point. The
first objection, they retort, is insufficient ; no one can properly oppose the enrichment of the language by a synonym,
which may yet be made to distinguish a valuable shade of
meaning—which, indeed, already shows signs of doing so, as
we tend to say " a *trustworthy* witness," but " *reliable* testimony." The second is false : English etymology is by no
means so precise in its application of the suffix *able* as the
objectors claim ; it admits *laughable*, meaning ' worthy to be
laughed *at*,' *unaccountable*, ' not to be accounted *for*,' *indispensable*, ' not to be dispensed *with*,' as well as many other
words of the same kind ; and even *objectionable*, ' liable to
objection,' *marriageable*, ' fit for marriage,' and so forth. As
for the third objection, whatever A, B, and C may do, it is
certain that D, F, and H, with most of the lower part of the
alphabet (including nearly all the X's, Y's, and Z's, the unknown quantities), use the new form freely ; and it is vain
to stand out against the full acceptance of a word which is
supported by so much and so respectable authority. How
the dispute is likely, or ought, to terminate, need not concern
us here ; it is only referred to because, while itself carried
on in full consciousness, and on paper, it is a typical illustration of a whole class of discussions which go on silently,
and even more or less unconsciously, in the minds before
which is presented, for acceptance or rejection, any proposed
alteration in the subsisting usages of speech. Is it called
for ? is it accordant with the analogies of the language ? is
it offered or backed by good authority ? these are the considerations by which general consent is won or repelled ; and
general consent decides every case without appeal.

   Downright additions, however, to the vocabulary of a
spoken tongue, even those who hold to the doctrine of the
organic life of language will probably be willing to ascribe
to human agency ; since no man in his sober senses, it would

seem, could possibly maintain that, when some individual mind has formed a conception or drawn a deduction, or when some individual ingenuity has brought forth a product of any of the modes of activity of which man is capable, language itself spontaneously extrudes a word for its designation! He who sees is likewise he who says; the ingenuity that could find the thing was never at a loss to devise also its appellation.

But the case is not otherwise with those gradual changes which bring about the decay of grammatical structure, or the metamorphosis of phonetic form, in a language. Though they go on in a more covert and unacknowledged way than the augmentations of a vocabulary, they are due to the action of the same forces. If we write *knight*, and pronounce it *nit*, while our ancestors spelled the word *cniht*, and made its every letter distinctly audible (giving the *i* our short *i*-sound, as in *pin*)—just as the Germans even now both write and speak the same word *knecht*—we know that it is not because, by any force inherent in the word itself, the fuller form grew into the simpler, but because the combination *kn*, as initial, was somewhat difficult for men's organs to utter, and therefore began to lose its *k*, first, in the mouths of careless and easy speakers; and the corruption went on gaining in popularity, until it became the rule of our speech to silence the mute before the nasal in all such words (as in *knife, knit, gnat, gnaw*, etc.); because, moreover, the sound of the guttural *h* after a vowel became unpopular, men's organs shrinking from the effort of producing it, and was finally got rid of everywhere (being either left out entirely, as in *nigh, ought*, or turned into *f*, as in *laugh, cough*); while, at the same time, the loss of this consonant led to a prolongation of the vowel *i*, which was changed into the diphthongal sound we now give it; in company, too, with so many other of the "long *i*'s" of the older language, that our usual name at present for the diphthong is "long *i*." And so in all the multitude of similar cases. There is no necessity, physiological or other, for the rustic's saying *kău* for *cow;* only the former is a lazy drawling utterance, which opens the mouth less widely than the latter. A precisely similar flattening of the simple sound of *a*, in such words as *grăsp*, *grăft*, *dănce*—which but a brief time since were universally pronounced *grásp*, *gráft*, *dánce* (*á* as in *far*), and are so still in certain localities—is now so common as to have become the accepted mode of utterance ; but no one fails to recognize in it a corruption of the previous pronunciation, made current by example and imitation, prompted and recommended by that lazy habit of mouth which has occasioned the dimming of so many of our clear vowels. The pronunciation *eïther* and *neïther* seems at the present time to be spreading in our community, and threatening to crowd out of use the better-supported and more analogical * *ëither* and *nëither ;* but it is only by the deliberate choice of persons who fancy that there is something nicer, more *recherché*, more "English," in the new sound, and by imitation of these on the part of others. Such phonetic changes, we are accustomed to say, are inevitable, and creep in of themselves ; but that is only another way of saying that we know not who in particular is to blame for them. Offences must needs come, but there is always that man by whom they come, could we but trace him out.

It is unnecessary to dwell longer upon this point, or to illustrate it more fully, inasmuch as even those who teach the independent existence and organic growth of language yet allow that phonetic change is the work of men, endeavouring to make things easy to their organs of speech.

A language in the condition in which ours is at present, when thousands of eyes are jealously watching its integrity, and a thousand pens are ready to be drawn, and dyed deep in ink, to challenge and oppose the introduction into it of any corrupt form, of any new and uncalled-for element, can, of course, undergo only the slowest and the least essential alteration. It is when the common speech is in the sole keeping of the uncultivated and careless speakers, who care little for classical and time-honoured usages, to whom the preferences of the moment are of more account than any-

---

* The only English word in which *ei* has the "long *i*" sound is *height*, and even there it is nothing but an old orthographical blunder; there was no reason for divorcing the derivative noun in spelling from its theme, *hıgh*.

thing in the past or in the future, that mutation has its full
course. New dialects are wont to grow up among the common people, while the speech of the educated and lettered
class continues to be what it has been. But the nature of
the forces in action is the same in the one case as in the
other : all change in language is the work of the will of its
speakers, which acts under the government of motives,
through the organs of speech, and varies their products
to suit its necessities and its convenience. Every single
item of alteration, of whatever kind, and of whatever degree
of importance, goes back to some individual or individuals,
who set it in circulation, from whose example it gained a
wider and wider currency, until it finally won that general
assent which is alone required in order to make anything in
language proper and authoritative. Linguistic change must
be gradual, and almost insensible while in progress, for the
reason that the general assent can be but slowly gained, and
can be gained for nothing which is too far removed from
former usage, and which therefore seems far-fetched, arbitrary, or unintelligible. The collective influence of all the
established analogies of a language is exerted against any
daring innovation, as, on the other hand, it aids one which
is obvious and naturally suggested. It was, for instance,
no difficult matter for popular usage to introduce the new
possessive *its* into English speech, nor to add *worked* to
wrought, as preterit of *work*, nor to replace the ancient
plural *kye* or *kine* (Anglo-Saxon *cy*, from *cu*, 'cow') by a
modern one, *cows*, formed after the ordinary model : while
to reverse either process, to crowd *its*, *worked*, and *cows* out
of use by substitution of *his*, *wrought*, and *kine*, would have
been found utterly impracticable. The power of resistance
to change possessed by a great popular institution, which is
bound up with the interests of the whole community, and is
a part of every man's thoughts and habitual acts, is not
easily to be overestimated. How long has it taken to persuade and force the French people, for instance, into the
adoption of the new decimal system of weights and mea-
sures ! How have they been baffled and shamed who have
thought, in these latter days, to amend in a few points, of

obvious desirability, our English orthography ! But speech
is a thing of far nearer and higher importance ; it is the
most precious of our possessions, the instrument of our
thoughts, the organ of our social nature, the means of our
culture ; its use is not daily or hourly alone, but momently ;
it is the first thing we learn, the last we forget ; it is the
most intimate and clinging of our habits, and almost a
second nature : and hence its exemption from all sweeping
or arbitrary change. The community, to whom it belongs,
will suffer no finger to be laid upon it without a reason ;
only such modifications as commend themselves to the
general sense, as are virtually the carrying out of tendencies
universally felt, have a chance of winning approval and
acceptance, and so of being adopted into use, and made
language.

Thus it is indeed true that the individual has no power
to change language. But it is not true in any sense which
excludes his agency, but only so far as that agency is confessed to be inoperative except as it is ratified by those
about him. Speech and the changes of speech are the work
of the community ; but the community cannot act except
through the initiative of its individual members, which it
follows or rejects. The work of each individual is done un-
premeditatedly, or as it were unconsciously ; each is intent
only on using the common possession for his own benefit,
serving therewith his private ends ; but each is thus at the
same time an actor in the great work of perpetuating and of
shaping the general speech. So each separate polyp on
a coral-bank devotes himself simply to the securing of his
own food, and excretes calcareous matter only in obedience
to the exigencies of his individual life ; but, as the joint result of the isolated labours of all, there slowly rises in the
water the enormous coral cliff, a barrier for the waves to
dash themselves against in vain. To pick out a single man,
were he even an emperor, and hold him up to view in his
impotence as proof that men cannot make or alter language,
is precisely equivalent to selecting one polyp, though the
biggest and brightest-coloured of his species, off the growing reef, and exclaiming over him, " See this weak and puny

creature! how is it possible that he and his like should
build up a reef or an island?" No one ever set himself
deliberately at work to invent or improve language—or did
so, at least, with any valuable and abiding result; the work
is all accomplished by a continual satisfaction of the need of
the moment, by ever yielding to an impulse and grasping
a possibility which the already acquired treasure of words
and forms, and the habit of their use, suggest and put
within reach. In this sense is language a growth; it is not
consciously fabricated; it increases by a constant and im-
plicit adaptation to the expanding necessities and capacities
of men.

This, again, is what is meant by the phrases "organic
growth, organic development," as applied to language. A
language, like an organic body, is no mere aggregate of
similar particles; it is a complex of related and mutually
helpful parts. As such a body increases by the accretion of
matter having a structure homogeneous with its own, as its
already existing organs form the new addition, and form it
for a determinate purpose—to aid the general life, to help
the performance of the natural functions, of the organized
being—so is it also with language : its new stores are formed from, or assimilated to, its previous substance ; it enriches
itself with the evolutions of its own internal processes, and
in order more fully to secure the end of its being, the expression of the thought of those to whom it belongs. Its
rise, development, decline, and extinction are like the birth,
increase, decay, and death of a living creature.

There is a yet closer parallelism between the life of language and that of the animal kingdom in general. The
speech of each person is, as it were, an individual of a species,
with its general inherited conformity to the specific type, but
also with its individual peculiarities, its tendency to variation
and the formation of a new species. The dialects, languages,
groups, families, stocks, set up by the linguistic student,
correspond with the varieties, species, genera, and so on, of
the zoölogist. And the questions which the students of
nature are so excitedly discussing at the present day—the
nature of specific distinctions, the derivation of species by

individual variation and natural selection, the unity of origin
of animal life—all are closely akin with those which the
linguistic student has constant occasion to treat. We need
not here dwell further upon the comparison : it is so naturally suggested, and so fruitful of interesting and instructive
analogies, that it has been repeatedly drawn out and
employed, by students both of nature and of language.*

Once more, a noteworthy and often-remarked similarity
exists between the facts and methods of geology and those
of linguistic study. The science of language is, as it were,
the geology of the most modern period, the Age of Man,
having for its task to construct the history of development
of the earth and its inhabitants from the time when the
proper geological record remains silent ; when man, no longer
a mere animal, begins by the aid of language to bear witness
respecting his own progress and that of the world about him.
The remains of ancient speech are like strata deposited in
bygone ages, telling of the forms of life then existing, and of
the circumstances which determined or affected them ; while
words are as rolled pebbles, relics of yet more ancient formations, or as fossils, whose grade indicates the progress of
organic life, and whose resemblances and relations show the
correspondence or sequence of the different strata ; while,
everywhere, extensive denudation has marred the completeness
of the record, and rendered impossible a detailed exhibition
of the whole course of development.

Other analogies, hardly less striking than these, might
doubtless be found by a mind curious of such things. Yet
they would be, like these, analogies merely, instructive as
illustrations, but becoming fruitful of error when, letting our
fancy run away with our reason, we allow them to determine
our fundamental views respecting the nature of language
and the method of its study ; when we call language a living

* For instance, by Lyell (Antiquity of Man, chapter xxiii.), who has founded
upon it a lucid and able analogical argument bearing on the Darwinian
theory of the mutation of species.   Professor August Schleicher (Die Darwin-
sche Theorie und die Sprachwissenschaft, Weimar, 1863) attempts absolutely
to prove by its aid the truth of the Darwinian theory, overlooking the fact
that the relation between the two classes of phenomena is one of analogy
only, not of essential agreement.

and growing organism, or pronounce linguistics a physical
science, because zoölogy and geology are such. The point
is one of essential consequence in linguistic philosophy. We
shall never gain a clear apprehension of the phenomena of
linguistic history, either in their individuality or in their totality, if we mistake the nature of the forces which are active
in producing them. Language is, in fact, an institution—
the word may seem an awkward one, but we can find none
better or more truly descriptive—the work of those whose
wants it subserves ; it is in their sole keeping and control ;
it has been by them adapted to their circumstances and wants,
and is still everywhere undergoing at their hands such adaptation ; every separate item of which it is composed is, in its present form—for we are not yet ready for a discussion of the
ultimate origin of human speech—the product of a series of
changes, effected by the will and consent of men, working
themselves out under historical conditions, and conditions of
man's nature, and by the impulse of motives, which are, in
the main, distinctly traceable, and form a legitimate subject
of scientific investigation.

These considerations determine the character of the study
of language as a historical or moral science. It is a branch
of the history of the human race and of human institutions.
It calls for aid upon various other sciences, both moral and
physical : upon mental and metaphysical philosophy, for an
account of the associations which underlie the developments
of signification, and of the laws of thought, the universal
principles of relation, which fix the outlines of grammar ;
upon physiology, for explanation of the structure and mode
of operation of the organs of speech, and the physical relations of articulate sounds, which determine the laws of
euphony, and prescribe the methods of phonetic change ;
upon physical geography and meteorology, even, for information respecting material conditions and climatic aspects,
which have exerted their influence upon linguistic growth.
But the human mind, seeking and choosing expression for
human thought, stands as middle term between all determining causes and their results in the development of language.
It is only as they affect man himself, in his desires and tend-

encies or in his capacities, that they can affect speech : the
immediate agent is the will of men, working under the joint
direction of impelling wants, governing circumstances, and
established habits.   What makes a physical science is that
it deals with material substances, acted on by material forces.
In the formation of geological strata, the ultimate cognizable
agencies are the laws of matter ; the substance affected is
tangible matter ; the product is inert, insensible matter.   In
zoology, again, as in anatomy and physiology, the investigator
has to do with material structures, whose formation is dependent on laws implanted in matter itself, and beyond the
reach of voluntary action.   In language, on the other hand,
the ultimate agencies are intelligent beings, the material is—
not articulated sound alone, which might, in a certain sense,
be regarded as a physical product, but—sound made significant of thought ; and the product is of the same kind, a system of sounds with intelligible content, expressive of the
slowly accumulated wealth of the human race in wisdom,
experience, comprehension of itself and of the rest of creation.   What but an analogical resemblance can there
possibly be between the studies of things so essentially dissimilar ?
    There is a school of modern philosophers who are trying
to materialize all science, to eliminate the distinction between
the physical and the intellectual and moral, to declare for
naught the free action of the human will, and to resolve the
whole story of the fates of mankind into a series of purely
material effects, produced by assignable physical causes, and
explainable in the past, or determinable for the future, by
an intimate knowledge of those causes, by a recognition of
the action of compulsory motives upon the passively obedient
nature of man.   With such, language will naturally pass,
along with the rest, for a physical product, and its study for
a physical science ; and, however we may dissent from their
general classification, we cannot quarrel with its application
in this particular instance.   But by those who still hold to
the grand distinction of moral and physical sciences, who
think the action of intelligent beings, weighing motives and
selecting courses of conduct, seeing ends and seeking means

4

to their attainment, to be fundamentally and essentially different from that of atoms moved by gravity, chemical affinity, and the other immutable forces of nature, as we call them—by such, the study of language, whose dependence upon voluntary action is so absolute that not one word ever was or ever will be uttered without the distinct exertion of the human will, cannot but be regarded as a moral science ; its real relationship is with those branches of human knowledge among which common opinion is accustomed to rank it—with mental philosophy, with philology, with history.

While, however, we are thus forced to the acknowledgment that everything in human speech is a product of the conscious action of human beings, we should be leaving out of sight a matter of essential consequence in linguistic investigation if we failed to notice that what the linguistic student seeks in language is not what men have voluntarily or intentionally placed there. As we have already seen, each separate item in the production or modification of language is a satisfaction of the need of the moment; it is prompted by the exigencies of the particular case; it is brought forth for the practical end of convenient communication, and with no ulterior aim or object whatsoever ; it is accepted by the community only because it supplies a perceived want, and answers an acknowledged purpose in the uses of social intercourse. The language-makers are quite heedless of its position and value as part of a system, or as a record with historical content, nor do they analyze and set before their consciousness the mental tendencies which it gratifies. A language is, in very truth, a grand system, of a highly complicated and symmetrical structure ; it is fitly comparable with an organized body; but this is not because any human mind has planned such a structure and skilfully worked it out. Each single part is conscious and intentional; the whole is instinctive and natural. The unity and symmetry of the system is the unconscious product of the efforts of the human mind, grappling with the facts of the world without and the world within itself, and recording each separate result in speech. Herein is a real language fundamentally different from the elaborate and philosophical structures

with which ingenious men have sometimes thought to replace
them.* These are indeed artful devices, in which the character and bearing of each part is painfully weighed and
determined in advance: compared with them, language is a
real growth; and human thought will as readily exchange
its natural covering for one of them as the growing crusta-
cean will give up its shell for a casing of silver, wrought by
the most skilful hands. Their symmetry is that of a mathematical figure, carefully laid out, and drawn to rule and line;
in language, the human mind, tethered by its limited capacities in the midst of creation, reaches out as far as it can in
every direction and makes its mark, and is surprised at
the end to find the result a circle.

In whatever aspect the general facts of language are
viewed, they exhibit the same absence of reflection and
intention. Phonetic change is the spontaneous working
out of tendencies which the individual does not acknowledge
to himself, in their effects upon organs of whose structure
and workings he is almost or wholly ignorant. Outward
circumstances, historical conditions, progress of knowledge
and culture, are recorded in speech because its practical
uses require that they should be so, not because any one has
attempted to depict them. Language shows ethnic descent,
not as men have chosen to preserve such evidence of their
kindred with other communities and races, but as it cannot
be effaced without special effort directed to that end. The
operations of the mind, the development of association, the
laws of subjective relation, are exhibited there, but only
as they are the agencies which govern the phenomena of
speech, unrecognized, in their working, but inferrible from
their effects.

Now it is this absence of reflection and conscious intent
which takes away from the facts of language the subjective
character that would otherwise belong to them as products
of voluntary action. The linguistic student feels that he is
not dealing with the artful creations of individuals. So far

* For an account of some of these attempts at an artificial language,
of theoretically perfect structure, and designed for universal use, see Professor
Max Müller's Lectures on Language, second series, second lecture.

as concerns the purposes for which he examines them, and the results he would derive from them, they are almost as little the work of man as is the form of his skull, the outlines of his face, the construction of his arm and hand. They are fairly to be regarded as reflections of the facts of human nature and human history, in a mirror imperfect, indeed, but faithful and wholly trustworthy ; not as pictures drawn by men's hands for our information. Hence the close analogies which may be drawn between the study of language and some of the physical sciences. Hence, above all, the fundamental and pervading correspondence between its whole method and theirs. Not less than they, it founds itself upon the widest observation and examination of particular facts, and proceeds toward its results by strict induction, comparing, arranging, and classifying, tracing out relations, exhibiting an inherent system, deducing laws of general or universal application, discovering beneath all the variety and diversity of particulars an ever-present unity, in origin and development, in plan and purpose. Beyond all question, it is this coincidence of method which has confused some of the votaries of linguistic science, and blinded their eyes to the true nature of the ultimate facts upon which their study is founded, leading them to deny the agency of man in the production and change of language, and to pronounce it an organic growth, governed by organic forces.

Another motive—a less important one, and in great part, doubtless, unconscious in its action — impelling certain students of language to claim for their favourite branch of investigation a place in the sisterhood of physical sciences, has been, as I cannot but think, an apprehension lest otherwise they should be unable to prove it entitled to the rank of a science at all. There is a growing disposition on the part of the devotees of physical studies—a class greatly and rapidly increasing in importance and influence—to restrict the honourable title of science to those departments of knowledge which are founded on the unvarying laws of material nature, and to deny the possibility of scientific method and scientific results where the main element of action is the varying and capricious will of man. The considerations adduced above, it is hoped, will remove this apprehension. Nor was it ever otherwise than needless, as the tendency which called it forth is mistaken and unjustifiable. The name " science " admits no such limitation. The vastness of a field of study, the unity in variety of the facts it includes, their connection by such ties that they allow of strict classification and offer fruitful ground for deduction, and the value of the results attained, the truth deduced—these things make a science. And, in all these respects, the study of language need fear a comparison with no one of the physical sciences. Its field is the speech of all mankind, cultivated or savage ; the thousands of existing dialects, with all their recorded predecessors ; the countless multitudes of details furnished by these, each significant of a fact in human history, external or internal. The wealth of languages is like the wealth of species in the whole animal kingdom. Their tie of connection is the unity of human nature in its wants and capacities, the unity of human knowledge, of existing things and their relations, to be apprehended by the mind and reflected in speech—a bond as infinite in its ramifications among all the varieties of human language, and as powerful in its binding force, as is the unity of plan in vegetable or animal life. The results, finally, for human history, the history of mind, of civilization, of connection of races, for the comprehension of man, in his high endowments and in his use of them, are of surpassing interest. To compare their worth with that of the results derivable from other sciences were to no good purpose : all truth is valuable, and that which pertains to the nature and history of man himself is, to say the least, not inferior in interest to that which concerns his surroundings. Linguistic science, then, has in itself enough of dignity and true scientific character not to need to borrow aught of either from association with other branches of inquiry, which differ from it in subject and scope, while yet they seek by corresponding methods the same ultimate object, the increase of knowledge, and the advancement of man in comprehension of himself and of the universe.

We return, now, from this necessary digression, to follow
onward our leading inquiry, "Why we speak as we do?"
And we have to push the question a step further than in the
last lecture, asking this time, not simply how we ourselves
came into possession of the signs of which our mother-
tongue is made up, but also how those from whom we
learned them came into possession of them before us; how
the tradition from whose hands we implicitly accepted them
got them in the form in which it passed them on to us;
why our words, in short, are what they are, and not otherwise. We have seen that every part and particle of every
existing language is a historical product, the final result of a
series of changes, working themselves out in time, under
the pressure of circumstances, and by the guidance of
motives, which are not beyond the reach of our discovery.
This fact prescribes the mode in which language is to be
fruitfully studied. If we would understand anything which
has *become* what it is, a knowledge of its present constitution is not enough: we must follow it backward from stage
to stage, tracing out the phases it has assumed, and the
causes which have determined the transition of one into the
other. Merely to classify, arrange, and set forth in order
the phenomena of a spoken tongue, its significant material,
usages and modes of expression, is grammar and lexicography,
not linguistic science. The former state and prescribe only;
the latter seeks to explain. And when the explanation is
historical, the search for it must be of the same character.
To construct, then, by historical processes, with the aid of
all the historical evidences within his reach, the history of
development of language, back to its very beginning, is the
main task of the linguistic student; it is the means by
which he arrives at a true comprehension of language, in its
own nature and in its relations to the human mind and
to human history.

Furthermore, it is hardly necessary to point out that the
history of language reposes on that of words. Language is
made up of signs for thought, which, though in one sense
parts of a whole, are in another and more essential sense
isolated and independent entities. Each is produced for its

own purpose ; each is separately exposed to the changes and
vicissitudes of linguistic life, is modified, recombined, or
dropped, according to its own uses and capacities.   Hence
etymology, the historical study of individual words, is the
foundation and substructure of all investigation of language ;
the broad principles, the wide-reaching views, the truths of
universal application and importance, which constitute the
upper fabric of linguistic science, all rest upon word-genealogies.   Words are the single witnesses from whom etymology
draws out the testimony which they have to give respecting
themselves, the tongue to which they belong, and all human
speech.

How the study of words is made the means of bringing
to light the processes of linguistic growth, and what those
processes are, it will, accordingly, be our next duty to examine and set forth by suitable examples.   Having only
illustration in view, we will avoid all cases of a difficult or
doubtful character, noticing only words whose history is
well known ; choosing, moreover, those which, while they
truly exhibit the principles we seek to establish, are at the
same time of the simplest kind, and most open to general
comprehension.

There is no word or class of words whose history does
not exemplify, more or less fully, all the different kinds of
linguistic change.   It will be more convenient for us, however, to take up these kinds in succession, and to select our
instances accordingly.   And, as the possibility of etymological analysis depends in no small part on the nature of
words as not simple entities, but made up of separate elements, this composite character of the constituents of speech
may properly engage our first attention.

That we are in the constant habit of putting together two
independent vocables to form a compound word, is an obvious and familiar fact.   Instances of such words are *fear-inspiring, god-like, break-neck, house-top.*   They are substitutes
for the equivalent phrases *inspiring fear, like a god, apt to
break one's neck, top of a house.*   For the sake of more compact and convenient expression, we have given a closer
unity to the compound word than belongs to the aggregate

which it represents, by omission of connectives, by inversion
of the more usual order of arrangement, but most of all by
unity of accent: this last is the chief outward means of
composition; it converts two entities into one, for the
nonce, by subordinating the one of them to the other. Our
common talk is strewn with such words, and so gradual is
the transition to them from the mere collocations of the
phrase, that there are couples, like *mother-tongue*, *well-
known*, which we hardly know whether to write separately,
as collocations only, or with a hyphen, as loose compounds;
others, like *dial-plate, well-being,* usage so far recognizes for
compounds that they are always written together, sometimes
with the hyphen and sometimes without; others yet, like
godlike, herself, are so grown together by long contact, by
habitual connection, that we hardly think of them as having
a dual nature. And even more than this : we have formed
some so close combinations that it costs us a little reflection
to separate them into their original parts. Of such a
character is *forehead*, still written to accord with its derivation, as a name for the *fore* part of the *head*, but so altered
in pronunciation that, but for its spelling, its origin would
certainly escape the notice of nineteen-twentieths of those
who use it. Such, again, is *fortnight*, altered both in pronunciation and in spelling from the *fourteen nights* out of
which it grew. Such, once more, is our familiar verb *breakfast*. We gave this name to our morning meal, because it
broke, or interrupted, the longest *fast* of the day, that which
includes the night's sleep. We said at first *breāk fāst*—" *I*
broke fast at such an hour this morning :" he, or they, who
first ventured to say *I breakfasted* were guilty of as heinous
a violation of grammatical rule as he would be who should
now declare *I takedinnered*, instead of *I took dinner ;* but
good usage came over to their side and ratified their blunder,
because the community were minded to give a specific name
to their earliest meal and to the act of partaking of it, and
therefore converted the collocation *breākfāst* into the real
compound *breăkfast*.

Yet once more, not only are those words in our language
of composite structure, of which at first sight, or on second

thought, we thus recognize the constituent elements; not a
few, also, which we should not readily conjecture to be other
than simple and indivisible entities, and which could not be
proved otherwise by any evidence which our present speech
contains, do nevertheless, when we trace their history by the
aid of other and older languages than ours, admit of analysis
into component parts. We will note, as instances, only a
familiar word or two, namely *such* and *which*. The forms of
these words in Anglo-Saxon are *swylc* and *hwylc*: with the latter of them the Scottish *whilk* for *which* quite closely agrees,
and they also find their near correspondents in the German
solch and *welch*. On following up their genealogy, from language to language of our family, we find at last that they
are made up of the ancient words for *so* and *who*, with the
adjective *like* added to each: *such* is *so-like*, ' of that likeness
or sort;' *which* is *who-like*, ' of what likeness or sort.'

But we turn from compounds like these, in which two
originally independent words are fully fused into one, in
meaning and form, to another class, of much higher importance in the history of language.

Let us look, first, at our word *fearful*. This, upon reflection, is a not less evident compound than *fear-inspiring*:
our common adjective *full* is perfectly recognizable as its
final member. Yet, though such be its palpable origin, it
is, after all, a compound of a somewhat different character
from the other. The subordinate element *full*, owing to its
use in a similar way in a great number of other compounds,
such as *careful, truthful, plentiful, dutiful*, and the frequent
and familiar occurrence of the words it forms, has, to our
apprehension, in some measure lost the consciousness of its
independent character, and sunk to the condition of a mere
suffix, forming adjectives from nouns, like the suffix *ous* in
such words as *perilous, riotous, plenteous, duteous*. It approaches, too, the character of a suffix, in that its compounds
are not, like *fear-inspiring* and *house-top*, directly translatable
back into the elements which form them: *plentiful* and *dutiful* do not mean ' full of plenty ' and ' full of duty,' but are
the precise equivalents of *plenteous* and *duteous*. We could
with entire propriety form an adjective from a new noun by

adding *ful* to it, without concerning ourselves as to whether the corresponding phrase, " full of so and so," would or would not make good sense.   And when we hear a Scotchman say *fearfu'*, *carefu'*, we both understand him without difficulty, and do not think of inquiring whether he also clips the adjective *full* to *fu'*.

The word of opposite meaning, *fearless*, is not less readily recognizable as a compound, and our first impulse is to see in its final element our common word *less*, to interpret *fearless* as meaning ' *minus* fear,' 'deprived of fear,' and so ' exempt from fear.'   A little study of the history of such words, however, as it is to be read in other dialects, shows us that this is a mistake, and that our *less* has nothing whatever to do with the compound.   The Anglo-Saxon form of the ending, *leas*, is palpably the adjective *leas*, which is the same with our word *loose ;* and *fearless* is primarily ' loose from fear,' ' free from fear.'   The original subordinate member of the compound has here gone completely through the process of conversion into a suffix, being so divorced from the words which are really akin with it that its derivation is greatly obscured, and a false etymology is suggested to the mind which reflects upon it.

Take, again, such words as *godly, homely, brotherly, lovely.* Here, as in the other cases, each is composed of two parts ; but, while we recognize the one as a noun, having an independent existence in the language, we do not even feel tempted to regard the other as anything but an adjective suffix, destitute of separate significance ; it appears in our usage only as an appendage to other words, impressing upon them a certain modification of meaning.   What, however, is its history ?   Upon tracing it up into the older form of our speech, the Anglo-Saxon, we find that our modern usage has mutilated it after the same fashion as the Scottish dialect now mutilates the *ful* of *fearful*—by dropping off, namely, an original final consonant: its earlier form was *lic*.   The final guttural letter we find preserved even to the present day in the corresponding suffixes of the other Germanic languages, as in the German *lich*, Swedish *lig*, Dutch *lijk*. These facts lead us naturally to the conjecture that the so-

called suffix may be nothing more than a metamorphosis of
our common adjective *like;* and a reference to the oldest
Germanic dialect, the Mœso-Gothic, puts the case beyond
all question ; for there we find the suffix and the independent adjective to be in all respects the same, and the derivatives formed with the suffix to be as evident compounds with
the adjective as are our own *godlike, childlike,* and so on.
Words thus composed are common in all the Germanic
tongues; but we who speak English have given the same
suffix a further modification of meaning, and an extension of
application, which belong to it nowhere else. In our usage
it is an adverbial suffix, by which any adjective whatever
may be converted into an adverb, as in *truly, badly, fearfully,
fearlessly.* In the old Anglo-Saxon, such adverbs were oblique cases of adjectives in *lic,* and so, of course, were
derived only from adjectives formed by this ending ; the full
adverbial suffix was *lice,* the *e* being a case-termination : instances are *ánlíce,* ' only, singularly,' from *ánlíc,* ' sole, singular,' literally ' one-like ; ' *leóflíce,* 'lovelily,' from *leóflíc,*
' lovely.' We moderns, now, have suffered the ending to go
out of use as one forming adjectives, only retaining the adjectives so formed which we have inherited from the ancient
time ; but we have taken it up in its adverbial application,
and, ignoring both its original character and its former
limitation to a single class of adjectives, apply it with un-
restricted freedom in making an adverb from any adjective
we choose ; while, at the same time, we have mutilated its
form, casting off as unnecessary the vowel ending, along
with the consonant to which it was appended. The history
of this adverbial suffix is worthy of special notice, inasmuch
as the suffix itself is the latest addition which our grammatical system has gained in the synthetic way, and as its
elaboration has taken place during the period when the
growth of our language is illustrated by contemporary
documents. The successive steps were clearly as follows :
the adjective *like* was first added to a number of nouns,
forming a considerable class of adjective compounds, like
those now formed by us with *full* ; then, like the latter word,
it lost in a measure the consciousness of its origin, and was

regarded rather as a suffix, forming derivative adjectives ; one of the oblique cases of these adjectives was next often employed in an adverbial sense ; and the use of the suffix in its extended form and with its modified application grew in importance and frequency, until finally it threw quite into the shade and supplanted the adjective use—and the independent adjective had become a mere adverbial ending. The mutilation of its form went hand in hand with this obliviousness of its origin and with its transferral to a new office ; each helped on the other.

Another Germanic suffix, *ship*, as in *friendship*, *worship*, *lordship*, is distinctly traceable to its origin in the independent word *shape ;* and its transition of meaning, from ' form ' to ' aspect, condition, *status*, rank,' though perhaps less obvious than those which we have already noted, is evidently a natural and easy one.

A case of somewhat greater difficulty is presented us in such forms as *I loved.* Here the final *d* is, as we say, the sign of the preterit tense, added to the root *love* in order to adapt it to the expression of past time ; and, from the evidence presented in our own language, no suspicion of its derivation from an independent word would ever cross our minds. Nor does the Anglo-Saxon, nor any other of the Germanic dialects of the same period, cast any light upon its origin. Since, however, such a sign of past time is one of the distinctive features of the Germanic group of languages, and is found nowhere else in the greater family to which these belong, we cannot help assuming that it has grown up in them since their separation from the rest of the family : just as the adverbial suffix *ly*, which is peculiar to our own tongue, has grown up in it since its separation from the other Germanic tongues. It is therefore a form of comparatively modern introduction, and we might hope to trace out its genesis. This is, in fact, disclosed to us by the Mœso-Gothic, the most ancient Germanic dialect, which stands toward the rest in somewhat the same relation as the Anglo-Saxon to the English ; in its primitive and uncorrupted forms we see clearly that the preterits in question are made by appending to the root of the verb the past

tense of another verb, namely *did*, from *to do*. *We tamed* is
in Mœso-Gothic *tamidêdum*, which means not less evidently
tame-did-we than the Anglo-Saxon *sóthlíce*, ' soothly, truly,'
means ' in a sooth-like (truth-like) way.' *I loved* is, then,
originally *I love did*, that is, *I did love*—as, unconsciously
repeating in another way the same old act of composition,
we now almost as often say. The history of the suffix has
been quite like that of the *ly* of *truly*, save that it happened
longer ago, and is therefore more difficult to read.

All our illustrations hitherto have been taken from the
Germanic part of our language, and they have all been forms
which are peculiar to the Germanic dialects, and which we
have therefore, as already remarked, every reason to believe
of later date than the separation of that group of dialects
from the other tongues with which it stands related. Yet,
with the exception of the adverbial application of the suffix
ly, they are all anterior to the time at which we first make
acquaintance with any Germanic tongue in contemporary
records. Our confidence in the reality of our etymological
analysis, and in the justness of the inferences drawn from it,
is not on that account any the less : we feel as sure that the
words in question were made by putting together the two
parts into which each is still resolvable as if the whole process of composition had gone on under our own observation.
If this were not so, if our conclusions respecting the growth
of language were to be limited by the possession of strict
documentary evidence, our researches in linguistic history
would be stopped almost at the outset. Few languages
have any considerable portion of their development illustrated by contemporary records ; literature is wont, at the
best, to cast light upon certain distinct epochs in the history of a dialect, leaving in obscurity the intervening periods ;
nor do we ever, by such help, reach a point at all nearly
approaching that of the actual origin of speech. Hence the
necessity resting upon the etymologist of interrogating the
material of language itself, of making words yield up, on
examination, their own history. He applies the analogy of
processes of change and development which are actually
going on in language to explain the earlier results of the

same or like processes. And, if he work with due caution and logical strictness, his results are no more exposed to question than are those of the geologist, who infers, from the remains of animal and vegetable organisms in deeply-buried rocks, the deposition of those rocks in a period when animal and vegetable life, analogous with that of our own day, was abundant.

If, now, we turn our attention to other portions of our English speech, to those which come to us from the Latin, or which are of an ancient and primitive growth, we note the same condition of things as prevailing there also. The subject admits of the most abundant and varied illustration, but we must limit ourselves to but an instance or two.

In the series of multiplicative numerals, *double, triple, quadruple, quintuple,* and so on, we have a suffix *ple,* which is the principal indicator of the grammatical quality of the words. On following them up into the Latin, whence we derive them, we find this brief ending to be a mutilated remnant of the syllable *plic,* which is a well-known root, meaning ' to bend, to fold.' *Double* is thus by origin *duplic,* by abbreviation from *duo-plic,* and is, in sense, the precise Latin equivalent of our Germanic word *two-fold.* We still retain the fuller form in *duplicate,* the learned synonym of *double.*

Again, one of the oldest words in our familiar speech is *am,* the first person of the verb *to be,* nor do we see in it any signs of being otherwise than simple and indivisible. As, however, we trace its history of changes backward, from one to another of the languages with which our own claims kindred, we are enabled to discover that its two sounds are the scanty relics of two separate elements : the first, *a,* is all that remains of an original syllable *as,* which expressed the idea of existence; the other, *m,* represents an ending, *mi,* which, originally a pronoun, and having the same meaning as the same word, *me,* still has with us, was employed to limit the predicate of existence to the person speaking : it was, in fact, the suffix universally employed, during the earliest period in the history of our family of languages, to form the first persons singular of verbs. *Am,* then, really contains a

verb and its subject pronoun, and means 'be-I;' that is, 'I
exist.' The third person of the same verb, *is*, possesses
virtually a similar character, although linguistic usage, in its
caprice, has dealt somewhat differently with it. As *am*
stands for *as-mi*, 'be-I,' so *is* stands for *as-ti*, 'be-that:' we
have, indeed, worn off the second element altogether, so that
our *is* is the actual representative only of the radical syllable *as;* but by far the greater number of the Germanic dialects, and of the other descendants from the primitive
tongue in which was first formed the compound *asti*, have
retained at least the initial consonant of the pronominal
suffix: witness the German *ist*, the Slavonian *yest*, the Latin
est, the Greek and Lithuanian *esti*, the Sanscrit *asti*, and so
on. It is the same *t* which, in the form of *th* or *s*, still does
service in the regular scheme of conjugation of our verbs, as
ending of the third person singular present: thus, he *loveth*
or *loves*.

The examples already given may sufficiently answer our
purpose as illustrations of the way in which suffixes are produced, and grammatical classes or categories of words created.
The adjectives in *ful*, or the adjectives in *less*, form together
a related group, having a common character, as derivatives
from nouns, and derivatives possessing a kindred significance,
standing in a certain like relation to their primitives, filling
a certain common office in speech, an office of which the sign
is the syllable *ful*, or *less*, their final member or suffix. With
ly, this is still more notably the case: the suffix *ly* is the
usual sign of adverbial meaning; it makes much the largest
share of all the adverbs we have. A final *m*, added to a
verbal root, in an early stage of the history of our mother-
tongue, and yet more anciently an added syllable *mi*, made
in like manner the first persons singular present of verbs;
as an added *s*, standing for an original syllable *ti*, does even
to the present day make our third persons singular. All
these grammatical signs were once independent elements,
words of distinct meaning, appended to other words and compounded with them—appended, not in one or two isolated
cases only, but so often, and in a sense so generally applicable, that they formed whole classes of compounds. There

was nothing about them save this extensibility of their application and frequency of their use to distinguish their compounds from such as *house-top, break-neck, forehead, fortnight,* and the others of the same class to which we have already referred. Yet this was quite enough to bring about a change of their recognized character, from that of distinct words to that of non-significant appendages to other words. Each passed over into the condition of a *formative element ;* that is to say, an element showing the logical form, the grammatical character, of a derivative, as distinguished from its primitive, the word to which the sign was appended. There was a time when *fear-full, fear-loose, fear-free, free-making, fear-struck, love-like, love-rich, love-sick, love-lorn,* were all words of the same kind, mere lax combinations ; it was only their different degree of availability for answering the ends of speech, for supplying the perceived needs of expression, that caused two or three of them to assume a different character, while the rest remained as they had been.

Often, as every one knows, there is an accumulation of formative elements in the same word. In *truthfully,* for example, we have the adverbial suffix *ly* added to the primitive *truthful ;* in which, again, the adjective suffix *ful* has performed the same office toward the remoter primitive *truth.* By the use of a formative element of another kind, a prefix, we might have made the yet more intricate compound *untruthfully.* Nay, further, *truth* itself contains a suffix, and is a derivative from the adjective *true,* as appears from its analogy with *wealth* from *well, width* from *wide, strength* from *strong,* and many other like words ; and even *true,* did we trace its history to the beginning, we should find ending in a formative element, and deriving its origin from a verbal root meaning ' to be firm, strong, reliable.' The Latin part of our language, which includes most of our many-syllabled words, offers abundant instances of a similar complicated structure. Thus, the term *inapplicabilities* contains two prefixes, the negative *in* and the preposition *ad* which means ' to,' and three suffixes, *able,* forming adjectives, *ty,* forming abstract nouns from adjectives, and *s,* the plural ending, all clustered about the verbal root *plic,* which we have already seen itself forming a suffix, in *double, triple,* and so forth, and which conveys the idea of ' bending ' or ' folding.' By successive extensions and modifications of meaning, by transferral from one category to another through means of their appropriate signs, we have developed this simple idea into a form which can only be represented by the long paraphrase ' numerous conditions of being not able to bend (or fit) to something.'

With but few exceptions—which, moreover, are only apparent ones—all the words of our language admit of such analysis as this, which discovers in them at least two elements, whereof the one conveys the central or fundamental idea, and the other indicates a restriction, application, or relation of that idea. Even those brief vocables which appear to us of simplest character can be proved either to exhibit still, like *am* for *as-mi,* the relic of a mutilated formative element, or, like *is* for *as-ti,* to have lost one which they formerly possessed. This, then, in our language (as in the whole family of languages to which ours is related), is the normal constitution of a word : it invariably contains a radical and a formal portion ; it is made up of a root combined with a suffix, or with a suffix and prefix, or with more than one of each. In more technical phrase, no word is *unformed;* no one has been a mere significant entity, without designation of its relation, without a sign putting it in some class or category.

It is plain, therefore, that a chief portion of linguistic analysis must consist, not in the mere dismembering of such words as we usually style compounded, but in the distinction from one another of radical and formal elements ; in the isolation of the central nucleus, or root, from the affixes which have become attached to it, and the separate recognition of each affix, in its individual form and office. But our illustrations have, as I think, made it not less plain that there is no essential and ultimate difference in the two cases : in the one, as in the other, our process of analysis is the re-tracing of a previous synthesis, whereby two independent elements were combined and integrated. That this is so to a certain extent is a truth so palpable as to admit of neither

denial nor doubt. Had there been in the Germanic languages no such adjective as *full*, no such derivative adjectives
as *fearful* and *truthful* would have grown up in them ; if they
had possessed no adjective *like*, they would never have gained
such adjectives as *godly* and *lovely*, nor such adverbs as *fearfully* and *truly*. So also with *friendship*, with *loved*, with
am and *is*, and the rest. No inconsiderable number of the
formative elements of our tongue, in every department of
grammar and of word-formation, can be thus traced back to
independent words, with which they were at first identical,
out of which they have grown. It is true, at the same time,
that a still larger number do not allow their origin to be
discovered. But we have not, on that account, the right to
conclude that their history is not of the same character. In
grammar, as everywhere else, like effects presuppose like
causes. We have seen how the formative elements are
liable to become corrupted and altered, so that the signs of
their origin are obscured, and may even be obliterated. The
full in *truthful* is easy enough to recognize, but a little historical research is necessary in order to show us the *like*
which is contained in *truly*. *Hateful* is, for aught we know,
as old a compound as *lovely*, but linguistic usage has chanced
to be more merciful to the evidence of descent in the former
case than in the latter. A yet more penetrating investigation is required ere we discover our pronoun *me* in the word
am, or our imperfect *did* in *I loved;* and, but for the happy
chance that preserved to us the one or two fragmentary
manuscripts in which are contained our only records of
Mœso-Gothic speech, the genesis of the latter form would
always have remained an unsolved problem, a subject for ingenious conjecture, but beyond the reach of demonstration.
The loss of each intermediate stage, coming between any
given dialect and its remotest ancestor, wipes out a portion
of the evidence which would explain the origin of its forms.
If English stood all alone among the other languages of the
earth, but an insignificant part of its word-history could be
read ; its kindred dialects, contemporary and older, help us
to the discovery of a much larger portion ; and the preservation of authentic records of every period of its life would,

as we cannot hesitate to believe, make clear the rest. There
is no break in the chain of analogical reasoning which com-
pels the linguistic student to the conviction that his analyses
are everywhere real, and distinguish those elements by the
actual combination of which words were originally made up.
On this conviction rests, for him, the value of his analytical
processes : if they are to be regarded as in part historical
and real, in part only theoretical and illusory, his researches
into the history of language are baffled ; he is in pursuit of
a phantom, and not of truth.

Wherever, then, our study of words brings us to the recognition of an element having a distinct meaning and office,
employed in combination with other elements for the uses of
expression, there we must recognize an originally independent entity.   The parts of our words were once themselves
words.

Some of the remoter consequences involved in this principle will engage our attention at a more advanced stage of
our inquiries into the history of human speech : our present
purpose only requires us to notice that, since all known
words have been constructed by putting together previously
existing items of speech, the combination of old materials
into new forms, the making of compounds, with frequent accompanying reduction of one of their members to a merely
formal significance, is a very prominent part of the mechanism of language, one of the most fundamental and important
of the processes by which are carried on its perpetual
growth and change, its organic development.   What other
processes are the concomitants and auxiliaries of this one
we shall go on to inquire in the next lecture.

LECTURE III.

Phonetic change; its ground, action on compound words, part in word-
making, and destructive effects. Replacement of one mode of formal
distinction by another. Extension of analogies. Abolition of valuable
distinctions. Conversion of sounds into one another. Physical characters of alphabetic sounds; physical scheme of the English alphabet.
Obsolescence and loss of words. Changes of meaning; their ground
and methods. Variety of meanings of one word. Synonyms.
Conversion of physical into spiritual meaning. Attenuation of meaning; production of form-words. Variety of derivatives from one
root. Unreflectiveness of the process of making names and forms.
Conceptions antedate their names. Reason of a name historical, and
founded in convenience, not necessity. Insignificance of derivation
in practical use of language.

It will be our present task to continue the examination
and illustration of the processes of linguistic growth which
we began at our last interview. We completed at that time
our preliminary inquiries into the mode of preservation and
transmission of language, and were guided by them to a
recognition of the true nature of the force which alone is
efficient in all the operations of linguistic life—the events,
as we may more properly style them, of linguistic history. It
was found to be the will of men : every word that exists,
exists only as it is uttered or written by the voluntary effort
of human organs ; it is changed only by an action proceeding
from individuals, and ratified by the general consent of speakers and writers. Language, then, is neither an organism
nor a physical product ; and its study is not a physical but
a moral science, a branch of the history of the human race
and of human institutions. The method of its investigation

is historical, an endeavour to trace backward—even to the
beginning, if the recorded evidence permit—the processes
by which our own speech, or human speech in general, has
become what it is, and to discover the *rationale* of those processes, the influences under which they have been carried
on, and the ends which they have been intended to subserve.
We took up first, accordingly, the process of combination
of old material in language into new forms, and exhibited its
universal agency in the production of the present constituents of speech. Not only are words put together to form
what to our sense are and still remain ordinary compounds,
but such compounds are further fused into a deceitful likeness to simple vocables; or, what is of yet more frequent
occurrence and more important bearing, one of their members sinks to a subordinate position, and becomes a suffix,
without recognized separate signification. This, it was
claimed, is the way in which all formative elements, all signs
of grammatical categories, have originated; and as every
word in our language either contains, or has contained and
been deprived of, a formative element, or more than one, the
process of composition is one whose range and importance
in linguistic history cannot easily be over-estimated.

But the same examples on which we relied to show how,
and how extensively, words are compounded together and
forms produced, have shown us not less clearly that mutilation and loss of the elements employed by language, and of
the compounds and forms into which they enter, are also
constant accompaniments of linguistic growth. "All that
is born must die" seems a law almost as inexorable in the
domain of speech as in that of organic life. We have next
to turn our attention to the principles underlying this department of linguistic change, and to some of the modes of
its action and the effects which it produces.

And the first and most important principle which we
have to notice, the one which lies at the bottom of nearly
all phonetic change in language, is the tendency, already
alluded to and briefly illustrated in our first lecture, to make
the work of utterance easier to the speaker, to put a more
facile in the stead of a more difficult sound or combination

of sounds, and to get rid altogether of what is unnecessary in the words we use. All articulate sounds are produced by effort, by expenditure of muscular energy, in the lungs, throat, and mouth. This effort, like every other which man makes, he has an instinctive disposition to seek relief from, to avoid: we may call it laziness, or we may call it economy; it is, in fact, either the one or the other, according to the circumstances of each separate case: it is laziness when it gives up more than it gains; economy, when it gains more than it abandons. Every item of language is subject to its influence, and it works itself out in greatly various ways; we will give our first consideration to the manner in which its action accompanies, aids, and modifies that of the process of composition of old material into new forms, as last set forth. For it is composition, the building up of words out of elements formerly independent, that opens a wide field to the operation of phonetic change, and at the same time gives it its highest importance as an agency in the production and modification of language. If all words were of simple structure and brief form, their alterations would be confined within comparatively narrow limits, and would be of inferior consequence as constituting one of the processes of linguistic growth. Our adjective *like*, for example, is but slightly altered in our usage from the form which it had in the Anglo-Saxon *(lîc)* and the Mœso-Gothic *(leik)*; while, in the compounds into which it has entered, it is mutilated even past recognition: in the adjectives and adverbs like *godly* and *truly*, it has been deprived of its final consonant; in *such* and *which* (A.-S. *swylc, hwylc;* M.-G. *swaleik, hwaleik),* it has saved only the final consonant, and that in a greatly modified shape. Our preterit *did* is, indeed, but a remnant of its older self, but in *love-d* it has reached a much lower stage of reduction.

The reason which makes phonetic change rifest in linguistic combinations is the same with that which creates the possibility of any phonetic change at all in language. It is inherent in the nature of a word, and its relation to the idea which it represents. A word, as we have already seen, is not the natural reflection of an idea, nor its description,

nor its definition ; it is only its designation, an arbitrary
and conventional sign with which we learn to associate it.
Hence it has no internal force conservative of its identity,
but is exposed to all the changes which external circumstances, the needs of practical use, the convenience and
caprice of those who employ it, may suggest. When we
have once formed a compound, and applied it to a given
purpose, we are not at all solicitous to keep up the memory
of its origin ; we are, rather, ready to forget it. The word
once coined, we accept it as an integral representative of
the conception to which we attach it, and give our whole
attention to that, not concerning ourselves about its derivation, or its etymological aptness. Practical convenience becomes the paramount consideration, to which every other is
made to give way. Let us look at an example or two. There
is a certain class of insects, the most brilliant and beautiful
which the entomologist knows. Its most common species,
both in the Old world and the New, are of a yellow colour ;
clouds of these yellow flutterers, at certain seasons, swarm
upon the roads and fill the air. Because, now, butter is or
ought to be yellow, our simple and unromantic ancestors
called the insect in question the *butterfly*, as they called a certain familiar yellow flower the *buttercup*. In our usage, this
word has become the name, not of the yellow species only,
but of the whole class. And, though its form is unmutilated,
and its composition as clear as on the day when the words
were first put together to make it, probably not one person
in a hundred of those who employ it has ever thought of its
origin, or considered why it was applied to the use in which
it serves him. We no longer invest it with the paltry and
prosaic associations which, from its derivation, would naturally
cluster about it; it has become, from long alliance in our
thoughts with the elegant creatures which it designates, instinct with poetic beauty and grace.

Again, some ancient navigator, who discovered a certain
huge island on the north-eastern coast of America, had not
ingenuity enough to devise a better appellation for it than
the new-found land. Such a name was evidently no more
applicable to this than to any other of the newly-discovered

regions in that age of discovery, yet men learned by degrees
to employ it as the proper title of this particular island.
At first, doubtless, they pronounced it distinctly, *new-found
land;* but no sooner had the words fully acquired the character of a specific name for a single thing, than they began to
receive the stamp of formal unity, by the accentuation of one
of the three syllables, and the subordination of the rest, in
quantity and distinctness of tone. There was, to be sure, a
difficulty about deciding which of three constituents of so
nearly equal value should receive the principal stress of
voice, and our practice varies even now between *Newfoúnd-
land* and *Néwfoŭndland,* while we occasionally even hear *New-
foŭndlánd:* but good usage will finally decide in favour of
one of these modes, and will reject the others. How little
is the primary meaning of the compound present to the
minds of those who utter it! And when, transferring the
name of the island to one of its most noted products, we
speak of some one as "the fortunate owner of a fine Newfoundland," how little we realize that, in terms, we are as-
serting his lordship over a recently discovered territory!
The two words which we have instanced have suffered no
modification, or only a very slight one, of their original form
since they were put together out of separate elements. But it
is clear enough that this readiness to forget the etymological meaning of a word in favour of its derivative application,
to sink its native condition in its official character, prepares
the way for mutilation and mutation. We have put together, to form the title of a certain petty naval officer, the
two words *boat* and *swain,* and we know what the word
means, and why : the sailors, too, know what, but the why
is a matter of indifference to them ; they have no leisure for
a full pronunciation of such cumbrous compounds as *bōat-
swāin;* they cut it down to *bos'n;* and it is a chance if a
single one among them who has not learned to read and
write can tell you how he of the whistle comes by such a title.
So also, the mariner calls *to'gal'nts'ls* what we land-lubbers
know by the more etymologically correct, but more lumbering, name of *topgallantsails.* And these are but typical examples of what has been the history of language from the

beginning. No sooner have men coined a word than they
have begun—not, of course, with deliberate forethought,
but spontaneously, and as it were unconsciously—to see
how the time and labour expended in its utterance could be
economized, how any complicated and difficult combination
of sounds which it presented could be worked over into a
shape better adapted for fluent utterance, how it could be
contracted into a briefer form, what part of it could be
spared without loss of intelligibility.

Thus—to recur to some of our former illustrations—as
soon as we are ready to forego our separate memory of the
constituents of such compounds as *breāk-fắst, fŏre-hĕad, four-
teen-night*, that we may give a more concentrated attention to
the unity of signification which we confer upon them, we begin to convert them into *brĕakfast, fŏre'd, fŏrtnĭt*. And the
case is the same with all those combinations out of which grow
formative elements and forms. While we have clearly in mind
the genesis of *god-like, father-like*, and so forth, we are little
likely to mutilate either part of them : our apprehension of
the latter element as no longer coördinate with the former,
but as an appendage to it, impressing upon it a modification
of meaning, and our reduction of the subordinate element to
ly, thus turning the words into *godly* and *fatherly*, are processes that go hand in hand together, each helping the other.

This brings us to a recognition of the important and valuable part played by the tendency to ease of utterance, and
by the phonetic changes which it prompts, in the construction of the fabric of language. If a word is to be taken
fully out of the condition of constituent member of a compound, and made a formative element, if a compound is thus
to be converted into a form, or otherwise fused together into
an integral word, it must be by the help of some external
modification. Our words *thankful, fearful, truthful*, and
their like, are, by our too present apprehension of the independent significance of their final syllable, kept out of the
category of pure derivatives. Phonetic corruption makes
the difference between a genuine form-word, like *godly*, and
a combination like *godlike*, which is far less plastic and
adaptable to the varying needs of practical use ; it makes the

difference between a synthetic combination, like *I loved*, and
a mere analytic collocation, like *I did love.* It alone renders
possible true grammatical forms, which make the wealth and
power of every inflective language. We sometimes laugh at
the unwieldiness of the compounds which our neighbour language, the German, so abundantly admits; words like *Ritter-
gutsbesitzer*, 'knight's-property-possessor,' or *Schuhmacher-
handwerk*, 'cobbler's-trade,' seem to us too cumbrous for use;
but half the vocables in our own tongue would be as bulky
and awkward, but for the abbreviation which phonetic change
has wrought upon them. Without it, such complicated derivatives as *untruthfully, inapplicabilities*, would have no
advantage over the tedious paraphrases with which we should
now render their precise etymological meaning.

Change, retrenchment, mutilation, disguise of derivation is,
then, both the inevitable and the desirable accompaniment of
such composition as has formed the vocabulary of our spoken
tongue. It stands connected with tendencies of essential
consequence, and is part of the wise economy of speech. It
contributes to conciseness and force of expression. It is the
sign and means of the integration of words. It disencum-
bers terms of traditional remembrances, which would otherwise disturb the unity of attention that ought to be concentrated upon the sign in its relation to the thing signified. It
makes of a word, instead of a congeries of independent entities, held together by a loose bond and equally crowding
themselves upon the apprehension, a unity, composed of duly
subordinated parts.

But the tendency which works out these valuable results
is, at the same time, a blind, or, to speak more exactly, an
unreflecting one, and its action is also in no small measure
destructive; it pulls down the very edifice which it helps to
build. Its direct aim is simply ease and convenience; it
seeks, as we have seen, to save time and labour to the users
of language. There may be, it is evident, waste as well as
economy in the gratification of such a tendency; abbreviation
may be carried beyond the limits of that which can be well
dispensed with; ease and convenience may be consulted by
the sacrifice of what is of worth, as well as by the rejection

of what is unnecessary. No language, indeed, in the mouths of a people not undergoing mental and moral impoverishment, gives up, upon the whole, any of its resources of expression, lets go aught of essential value for which it does not retain or provide an equivalent. But an item may be dropped here and there, which, upon reflection, seems a regrettable loss. And a language may, at least, become greatly altered by the excessive prevalence of the wearing-out processes, abandoning much which in other and kindred languages is retained and valued. It is the more necessary that we take notice of the disorganizing and destructive workings of this tendency, inasmuch as our English speech is, above all other cultivated tongues upon the face of the earth, the one in which they have brought about the most radical and sweeping changes.

It has already been remarked (p. 62) that, in the earliest traceable stage of growth of our language, the first person singular of its verbs was formed by an ending *mi*, of which the *m* in *am* is a relic, and the only one which we have left. In Latin, too, it remains in the present indicative of only two words, *sum* and *inquam*, and in Greek, in the comparatively small class of " verbs in *mi*," like *tithēmi, didōmi*. But the history of verbal conjugation can be better illustrated by considering the changes wrought upon another set of endings, those of the plural. At the same early period of its development, the tongue from which ours is descended had an elaborate series of terminations to denote the first, second, and third persons plural of its verbs. In the oldest form in which we can trace them—when, however, they had already acquired the character of true formative elements—they were *masi, tasi*, and *nti*. By origin, they were pronominal compounds, which had " grown on " to the end of the verbal root—that is to say, had first been habitually spoken in connection with the root, then attached to it, and finally integrated with it, in the manner already illustrated : they meant respectively, ' I and thou ', i.e. ' we ' ; ' he and thou ', i.e. ' ye '; and ' they '. Thus *lagamasi, lagatasi, laganti*, for instance, signified at first, in a manner patent to every speaker's apprehension, ' lie-we ', ' lie-ye ', ' lie-they' : it would

have seemed as superfluous, in using these forms, to put the
subject pronouns a second time before them, as it would seem
to us now to say *I did loved*, for *I loved*. But the consciousness of the origin of the endings becoming dimmed, and their
independent meaning lost from view, they were left to undergo the inevitable process of reduction to a simpler form.
As they appear in the Latin, they have suffered a first process of abbreviation, by rejection of the final vowel of each :
they have become *mus, tis*, and *nt*, as in *legimus, legitis, le-
gunt*, 'we read, ye read, they read.' The ancient Gothic,
the most primitive of the Germanic dialects, exhibits them in
a yet succincter form, the first two having been cut down to
their initial letter only : thus, *ligam, ligith, ligand*. Thus far,
each ending has, through all its changes, preserved its identity,
and is adequate to its office ; however mutilated and corrupted
in form, they are still well distinguished from one another,
and sufficiently characteristic.   But it was now coming to be
usual to put the pronouns before the verb in speaking.   At
first added occasionally, for greater emphasis, they had, as the
pronominal character of the endings faded altogether from
memory, become customary attendants of the verb in all the
persons—save as, in the third person, their place was taken
by the more varied subjects which that person admits. Since,
then, the expressed subjects were of themselves enough to
indicate the person, distinctive endings were no longer
needed.   Under the influence of this consideration, the Anglo-Saxon had reduced all the plural terminations to one—*ath*
in the present, *on* in the imperfect—saying *we licgath, ge licgath, hi licgath*. Although this last was, in its inception,
much such a blunder as is now committed by the vulgar among
ourselves who say *I is, says I*, and so on, it was adopted and
ratified by the community, because it was only a carrying out
of the legitimate tendency to neglect and eliminate distinctions
which are practically unnecessary ; and all the other Germanic dialects have done the same thing, in whole or in part.
We, finally, have carried the process to its furthest possible limit, by casting off the suffixes altogether ; and with
them, in this particular verb, even the final consonant of the
root : as we say *I lie*, so we also say *we lie, ye lie, they lie*.

We do not feel that we have thus sacrificed aught of that distinctness of expression which should be aimed at in language ; *we lie* is not less unambiguous than *laɡamasi ;* it is, in fact, a composition of equivalent elements in another mode ; just as *I did love* is, in a different form, the same combination with *I loved.*

In the declension of our nouns we have effected a more thorough revolution, if that be possible, than in the conjugation of our verbs. The ancient tongue from which our English is the remote descendant inflected its nouns, substantive and adjective, in three numbers, each containing eight cases. Of the numbers, the Anglo-Saxon had almost wholly given up one, the dual, retaining only scanty relics of it in the pronouns ; and, of the cases, it had in familiar use but four—the nominative, genitive, dative, and accusative—with traces of a fifth, the instrumental. The dual, indeed, on account of its little practical value, has disappeared in nearly all the modern languages of our family, its duties being assumed by the plural; and the prepositions have long been usurping the office of the case-endings, and rendering these dispensable. In English, now, all inflection of the adjective has gone out of use, and we have saved for our substantives only one of the cases, the genitive or possessive—to which a few of the pronouns add also an accusative or objective : thus, *he, his, him, they, their, them,* etc. Here, too, we should be loth to acknowledge that we have given up what the true purposes of language required us to keep, that we can speak our minds any less distinctly than our ancestors could, with all their apparatus of inflections.

A remarkable example of the total abandonment of a conspicuous department of grammatical structure, without any compensating substitution, is furnished in our treatment of the matter of gender. The grammatical distinction of words as masculine, feminine, or neuter, by differences of termination and differences of declension, had been from the very earliest period the practice of all the languages of the family to which the English belongs. It was applied not alone to names of objects actually possessed of sex, but to all, of whatever kind, even to intellectual and abstract terms ; the whole language was the scene of an immense personification, where-

by sexual qualities were attributed to everything in the world
both of nature and of mind: often on the ground of conceptions and analogies which we find it excessively difficult to
recognize and appreciate. This state of things still prevailed
in the Anglo-Saxon: nouns were masculine, feminine, and
neuter, according to the ancient tradition (for example, *tóth*,
'tooth,' was masculine; *syn*, 'sin,' was feminine; and *wíf*,
'wife, woman,' was neuter); and every adjective and adjec-
tive-pronoun was declined in the three genders, and made to
agree with its noun in gender as well as in number and case,
just as if it were Latin or Greek. But in that vast decay
and ruin of grammatical forms which attended the elaboration
of our modern English out of its Saxon and Norman elements,
the distinctive suffixes of gender and declension have disappeared along with the rest; and with them has disappeared
this whole scheme of artificial distinctions, of such immemorial
antiquity and wide acceptance. It has completely passed from
our memory and our conception, leaving not a trace behind;
the few pronominal forms indicative of sex which we have
saved—namely, *he*, *she*, *it*, *his* and *him*, *her*, and *its*—we use
only according to the requirements of actual sex or its
absence, or to help a poetic personification; and we think it
very inconvenient, and even hardly fair, that, in learning
French and German, we are called upon to burden ourselves
with arbitrary and unpractical distinctions of grammatical
gender.

The disposition to rid our words of whatever in them
is superfluous, or can be spared without detriment to distinctness of expression, has led in our language, as in many
others, to curious replacements of an earlier mode of indicating meaning by one of later date, and of inorganic origin—
that is to say, not produced for the purpose to which it
is applied.   Thus we have a few plurals, of which *men* from
man, *feet* from *foot*, and *mice* from *mouse* are familiar examples, which constitute noteworthy exceptions to our
general rule for the formation of the plural number.   Comparison of the older dialects soon shows us that the change
of vowel in such words as these was originally an accident
only; in was not significant, but euphonic; it was called out

by the vowels of certain case-endings, which assimilated the vowels of the nouns to which these were attached. So little was the altered vowel in Anglo-Saxon a sign of plurality, that it was found also in one of the singular cases, while two of the plural cases exhibited the unchanged vowel of the theme. *Man*, for instance, was thus declined:

	Singular.		Plural.	
Nom.	*man*,	'man':	*men*,	'men.'
Gen.	*mannes*,	'man's';	*manna*,	'men's.'?
Dat.	*men*,	'to man';	*mannum*,	'to men.'
Accus.	*man*,	'man';	*men*,	'men.'

But the nominative and accusative singular exhibited one vowel, and the nominative and accusative plural another; and so this incidental difference of pronunciation between the forms of most frequent occurrence in the two numbers respectively came to appear before the popular apprehension as indicative of the distinction of number; its genesis was already long forgotten, as the case-endings which called it out had disappeared; and now it was fully invested with a new office—though only in a few rather arbitrarily selected cases: the word *book*, for example, has the same hereditary right to a plural *beek*, instead of *books*, as has *foot* to a plural *feet*, instead of *foots*.* The case is quite the same as if, at present, because we pronounce *nătional* (with "short *a*") the adjective derived from *nātion*, we should come finally to neglect as unnecessary the suffix *al*, and should allow *nātion* and *nătion* to answer to one another as corresponding substantive and adjective.

A very similar case of substitution of distinctions originally accidental for others of formal and organic growth appears also in some of our verbs. From *dœlan*, 'to deal,' the Anglo-Saxon formed, by the usual suffixes of conjugation, the imperfect *dœlde* and the participle *dœled*. In our mouthing over of these forms to suit our ideas of convenient pronunciation, we have established a difference of vowel sound among them, saying *I dĕal*, but *he dĕalt* and *we have dĕalt*. Here is an internal distinction, of euphonic

---

* The plural of *bôc* in Anglo-Saxon is *bêc*, as that of *fôt* is *fêt*.

origin, accompanying and auxiliary to the external distinction of conjugational endings. But, among the not inconsiderable number of verbs exhibiting this secondary change of vowel, there are a few, ending in *d*, in which we have elevated it to a primary rank, casting away the endings as inconvenient and unnecessary. Thus, where the Anglo-Saxon says *lædan, lædde, læded*, and *rædan, rædde, ræded*, we say *I lēad, he lĕd, we have lĕd*, and *I rēad, he rĕad, we have rĕad*—not even taking the trouble, in the latter instance, to vary the spelling to conform to the pronunciation.

Yet another analogous phenomenon has a much higher antiquity, wider prevalence, and greater importance, among the languages of the Germanic family : it is the change of radical vowel in what we usually call the "irregular" conjugation of verbs. The imperfect and participle of *sing*, for example, are distinguished from one another and from the present solely by a difference of vowel : thus, *sing, sang, sung*. Other verbs exhibit only a twofold change, their participle agreeing with either the present or the imperfect; thus, *come, came, come; bind, bound, bound*. That this mode of conjugation is Germanic only, proves that it arose after the separation of the Germanic languages from the greater family of which these form a branch. It is, in fact, like the other changes of vowel in declension and conjugation which we have just been considering, of euphonic origin, and it has acquired its present value and significance in comparatively modern times : indeed, the English alone has suffered it to reach its full development as a means of grammatical expression, by generally rejecting all aid from other sources than the variation of vowels in distinguishing the verbal forms from one another. In the Anglo-Saxon, it still wore in great measure a euphonic aspect: that language had its separate affixes for the infinitive and participle; it said *singan*, 'to sing,' and *sungen*, ' sung ;' and its present, *ic singe*, and its preterit, *ic sang*, were distinguished in every person but one by terminations of different form : the varying scale of vowels, then, was only auxiliary to the sense, not essential —and it had, and still has, to a considerable extent, the

same value in the other Germanic dialects, ancient and
modern. Moreover, there were other frequent changes of
vowel in verbal conjugation, in other forms than these : the
second and third persons singular present often differed
from the first, and in a very large class of verbs the preterit
plural differed from the singular. Thus, from *helpan*, ' to
help', for example, we have *ic helpe*, 'I help '; *he hylpth*,
' he helpeth ' ; *ic healp*, 'I helped '; *we hulpon*, ' we helped ';
and finally *holpen*, ' helped '—a fivefold play of vowel change.
We, in our unconscious endeavour to utilize what was
practically valuable in this condition of things, and to reject
the rest from use, have retained and now admit, at most, a
threefold variation, and have made it directly and independently significant, by casting away the needless terminations.

An interesting illustration of the way in which phonetic
corruption sometimes creates a necessity for new forms, and
leads to their production, is to be noted in connection with
this subject. The Germanic preterits were originally formed by means of a reduplication, like the Greek and some of
the Latin perfects ;* but the variation of a radical vowel
had, to no small extent, supplanted it, assuming its office
and causing its disappearance in the great majority of ancient verbs. Its recognition as the sign of past meaning,
and its application to the formation of preterits from new
verbs, were thus broken up and rendered ineffective. At
the same time, the change of vowel was too irregular and
seemingly capricious to supply its place in such uses ; there
was no single analogy presented before the minds of the
language-makers, which could be securely and intelligently
followed. Hence, for all derivative and denominative verbs
—additions by which every language is constantly enriching
its stores of verbal expression—a new kind of past tense
had to be formed, by composition with the old reduplicated
preterit *did*, as has been already explained. This being soon
converted into a suffix, and the number of preterits formed by
means of it increasing greatly and rapidly, it became by
degrees the more common indicator of past action, and was

* See below, lecture vii. p. 268.

recognized as such by the popular apprehension. From
that time, it began to exhibit a tendency to extend its sphere
of application at the expense of the more ancient modes of
forming the preterit tense—the same tendency which shows
itself so noticeably now in every child who learns the English language, inclining him to say *I bringed, I goed, I seed,*
until with much pains he is taught the various " irregular "
forms, and is made to employ them as prevailing usage
directs. Prevailing usage has in our language already ratified a host of such blunders ; a large portion of the ancient
Germanic verbs, formerly inflected after the analogy of *sing,
come, bind, give,* and their like, we now conjugate " regularly." One instance we have had occasion to notice above—
the verb *help,* of which the ancient participle *holpen,* instead
of *helped,* is still to be found in our English Bibles : others
are *bake, creep, fold, leap, laugh, smoke, starve, wade, wield.*

Further examples of the same tendency toward extension
of prevailing analogies beyond their historically correct
limits are to be seen in the present declension of our nouns.
The letter *s* is, with us, the sign of all possessive cases, not
in the singular number alone, but in the plural also of such
words as do not form their plural in *s ;* thus, *man's, men's ;
child's, children's.* In the Anglo-Saxon, it was the genitive
ending of the singular only, and by no means in all nouns :
the feminines, without exception, and many masculines and
neuters, formed their genitives in other ways. But it was
the possessive sign in a majority of substantives, and there
was no other distinctive ending which had the same office ;
and accordingly, it came to be so associated with the relation of possession in the minds of English speakers, that, in
the great change and simplification of grammatical apparatus
which attended the transition of Anglo-Saxon into English,
its use was gradually extended, till at last no exceptions
were left. A like treatment has given our plural suffix the
range of application which it now exhibits. Less than half
the Anglo-Saxon nouns had plurals in *s :* it was restricted
to a single gender, the masculine, nor did it even form all
the masculine plurals ; while, in our usage, it is almost universal, the only exceptions being the anomalous forms already

referred to (*men, mice, feet,* etc.), and the few words, like
oxen from *ox,* in which we have retained relics of another
mode of declension, once belonging to a large class of nouns.
The prevalence which this suffix has attained in our language has been plausibly conjectured to be in part due to
the influence of the French-speaking Normans, in whose
own tongue *s* was the plural-sign in all nouns, having become
such by a similar extension of its original Latin use.
This extensibility of application is a part of the essential
and indispensable character of a formative element. We
have not to go over and over again with the primitive act
of composition and the subsequent reduction, in each separate case. It needs only that there be words enough in
familiar use in a language, in which a certain added element
distinctly impresses a certain modification of meaning upon
certain plainly recognizable primitives, and we establish a
direct association between that element and the given modification of meaning, and are ready to apply the former wherever we wish to signify the latter. The ending *ly,* for instance, we use when we want to make an adverb, without
any thought of whether the adjective *like* would or would
not be properly combinable with the word to which we add
the ending. This alone makes it possible to mobilize, so
to speak, our linguistic material, to use our old and new
words in all the circumstances among which they are liable
to fall. We adopt into our common speech a new term like
telegraph ; it was manufactured out of the stores of expression of the ancient Greek language, by some man versed in
that classic tongue, and is implicitly accepted, under the
sanction and recommendation of the learned, by the public
at large, who neither know nor care for its etymology, who
know only that they want a name for a thing, and that this
answers their purpose. It thus becomes to all intents and
purposes an English word, a naturalized citizen in our tongue,
invested with all the rights and duties of a native—and divest-
ed, also, of those which belonged to it by hereditary descent,
among its own kith and kin. We proceed, accordingly, to
apply to it a whole apparatus of English inflections, long
since worked out by the processes of linguistic change, and

6 *

not yet destroyed by the same processes. We make of it a
verb, in various forms: *he telegraphs, they telegraphed, I shall
telegraph, we are telegraphing*, the art of *telegraphing;* other
nouns come from it, as *telegrapher, telegraphist, telegraphy;*
we can turn it into an adjective, *telegraphic;* and this, again,
into an adverb, *telegraphically.* Historical congruency is the
last thing we think of in all this. To a Greek word we add,
without compunction, endings of wholly diverse descent:
the greater part are Germanic, coming down to us from the
Anglo-Saxon; but one or two, *ic, ical*, are Latin; and at
least one, *ist*, comes ultimately from the Greek. Made up,
as our English language is, out of two diverse tongues,
Anglo-Saxon and Norman-French, and with more or less intermixture of many others, such a condition of things could
not be avoided; it is, while practically one homogeneous
tongue, historically a composite structure, both in vocabulary
and in grammar. Its grammatical apparatus, its system of
mobile endings, whereby words may be derived, inflected,
and varied, is, indeed, in its larger and more essential part
Germanic; but it is also in no insignificant measure Latin;
while hosts of Latin words receive Germanic endings, not a
few Germanic words appear invested with Latin and French
affixes, which have more or less fully acquired in our use the
value of formative elements: such are *dis-belief, re-light, for-
bear-ance, atone-ment, odd-ity, huntr-ess, eat-able, talk-ative.*[*]
   Hitherto we have taken note only of those effects of the
wearing-out process in language which lead to the substitution of one means of expression for another, or which, as in
the case of grammatical gender, do away with luxuries of
expression which any tongue can well afford to dispense
with. But that popular use is not content with abolishing
distinctions which are wanting in practical value, with giving
up what is otherwise replaced, or can be spared without loss,
we shall be fully persuaded, if we merely note what is all
the time going on around us. The wholly regrettable inaccuracies of heedless speakers, their confusion of things
which ought to be carefully held apart, their obliteration of

---

[*] These examples are taken from Professor Hadley's " Brief History of
the English Language, " prefixed to the latest edition of Webster's Dictionary.

valuable distinctions—all these are part and parcel of the
ceaseless changes of language, and not essentially different
from the rest; they are only that part against which the
best public sentiment, a healthy feeling for the conservation
of linguistic integrity, arrays itself most strongly, and which
therefore are either kept down altogether, or come but
slowly and sparingly to acceptance. Let us note a few instances of such linguistic degeneration.

There is in English a long-standing tendency to efface the
distinction of form between the imperfect and participle,
usually assimilating the former to the latter, though not infrequently also the latter to the former. *Spoke* and *broke*,
for *spake* and *brake*, *held* for *holden*, and many others, are of
recent acceptance, but now impregnably established; from
begin, and a considerable class of like verbs, the two forms
he began and *he begun*, and so forth, are in nearly equal
favour;* *he come* for *he came*, *I done* for *I did*, and others
like them, are still blunders and vulgarisms; and we may
hope that they will always continue such. These alterations
find support in one of the analogies of the language, which
has doubtless done much to call them forth. In our regular
verbs, namely, there is an entire coincidence of form between
the preterit and participle. The careless speaker reasons—
not consciously, but in effect—thus: If I say *I gained* and
I have gained, *I dealt* and *I have dealt*, why not also *I sung*
and *I have sung*, *he drank* and *he has drank*, *we held* and *we
have held*, *they done* and *they have done?*

It is not often, perhaps, that the preterit and participle
will stand in connections which fail to show distinctly which
form is meant by the speaker or writer. But we have also
a few verbs—of which *put* is a familiar example—in which
all distinction of present and preterit is likewise lost: if we
say *they put*, the general requirements of the sense alone
can point out the tense, just as if the phrase were so much
Chinese.

---

* This variation is of ancient date, and doubtless founded upon the fact
that, in many verbs of the class, the vowels were unlike in the singular and
plural of the preterit: thus, from *singan*, the Anglo-Saxon has *he sang*, but
we sungon.

The common confusion of *learn* and *teach*, as in "*I learnt
him to swim*," is another case of a somewhat similar character, being also favoured by a recognized usage of our language, which permits us in numerous instances to employ a
verb in both a simple and a causative sense. We say correctly
"the ship *ran* aground" and "they *ran* it aground"; why
not as well "the boy *learned* his lesson" and "they *learned*
him his lesson"?

A reprehensible popular inaccuracy—commencing in this
country, I believe, at the South or among the Irish, but
lately making very alarming progress northward, and through
almost all classes of the community—is threatening to wipe
out in the first persons of our futures the distinction between
the two auxiliaries *shall* and *will*, casting away the former,
and putting the latter in its place. The Southerner says:
"It is certain that we *will* fail," "I *would* try in vain to
thank you." To say *I shall* in circumstances where we
should say *he will*, to put *we should* where good usage would
require *they would*, seems to these people, who have never
investigated either the history or the philosophy of the
difference of the phraseology in the two persons, an incon-
sistency which may and should be avoided. The matter,
however, is one which implies a violation not only of good
English usage, but also of sound etymological morality: *shall*
originally and properly contains the idea of duty, and *will*
that of resolve; and to disregard obligation in the laying out
of future action, making arbitrary resolve the sole guide, is a
lesson which the community ought not to learn from any
section or class, in language any more than in political and
social conduct.

Once more, our verb has long been undergoing a process of
impoverishment by the obliteration of its subjunctive mood.
This had begun even in the Anglo-Saxon, by the partial loss
of the distinctive signs of subjunctive meaning, and the
assimilation of the subjunctive and indicative forms. The
wearing-off of inflections since that period has nearly finished
the work, in wiping out, in almost every verb in the language,
all formal distinction between the two moods, except in the
second and third persons singular present and the second

singular preterit: there, it was still possible to say *if thou love*, *if he love*, *if thou loved*, instead of *thou lovest, he loves, thou lovedst*. But the second persons have become of so rare use with us that they could render little aid in keeping alive in the minds of speakers the apprehension of the subjunctive: it virtually rested solely upon the single form *if he love*. No wonder, then, that the distinction, so weakly sustained, became an evanescent one ; in *if they love, if we loved*, and so on, forms apparently indicative answered sufficiently well the purpose of conditional expression ; why not also in the third person singular ? Under the influence of such considerations, it has become equally allowable to write *if he loves* and *if he love*, even in careful and elegant styles of composition, while the latter is but very rarely heard in colloquial discourse. Only in the verb *to be*, whose subjunctive forms were more plainly, and in more persons, distinguished from the indicative, have they maintained themselves more firmly in use: to say *if I was, if he was*, for *if I were, if he were*, is even now decidedly careless and inelegant.

What has been given must suffice as illustration of the abbreviation of forms, the mutilation and wearing out of formative elements. But this, though a fundamentally and conspicuously important part of the phonetic history of a language, is only a part: the same tendency, to economize the time and labour expended in speaking, to make the utterance of words more easy and convenient, shows itself in a great variety of other ways. None of the articulate elements of which our vocables are composed are exempt from alteration under the operation of this tendency ; while a word continues to maintain its general structure and grammatical form, it is liable to change by the conversion of some of its sounds into others, by omission, even by addition or insertion. The subject of phonetic change in language is too vast, and runs out into a too infinite detail, to be treated here with any fulness : we can only attempt to direct our attention to its most important features and guiding principles.

Each one of the sounds composing our spoken alphabet is produced by an effort in which the lungs, the throat, and the organs of the mouth bear a part. The lungs furnish the rough material, an expulsion of air, in greater or less force ; the vocal cords in the larynx, by their approximation and vibration, give to this material resonance and tone ; while it receives its final form, its articulate character, by the modifying action of the tongue, palate, and lips. Each articulation thus represents a certain position of the shaping organs of the mouth, through which a certain kind and amount of material is emitted. A word is composed of a series of such articulations, and implies a succession of changes of position in the mouth-organs, often accompanied by changes in the action of the larynx upon the passing column of air. Thus, for example, in the word *friendly*. At first, the tips of the upper teeth are pressed upon the edge of the lower lip, and simple breath, not intonated in the larynx, is forced out between the two organs : the rustling thus produced is the *f*-sound. The teeth and lips are now released from service, and the tip of the tongue is brought near to the roof of the mouth at a point a little way behind the gums ; at the same instant, the vocal cords are raised and strained, so that the escaping air sets them in vibration and becomes sonant; tone, instead of mere breath, is expelled; and the sound of *r* is heard. Next the tongue is moved again ; its point is depressed in the mouth, and its middle raised toward the palate, yet not so near but that the sonant breath comes forth freely, giving an opener, a more sonorous and continuable tone than either of the preceding positions yielded : this we call a vowel, short *e*. Once more the tip of the tongue approaches the upper part of the mouth behind the teeth, and this time forms a close contact there, cutting off all exit of the breath through the oral passage ; but the passage of the nose is opened for its escape, and we hear the nasal *n*. To produce the next sound, *d*, the only change needed is the closure of the nasal passage ; the mouth and nose being both shut, no emission of breath is possible ; yet the tone does not cease ; breath enough to support for an instant the sonant vibration of the vocal cords is forced up into the closed cavity of the mouth, behind the tongue : were the vibration and tone intermitted during the instant of closure, the sound uttered would be a *t*, instead of a *d*. Before the oral cavity is so full that the sonant utterance can be no longer sustained, the contact of the tongue with the roof of the mouth is broken at its sides, but kept up at its tip, in which position the continuance of intonated emission generates an *l*. Finally, the tongue is released at the tip and elevated in the middle, to a posture nearly the same with that in which the former vowel was spoken, only a little closer, and we have another vowel, a short *i*. Here, unless some other word immediately follows, the process is ended, and inarticulate breathing is commenced again. Thus, during the pronunciation of so brief and simple a word, the mouth-organs have been compelled to assume in succession seven different positions: but all their movements have been made with such rapidity and precision, one position has followed another so closely and accurately, that no intermediate sounds, no slides from one to another, have been apprehended by the ear; it has heard only the seven articulations. The action of the throat has varied once; passing without modification the breath expended in uttering the *f*, it has intonated, in one unbroken stream, all that followed. The general effort of utterance, too, the degree of exertion put forth by the lungs, has not been the same throughout: the former part of the word has been accented—that is to say, spoken with a fuller and stronger tone —with which effect, when not contravened by the emphasis, or tone of the sentence, a slight rise of musical pitch is wont to ally itself. And yet once more, we have to note that our word, whether we regard it as seven-fold or as one-fold in respect to the action of the articulating organs, presents itself to our apprehension as a two-fold entity: it is dissyllabic. This property, the foundation of which is in the ear of the hearer rather than in the mouth of the speaker, depends upon the antithesis of the opener and closer sounds composing the word: the comparatively open and resonant vowels strike the ear as the prominent and principal constituents of the series, while the closer consonants appear as their adjuncts, separating at the same time that they connect them.

This example brings to light the principal elements which enter into the structure of spoken signs for ideas, and which have to be taken into account in all inquiries into the phonetic history of language. Each constituent of the spoken alphabet requires, in order to its production, a certain kind and amount of effort on the part of the various organs concerned in articulate utterance. Some of them call for greater change from the quiescent condition of the organs, and so are in themselves harder to utter, than others. And again— what is of far higher importance in phonology—some are much harder to utter than others in connection with one another ; the changes of position and mode of action of the articulating organs which they imply are more difficult of production and combination. Thus, it is perfectly practicable to arrange the sounds composing the word *friendly* in such ways as to give very harsh combinations, which, although we may make shift to utter them by a great effort, we should ordinarily and properly call unpronounceable : for example, *nfdrely, lrefdny, yrfdnle.* And our word itself, easy as it seems to us, would be deemed harsh and unpronounceable by many a race and nation of men. It is all a question of degree, of the amount of labour to which we are willing to subject our articulating organs in speaking. Hosts of series of sounds may be made up which, though not unutterable by dint of devoted and vehement exertion, never appear in actual speech, because they are practically too hard ; their cost is greater than their value ; the needs of speech can be supplied without resorting to them. And half the languages in the world have sounds and combinations of sounds which other tongues eschew as being harder than they choose to utter. No word that a community has once formed and uttered is incapable of being kept unchanged in their use ; yet use breeds change in all the constituents of every language : each sound in a word exercises an assimilating influence over the others in its neighbourhood, tending to bring them into some other form which is more easily uttered in connection with itself. The seat of " euphony," as we somewhat mistakenly term it, is in the mouth, not in the ear ; words are changed in phonetic structure, not according to the impression they make upon the organs of hearing, but according to the action which they call for in the organs of speaking ; physiological, not acoustic relations determine how sounds shall pass into one another in the process of linguistic growth.

A spoken alphabet, then, in order to be understood, must be arranged upon a physiological plan. It is no chaos, but an orderly system of articulations, with ties of relationship running through it in every direction. It has its natural limits, divisions, and lines of arrangement. It is composed of series of sounds, produced each in its own part of the mouth, by different degrees of approximation of the same organs. According to these different degrees of approximation, mainly, it is separated into classes: the opener sounds we call vowels; the closer, consonants; and, upon the limit between the two are sounds—like *l*, *r*, *n* in English—which are capable of use as either consonants or vowels. The consonants, again, are subdivided into classes of lesser extent, also determined by their correspondence in respect to measure of openness, resonance, and continuability: such are the semivowels, the nasals, the fricatives (which may be further subdivided into sibilants and spirants), and the mutes. And, after a certain grade of closeness is reached, each position of the mouth-organs gives rise to two distinct sounds, sonant and surd, according as intonated or unintonated breath is expelled through it.

The English spoken alphabet, arranged according to this method, presents the following scheme:*

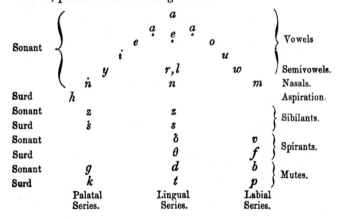

	Palatal Series.	Lingual Series.	Labial Series.	
Sonant				Vowels
		y	*r, l*	*w*	Semivowels.
	ṅ		*n*	*m*	Nasals.
Surd	*h*				Aspiration.
Sonant	*z*		*z*		Sibilants.
Surd	*s̀*		*s*		
Sonant			*δ*	*v*	Spirants.
Surd			*θ*	*f*	
Sonant	*g*		*d*	*b*	Mutes.
Surd	*k*		*t*	*p*	

* For a fuller explanation and establishment of this method of arrange-

The scale of these lectures does not require us to enter into a more detailed examination of the organs of speech and their product, articulate sounds, or a more exact definition of the physical relations of articulate sounds, than has thus been given. The principal and most frequent phonetic transitions are sufficiently explained by our alphabetic scheme. Let us notice a few of them.

The conversion of a surd letter into its corresponding sonant, or of sonant into surd, is abundantly illustrated in the history of every language. Our own plural sign, *s*, is pronounced as *s* only when it follows another surd consonant, as in *plants, cakes;* after a sonant consonant or a vowel, it becomes *z*, as in *eyes, pins, pegs.* A like change is common between two vowels, as in *busy;* the vowel intonation being continued through the intervening consonant, instead of intermitted during its utterance. So, on the other hand, we turn a *d* into a *t* after another surd consonant, where a sonant would be only with difficulty pronounced, as in *looked* (*lookt*); and the German eliminates the intonation from all his final mutes, speaking *kind, kalb,* as if they were written *kint, kalp.* Sounds of the same series, but of different classes, easily pass into one another: thus, the spirants (*f, th,* and so on) are almost universally derived from the full mutes, by a substitution of a close approximation (usually accompanied, it is true, by a slight shifting of position) for the full mute contact; and they

ment of the alphabet, see the author's papers on the Standard Alphabet of Professor Lepsius, in the Journal of the American Oriental Society, vol. vii., pp. 299—332, and vol. viii., pp. 335—373. The signs used in the scheme are those of the Lepsian system. Thus, *a* represents the sound in *far; a̞,* in *făt; e,* in *thĕn* and *thēy; i,* in *pĭn* and *pīque; a̞,* in *whăt* and *āll; o,* in *nōte; u,* in *fŭll* and *rūle; e̞,* in *bŭn* and *bŭrn; z̧,* the *z* of *azure; s̨,* the *sh* of *shun; ð,* the *th* of *that; θ,* the *th* of *thin.* The distinction of long and short vowels, although it is in every case founded on a difference of quality as well as quantity, is here, for convenience's sake, omitted; as are also the diphthongs *ai, au,* and *a̞i,* as in *pint, pound, point* (of which the two first are rather vocal slides than diphthongs). The compound consonants *ch* and *j,* in *church, judge,* have also strictly a right to separate representation; since, though their final element respectively is *s̨* and *z̧,* their initial element is not precisely our usual *t* and *d,* but one of another quality, more palatal. Were all these differences of utterance noted by separate characters, our written alphabet would contain forty-two signs, instead of the thirty given above.

come especially from such mutes as were originally aspirated—
that is to say, had an audible bit of an *h* pronounced after
them, before the following sound: the way in which they are
often written, as *ph*, *th*, *ch* (German), is a result and evidence
of this their origin. A *v*, too, has in many languages taken
the place of an earlier semivowel *w*. Of the transition of
the spirant *th* into the sibilant *s* a notable example is offered
in our substitution—now become universal except in antiquated and solemn styles—of *he loves* for *he loveth : s* as
ending of the third person singular of verbs is rare in
Chaucer, and quite unknown a little earlier. An *s* between
vowels, instead of being turned into its own corresponding
sonant, *z*, becomes sometimes the next opener sonant of the
same series, namely *r :* this change prevails very extensively
in many tongues, as the Sanskrit, Latin, Germanic ; a familiar
example of its effect is seen in our *were*, plural and subjunctive of *was*, which has retained the original sibilant. A less
frequent and regular change puts in place of a letter of one
series one belonging to the same class but a different series.
Thus, when the English gave up in pronunciation its palatal
spirant—still written in so many of our words with *gh*—
while it usually simply silenced it, prolonging or strengthening, by way of compensation, the preceding vowel, as in *light,
bough, Hugh*, it sometimes substituted the labial spirant *f*, as
in *cough, trough ;* and, in the latter word, a common popular
error, doubtless going back to the time of first abandonment
of the proper *gh* sound, substitutes the lingual spirant, *th*,
pronouncing *troth*. So the Russians put *f* for *th*, turning
Theodore into *Fedor*. Exchanges of the mutes of different
organs with one another are not very seldom met with,
though not so easy to illustrate with English instances: the
pent of *pentagon* and the *quinq* of *quinquennial* are Greek and
Latin versions of the same original word, which in our own
tongue, moreover, has become *five*. We often hear persons
who have a constitutional or habitual inaptness to pronounce
an *r*, and who turn it into a *w*, or an *l : r* and *l*, indeed,
throughout the history of language, are the most interchangeable of sounds. Combination of consonants leads with espe-
cial frequency to the assimilation of the one to the other :

our *ditto* is the Latin *dictum*, ' said ' ; we say *dis-join*, but *dif-fuse ; in-different*, but *im-possible ; ad-dict*, but *an-nul*, *ap-pend*, *as-sign*, *ac-cede*, *af-firm*, *ag-gress*, *al-lude*, *am-munition*.

If the consonants are thus variously liable to pass into one another, a yet higher degree of mobility belongs to the vowels. It is needless to go into particulars upon this point: the condition of our own vowel-system is a sufficient illustration of it. The letters *a, e, i, o, u* were originally devised and intended to represent the vowel-sounds in *far, prey, pique, pole*, and *rule*, respectively, and they still have those values, constantly or prevailingly, in most of the other languages which employ them. But, during the written period of our own tongue, the pronunciation of its vowels has undergone—partly under the influence of circumstances which are still clearly to be pointed out—very sweeping and extensive changes, while our words have continued to be spelt nearly as formerly ; and the consequence has been a grand dislocation of our orthographical system, a divorcement of our written from our spoken alphabet. Our written vowels have from three to nine values each, and they are supplemented in use by a host of digraphs, of equally variable pronunciation ; our spoken vowels have each from two to twelve written representatives. All the internal relations of our sounds are turned awry ; what we call " long " and " short " *a*, or *i*, or *u*, or *e*, or *o*, are really no more related to one another as corresponding long and short, than *dog* and *cat*, *sun* and *moon*, are related to one another as corresponding male and female. With our consonants, also, the case is but little better than with our vowels : our words, as we write them, are full of silent and ambiguous signs of every class, unremoved ruins of an overthrown phonetic structure. And our sense of the fitness of things has become so debauched by our training in the midst of these vicious surroundings, that it seems to us natural and proper that the same sound should be written in many different ways, the same sign have many different sounds; the great majority of us seriously believe and soberly maintain that a historical is preferable to a phonetic spelling— that is to say, that it is better to write our words as we imagine that somebody else pronounced them a long time

since, than as we pronounce them ourselves; and an ortho-
epical corruption or anomaly, like *kyind* for *kind, dănce* for
dânce, neïther for *nëither*, is less frowned on by public
opinion, and has a better chance for adoption into general
use, than any, the most obvious, improvement of orthography.

The illustrations of phonetic change which we have been
considering concern, as was claimed for them at the outset,
only the most frequent and easily explainable phenomena of
their kind, those which are found to prevail more or less in
almost every known language. But every language has its
own peculiar history of phonetic development, its special laws
of mutation, its caprices and idiosyncrasies, which no amount
of learning and acuteness could enable the phonologist to
foretell, and of which the full explanation often baffles his
art. His work is historical, not prescriptive. He has to
trace out the changes which have actually taken place in the
spoken structure of language, and to discover, so far as he is
able, their ground, in the physical character and relations of
the sounds concerned, in the positions and motions of the
articulating organs by which those sounds are produced. He
is thus enabled to point out, in the great majority of cases,
how it is that a certain sound, in this or that situation, should
be easily and naturally dropped, or converted into such and
such another sound. But with this, for the most part, he is
obliged to content himself; his power to explain the motive
of the change, why it is made in this word and not in that,
why by this community and not by that other, is very limited.
He cannot tell why sounds are found in the alphabet of one
tongue which are unutterable by the speakers of another;
why combinations which come without difficulty from the
organs of one people are utterly eschewed by its neighbour
and next of kin; why, for example, the Sanskrit will tolerate
no two consonants at the end of a word, the Greek no consonant but *n, s,* or *r,* the Chinese none but a nasal, the Italian
none at all: why the Polynesian will form no syllable which
does not end with a vowel, or which begins with more than one
consonant, while the English will bear as many as six or seven
consonants about a single vowel (as in *splints, strands, twelfths*);
why the accent in a Latin word has its place always determined by the quantity of the syllable before the last, and rests

either upon that syllable or the one that precedes it, while in
Greek it may be given to either of the last three syllables, and
is only partially regulated by quantity; why, again, the Irish
and Bohemian lay the stress of voice invariably upon the first
syllable of a word, and their near relations, the Welsh and
Polish, as invariably upon the penult; others still, like the
Russian and Sanskrit, submitting it to no restriction of place
whatever. These, and the thousand other not less striking
differences of phonetic structure and custom which might
readily be pointed out, are national traits, results of differences
of physical organization so subtile (if they exist at all), of influences of circumstance so recondite, of choice and habit so
arbitrary and capricious, that they will never cease to elude
the search of the investigator. But he will not, in his perplexity, think of ascribing even the most obscure and startling
changes of sound to any other agency than that which brings
about those contractions and conversions which are most
obviously a relief to the organs of articulation : it is still the
speakers of language, and they alone, who work over and
elaborate the words they utter, suiting them to their convenience and their caprice. The final reason to which we
are brought in every case, when historical and physical study
have done their utmost, is but this : it hath pleased the community which used this word to make such an alteration in its
form; and such and such considerations and analogies show
the change to be one neither isolated nor mysterious.
Except in single and exceptional cases, there is no such difference of structure in human mouths and throats that any
human being, of whatever race, may not perfectly master the
pronunciation of any human language, belonging to whatever
other race—provided only his teaching begin early enough,
before his organs have acquired by habit special capacities
and incapacities. The collective disposition and ability of a
community, working itself out under the guidance of circumstances, determines the phonetic form which the common
tongue of the community shall wear. And as, in the first
essays of any child at speaking, we may note not only natural
errors and ready substitutions of one sound for another, common to nearly all children, but also one and another peculiar
conversion, which seems the effect of mere whim, explainable

by nothing but individual caprice, so in the traditional transmission of language—which is but the same process of teaching children to speak, carried out upon a larger scale—we
must look for similar cases of arbitrary phonetic transitions.

So important a part of the history of a language are its
special methods of phonetic change, that, in investigating the
relations of any dialect with its kindred dialects, the first step
is to determine to what sounds in the latter its own sounds
regularly correspond. Thus, on comparing English and
German, we find that a *d* in the former usually agrees, not
with a *d*, but with a *t*, in the latter ; as is shown by *dance* and
tanz, day and *tag, deep* and *tief, drink* and *trink*, and so on.
In like manner, the German counterpart of an English *t* is *s*
or *z :* compare *foot* and *fuss, tin* and *zinn, to* and *zu, two* and
zwei, and the like ; and a German *d* answers to our *th*, as in
die for *the, dein* for *thine, bad* for *bath*. What is yet more
extraordinary is the fact that, if we compare English with the
older languages of our family—as with Latin, Greek, and
Sanskrit—we discover the precise converse of this relation :
as German *t* is English *d*, so English *t* is Latin *d* (compare
two and *duo*) ; as German *d* is English *th*, so English *d* is
Greek *th* (compare *door* and *thura, daughter* and *thugatr*) ;
as German *s* or *z* is English *t*, so English *th* (the lisped letter
instead of the hissed, the spirant for the sibilant) is Latin,
Greek, and Sanskrit *t* (compare *three* and *tres, treis, tri ;
that* and *-tud, to, tad*). In short, taking the series of three
dental mutes, surd, aspirate, and sonant, *t, th*, and *d*, we find
that the Germanic languages in general, including the English, have pushed each of them forward one step, while the
High-German dialects, chiefly represented by the literary
German, have pushed each of them forward two steps.
Thus, in tabular form :

1.	*t*	S.	*tad* (3),				
2.	*th*	E.	*that* (1),	Gr. *thura*,			
3.	*d*	G.	*das* (2).	E. *door*,	L.	*dent-em*	(1),
1.	*t*			G. *tór**.	E.	*tooth*	(2),
2.	*th*				G.	*zand**	(3).

* I give here the Old High-German forms, as illustrating the change more
distinctly and fully than the corresponding modern German words.

And a similar rule of permutation holds good also among the consonants of the two other series, the palatal and labial : *k*, *kh*, *g* ; *p*, *ph*, *b*—the whole, with certain variations and exceptions, of which we do not need here to take account. This intricate method of correspondence without identity is generally styled, after its discoverer, " Grimm's Law of Permutation of Consonants ; "* it is a fact of prime consequence in the history of the group of languages to which ours belongs, and, at the same time, one of the most remarkable and difficult phenomena of its class which the linguistic student finds anywhere offered him for explanation. Nor has any satisfactory explanation of it been yet devised ; while, nevertheless, we have no reason to believe it of a nature essentially different from other mutations of sound, of equally arbitrary appearance, though of less complication and less range, which the history of language everywhere exhibits. The Armenian, for example, has converted its ancient surd mutes prevailingly into sonants, and its sonants into surds ; the cockney drops his initial *h*'s, and aspirates his initial vowels : neither of these, any more than the permutation of consonants in the Germanic languages, is referable to a tendency toward ease of utterance, in any of its ordinary modes of action ; yet no sound linguist would think of doubting that all the three phenomena are alike historical in their nature, results of the working out of tendencies which existed and operated in the minds of those who spoke the several languages in which they have made their appearance.

We need give but a moment's attention to another process of linguistic change, whereby not letters, parts of words, formative elements, alone are lost, but whole words, signs of ideas, disappear from among the stores of expression of a language. This, too, is always and everywhere going on. Evidence of it is to be seen in the obsolete and obsolescent material found recorded on almost every page of our dictionaries, and still more abundantly in the monuments of our literature, of periods to which our dictionaries do not pretend to go back, among the works of the earliest English writers ; and, above all, in the Anglo-Saxon literature. As

* In German, simply the *Lautverschiebung.*

new thought and knowledge calls for new words and phrases, in order to its expression, so, when old thought and knowledge becomes antiquated, is superseded, and loses its currency, the words and phrases which expressed it, unless converted to other purposes, must also go out of use. It is sufficient that any constituent of language come to appear to those who have been accustomed to use it unnecessary and superfluous, and they cease to employ and transmit it; and, as tradition and use are the only means by which the life of language is kept up, it drops out of existence and disappears for ever—unless, indeed, it be maintained in artificial life by the preservation of records of the dialect in which it figured, or its mummy, with due account of its history and departed worth, be deposited, labelled "obsolete," in a dictionary. In part, things themselves pass out of notice and remembrance, and their names along with them; in part, new expressions arise, win their way to popular favour, and crowd out their predecessors; or, of two or more nearly synonymous words, one acquires a special and exclusive currency, and assumes the office of them all; in part, too, even valuable items of expression fall into desuetude, from no assignable cause save the carelessness or caprice of the language-users, and pass away, leaving a felt void behind them. Of course, those departments of a vocabulary which are liable to most extensive and rapid change by expansion are also most exposed to loss of their former substance, since the growth of human knowledge consists not merely in addition, but also in the supersession and replacement of old ideas by new: the technical phraseology of the arts, sciences, and handicrafts shows most obsolete words, as it shows most new words; yet, in the never-ending adjustment of human speech to human circumstances and needs, every part is in its own degree affected by this kind of change, as well as by the others. Rarely has any cultivated tongue, during a like period of its history, given up more of its ancient material than did the English during the few centuries which succeeded the Norman invasion; a large portion of the Anglo-Saxon vocabulary was abandoned; but this was only the natural effect of the intrusion of so many Norman-French words, an enrichment beyond all due measure, rendering necessary the relinquishment of some part of resources which exceeded the wants of the community. If, upon the whole, we have gained by the exchange, it has not been without some regrettable losses, of the significant as well as of the formative elements of expression.

The processes which we have thus examined and illustrated —on the one hand, the production of new words and forms by the combination of old materials ; on the other hand, the wearing down, wearing out, and abandonment of the words and forms thus produced, their fusion and mutilation, their destruction and oblivion—are the means by which are kept up the life and growth of language, so far as concerns its external shape and substance, its sensible body : by their joint and mutual action, greatly varying in rate and kind among different peoples, at different times, and under different circumstances, spoken tongues have been from the beginning of their history, and are still, everywhere becoming other than they were. Yet they together constitute but one department of linguistic change ; another, affecting the internal content of language, the meaning of its words, equally demands notice from us. To this we have not yet distinctly directed our attention, although our illustrations have necessarily set forth, to a certain extent, its action and effects, along with those of the external modifications which we have been especially considering. It is a part of linguistic history which, to say the least, possesses not less interest and importance than the other. To trace out the changes of signification which a word has undergone is quite as essential a part of the etymologist's work as to follow back its changes of phonetic form ; and the former are yet more rich in striking and unexpected developments, more full of instruction, than the latter : upon them depend in no small measure the historical results which the student of language aims at establishing. It may even be claimed with a certain justice that change and development of meaning constitute the real interior life of language, to which the other processes only furnish an outward support. In their details, indeed, the outer and inner growth are to a great extent in-

dependent of one another: a word may suffer modification
of form in any degree, even to the loss or mutation of every
phonetic element it once contained, with no appreciable
alteration of meaning (as in our *I* for Anglo-Saxon *ic*, *eye*
for *eage*) ; and, again, it may be used to convey a totally
different meaning from that which it formerly bore, while
still maintaining its old form. Yet, upon the whole, the two
must correspond, and answer one another's uses. That
would be but an imperfect and awkward language, all whose
expansion of significant content was made without aid from
the processes which generate new words and forms ; and the
highest value of external change lies in its facilitation of internal, in its office of providing signs for new ideas, of expanding a vocabulary and grammatical system into a more
complete adaptedness to their required uses. But change
of meaning is a more fundamental and essential part of linguistic growth than change of form. If, while words grew
together, became fused, integrated, abbreviated, their signification were incapable of variation, no phonetic plasticity
could make of language aught but a stiff dead structure, incapable of continuously supplying the wants of a learning
and reasoning people. If for every distinct conception language were compelled to provide a distinct term, if every
new idea or modification of an idea called imperatively for a
new word or a modification of an old one, the task of language-making would be indefinitely increased in difficulty.
The case, however, is far otherwise. A wonderful facility of
putting old material to new uses stands us in stead in dealing with the intent as well as the form of our words. The
ideal content of speech is even more yielding than is its external audible substance to the touch of the moulding and
shaping mind. In any sentence that may be chosen, as we
shall find that not one of the words is uttered in the same
manner as when it was first generated, so we shall also find
that not one has the same meaning which belonged to it at
the beginning. The phonetists claim, with truth, that any
given articulated sound may, in the history of speech, pass
over into any other ; the same may with equal truth be
claimed of the ideas signified by words : there can hardly be

two so disconnected and unlike that they may not derive themselves historically, through a succession of intermediate steps, from one another or from the same original. The varieties of significant change are as infinite as those of phonetic change; and, as in dealing with the latter, so here again, we must limit ourselves to pointing out and exemplifying the leading principles and more prominent general methods.

The fundamental fact which makes words to be of changeable meaning is the same to which we have already had to refer as making them of changeable form : namely, that there is no internal and necessary connection between a word and the idea designated by it, that no tie save a mental association binds the two together. Conventional usage, the mutual understanding of speakers and hearers, allots to each vocable its significance, and the same authority which makes is able to change, and to change as it will, in whatever way, and to whatever extent. The only limit to the power of change is that imposed by the necessity of mutual intelligibility ; no word may ever by any one act be so altered as to lose its identity as a sign, becoming unrecognizable by those who have been accustomed to employ it. *Eleēmosunē* is reducible to *a'ms*, but only through a series of intermediate stages, of which the German *almosen*, the Anglo-Saxon *almes*, and our spelling *alms* are representatives ; the change of significant content which it has at the same time undergone, from ' feeling of pity or compassion ' to one of the practical results of such a feeling, is comparatively inconsiderable, not more than we are in the constant habit of making at a single step. Our corresponding word of Latin derivation, *charity*, while little altered in form from its original, *caritas*, ' dearness,' has suffered a much more distant transfer of signification. *Priest*, again, from the Greek *presbūteros*, ' an older person,' has wandered from its primitive to about equal distance in form and in meaning ; the one departure taking place under physical inducements, brought about by an impulse to economize physical effort on the part of those who had to utter the word ; the other accompanying a historical change in the character and functions of an official originally chosen

simply as a person of superior age and experience to oversee
the concerns of a Christian community. These are but ordinary examples of the indefinite mutability of words, such as
might be culled out of every sentence which we speak. Let
us look at one or two further instances, which go back to a
remoter period in the history of speech, and illustrate more
fully the normal processes of word-making.

The word *moon*, with which are akin the names for the
same object in many of the languages connected with our
own, comes from a root *(má)* signifying 'to measure', and,
by its etymology, means 'the measurer'. It is plainly the
fact—and one of some interest, as indicating the ways of
thinking of our remote ancestors—that the moon was looked
upon as in a peculiar sense the measurer of time : and, indeed, we know that primitive nations generally have begun
reckoning time by moons or months before arriving at a
distinct apprehension of the year, as an equally natural and
more important period. By an exception, the Latin name
luna (abbreviated from *luc-na*) means 'the shining one.' In
both these cases alike, we have an arbitrary restriction and
special application to a single object of a term properly bearing a general sense ; and also, an arbitrary selection of a
single quality in a thing of complex nature to be made a
ground of designation for the whole thing. In the world of
created objects there are a great many "measurers", and a
great many "shining ones"; there are also a great many
other qualities belonging to the earth's satellite, which have
just as good a right as these two to be noticed in her name :
yet the appellation perfectly answers its purpose ; no one,
for thousands of years, has inquired, save as a matter of
learned curiosity, what, after all, the word *moon* properly
signifies : for us it designates our moon, and we may observe
and study that luminary to the end of time without feeling
that our increased knowledge furnishes any reason for our
changing its name. The words for 'sun' have nearly the
same history, generally designating it as 'the brilliant or
shining one', or as 'the enlivener, quickener, generator'.
There are hardly two other objects within the ordinary
range of human observation more essentially unique than

the sun and the moon, and their titles were, as nearly as is
possible in language, proper names. But such they could
not continue to be. No constituent of language is the appellation of an individual existence or act; each designates
a class; and, even when circumstances seem to limit the
class to one member, we are ever on the watch to extend its
bounds. The same tendency which, as already pointed out,
leads the child, when it has learned the words *papa* and *sky*, to
take the things designated by those words as types of classes,
and so—rightly enough in principle, though wrongly as regards the customary use of language—to call other men
papa, and to call the ceiling *sky*, is always active in us.
Copernicus having taught us that the sun is the great centre
of our system, that the earth is not the point about which
and for which the rest of the universe was created, the
thought is at once suggested to us that the fixed stars also
may be centres of systems like our own, and we call them
suns. And no sooner does Galileo discover for us the lesser
orbs which circle about Jupiter and others of our sister-
planets, than, without a scruple, or a suspicion that we are
doing anything unusual or illegitimate, we style them *moons*.
Each word, too, has its series of figurative and secondary
meanings. "So many *suns*", "so many *moons*", signify the
time marked by so many revolutions of the two luminaries
respectively; in some languages the word *moon* itself (as in
the Greek *mēn*), in others, a derivative from it (as the Latin
mensis and our *month*), comes to be the usual name of the
period determined by the wax and wane of our satellite—
and is then transferred to designate those fixed and arbitrary
subdivisions of the solar year to which the natural system of
lunar months has so generally been compelled to give place.
By a figure of another kind, we sometimes call by the name
sun one who is conspicuous for brilliancy and influence:
"made glorious summer by this *sun* of York." By yet another, but which has now long lost its character as a figure,
and become plain and homely speech, we put *sun* for *sunlight*,
saying, "to walk out of the *sun*", "to bask in the *sun*", and
so on. In more learned and technical phrase, the Latin
name of the moon, *lune*, or its diminutive, *lunette*, is made

the designation of various objects having a shape roughly resembling some one of the moon's varying phases. A popular
superstition connects with these last some of the phenomena
of insanity, and so the same word *lune* has to signify also 'a
crazy fit', while a host of derivatives—as *lunatic, lunacy ;* as
moon-struck, mooning, mooner—attest in our common speech
the influence of the same delusion.

This elasticity of verbal significance, this indefinite con-
tractibility and extensibility of the meaning of words, is
capable of the most varied illustration. Among all the
various workmen who take rough materials and make them
supple or *smooth,* the arbitrary choice of our Germanic
ancestors, ages ago, designated the worker in metal as the
one who should be styled the *smith.* At a much later period,
when the convenience of a more developed social condition
created a demand for surnames, certain individuals of this
respectable profession took from it the cognomen of *Smith.*
Then, just as the name *smith* had been divorced from its connection with the more general idea of *smooth,* and restricted
to a certain class of smoothers, so now, the name *Smith* was
cut loose from the profession, and limited to these particular
individuals and their belongings. Yet, as such, it became
the nucleus of a new class-extension, in which the tie of consanguinity was substituted for that of common occupation ;
and, although all *smiths* are not *Smiths,* the *Smiths* are
now even more numerous than the *smiths.*   Every proper
name, not less than every common noun, goes back thus to an
individual appellation, having a historical ground, and is
determined in its farther application by historical circumstances. Thus, to take a more dignified example, the first
Cæsar was so styled from some fact in his life—the authorities are at issue from what particular one: whether from his
unnatural mode of birth *(a* cæso *matris utero),* or from his
coming into the world with long hair *(cæsaries),* or from his
slaying a Mauritanian elephant *(cæsar* in Mauritanian
speech).   His descendants then inherited from him the same
name, without having to show the same reason for it; and
the preëminent greatness and power of one among them
made it a part of the permanent title of him who ruled the

Roman state, of whatever race he might be ; while from here
it not only passed to the emperor *(kaiser)* of Germany,
whose throne pretends to be the modern representative of
that of Rome, but also to the autocrat *(czar)* of distant and
barbarous Russia—thus becoming the equivalent of 'emperor'
in two of the most important languages of modern Europe.

These examples are of themselves sufficient to place before
our eyes the most important features in the history of significant change of words, the principal processes by which—
even apart from combination or phonetic change, but yet
more effectively in connection with these—the existing
vocabulary of a language is adaptable to the growing knowledge and varying needs of those who use it.   We see that,
in finding a name by which to designate a new conception,
we may either pitch upon some one of the latter's attributes,
inherent or accidental, and denominate it from that, limiting
and specializing for its use an attributive term of a more
general meaning ; or, on the other hand, we may connect it
by a tie of correspondence or analogy with some other conception already named, and extend so as to include it the
sphere of application of the other's designation ; while, in
either case, we may improve or modify to any extent our apprehension of the object conceived of, both stripping it of
qualities with which we had once invested it and attributing
to it others, and may thus pave the way to the establishment
of new relations between it and other objects, which shall become fruitful of further changes in our nomenclature.   These
two, in fact—the restriction and specialization of general
terms, and the extension and generalization of special terms
—are the two grand divisions under which may be arranged
all the infinite varieties of the process of names-giving.
Some of these varieties and their effects, however, it will be
desirable for us to examine and illustrate more fully, before
going on to consider farther the general character of the
process.   We will not attempt in our illustrations a strictly
systematic method, but will take something of the same freedom which linguistic usage assumes in dealing with the
material of speech.

It is obvious how vastly the resources of a language for

the expression of thought are increased by attribution to the
same word of different meanings. Not only does a term exchange one well-defined meaning for another, but it acquires
new uses while yet retaining those it formerly possessed.
For example, *board* appears to be originally connected with
broad, and to designate etymologically that form of timber
which is especially characterized by breadth rather than
thickness. Here we have the customary and normal genesis of the name of a specific thing, by restriction of a general
term expressing one of its attributes. Then follow yet other
individualizations and transfers. The word is applied to designate a table : on the one hand, the table upon which our
food is spread, and we sit around the festive *board ;* whence,
then, a metaphor makes it mean provision or entertainment;
and we seek bed and *board*, or work for our *board :* on the
other hand, the table about which a body of men sit for the
transaction of business, and so, by another metaphor, those
who sit about it, a constituted body of trustees or commis-
sioners, the Board of Trade, or of Commerce, or of Admiralty.
Again, it is specifically used to denote the plank covering of
a vessel, and generates in this sense a new group of phrases,
like *aboard* and *overboard*. The paper-maker, too, has his technical uses for the term ; to him it signifies the stiffest and
thickest, the most board-like, of his fabrics. *Post* (Latin
positum, from *pono*, ' I place ') means by derivation nothing
more than ' put, placed, stationed ' ; all its varied and diverse
senses—so diverse that we can not only say " as immovable as
a *post* ", but also " to travel *post*-haste "—we developed out
of this, along with the historical growth of human institutions. The establishment of a series of stations, *posts*, for
the trusty and rapid transmission of passengers and mails
along a road, leads finally to the familiar use of such terms
as *post-coach*, *post-master*, and *postage*. What a cluster of
derived uses is gathered about the word *head*, as illustrated
in the phrases the *head* of a pin, a *head* of cabbage, the *head*
of a bed, the *head* of a household or of a sect, the *head* of a
river, the *heads* of a discourse, a *head* of hair, so many *head*
of sheep, of one's own *head*, to come to a *head*, to make *head!*
Half the whole list of figures of rhetoric are exemplified in

the history of this one word. In *court*, the secondary significations have almost effaced the primitive, and, to be clear,
we say rather the *court-yard* than the *court* of a castle ; but
a nobleman of the *court*, a case in *court*, the *court* instructs
the jury, to pay *court ;* and the derivative words *courtly,
courteous*, a *courtesy, courtship, courtier, courtesan*, all coming
from one of the specific applications of *court*, tell us of the
manners of those who walk in kings' houses.

Not seldom, the proper meaning of a word is altogether
lost, and it diverges into others so unlike that the common
apprehension is unable to connect them by any tie. *Become*
contains *come*, but not *to be*, although we may often render it
by ' come to be '. Its *be* is the same with that of *befall, beset,
bemoan*, a prefix giving a transitive meaning to an intransitive
verb : to *become* is originally ' to come upon, to come by, to
obtain, to get '. The transfer of meaning, from ' obtain ' to
' come to be ', is a somewhat peculiar one ; but that it is
natural enough is shown by the fact that we have gone on to
treat in the same way the equivalent verb *to get*, saying he
gets tired for he *becomes* tired, and so on. From the same
primitive sense of ' come upon ', we have taken a step in
another direction to ' sit well upon, be adapted to, suit ', as
when we say " such conduct does not *become* one in high
station". To trace the relation between these two meanings
of *become* is out of the power of most of those who use them ;
even the dictionaries enter them as two separate words. Not
much less difficult is the connection of *kind*, 'well-disposed,
friendly ', with *kind*, ' a sort of species ' ; or of *like*, ' to be
fond of ', with *like*, ' resembling '—although both are but a
working out, in the minds of the language-makers, of the
thought " a fellow-feeling makes us wondrous kind " : the
idea of kindred or resemblance leading naturally to that of
consideration and affection. So, once more, how *second*, ' the
sixtieth of a minute ', and *second* as ordinal of *two*, come to
be the same word, would be a puzzle for most English
speakers : the fact that *seconds* constitute the *second* order in
the sexagesimal subdivision of the hour and of the degree
being by no means a conspicuous one ; and the act which
stamped this particular second order of division with the name

second being not less arbitrary than that which applied the
same term—coming, as it does, from *sequor*, ' I follow', and
so signifying only ' the one next following '—to designate the
ordinal which succeeded the first, rather than any other of
the series.
   But it is needless to multiply illustrations of this point ;
every one knows that it is the usual and normal character of
a word to bear a variety, more or less considerable, of meanings and applications, which often diverge so widely, and are
connected so loosely, that the lexicographer's art is severely
taxed to trace out the tie that runs through them, and exhibit
them in their natural order of development. Hardly a term
that we employ is not partially ambiguous, covering, not a
point, but a somewhat extended and irregular territory of
significance ; so that, in understanding what is said to us, we
have to select, under the guidance of the context, or general
requirement of the sense, the particular meaning intended.
To repeat a simile already once made use of, each word is,
as it were, a stroke of the pencil in an outline sketch ; the
ensemble is necessary to the correct interpretation of each.
The art of clear speaking or writing consists in so making up
the picture that the right meaning is surely suggested for
each part, and directly suggested, without requiring any
conscious process of deliberation and choice. The general
ambiguity of speech is contended against and sought to be
overcome in the technical vocabulary of every art and science:
in chemistry, for instance, in mineralogy, in botany, by the
observation of minor differences, even back to the ultimate
atomic constitution of things, and by the multiplication and
nice distinction of terms, the classes under which common
speech groups together the objects of common life are broken
up, and each substance and quality is noted by a name which
designates it, and it alone. Mental philosophy attempts the
same thing with regard to the processes and cognitions of the
mind ; but since, in matters of subjective apprehension, it is impracticable to bring the meaning of words to a definite and
unmistakable test, the difficulty of distinctly denominating
one's ideas, of defining terms, amounts to an impossibility : no
two schools of metaphysics, no two teachers even, agree pre-

cisely in their phraseology ; nor can any one's doctrine upon
recondite points be fully understood save by those who have
studied longest and most thoroughly the entirety of his sys-
tem—nor always even by them. As the significant changes of language thus bring the same
word to the office of designating things widely different, so
they also bring different words to the office of designating the
same or nearly the same thing. Thus the resources of expression are enriched in another way, by the production of
synonyms, names partly accordant, partly otherwise, distinguishing different shades and aspects of the same general idea. I will refer to but a single instance. The feeling of
shrinking anticipation of imminent danger, in its most general manifestation, is called *fear* : but for various degrees and
manifestations of *fear* we have also the names *fright, terror,
dread, alarm, apprehension, panic, tremor, timidity, fearfulness,*
and perhaps others. Each of these has its own relations and
associations ; there is hardly a case where any one of them is
employed that one or other of the rest might not be put in
its place; and yet, there are also situations where only one
of them is the best term to use—though the selection can
only be made, or appreciated when made, by those who are
nicest in their treatment of language, and though no one who
does not possess unusual acuteness and critical judgment can
duly describe and illustrate the special significance of each
term.   We are not to suppose, however, that our synonymy
covers all the distinctions, in this or in any other case, that
might be drawn, and drawn advantageously.   On learning
another language, we may find in its vocabulary a richer
store of expressions for the varieties of this emotion, or a
notation of certain forms of it which we do not heed.
Hardly any word in one tongue precisely fills the domain
appropriated to the word most nearly corresponding with it
in another, so that the former may be invariably translated
by the latter.   The same territory of significance is differently parcelled out in different tongues among the designations which occupy it ; nor is it ever completely covered by
them all.   The varying shades of *fear* are practically infinite, depending on differences of constitutional impressi-

bility to such a feeling, on differences of character and habit
which would make it lead to different action. Hence the
impossibility that one should ever apprehend with absolute
truth what another, even with the nicest use of language,
endeavours to communicate to him. This incapacity of speech
to reveal all that the mind contains meets us at every point.
The soul of each man is a mystery which no other man can
fathom : the most perfect system of signs, the most richly
developed language, leads only to a partial comprehension,
a mutual intelligence whose degree of completeness depends upon the nature of the subject treated, and the acquaintance of the hearer with the mental and moral character
of the speaker.

It not infrequently happens that a variation of phonetic
form comes in to aid the variation of significant content of
a word. That *minúte* portion of time of which sixty make
an hour we call *mínute* (*mín-it*). *Of* and *off* are but different English forms of the same Anglo-Saxon word, the latter
retaining the full significance of the ancient preposition, the
former having acquired a greatly attenuated and extended
sense. *Can* is a variety of *ken*, 'to know,' and means
etymologically 'to know how;' the language-makers had
observed that "knowledge is power" long before it occurred
to Lord Bacon to make the remark. *Worked* and *wrought*,
owned, *owed*, and *ought*, are identical in all their constituent
elements, however differently understood and employed by
us. A yet more notable diversity, both of form and meaning, has been established between *also* and *as*. *Gentle*, *genteel*, and *gentile* all go back to the Latin *gentilis*, which
means simply 'pertaining to a *gens* or race.' So with *legal*,
loyal, and *leal*, so with *fragile* and *frail*, with *secure* and *sure*
—of which the former come more directly from the Latin,
the other from the corrupted French forms. So, too, with
manœuvre and *manure*, *corps* and *corpse*, *think* and *thank*,
and a host of other words which might readily be adduced.

Among the examples already given, not a few have illustrated the transfer of a word from a physical to a spiritual
significance. This method of change is one of such prominent importance in the development of language that it

requires at our hands a more special treatment. By it has
been generated the whole body of our intellectual, moral,
and abstract vocabulary; every word and phrase of which
this is composed, if we are able to trace its history back to
the beginning, can be shown to have signified originally
something concrete and apprehensible by the senses: its
present use is the result of a figurative transfer, founded
on the recognition of an analogy between a physical and a
mental act or product. Let us look, for example, at a few
of the terms which we have just been using. *Abstract* is
'drawn off, dragged away;' *concrete* is 'grown together,
compacted,' into something *substantial*, as we say; that is,
something that 'stands beneath,' constitutes a foundation.
Spirit is 'breath.' *Intellect* comes from a verb signifying
'to gather or select among, to choose between.' *Apprehend*
signifies literally 'to lay hold of,' and we still use it in that
sense, as when we say that the officer *apprehends* the felon;
but we much more often apply it to the laying hold, the
seizing or catching, of something set before our minds to be
received; and we even speak of an *apprehended* calamity,
as if our anticipations reached out and laid hold upon that
which has not yet come, and may never come, upon us.
Sympathy is good Greek for 'companionship in suffering;'
but if we say that two wounded men on neighbouring pallets
sympathize, we refer, not to their physical distress, but to
that unselfish emotional pain with which every noble heart,
forgetting so far its own griefs, is touched at the sight of
another's. To *possess* is 'to sit by, to beset' (like the German equivalent, *besitzen*). When we employ the phrase " I
propose to discuss an important subject," of what a medley
of metaphors should we be guilty, if we had not forgotten
the etymological meaning of the terms we use! To *propose*
is 'to set in front ' of us; to *discuss* is 'to shake to pieces;'
a *subject* is a thing 'thrown under,' something brought under
our notice; *important* means 'carrying within '—that is,
having a content, not empty or valueless.

This subject admits of easiest and most abundant illustration from the Latin side of our language, because so large a
share of our abstract phraseology comes to us from Latin

sources; yet our Germanic words are full of the same kind of meaning.   One of our commonest intellectual terms, *understand*, is also one presenting an exceptionally bold and difficult figure: as if to 'stand beneath' (or perhaps, according to the older meaning of *under*, to 'stand in the midst of') a thing were to take such a position of advantage with regard to it that it could not help disclosing to us its secrets. *Forget* is the opposite of *get*, and means to 'fail to get,' or, having gotten, to lose again from possession.   In this latter sense the language seizes upon it, but arbitrarily restricts its application to a mental possession, and makes the compound signify 'to lose from memory' only.   I *get* my lesson, and *forget* it again ; but the fortune I had once *gotten* I have by no means *forgotten*, when an unlucky venture has made it slip from my hands.   *Forgive* has had a somewhat similar history.   It signifies primarily to 'give up.'   I *forgive* a debt (in phrase now antiquated) when I magnanimously yield it up to him by whom it is due, waiving my claim against him on account of it: I *forgive* an offence when in like manner I voluntarily release the offender from obligation to make amends, from liability to penalty, for it.   It is only by what was originally a blunder of construction that we now talk of *forgiving* the offender, as well as the offence —a blunder like that which we have made in the treatment of more than one other word : for instance, in *please* and *like ;* we said "if you *please*," "if you *like*," i. e. 'if it *please* you,' 'if it *like* you,' until we forgot that the *you* was object of the verb used impersonally, and, apprehending it as subject, began to say also "if I please," "if they like ;" and again, in *reproach*, which means strictly to 'approach again,' to bring up anew before a person what he would fain forget, and, until its etymology was forgotten, took for direct object the offence, and for indirect the offender ; as, " I *reproached* to my friend his fault."   *Befall* is 'fall upon ;' but, if some unlucky person is crushed under the ruins of his dwelling, we speak, not of the house, but only of the accident, as having *befallen* him.   *Right* is 'straight, direct;' *wrong* is ' wrung, twisted;' *queer* is ' crosswise '—and so on, through the whole list of words of the same kind.

8

There is a large and important class of words, the history
of whose development of meaning illustrates, not so much
an elimination of the physical element, a transfer from a
sensible to an intellectual use, as an effacement of significance, a fading-out of distinctive colour, a withdrawal of sub-
stantiality, a reduction to the expression of relation rather
than of quality. Take as an instance the preposition *of*,
already referred to as having been, not long since, undistinguished from *off*, in either form or meaning.   *Off* still
retains its distinct physical sense, of removal in place; it
means 'from, away from, forth from;' in *of*, we have
attenuated this original idea of removal, procedure, derivation,
into the most general and indefinite one of possession,
appurtenance, connection : we say the top *of* the mountain,
though the former is not *off*, but *on*, the latter; we say the
father *of* the boy, as well as the son *of* the man ; we say a
sword *of* steel, pride *of* birth, the time *of* Moses, the city *of*
Athens, and so on.   *For*, from *fore*, ' in front of,' has
passed through a process closely similar.   *Also* (A.-S. *eal-
swa*) was made up of *all* and *so*, and meant ' altogether thus, in
just that way, in like wise;' now, like the abbreviated form
of the last expression, *likewise*, it simply adds a circumstance
coördinate with one already mentioned ; it is hardly more
than a particle of connection.   *As*, as was pointed out
above, is a mutilated form of the same word, with its demonstrative meaning usually converted into a relative : the act
of apprehension which, in a phrase like " he is *as* good *as* he
is great " (that is, ' he is in that degree or manner good in
which degree he is great '), attributes a demonstrative sense
to the former *as*, and a relative to the latter, is not less arbitrary than the one which attributes, in " *the* more, *the*
merrier " (that is, 'in what degree more, in that degree
merrier '), a relative sense to the former *the*, and a demonstrative to the latter.   All those relative words which bind
the parts of a sentence together into an organic whole,
instead of leaving it a congeries of independent clauses, are
of like origin, coming by a gradual change of meaning from
words originally demonstrative or interrogative.   " I knew
that he was ill " is but an altered form of " he was ill ; I

knew *that*," or " I knew *that* thing : viz. he was ill ;" " we saw the man *who* did it " represents " *who* did it ? we saw the man," or " we saw the man [of whom the inquiry is made] *who* did it ? " *Than* is historically the same word as *then* : " he is mightier *than* I " was once " he is mightier, *then* (that is, next after him) I." *Or* is a contracted form of *other.* The primary meaning of *and* is ' against ;' the simpler form of the latter, *again,* has made at least partially the same transition to a connective. Our articles are of quite modern development ; *an* or *a* is the numeral *one ; the* is the demonstrative *that.* We saw some time since how *head* has come to stand for ' individual ;' the butcher talks of "twenty *head* of sheep," as if that part of the animal were not the least valuable from his point of view. *Hand* is similarly applied : " the head-carpenter and his twenty *hands,*" if it do not describe one Briarean individual, ought at least to designate only eleven persons ; but in our usage it denotes twenty-one. Even the peculiarly corporal word *body* has been spiritualized, in *somebody, anybody,* " if a *body* meet a *body,*" and so on : to say " *nobody* was present " is equivalent to saying " not a soul was there," and would be true, however many corpses, or beasts, or bodies metallic, fluid, or aëriform, might have been within cognizance. The verb *grow* signifies properly ' to increase, to change from smaller to larger,' but we often use it in the simple sense of gradual change, of ' becoming,' and say to *grow* thin or small, to *grow* tired. By a farther extension of the same process, the verb which in our whole family of languages originally meant 'to grow ' (Sansk. *bhú,* Greek *phüö*) has in many of them passed through the idea of ' becoming ' to that of ' being ' simply : the Latin *fui,* our *be, been,* are its descendants. Indeed, our substantive verb *to be,* the most bodiless and colourless of all our words, the mere copula between subject and predicate, is made up of the relics of several verbs which once had a distinct physical significance : *be* and *been,* as just noticed, contained the idea of ' growing ;' *am, art, is,* and *are,* that of ' sitting ;'* *was* and *were,* that of ' dwelling, abiding.'

* I connect, namely, the root *as* with *âs,* ' sitting,' as being most probably a different form of the same original. Others conjecture the primitive signification to have been that of ' breathing.'

The corresponding verb in modern French is partly filled up (*être, étais, éte*) from the Latin *stare*, ' to stand.'

Not only are certain words thus stripped by the users and makers of language of the substantial meaning with which they once were invested, but phrases are also formed, of two or more words, and applied to uses widely remote from those which their constituents more generally and properly subserve. An event, we say, *takes place*, or *comes to pass ;* a young man *turns out* ill ; his foibles are tellingly *hit off*, or *taken off ;* though they had seriously *fallen out*, they *made up* their quarrel, and a good understanding was *brought about* between them ; they *gave up* further attempts ; at every new turn, he was *headed off* anew ; I was *put up* to it, but woefully *put upon*, and shall *put up with* such treatment no longer ; don't *take on* so, my good fellow—and so on indefinitely. Phrases such as these are abundant in every part of language, and are of every kind and degree of removal from literalness : in some, a moment's reflection points out the figure or the implication which has led the way to their establishment in current use ; in others, the transfer has been so distant, and some of its steps so bold or so obscure, that even a careful investigation fails fully to show us how it has been accomplished. In phrases, as is well known, consists no small part of the idiom of a language ; use determines, not merely the significance which each word shall bear, but how it shall be combined with other words, in order to something more than intelligibility—to expressiveness, to force, to elegance of style.

All word-making by combination, as illustrated in the last lecture, is closely analogous with phrase-making : it is but the external and formal unification of elements which usage has already made one in idea. The separate and distinctive meaning of the two words in *take place* is as wholly ignored by us who use the expression as is that of the two in *break-fast ;* that we may allow ourselves to say *he breakfasted*, but not *it takeplaced*, is only an accident ; it has no deeper ground than the arbitrariness of conventional usage. To *hit off* is as much one idea as *doff* (from *do off*), to *take on* as *don* (from *do on*), although we are not likely ever to fuse the

two former into single words, like the two latter. It is
clear that, as formerly claimed, the significant content of
words is more plastic than their external form: while our
language has nearly lost the habit, and so the "power," as
we call it, of making new vocables out of independent elements, it is still able to combine and integrate the meanings
of such elements, to no small extent.

But again, all form-making includes as an essential part
something of the same attenuation of meaning of the formative element, the same withdrawal of its distinctive substantial significance and substitution of one which is relational and formal, which we have been illustrating in the
history of independent words. The *ly* of *godly, homely,
lively*, and so on, no longer means 'like;' still less does
that of *fully, mostly*, etc. In the *ship* of *lordship*, the independent word *shape* is no more to be recognized by its significance than by its form. Even the *ful* of *healthful* and
cheerful has been weakened in intent from 'full of' to
'possessed of, characterized by.' But there are other
phrases which exhibit a closer resemblance and more intimate connection with form-making than any hitherto cited.
The *d* of *loved*, as we have already seen, is by origin the
imperfect *did; I loved* means etymologically 'I did or performed a loving;' the *d* has been converted from an independent word into a formative element, indicative of past
action, by being compounded with *love*, and then, in the
relation which it sustained toward that word, losing its distinctive force and meaning, and assuming the value of a
temporal modification merely. With the form *I loved*, now,
the phrase *I did love* is virtually equivalent: it contains the
same elements, and they have the same logical value: the
did is there for no other purpose than the *d*, its hereditary
representative, and is in idea, not less than the latter, a
formative element; it impresses a modification of temporal
form upon the word with which it is connected, and has no
other office. That it still maintains its grammatical standing
as a separate word constitutes only a formal, not an essential,
distinction between the two equivalent expressions. So also
with the verb *have*, by the aid of which we form other of

our past tenses, and of which the primitive significance is
'possession.' It is easy to see how "I *have* my arms
stretched out" might pass into "I *have* stretched out my
arms," or how, in such phrases as "he *has* put on his coat,"
"we *have* eaten our breakfast," "they *have* finished their
work," a declaration of possession of the object in the condition denoted by the participle should come to be accepted.
as sufficiently expressing the completed act of putting it
into that condition ; the present possession, in fact, implies
the past action, and, if our use of *have* were limited to the
cases in which such an implication was apparent, the expressions in which we used it would be phrases only. When,
however, we extend the implication of past action to every
variety of case—as in "I *have* discharged my servant," "he
has lost his breakfast," "we *have* exposed their errors,"
where there is no idea of possession for it to grow out of;
or with neuter verbs, "you *have* been in error," "he *has*
come from London," "they *have* gone away," where there is
even no object for the *have* to govern, where condition, and
not action, is expressed, and "you *are* been," "he *is* come,"
"they *are* gone" would be theoretically more correct (as
they are alone proper in German)—then we have converted
have from an independent part of speech into a purely
formative element. The same word, by a usage not less
bold and pregnant, though of less frequent occurrence, we
make to signify causation of action, as in the phrases "I
will *have* him well whipped for his impertinence," "he *has*
his servant wake him every morning."   And, yet once more,
we turn it into a sign of future action, with further implication of necessity, as in "I *have* to go to him directly."
As is well known, the modern European languages which
are descended from the Latin have formed their simple
futures by means of this phrase, eliminating from it the implication of necessity : the French *j'aimerai*, 'I shall love,'
for instance, is by origin *je aimer ai*, i.e. *j'ai à aimer*, 'I have
to love.' Nor is our own "I *shall* love" of different history, for I *shall* means properly 'I owe, am under obligation;' and the *will* of "he *will* love," although we now so
commonly employ it as the mere sign of futurity, conveys

the idea of 'wish, intent, determination.' The Anglo-Saxon had no future tense, but habitually employed its present in the sense of both present and future; we have struck out, in our modern usage, a peculiarly rich synonymy of expressions for future action: there are the two already mentioned, I *will* go, and I *shall* go, each of which is capable of use as simple future, or with a modal implication; further, I *have* to go, with the nearly equivalent I *am* to go; I *am going* to go (to which the French adds the closely correlative expression " I am coming from going," *je viens d'aller*, that is, ' I have just gone '); I *am on the point* of going, and I *am about* to go—with which is nearly allied the Hibernicism, I *am after* going, for ' I have gone.' These phrases will illustrate the ease with which are found, in the resources of a rich and flexible language, means of denoting a given relation, the variety in which they may be produced, and the arbitrariness with which certain ones are selected for most frequent and familiar employment.

An instance of a purely formal word of a different character is furnished us in the preposition *to* as " sign of the infinitive." The infinitive is originally and properly the verbal noun, and, as a noun, should be governed by any preposition which the sense may require. The present usage of our language, however, forbids this freedom of construction, and assigns to the infinitive *to* as its almost constant accompaniment. At first, the *to* was only employed where it had its proper significance, as in phrases like " I am here *to* help him," that is, ' in order *to* the helping him,' " lawful for him *to* eat," that is, ' *to* the eating; ' * now, no regard whatever is had to this consideration, and, to the apprehension of every speaker of English, *to* is as arbitrary and non-significant a sign of this form of the verb as is the ending *en* of the German *essen*, or *re* of the Latin *edere*.

Yet another class of words having the grammatical *status* of independent members of the sentence, but the logical

---

* ' In Anglo-Saxon, *him alyfede to etanne*, ' allowed him unto eating,' the Anglo-Saxon putting the infinitive after *to* into a distinct dative case, but leaving it uninflected when the object of a verb; as in *hi ongunnon etan*, ' they began eating.'

value of formative elements, is exemplified in the preposition *of*, as already noticed.   The *of* in "a crown *of* gold" is equivalent to the adjective suffix *en* in "a gold*en* crown;" that in "the son *of* the king" to the genitive ending *s* in "the king'*s* son."

We have paid the more attention to this kind of words, because of their importance in the history of language. Such shadowy and half-formal parts of speech as *an* and *the*, such *quasi* formative elements as *do* and *have*, as *to* and *of*, are products of the development of language which by their prevalence mark a distinct tendency, known as the "analytical," and characteristic, in a greater or less degree, of many of the modern tongues with which ours is related.   We shall have to take it into further account in connection with another department of our subject (see lecture seventh).

Let us now look at a single example going to show to what a rich variety the processes of development of meaning may lead among the derivatives of a single verb.   *Pono*, in Latin, signifies 'put,' or 'place,' but we might well spend an hour in tracing out all the store of ideas which it has been made in our language the means of designating.   Some of its uses we have inherited from the Latin; others were struck out during the later period of the French; yet others have grown up on English soil; and we are even now far from having exhausted its capabilities of expression.   From the uncompounded root come *pose*, a *poser*, *position*, with its many applications, *post*, with its still more various and special uses, *posture*, *positive*, and so forth.   Then, as combined with prefixes, for the most part significant merely of place and direction, it gives us an *apposite* remark; *apposition* of nouns; *component* parts; *composure* of mind; a great *composer; compositions* and declamations; a *composing*-stick; *compost*-heaps; *compound* interest; to *compound* a felony; a *deponent* verb; the *deponent* saith; a *deposed* king; *depositions* from water; a school-book *depository;* removal of the *deposits;* a railway *depot;* an *exponent* of democratic principles; to *expose* a fraud; *exposed* to attack; clear *exposition* of a hard text; a lawn with southern *exposure;* an *imposing* figure; *imposts* and customs; miserable *impostor;* consecrated by *imposition* of hands ; to *impound* stray cattle ; an *imposing-*stone ; all his *disposable* forces ; *disposed* to sleep ; an amiable *disposition;* the prima donna is *indisposed;* troops *disposed* in three lines ; God *disposes;* a worthy *opponent;* the house *opposite;* member of the *opposition;* divine *interposition;* he *proposed* to her ; fifth *proposition*, first book ; *propounded* for admission ; locked in sweet *repose;* to *repose* confidence ; what do you *purpose?* he did it on *purpose;* an effect *supposes* a cause ; at least, I *suppose* so ; a *supposititious* heir ; and so on. Here is but a selection from among the multitude of expressions for heterogeneous conceptions which have grown out of the sign for the simple idea of ' putting ' or ' placing ; ' but, though a striking, they are not an exceptional instance of the manner in which linguistic usage deals with all the material of language. As new experiences are met with, new deductions drawn, new opinions formed, new mental combinations made, new products brought forth, new existences discovered, language finds no difficulty in enlarging itself to represent them. The material which lies most conveniently at hand, even if it be not very near, is seized and applied to the purpose : that which was general is individualized ; that which was individual is generalized ; the concrete becomes the abstract ; every variety of metaphor, of elliptical and pregnant expression, is resorted to, and, however bold and even startling at first, sinks by degrees to the level of ordinary prosaic appellation ; and delicate shades of meaning are distinguished by the gradual separation of words at first equivalent. The multiplicity of these changes, and the variety of their results, our examples have been wholly inadequate to set forth with any fulness or completeness ; only enough has been said to bring to light the leading facts and principles, to show what a fertile power of modification and adaptation is inherent in our speech, and that, in seeking and finding names for individual objects of conception, it is restrained within no narrow limits of action.

It must not fail to be observed that these processes of word-making, of names-giving, in all their variety, are not, in the fullest sense, consciously performed : that is to say, they are not, for the most part, premeditated and reflective.

There may be found among them, indeed, every degree of reflection, sometimes rising even to full premeditation. When there is first brought to the knowledge of a community some new substance or product, either natural or artificial, some result of invention or discovery, some process formerly unknown, people ask themselves deliberately "what shall we call it?" and it is by a conscious effort that they devise and assign its appellation—there being, at the same time, an unconscious part to the process; namely, the manner in which their selection is guided and determined by the already subsisting usages and analogies of their speech, and by the limitations of their intelligence. The zoölogist, the chemist, the geologist, when they want a new technical term or distinctive name, go of set purpose to such sources as their Greek and Latin dictionaries, or search out local or personal associations upon which to found their choice; they con over the various distinctive qualities or accidental circumstances of the thing to be denominated, and weigh the capabilities and advisabilities of the case as deliberately as does the father when deciding after which rich uncle, or what noted public character, he shall have his son christened. Sometimes the scientific man has put upon him the task of devising a terminology, as well as a nomenclature—as was the case with those French chemists, at the end of the last century, who fixed the precise scientific meaning to be thenceforth signified by a whole apparatus of formative elements, of suffixes and prefixes : for example, in *sulphuret, sulphuric, sulphurous, sulphate, sulphite, sulphide, bisulphate, sesquisulphide,* and so on. This is, indeed, of the nature of an artificial universal language, built up of precise, sharply distinguished, and invariably regular signs for the relations of ideas—such a language as some have vainly imagined it possible to invent and teach for all the infinitely varied needs of speech, and for the use of the whole human race : the chemical terminology is, in its own sphere, of universal applicability, and is adopted by chemists of various race and native tongue. But human language is not made in this way. The most important and intimate part of linguistic growth, that which affects the vocabulary of general and daily use, learned by every child, used in the common intercourse of life, goes on in a covert and unacknowledged manner; it is almost insensibly slow in its progress; it is the effect of a gradual accumulation of knowledge and quickening of insight; it is wrought out, as it were, item by item, from the mass of the already subsisting resources of expression: the mind, familiar with a certain use of a term, sees and improves a possibility of its extension, or modification, or nicer definition; old ideas, long put side by side and compared, prompt a new one; deductions hitherto unperceived are drawn from premises already known; a distinction is sharpened; a conception is invested with novel associations; experience suggests a new complex of ideas as calling for conjoint expression. Speech is the work of the mind coming to a clearer consciousness of its own conceptions and of their combinations and relations, and is at the same time the means by which that clearer consciousness is attained; and hence, it works its own progress; its use teaches its improvement; practice in the manipulation of ideas as represented by words leads the way to their more adroit and effective management. A vocabulary, even while undergoing no extension in substantial content of words and forms, may grow indefinitely in expressiveness, becoming filled up with new senses, its words and phrases made pregnant with deeper and more varied significance. It may do so, and it will, if there lie in the nature and circumstances of the people who speak it a capacity for such growth. The speech of a community is the reflex of its average and collective capacity, because, as we have already seen, the community alone is able to make and change language; nothing can become a part of the common treasure of expression which is not generally apprehended, approved, and accepted. It is not true, as is sometimes taught or implied, that a genius or commanding intellect, arising among a people, can impress a marked effect upon its language—least of all, in the earlier stages of linguistic development, or amid ruder and more primitive conditions of culture. No individual can affect speech directly except by separate items of change in respect to which he sets an example for others to follow, and an example which will be followed in proportion as the changes are accordant with already prevailing usage and naturally suggested by it: the general structure and character of language are out of his reach, save as he can raise the common intellect, and quicken and fertilize the minds of his fellows, thus sowing seed which may spring up and bear fruit in language also. If he attempt anything like innovation, the conservatism of the community will array itself against him with a force of resistance against which he will be powerless. The commanding intellect has much the better opportunity to act effectively in a cultivated and lettered people, inasmuch as his inciting and lifting influence can be immediately exerted upon so many more of his fellows, and even upon more than one generation.

Especially is it true that all form-making is accomplished by a gradual and unreflective process. It is impossible to suppose, for instance, that, in converting the adjective *like* into the adverbial suffix *ly*, there was anything like intention or premeditation, any looking forward, even, to the final result. One step simply prepared the way for and led to another. We can trace the successive stages of the transfer, but we cannot see the historical conditions and linguistic habits which facilitated it, or tell why, among all the Germanic races, the English alone should have given the suffix this peculiar application; why the others content themselves without any distinctive adverbial suffix, nor feel that their modes of expressing the adverbial relation are less clear and forcible than ours. And so in every other like case. An aptitude in handling the elements of speech, a capacity to perceive how the resources of expression can be applied to formative uses, a tendency toward the distinct indication of formal relations rather than their implication merely— these, in their natural and unconscious workings, constitute the force which produces grammatical forms, which builds up, piece by piece, a grammatical system, more or less full and complete. Every language is the product and expression of the capacities and tendencies of a race as bearing upon the specific work of language-making; it illustrates what they could do in this particular walk of human effort ; and the variety of product shows the difference of human endowment in this regard, even more strikingly than the variety of the art-products of different peoples exhibits their diverse grade and kind of artistic power to conceive and execute.

For, as has been already pointed out, and must here again be insisted on, every single act in the whole process of making words and forming language, at every period of linguistic development, has been a human act. Whether more or less deliberately performed, it was always essentially of the same kind ; it was something brought about by the free action of men. Its reasons lay in human circumstances, were felt in human minds, and prompted human organs to effort. No name was ever given save as a man or men apprehended some conception as calling for expression, and expressed it. Every idea had its distinct existence before it received its distinctive sign ; the thought is anterior to the language by which it is represented. To maintain the opposite, to hold that the sign exists before the thing signified, or that a conception cannot be entertained without the support of a word, would be the sheerest folly ; it would compel us to assert that *galvanism* could not be recognized as a new form of natural force, hitherto undescribed, until its discoverers had decided what to style it ; that Neptune was not visible in the astronomer's glass till it had been determined after which of the Grecian divinities it should be christened ; that the spinner's *mule* and *jenny* were not built till the inventor had chosen a name for them ; that the aniline colours made upon the eye no impressions distinguishable from those of hues long familiar until the battle-fields had been pitched upon whose names they should bear ; that the community had no appreciation of the frequent tediousness and impertinence of official forms until they had agreed to call it *red tape ;* that the human race did not see that the colour of growing things like leaves and grass was different from those of the clear sky, of blood, of earth, of snow, until, from the name for *growing*, they had worked out for it a name *green*, as well as, by some similar process, like names for the

others. Men do not lay up in store a list of ideas, to be
provided with spoken signs when some convenient season
shall come; nor do they prepare a catalogue of words, to
which ideas shall be attached when found: when the thing
is perceived, the idea conceived, they find in the existing
resources of speech the means of its expression—a name
which formerly belonged to something else in some way
akin with it; a combination of words, a phrase, which perhaps remains a phrase, perhaps is fused into, or replaced by,
a single word. Thus, for example, men were proposed in
ancient Rome for the free suffrages of their fellow-citizens,
and were, without difficulty, variously described as such,
before any distinctive appellation for one in such a plight
had been established; but the fortuitous circumstance that
Roman usage required those who were openly seeking office
to be *candidatos*, ' dressed in *white* (*candidus*),' led by degrees
to their designation, pregnantly, as *candidati;* and now,
through nearly the whole civilized world, he who aspires to
election or selection to any place or station is styled a
candidate.

Thus it is that the reason why anything is called as we are
accustomed to call it is a historical reason; it amounts to
this: that, at some time in the past—either when the thing
was first apprehended, or at some later period—it was convenient for men to apply to it this name. And the principal
item in this convenience was, that certain other things were
already named so and so. Until we arrive at the very
beginnings of speech (the character and origin of which must
be reserved for discussion at a later period of these lectures),
every name comes, by combination, derivation, or simple
transfer of meaning, from some other name or names : men
do not create new words out of hand; they construct them
of old material. At the time and under the circumstances,
then, when each term acquired its given significance, the
possession of certain other resources of expression, combined
with certain usages of speech and habits of thought, and
influenced by external circumstances, caused men's choice to
fall upon it rather than upon any other combination of
sounds. Thus every word has its etymology or derivation,

and to trace out its etymology is to follow up and exhibit its
transfers of meaning and changes of form, as far back and as
completely as the nature of the case allows. To recur to
our last example—*candidate* is the modern abbreviated form
of *candidatus*, participle of the (implied) Latin derivative
verb *candidare*, 'to whiten,' from *candidus*, 'white ; ' and the
historical circumstance which suggested its selection and
application to its purpose has been pointed out. *Candidus*
is itself a derivative adjective, coming from the verb *candeo*,
which means 'to shimmer, to shine ; ' it designates properly a
glittering or sheeny white. We have this also in our language, little altered in form, as the word *candid ;* but, though
it may be found here and there in old authors employed in
its sensible, physical signification of 'white,' it has in our
ordinary use been transferred, by a figure of which every one
appreciates the naturalness, to indicate a mental quality,
freedom from bias or prejudice, from dissimulation, from
deceit—those dark shades and spots on a character. Few
of us ever think of a connection of idea between *candid* and
candidate ; and the less, as the position indicated by the
latter word is by no means favourable to the development of
the virtue expressed by the former. The verb *candeo* we are
able to trace one or two steps farther back, through *caneo* and
canus, to a root *can*, which signifies ' shining ;' this, to our
analysis, is an ultimate fact, beyond which we cannot at
present penetrate.

But, while words thus have their historical grounds, while
the etymologist can explain how they came to receive the
value which we attribute to them, we must beware of ascribing too cogent or too permanent a force to the etymological
reason. It was not a necessary reason ; there was no
element of compulsion in it. The Roman seeker for office
might just as well have gotten some such name as *proponent*,
' proposer,' or *petent*, ' seeker,' as the one by which he actually came to be called ; either of these, it may be claimed, is
more truly significant than *candidate*, which expresses only a
fortuitous circumstance of external garb, and was applicable
to any one who should choose to wear a white dress. All
that can be said in reply is that the Romans were in fact

guided by the fortuitous rather than the more significant circumstance to their selection of a name. So, also, the Latin word *albus* or the Germanic word *white* might have been not less readily than *candidus* applied to designate the possession of candour; only the language-makers, for reasons which they themselves could not have explained, willed it otherwise. Among the various metaphors by which such a quality was signifiable and from time to time signified, this chanced to be the one which established itself in frequent use, and of which the metaphorical origin was by degrees forgotten. From among many possible expedients, it was the one pitched upon for filling this special need, for increasing in this direction the resources of expression. And then, when the expedient is once found, when the name is accepted by the community and installed in its office, the etymological reason becomes no longer operative; the sole and sufficient authority for the use of the term is the common assent and custom. Individuals do not go on indefinitely to repeat the act of transfer which first allotted a word to its use; they establish a direct mental association between the idea and the sign, and depend upon that. As was pointed out in the first lecture (p. 14), the child does not concern himself with questions of etymology when learning to talk; the words which he acquires he receives and employs implicitly, for the sole reason that those about him employ them. As he grows older, he will, in varying degree, according to his turn of mind, his general culture, and his particular education, turn his attention to etymological inquiries, and please himself with tracing out why the words which he has learned or learns were elected to the office in which they serve him. But it is always a matter of reflection, of learned curiosity; it concerns, not the general users of speech, but him who would study its history. To the greatest etymologist who lives, not less than to the most ignorant and unreflective speaker, the reason why he calls a certain idea by a certain name is simply that the community in which he lives so call it, and will understand him when he does the same. It is quite worth while to know how *candidate* and *candid* came to mean as they do; but our knowledge or our ignorance of their

etymology do not determine our use and understanding of
the terms.   It is, no doubt, an interesting and valuable bit
of information for the physicist that *galvanism* was named
after its first discoverer ; the fact is one of which no student,
no well-informed man even, should be ignorant ; but one may
use the word *galvanism* as well for all practical purposes
without ever having heard of Galvani ; and thousands do it
every day.   How few of those who talk about *electricity* are
aware that it signifies by derivation ' the quality of being like
amber (Greek, *elektron*),' and has no better ground than the
accidental circumstance that the first recognized manifestation of this potent force was the power of attracting light
objects exhibited by a piece of amber when rubbed ? And as
to the etymological reason of *elektron* itself, as Greek designation of ' amber,' it is irrecoverably lost.   It is, however,
far from being at our option to declare the etymology of
electricity a paltry and insufficient one, and to resolve that
we will have a name which shall denote some more essential
quality of the force, and of which we can trace the history
back to the very beginning ; he would be laughed at for a
fool who should attempt such a revolution ; a designation in
the use of which the community are agreed is good enough
for any one : it requires no other sanction.   If the case were
otherwise, if the right to use a word depended in any manner on its etymology, then every human being would have to
be an etymologist, prepared to render a reason, when called
upon, for everything he utters.   But, in fact, only the most
skilled and practised student of his native tongue can explain
the history of any considerable part of its vocabulary ; and
even his researches are apt to carry him back through no
more than the latest stages of its growth : the ultimate facts
are out of his reach.

We study, then, the history of words, not in order to assure
ourselves of our right to employ them as we do, but to satisfy
a natural curiosity respecting the familiar and indispensable
means of our daily intercourse, and to learn something of
the circumstances and character of those who established
them in use.   It is because every act of word-making is a
historical act, the work of human minds under the guidance

9

of human circumstances, that the investigation of language
is an inquiry into the internal and external history of men.
The results of such investigation are of the most varied
character. Sometimes we find at the basis of a word a mere
blunder of philosophy, as when we talk about *lunatics*, as if
we still believed the aberration of their wits to depend upon
the devious motions of the moon (*luna*) ; or a blunder of
natural history, as when we call our own native American
feathered biped a *turkey*, in servile imitation of that ill-
informed generation of Englishmen, which, not knowing
whence he came, but surmising that it might probably enough
be Turkey, dubbed him " the Turkey fowl ; " or a blunder of
geography, as when we style our aborigines *Indians*, because
the early discoverers of this continent set their faces westward from Europe to find India, and thought at first that
they had found it. *Copper*, the *magnet, parchment* commemorate for us the countries Cyprus, Magnesia, and Pergamos,
whence those substances were first brought to the founders
of our civilization. *Manumit*, like *candidate*, owes its existence to a peculiar Roman custom—of dismissing, namely,
with a slap of the hand a slave made free. *Money* and *mint*
(two different forms of the same original, *moneta*, the one
coming from the French *monnaie*, the other from the Anglo-
Saxon *mynet*) tell of Roman superstition and Roman convenience : within the imperial city was raised a temple to
Juno *Moneta*, ' Juno the *Monisher*,' in recognition of the
supernatural *monitions* the goddess had given them in certain
crises of their history ; and in this temple, as it chanced,
was set up the first stamp and die for coining money. We
say *calculate*, because the early Romans reckoned by the aid
of little pebbles (*calculi*). We call a truckling and unscrupulous parasite a *sycophant*, because it once pleased the men
of Athens to pass a law forbidding the exportation of figs
from Attica ; which, as is apt to be the case with such laws,
was little more than a dead letter ; while yet there were
found in the community certain mean fellows who sought to
gain their selfish ends by blabbing, or threatening to blab, of
those who violated it (*süko-phantēs*, ' fig-blabber '). We put
on a " pair of *rubbers*," because, when that most multifariously

valuable substance, caoutchouc, was first brought to us, we
could find for it no better use than the *rubbing* out of
pencil-marks. A whole chapter of literary history is
included in the derivation of *romantic* from *Rome*: it tells of
the rise of rude popular dialects, alongside the learned and
polished Latin, in the various provinces of the Roman
empire; and of the rise of modern European fiction, written
so distinctively in these dialects that it got its name from
them; and, finally, of the tone and style of fictitious writing,
and the characters it deals with. In like manner, a chapter of
religious history is summed up in the word *pagan* (literally,
'villager') : it tells of the obstinate conservation of heathen-
ism in the villages and hamlets under Roman dominion,
when the cities had already learned and embraced Christianity. And, once more, *slave* suggests a chapter in ethnological history : it tells of the contempt in which the *Slaves*
or Slavonians of eastern and central Europe were held by the
more powerful and cultivated Germans; and of the servitude
to which so many of them were reduced. Several among the
words we have thus instanced—as *lunatic, candidate, romantic, money*—farther include, as an essential part of their
history, the career of one great conquering and civilizing
power, the Roman, whose language, along with its knowledge
and institutions, has been spread to every part of the globe.
The etymology of *moon*, as signifying 'measurer,' has given
us an interesting glimpse of the modes of thought of that
primitive people who first applied this name to the earth's
satellite, and to whom her office as a divider of times was so
prominent among her attributes. And this is but one
among innumerable instances in which our conceptions of
olden times and peoples are aided, are made definite and
vivid, by like means. To study the moral and intellectual
vocabulary of any tongue is of high interest, and full of
instruction as to the laws and phenomena of association
which have led to its development out of the earlier signs
for physical and sensible things : we are constantly brought
to the recognition both of the unity of human nature, as
shown by the general resemblances which such study brings
to light, and of the diversity of human character and circum-

9 *

stance, as exhibited in the etymological variety of corresponding appellations. In this capacity of language to yield
to its historical investigator information concerning both the
internal life and external history and circumstances of those
who have made it what it is, lies, as was pointed out in the
outset of our inquiries, no small portion of the interest
attaching to linguistic study.

But etymological reminiscences, while thus of the highest
value to him who reflects upon language and examines its
history, are, as regards the practical purposes of speech, of
very subordinate consequence ; nay, they would, if more prominent before our attention, be an actual embarrassment to
us. Language would be half spoiled for our use by the
necessity of bearing in mind why and how its constituents
have the value we give them. The internal development of
a vocabulary, too, would be greatly checked and hampered by
a too intrusive etymological consciousness. All significant
transfer, growth of new meanings, form-making, is directly
dependent upon our readiness to forget the derivation of our
terms, to cut loose from historical connections, and to make
the tie of conventional usage the sole one between the thing
signified and its spoken sign. Much the greater part of the
resources of expression possessed by our language would be
struck off at a blow, if a perceived bond of meaning between
etymon and derivative were a requisite to the latter's existence and use. Those, then, are greatly in error who would
designate by the name " linguistic sense " (*sprachsinn*) a
disposition to retain in memory the original *status* and value
of formative elements, and the primary significance of transferred terms ; who would lay stress upon the maintenance
of such a disposition, and regard its wane as an enfeeble-
ment, a step downward toward the structural decay of language. On the contrary, the opposite tendency is the true
principle of lively and fertile growth, both of the form and
content of speech, and, as we shall see hereafter, it prevails
most in the languages of highest character and destiny. A
certain degree of vividness, of graphic and picturesque
quality, it is true, is conferred upon a term which has been
applied by a metaphor to a mental or philosophic use, by the

continued apprehension of the metaphor ; but vividness is a
quality which is dearly bought at the expense of any degree
of objective clearness, of dry and sober precision ; and it can
always be attained, when really wanted, by new figures, after
old figures have become prosaic appellations. As we rise,
too, in the scale of linguistic use, from that which is straight-
forward and unreflective to that which is elaborate, pregnant,
artistic, etymological considerations in many cases rise in
value, and constitute an important element in that suggestiveness which invests every word, giving it its delicacy of
application, making it full of significance and dignity where
another term, coarsely synonymous with it, would be tame
and ineffective. A pregnant implication of etymologic
meaning often adds strikingly to the force and impressive-
ness of an expression. Yet this is but one element among
many, and its degree of consequence is, I am convinced, apt
to be over-estimated. To recur once more to some of our
former illustrations—while an allusion to the *whiteness* of
soul signified in *candid* may touch and interest one whose
classical education enables him to recognize and appreciate
it, nothing but a joke or a conceit could well be extracted
from the etymology of *candidate ;* while *apprehend* affords
possible ground for a use in which both the physical and
intellectual meanings shall be clearly felt, the one enforcing
the other, *understand* would lend itself to no such treatment.
And most of our words are in the condition of *candid, candidate,* and *understand ;* either, as in the case of the two last,
the etymology is trivial or obscure, or, as in the case of the
first, it is within reach only of the learned, and cannot aid
the general speaker and hearer. On the whole, a word,
both in its direct significance and in its suggestiveness, is
just what our usage makes it. Hardly any two vocables
that we employ are more instinct with deep meaning, more
untranslatable into other tongues, than *home* and *comfort ;*
yet neither of them borrows aught from etymology ; the one
signifies by derivation nothing more intimate than the place
where one lives, the other, than the conferral of strength
(*con-fortare*) ; nor has either an etymon in English, discoverable without curious research. It is true that *fatherly,*

brotherly, womanly have, to our apprehension, a greater
depth and intimacy of significance than *paternal, fraternal,
feminine,* and so in many other like cases ; yet the part of
this which is due to the perceived connection of the former
with *father, brother, woman* is probably less than is usually
imagined ; the difference of the two classes consists much
more in their character as Anglo-Saxon and as Latin respectively, and in the more formal and learned use of the latter
class, as is usual with the Latin part of our language, when
compared with the other. How independent of all etymological aid is our conventional sense of the meaning of the
words we familiarly use may be shown by a great variety of
facts in our language.   It is convenient to have the various
conjugational and declensional parts of our verbs and nouns
agree in form as in sense : where we say *I·love,* to say also
he loves, we love, they loved, having loved ; where we say *man,*
to say also *man's, men, men's ;* yet we say I *am,* he *is,* we *are,*
they *were,* having *been,* and *I, my, we, our, she* and *her, go* and
went, think and *thought,* and so on, without any sense whatever of hesitation or difficulty.   So, on the other hand, it
gives us no manner of trouble to separate words which
ought, according to the usual analogies of the language, to
stand in a near relation of meaning together ; however close
may be their correspondence of form, it does not disturb the
independent act of association by which we bind together
each separate sign and its own conventional idea : take as
instances *home* and *homely, scarce* and *scarcely, direct* and
directly, lust and *lusty, naught* and *naughty, clerk* and *clergy,*
a *forge* and *forgery, candid* and *candidate, hospital* and *hospi-
tality, idiom* and *idiocy, light, alight,* and *delight, guard* and
regard, approach and *reproach, hold, behold,* and *beholden*—
and it would be easy to gather an indefinite list of such
words.   They furnish, indeed, only another illustration of
that power of the mind over its instruments which appears
in the facility and directness wherewith, as has been already
pointed out, we select from among the various and often
very diverse meanings of a single word—such as *kind, like,
become, court, head*—that one which the circumstances and
the connection require.   They help us to apprehend the

true relation of our speech to our thoughts, as being their assistant and means of communication, not their director or indispensable accompaniment.

Our review of the processes constituting the life of language is now completed : in the next lecture, we shall go on to consider the circumstances which hasten or retard their action, and their effect in bringing about the separation of languages into dialects.

LECTURE IV.

Varying rate and kind of linguistic growth, and causes affecting it.
Modes of growth of the English language. Influences conservative of
linguistic identity. Causes producing dialects; causes maintaining,
producing, or extending homogeneity of speech. Illustrations : history
of the German language ; of the Latin ; of the English. The English
language in America.

WE have, in the last two lectures, occupied ourselves with
tracing out and illustrating by typical examples the chief
processes of that incessant change, that linguistic growth,
which marks a language as living, as undergoing, in the
minds and mouths of a community, constant adaptation to
their needs, constant adjustment to their preferences and
caprices. These processes, as we saw, have to do both with
the external form of speech, its spoken and audible body,
and with its internal content, its intended and apprehensible
meaning. As regards the former, they appeared to be of
two general kinds or classes : on the one hand, they partake
of the nature of corruption and decay, consisting in the abbreviation and mutilation of existing words, the wearing off
of formative elements and consequent loss of forms, the
abandonment of old distinctions along with the means of
their expression, the dying out of words and phrases from
memory and use ; on the other hand, they are of the nature
of growth, providing for the repair of this waste, and the
supply of new additions to the resources of expression, by
the putting together of old material into fresh combinations,
the elaboration of formative elements out of words possess-

ing independent significance, and the application of accidental differences to the practical uses of significant distinction. And this external decay and growth is accompanied by, and accessory to, a rich and ever-progressing development of ideal content, which deals at its will with all the material of speech, which contracts, expands, and transfers the meanings of words, which converts the physical and concrete into the intellectual and abstract, which produces variety out of sameness, and is never at a loss for means whereby to provide with its suitable sign any fresh acquisition to the sum of things known, any new conception or deduction. In continuing at present our discussion of the life of language, we have first to note the varying rate at which the processes of growth go on, and to bring to light some of the circumstances which affect their progress.

The fact of variation in the rate of linguistic growth, it may be remarked by way of introduction, is a very obvious one. Our own English has changed much less during the past two hundred and fifty years than during the like period next preceding; and vastly less in the last five centuries than during the five which went before them. The German of the present day is not more altered from the ancient type of Germanic speech than was the English of six or seven centuries ago; nor the Icelandic now current than the Anglo-Saxon of King Alfred and his predecessors. The modern Romanic dialects—the Spanish, French, Italian, and the rest—have deviated far more widely from the Latin of Cicero and Virgil than has the dialect of the Greeks from that of Cicero's Hellenic contemporaries; and they differ from one another not a little in the degree, as well as in the mode, of their respective deviation. To go somewhat further from home, the Arabic of the Bedouin in this century is incomparably more nearly identical with that of the tribes through whose borders the children of Israel were led by Moses than is any one of our contemporary European tongues with its ancestor of the same remote period. And there are to be found upon the face of the earth dialects which are even now so rapidly changing that those who speak them would be unable to converse with either their ancestors or their descendants across an interval of four or five generations.

Now the particular modes and departments of linguistic change are so diverse that no one cause, or kind of causes, can affect them all, or affect them all alike, either to quicken or to retard them. But the plainest and most apprehensible influence is that which is exerted by change of external circumstances, surroundings, mode of life, mental and physical activity, customs and habits; and to this, accordingly, we will first direct our attention. How powerfully such causes may act upon language will be best shown, perhaps, by imagining an extreme case. Suppose an illiterate English family to be cast away upon a coral islet in the Pacific, and to be left there isolated through a succession of generations. How much of our language would at once begin to become useless to them! All that is connected with variety of scenery, as hill and dale, as rock and river; with diversity of season, of temperature, of skyey influences; with wealth of animal and vegetable life; with multifariousness of experience, of occupation, of material, of production—and much more, which it is needless to specify. For a certain period, some part of this might be kept alive by memory and tradition, but not for ever; it would lose its distinctness before the mind, become shadowy, and by degrees die out; and its loss would be facilitated by that stupefying effect which the climate and mode of life, with their restricted limits and dull uniformity, would unavoidably have upon the mind; vigour of thought and liveliness of sentiment would be likely to decline; and, after the lapse of a sufficient period to allow these causes their full effect, the wealth of English speech might be reduced to a poverty comparable with that of some among the present Polynesian dialects. But suppose, on the other hand, a Polynesian family set down in the midst of a country like Iceland, amid magnificent and terrible scenery, amid varieties of nature innumerable, where hard labour and prudent forethought, tasking all the moral and physical energies of man, are needed to preserve life and make it endurable—suppose them to be able to bear and adapt themselves to this tremendous change, and how rapidly would

their language grow in names and expressions for objects,
processes, experiences, emotions, relations !

This is but a magnified example of what is always and
everywhere going on in language : it expands and contracts
in close adaptation to the circumstances and needs of those
who use it ; it is enriched and impoverished along with the
enrichment or impoverishment of their minds. We have
already pointed out that the lowest and least educated classes
of English speakers use not a tenth of the words which
constitute to our apprehension the English tongue ; the reduction, then, of the English people in its entirety to the
condition of the classes referred to would imply the utter extinction of more than nine-tenths of its resources of expression : and all declension of civilization, decay of natural
vigour, intermission of instruction, tends, in its way and
measure, toward such a result ; while, on the other hand, a
race that is growing in knowledge and rising in character
makes its tongue richer and nobler at every step of its up-
ward career. But it is needless to insist farther upon a
truth so obvious : no one will think of denying that the content of any language, in words and phrases and their meanings, must correspond with and be measured by the mental
wealth of the community to whom it belongs, and must
change as this changes. It is but the simplest corollary
from the truth which we have already established, that men
make their own language, and keep it in existence by their
tradition, and that they make and transmit it for their own
practical uses, and for no other end whatsoever.

A vastly more subtle and difficult question is, in what
shall consist the linguistic growth which change of circumstance demands, or to which varying character and choice
impel : how far shall it lie in the accession or withdrawal
of words and meanings of words, and how far in development or decay of linguistic structure ? It was pointed out
in our first lecture that change of vocabulary, while it is the
most legitimate and inevitable of any that a language undergoes, is also the least penetrating, touching most lightly
the essential character of speech as the instrument of
thought. And we saw later (p. 83) how such words as

photograph and *telegraph* are brought in and naturalized,
fitted with all the inflectional apparatus which the language
possesses, without any further consequences. Such are
mere additions to speech, which may affect the sum and
aggregate value of its resources of expression, often to a
considerable extent, without modifying its organism, or altering its grammatical form, its apprehension of relations and
command of the means of signifying them. And yet, the
same circumstances which lead to the great and rapid development of a vocabulary—especially where it takes place out
of native resources, and in a less conscious and artificial way
—may have an indirect effect upon grammatical development also; where so much change is going on, so much
that is new coming into use, the influence will naturally be
felt in some measure in every part of the language. Hints
of such a possibility are discoverable even in the modern
history of our own speech : *graph,* for example, has been
brought in as the final member of so many new compounds
that it almost presents itself to the consciousness of English
speakers as a formative element, having a given office, and
so constituting a part of the apparatus of English derivation;
while *ism,* though of ultimate Greek origin, and coming to
us through the French, has become a thoroughly English
suffix, admitting of the most familiar and extended application in forming new words. So distinct, indeed, is our
apprehension of the specific value of the ending *ism* that we
are able to cut it off and make an independent word of it,
talking of a person's *isms,* or of his favourite *ism*—as we also
speak, less familiarly, of *ana,* ' personal reminiscence and
anecdote,' or, in a half-humorous way, of the *ologies,*
' branches of learned study.'

We cannot, perhaps, better illustrate this subject of the
modes of linguistic change as determined in their respective
degree of operation by the influence of circumstances, than
by briefly examining the way in which our own speech is
now adapting itself to the growing needs of its speakers.
The call upon it for increase of expressiveness during the
past century and at the present time has been and is hardly
less than would have been that upon the dialect of our

imagined Polynesians in their new Icelandic home. Doubtless there was never before in the history of the world a
time when men were accumulating with such rapidity knowledge of the past history and present constitution of the
whole universe of created things—knowledge which is not,
it is true, necessarily wisdom or virtue, but which can and
ought to turn to both. A part, now, of this new knowledge
—and a part of the highest importance to the general community—is such as calls for no change whatever in language,
because it consists only in the better understanding of things
long since observed and named. However much astronomy
and physics may teach us respecting the *sun* and the *planets*,
we continue to call them as of old ; the words *heat, cold,
light, green, blue, red* stand their ground in general use, notwithstanding the new vibratory theories, and the wonderful
discoveries lately made' in the spectrum of colours ; pudding-
stone is *pudding-stone*, and trap is *trap*, now as before the
geologist had explained the origin of either ; substances still
fall to the earth and *rise* and *float* in the air, even after the
discovery of gravitation ; rubbed amber and the loadstone
attract, as they did ere men had heard of electricity and
magnetism as cosmical forces. There is, and evidently in
the nature of the case can be, no limit to the extent to which
a language may thus become impregnated with clearer knowledge and deeper meaning ; and it has been already pointed
out (p. 21) that the speech of different individuals at the
same period may vary to almost any degree in the implication of these qualities, not less than the speech of the general
community at different periods. But in great part, also, the
modern additions to knowledge have been of such a sort as
to demand the provision of a store of new signs : they have
included an immense number of new particulars, things
before unobserved or confounded with others under the same
names, but which, being made the subject of distinct conceptions, have come to require specific appellations, that men
might communicate with one another respecting them.
Even this want has in some measure been filled without
external change of the language, by the internal development
of its resources, as illustrated in the preceding lecture, by the

application of a not inconsiderable number of old words to new uses. Whenever any branch of knowledge, any art or science, either originates or is extended and perfected, the natural impulse is always to subserve its new uses with our old phraseology. The new classifications, substances, processes, products are not so unlike·those already familiar to us that they may not be largely called by the same names, without fear of obscurity or error. Every technical vocabulary is thus made up to no small extent of the terms of common life, more precisely or more pregnantly used. The botanist talks of *leaves* and *flowers ;* but in either term he includes some things that the common man would exclude, and the contrary. *Current, conductor, induction,* in the mouth of the electrician, mean things of which he who knows nothing of physics has no conception. Many a man who is aware that *cohere* means ' stick together ' would be at a loss to distinguish *cohesion* from *adhesion*. *Atom, base, acid, salt, affinity, reaction,* are but instances of the words innumerable to which the chemist has given a new and special significance. In fact, the whole apparatus of common speech, as applied to the more definite and sharply distinguished uses of science, undergoes a kind of working-over and adaptation, which is of every degree, from such a conscious and artificial application as that of the word *salt,* used to express a large class of chemical compounds regarded as analogous with the substance formerly called by that name, down to such simple limitation or distincter apprehension of the true force of a term as is hardly separable from that change of implication without change of identity which we have illustrated above, by reference to the words *sun, heat, rise* and *fall,* etc. The mode of linguistic growth which we are now considering does, indeed, shade off into the former one, and is most nearly akin with it, in nature and in necessity. No language can possibly lose the capacity for it without losing its very life ; in some languages, as we shall see hereafter, it is compelled to do the whole work of linguistic adaptation, external growth being a thing unknown.

In our own tongue, however, external growth, as represented by the formation of new derivatives, and new combin-

ations of existing materials, is not altogether extinct,
though reduced to a comparatively low grade of activity, and
restricted in sphere. To its chief modes of action we have
already, in other connections, had occasion to refer. It
consists mainly in what we have called the *mobilization* of
our words, the application to them of those formative
elements which still remain to us with capacity of living use,
and by which we produce both inflections and derivative
words, as we have need of them. Increase of these our
means of internal development is all but impracticable. Our
most recent organically developed suffix is the adverbial ending *ly*, which has been found above so valuable in illustrating
the general method of suffix-formation.   Yet not a few elements of Latin origin have won by degrees the right to play
an active part in the making of new English words : such
are the prefixes *en, dis, re*, the suffixes *ment, ess, able, ous, ic,
ize, ism, fy*, and others ; nor, as we have seen, is the possibility even of farther additions to the list totally cut off.
An instance of a rather artificial and abnormal extension of
formative apparatus was afforded us by the introduction of
the chemical terminology referred to in the last lecture (p.
122); the modern history of scientific nomenclature presents other similar cases ; and the exigencies of common use,
directed by the custom and authority of the learned, may
yet cause some of these ingrafted elements to germinate
and flourish as integral parts of the general system of speech.
No such results are at all likely to follow from the combination and integration of elements of our own proper language which are now independent.   Of composition, as a
means of enrichment of our vocabulary, we make at present
but a limited use : *steamboat* and *railroad* are familiar representatives of a class which, though not inconsiderable in
numbers, forms a far less proportion of the modern growth
in our tongue than in most others of its kindred.
     Such of the needs of language-making as are not supplied
by us in the methods already noticed are satisfied by the
borrowing of words from other tongues ; and this, as every
one knows, is an expedient to which excessive resort is had
in English. Our dictionaries have been filled up with

thousands upon thousands of Greek and Latin words; and
thousands more, too purely technical as yet to be admitted
into the dictionaries, are current among certain classes of
our community. The circumstances, external and internal,
which give such prevalence among us to this mode of linguistic growth, are many and various. First among them,
we may refer to the scantiness of our formative apparatus,
and the indisposition to an extensive production of new compounds which characterizes our speech : these limitations to
the capacity of internal development compel a recurrence
to external wealth. Then, the combination into which our
originally Germanic dialect was forced, by pressure of historical conditions, with the Romanic tongue of the conquering Normans, while it brought immediately into general use
a host of terms of classical origin, opened the door for their
indefinite multiplication, by creating analogies to which
they could attach themselves,- giving them such support in
popular usage as took away the strangeness of aspect which
they would else have had. Yet it is true that the words of
common life, those which every English-speaking child learns
first and continues to use oftenest, are overwhelmingly of
Anglo-Saxon origin, are Germanic : Latin and Greek derivatives come in abundantly with culture, learning, special
scientific training. And this explains in part the modern
preponderance of such derivatives. The knowledge which
they are introduced to represent is of a learned cast, not
interesting in its details the general community of English
speakers, nor accessible to them ; belonging, rather, to a
special class, which feels itself more closely united by bonds
of community with like classes in other nations than with
the mass of its own countrymen. There is a fellowship, a
solidarity, among the chemists of Europe and America, for instance, which makes them name things on principles accepted
among themselves, and out of languages known alike to them
all, rather than out of the stores of expression, and in accordance with the usages, of their own vernaculars. It is doubtful whether any language that ever existed could have made
provision healthily, from its own internal resources, for the
expression of that infinite number of new particulars which

modern science has been pouring in of late upon the general
aggregate of knowledge.   Think, for example, of the perplexity of the naturalist who returns from an exploring tour
with a thousand new species of plants and animals, if he
were compelled to devise vernacular designations for them
all! And how useless the effort! They will remain for
ever unknown to nineteen twentieths, perhaps, of those who
speak his speech, and if one or another of them should ever
become introduced to general knowledge, they would easily
enough acquire familiar names.   No modern language, then,
whatever its superiority to the English in the capacity of
internal growth, attempts to fill such departments of expression otherwise than by borrowing from the Latin and Greek,
happy in the possession of stores so rich, so accessible, and
so manageable, to draw upon.   The names of animal and
vegetable species, of their parts and specific differences, of
mineral elements and compounds, of processes and relations,
and so forth, are Latin or Latinic through the whole civilized
world.   If the German is more inclined to favour terms of
native growth, and for *hydrogen, oxygen, acid,* says "water-sub-
stance" (*wasserstoff*), " sour-substance " (*sauerstoff*), " sour-
ness," (*säure*), and the like, it may be seriously doubted
whether the gain is of appreciable value.   We have seen how
little the act of association which binds together idea and sign
is dependent upon the aid of etymological suggestiveness; and
the forcing of a great variety of new specific meanings in a
brief space of time upon the old material of a tongue may
make quite as much for confusion as for intelligibility and
vividness of expression.   It is comparatively easy for a community to provide out of its vernacular resources of speech
for that ordinary growth of knowledge, experience, and
wisdom which comes in the main by the working over of
conceptions already acquired and named, and only in lesser
degree by the apprehension of new particulars; but we have
only to rejoice that our language is by fortunate circumstances saved from a strain which the present conditions
of our culture would otherwise have put upon it, and which
is more severe than any living tongue has ever been obliged
to endure.

10

But even things of the most common use and knowledge
come to bear with us designations of learned and artificial
make.   A certain showy flower, introduced not very long
ago by learned intervention to the parterres of the wealthy,
but now found in every poor man's garden, and almost as
familiar as the sun-flower or the rose, is known only by the
name *dahlia*, given it by its botanical describer in honour of
an earlier botanist, Dahl.   The *telegraph*, a scientific device,
keeps its foreign scientific title, not in our own country only,
but all over the globe, although it has become an institution
almost as universal and indispensable as the post.   A substance over whose discovery and application no small part of
our community has gone wild within the past few years, has
not retained its honest English appellation of *rock oil*,
or *mineral oil*, but has accepted from the learned the equivalent Latin name *petroleum*, and is so called by millions who
have no knowledge whatever of the derivation and meaning
of the term.   The influence of the learned class in the process of English names-giving has been for many centuries a
growing one, and has now become greatly predominant; and
with it has·grown, somewhat unduly, the introduction of
classic word and phrase, to supplement, or even to replace,
native English expression.   There is a pedantically learned
style which founds itself on the Latin dictionary rather than
the English, and discourses in a manner half unintelligible
except to the classically educated : but this is only the fool-
ish exaggeration of a tendency which has become by degrees
an integral part of English speech.   To draw in like manner
upon the resources of any other tongue (as, for instance,
upon the German) would be a fault of a very different character — a pure impossibility, an intolerable affectation,
because unsupported by anything in the previous usages of
our mother-tongue.
   We see, then, that the most obvious and striking peculiarity of English linguistic growth, the wholesale importation
of foreign terms, is one by which it differs only in degree
from other linguistic growth, ancient and modern, and that
this degree of difference is explained by the circumstances
of the case—the learned character of much of the knowledge

demanding representation, the sluggishness of the native processes of word-formation, and the presence of numerous words of classic origin in our familiar speech; all which circumstances have begotten and fostered a habit of resorting more and more for the supply of new needs to the accessible and abundant stores of classical expression. The determining causes are wholly historical. The inaptness for internal development, the aptness to borrow, which distinguish our language from others of Germanic origin, are both mainly traceable to the Norman invasion. In consequence of that event, the Anglo-Saxon was for a time in danger of extinction, or of reduction to the rank of a vulgar *patois*. Political conditions, severing Anglo-Norman interests from those of the continent, and originating a common English feeling in the whole population, notwithstanding its diverse elements, led to a fusion of Norman-French and Saxon-English, instead of a displacement of the latter by the former: but, when the new tongue came forth, it was found shorn of much of its grammatical power, greatly altered in its forms and modes of construction. The purity and directness of linguistic tradition had been broken up; the conservative influence exercised upon the foundation-language by the cultivated class of its speakers had been for a time destroyed, and popular inaccuracies and corruptions allowed full sway; a mode of speech was learned by considerable masses of a population to whose fathers it was strange and barbarous; the rest had admitted to their daily and familiar use a host of new words on which their old apparatus of inflection sat strangely: and this was the result. So is it likely ever to be, when the intermingling on nearly equal terms of races of diverse speech issues in the elaboration, by mutual accommodation and compromise, of a new mixed dialect which all shall learn and use alike.

We must be careful not to mistake the nature of the obstacle which prevents the liberal increase of our vocabulary by means of combination of old materials. It is wholly subjective, consisting in our habits and preferences. There is hardly a compound formed in German, for example, which would not, if literally translated by an English compound,

10 *

be understood, and which we might not therefore imitate, if intelligibility were all that we had to consult in our word-making. But we are obliged also to have in view the prepossessions of the community ; and this is not a thing which they are used to and will approve. The whole process of language-making and language-changing, in all its different departments, is composed of single acts, performed by individuals ; yet each act is determined, not alone by the needs of the particular case, but also by the general usages of the community as acting in and represented by the individual ; so that, in its initiation as well as its acceptance and ratification, it is virtually the act of the community, as truly conventional as if men held a meeting for its discussion and decision.

We have hitherto considered chiefly the effect of circumstances upon the growth of language, its enrichment with the means of designating new conceptions and representing new judgments. We have also briefly to examine their influence upon linguistic decay, upon phonetic change and grammatical corruption. These, as has been already sufficiently pointed out, are the result of the defective tradition of language ; by carelessness in the acquisition of words, or by inaccuracy in their reproduction, men change from generation to generation the speech which they transmit. It is evident, then, that everything which assists the accuracy of linguistic tradition tends to preserve the phonetic and grammatical structure of language from alteration. Where speech is most unconsciously employed, with most exclusive attention to the needs and conveniences of the moment, with least regard to its inherited usages, there its changes are rifest. Any introduction of the element of reflection is conservative in its effect. A people that think of their speech, talk about it, observe and deduce its rules and usages, will alter it but slowly. A tendency to do this sometimes forms a part of a nation's peculiar character, being the result of qualities and circumstances which it is well-nigh or quite impossible to trace out and explain ; but often it is called forth, or favoured and strengthened, by very obvious conditions ; by admiring imitation of the ways and words of

them of old time ; by the possession of a traditional literature ; but, most of all, by a recorded literature, the habit of
writing, and a system of instruction. Culture and education
are the most powerful of all the forces which oppose linguistic change. The smallest conceivable alterative influence
will emanate from one who has been trained to speak
correctly by a conscious effort, and who is accustomed to
write what he says almost as frequently and naturally as he
speaks it. Words, in their true form and independent
entity, are too distinctly present to his mind for him to take
part either in their fusion or mutilation. Hence the effect
of literary culture is to fix a language in the condition in
which it happens to be found, to assure to it the continued
possession of the formative processes which are then active
in its development, but to check or altogether prevent its
acquisition of any others ; to turn its prevailing habits into
unalterable laws ; and to maintain its phonetic character
against anything but the most gradual and insidious change.
    Thus far in the history of the world, this kind of con-
servative influence has usually been active only within the
limits of a class ; a learned or priestly caste has become the
guardian of the national literature and the conservator of the
tongue in which it was written ; while to the masses of the
people both have grown strange and unfamiliar. Deprived
of the popular support, the cultivated dialect has at once
begun to lose its vitality ; for no language can remain alive
which is not answering all the infinitely varied needs of a
whole community, and adapting itself in every part to their
changes ; it is stinted of its natural and necessary growth
when it is divorced from general use and made the exclusive
property of a class. Thus there come to exist among the
same people two separate tongues ; the one an inheritance
from the past, becoming ever more stiff and constrained,
and employable only for special uses ; the other the production of the present, growing constantly more unlike the
other by the operation of the ordinary processes of linguistic
change ; full of inaccuracies and corruptions, if we choose
to call them so, but also full of a healthy and vigorous life,
which enables it finally to overthrow and replace the learned

or sacred dialect of which it is the offspring. Such has been
the origin and such the fate of all the learned dialects which,
in various parts of the world, have been preserved as " dead
languages," for the purposes of learned communication, after
losing their character as the vernacular speech of a community : for instance, the ancient Egyptian, long kept up for
sacred uses, and written in the hieroglyphic signs, after both
language and letters had in popular use taken on another
form ; the Zend, in the keeping of the ministers of Zoroaster's doctrine ; the Sanskrit, even yet taught in the Brahmanic schools of India, amid the Babel of modern dialects,
its descendants ; the Latin, the common language of the
educated through all Europe, for centuries during which
the later forms of Romanic speech, now the vehicles of a
culture superior to that of Greece and Rome, were mere
barbarous *patois*.   Every dialect which is made the subject
of literary culture is liable to the fate of the Latin ; aris-
tocracy and exclusiveness tend to final overthrow, in language as in politics ; the needs and interests of the many
are more important than those of the few, and must in the
end prevail.   True linguistic conservatism consists in establishing an educated and virtuous democracy, in enlisting the
whole community, by means of a thorough and pervading
education, in the proper and healthy preservation of the
accepted usages of correct speech—and then in letting
whatever change must and will come take its course.   There
is a purism which, while it seeks to maintain the integrity
of language, in effect stifles its growth : to be too fearful of
new words and phrases, new meanings, familiar and colloquial expressions, is little less fatal to the well-being of a
spoken tongue than to rush into the opposite extreme.

It is hardly needful to point out that these desirable conditions are much more nearly realized in the case of our
modern cultivated and literary languages than in those of
olden time, and that the former have, in all human probability, a destiny before them very different from that of the
latter.   In the present constitution of society, among the
enlightened nations of Europe and America, the forces conservative of the general purity of language have attained a

development and energy to which only a distant approach was made under the most favourable circumstances in ancient times. The conscious and reflective users of speech, the instructed and cultivated, the writers of their thoughts, have become everywhere a class powerful in numbers as well as dominant in influence. Education, no longer confined to the upper layer, more or less pervades the whole mass of the people. Books are in every one's hands, assimilating and establishing the written and spoken usages of all. That form of the common speech in each country which has enlisted in its support the best minds, the sweetest and most sonorous tongues, is ever gaining ground upon the others, supplanting their usages, and promising to become and to continue the true popular language.

In America, the influences we have now been considering wear a somewhat peculiar form. On the one hand, the educated class nowhere else embraces so large a portion of the community, or has so vast a collective force ; on the other hand, and partly for this very reason, the highest and best-educated class have less power here than in the less democratic countries of the Old World : the low-toned party newspaper is too much the type of the prevailing literary influence by which the style of speech of our rising generation is moulding. A tendency to slang, to colloquial inelegancies, and even vulgarities, is the besetting sin against which we, as Americans, have especially to guard and to struggle. To attain that thorough democracy which is the best life and vigour of language, to keep our English speech vivid with the thought and feeling of a whole people, we should not bring down the tone and style of the highest, nor average those of all classes ; we should rather lift up the lower to the level of the higher.

Our review of the causes which determine the respective part played by the different processes of linguistic growth, and the rate at which they severally act, is far from being exhaustive. To treat the subject with thoroughness would require a treatise. Parts of it are of extreme subtlety and difficulty. Our attention has been directed almost solely to external historical circumstances, those of which the effect

is most easily traced. We have but hinted here and there
at the more recondite and most potent influences which are
deep-seated in the individual character of different tongues
and the qualities of the people who speak them. That
complex and intricate combination of native capacities and
dispositions, acquired and inherited habits, and guiding
circumstances, of which, in each individual community, the
form and development of the common speech is a product, is
in no two communities the same, and everywhere requires a
special and detailed study in order to its comprehension.
Ethnologists are obliged, in the main, to take the differences
of national character as ultimate facts, content with setting
them clearly forth, not claiming to explain them ; and a like
necessity rests upon the linguist as regards linguistic differences : not only can he not account for the presence of
peculiarities of character which determine peculiarities of
speech, but even their analysis eludes his search ; they
manifest themselves only in these special effects, and are not
otherwise demonstrable. To ascribe the differences of language and linguistic growth directly to " physical causes," to
make them dependent on "peculiarities of organization,"
whether cerebral, laryngal, or other, is wholly meaningless
and futile. Language is not a physical product, but a
human institution, preserved, perpetuated, and changed, by
free human action. Nothing but education and habit limits
any man to the idiom in the possession of which he has grown
up ; within the community of speakers of the same tongue
may readily be found persons with endowments as unlike, in
degree and kind, as those which characterize the average men
of distant and diverse races. Physical causes do, indeed,
affect language, but only in two ways : first, as they change
the circumstances to which men have to adapt their speech ;
and second, as they alter men's nature and disposition.
Every physical cause requires to be transmuted into a motive
or a mental tendency, before it can affect the signs by which
we represent our mental acts. It is universally conceded
that physical circumstances do produce a permanent effect
upon the characteristics of race, internal as well as external,
and so upon those, among the rest, which govern linguistic

development ; but in what measure, at what rate, and
through what details of change, is as yet matter of the widest
difference of opinion and the liveliest controversy. There
are headlong materialists who pronounce man the slave and
sport of nature, guided and controlled by the external forces
amid which he exists, and who claim that his history may be
explained and foretold by means of a knowledge of those
forces ; when as yet they have not found out even the A-B-
C of the modes in which human nature is moulded by its
surroundings.   These men have their counterparts also
among students of language. But, whatever may be hoped
from the future, it is certain that at present nothing of value
has been done toward showing how linguistic growth is
affected in its kind and rate by physical causes. There is no
human dialect which might not maintain itself essentially
unaltered in structure, though carried to climes very unlike
those in which it had grown up, and though employed by a
people whose culture and mode of life was rapidly varying ;
emigration, often assumed to be the chief and most powerful
cause of linguistic change, also often appears to exercise a
conservative influence.   And, on the other hand, a language
may rapidly disintegrate, or undergo phonetic transformation, or vary the substance of its vocabulary, without mov-
ing from the region of its origin, or becoming the organ of
other conditions of human life. When linguistic scholars
can fully account for such facts as that the Icelandic is the
most antique in form of the idioms of its family, that the
Lithuanian has preserved more of the primitive apparatus of
Indo-European inflection than any other known tongue of
modern times, that the Armenian has become with difficulty
recognizable as an Iranian dialect, that the Melanesian,
African, and American languages are the most changeful of
human forms of speech—then, perhaps, they may claim to
comprehend the circumstances that regulate the growth of
language.
     The variation of language in space, its change from
one region to another, is a not less obvious fact than its
variation in time, its change from one epoch to another.
The earth is filled with almost numberless dialects, differing

from one another in a greater or less degree, and some of
them, at least, we know by historical evidence to be descendants of a common original. This state of things finds its
ready and simple explanation in the principles which have
been already laid down ; they will demand, therefore, but a
brief application and further illustration.

We have been speaking, when treating of the growth of
language, of vital processes, as going on in the body of
speech itself, like the process of fermentation in bread, or of
the displacement and replacement of tissues in an animal
organism. But we have been careful, at the same time, to
bear in mind that the word "process" was thus used only in
a figurative sense. Every item of change which goes to
make up the growth of human speech is ultimately a result
of the conscious effort of human beings. In language, the
atoms which compose the fermenting mass and the growing
tissue are not inert matter, acted on by laws of combination
and affinity, but intelligent creatures, themselves acting for
a purpose. A process of linguistic growth, then, is only the
collective effect, in a given direction, of the acts of a number
of separate individuals, guided by the preferences, and controlled by the assent, of the community of which those individuals form a part. And upon the joint and reciprocal
action on language of the individual and the community
depend all the phenomena of dialectic separation and coalescence.

For, in the first place, it is evident that the infinite diversity of character and circumstance in the intelligent beings
who have language in charge must tend to infinite diversity
in their action and its products. Each independent mind,
working unrestrainedly according to its own impulses, would
impress upon the development of speech a somewhat different
history. It was shown almost at the beginning of our discussions (p. 22) that no two men speak exactly the same
tongue : of course, then, they would not propagate the same.
Each has his own vocabulary, his own pet words and phrases,
his own deviations from the normal standard of pronunciation,
of construction, of grammar ; the needs of each are in some
degree unlike those of others ; his mind is somewhat differ-

ently impressed and guided by feelings and experiences, differently swayed by the weight of existing analogies. Such tendency to variation is, to be sure, within comparatively narrow limits; individual speakers of English would not, if left to their own devices, rush madly off toward a Choctaw or Kamchatkan model of speech; yet its results are by no means imperceptible or insignificant; it is like the variation of the separate individuals of a species of plants or animals in respect to traits of structure and disposition, which, however slow its progress, would finally, if suffered to accumulate its effects, break up the species into well-marked varieties. Linguistic development is thus made up, as we may fairly express it, of an infinity of divergent or centrifugal forces.

But, in the second place, there is not wanting an effective centripetal force also, which holds all the others in check, which resolves them, giving value to that part of each which makes in a certain direction, and annulling the rest: this centripetal force is the necessity of communication. Man is no soliloquist: he does not talk for his own diversion and edification, but for converse with his fellows; and that would not be language which one individual alone should understand and be able to employ. Every one is, indeed, as we have already seen, engaged in his way and measure in modifying language; but no one's action affects the general speech, unless it is accepted by others, and ratified in their use. Every sign which I utter, I utter by a voluntary effort of my organs, over which my will has indefeasible control; I may alter the sign as I please, and to any extent, even to that of substituting for it some other wholly new sign; only, if by so doing I shock the sense of those about me, or make myself unintelligible to them, I defeat the very end for which I speak at all. This is the consideration which restrains me from arbitrariness and license in the modification of my speech, and which makes me exert my individual influence upon it only through and by the community of which I am a member. If those who form one community do not talk alike, and cannot understand one another, the fundamental and essential office of speech is not fulfilled. Hence, whatever changes a language may undergo, they must all be shared in by the whole community. The idiosyncrasies, the sharp angles and jutting corners, of every man's idiom must be worn off by attrition against those with which it comes in contact in the ordinary intercourse of life, that the common tongue may become a rounded unit. This does not imply an absolute identity of dialect, down to the smallest details, among all the constituent members of a community; within certain limits—which, though not strictly definable, are sufficiently distinct and coercive to answer their practical purpose perfectly well—each one may be as original as he pleases: he may push his oddity and obscurity to the very verge of the whimsical and the incomprehensible—or even beyond it, if he do not mind being misunderstood and laughed at; if his sense of his own individuality be so exaggerated that he is a whole community, a world, to himself. Nor must the word community, as used with reference to language, be taken in a too restricted or definite sense. It has various degrees of extension, and bounds within bounds: the same person may belong to more than one community, using in each a different idiom. For instance: I have, as we may suppose, a kind of home dialect, containing a certain proportion of baby-talk, and a larger of favourite colloquialisms, which would sound a little queerly, if they were not unintelligible, to any one outside of my family circle; as an artisan, pursuing a special branch of manufacture or trade, or as one engaged in a particular profession, or study, or department of art, I am a member of another community, speaking a language to some extent peculiar, and which would be understood neither by my wife and children nor by the majority of speakers of English. Thus, I may have dived deep into the mysteries of some scheme of transcendental philosophy, or searched and pondered the ultimate physical constitution of atoms; and, if I should discourse to a general audience of that which to me is full of profoundest significance and interest, while one out of twenty, perhaps, would follow me with admiring appreciation, to the other nineteen I should seem an incomprehensible ranter. But even as a general speaker of English,

qualified to meet and converse intelligently with others who
claim the same title, upon matters of import to us all, I
may have my speech marked more or less strongly with
local or personal peculiarities ; it may exhibit unusual tones
of utterance, or unusual turns of phrase, which, if I would
be readily and thoroughly understood, I must endeavour to
avoid. Now all these differences of speech, limited as their
range may be, are in their essential nature dialectic ; the
distinction between such idioms, as we may properly style
them, and well-marked dialects, or related but independent
languages, is one, not of kind, but only of degree. For I
also possess a considerable portion of my language in common with the Netherlander, the German, and the Swede, to
say nothing of my remoter relations, the Russian, the Persian, and the Hindu ; and if, in talking with any one of
them, I could only manage to leave out of my conversation
such words as belong to my dialect alone, and moreover, not
to pronounce the rest with such a local peculiarity of tone,
nor give them such special shades of meaning, he and I
might get along together famously, each of us understanding
all the other said. I can, indeed, make calculations and
compose mathematical formulas with him all day long ; or, if
we are chemists, we can compare our views as to the constitution of all substances, organic and inorganic, to our mutual edification ; since, as regards their mathematical and
chemical language, their systems of notation and nomenclature, all who share European civilization form but a single
community.

There is room, then, for all that diversity which was shown
in our first lecture to belong to the speech of different individuals and different classes in the same community, along
with that general correspondence which makes them speakers
of the same language. The influence of community works
in various degrees, and within various limits, according to
the nature and extent of the community by which it is
exercised. The whim of a child and the assent of its
parents may make a change in the family idiom ; the consent of all the artisans in a certain branch of mechanical
labour is enough to give a new term the right to stand in

their technical vocabulary ; the majority of good writers and
speakers of English is the only authority which can make
a word good English in the part of our tongue that we all
alike use and value ; while all the learned of Europe must
join together, in order to alter the notation of a number, or
the symbol of a chemical element. But the principle is
everywhere the same : as mutual intelligibility is the bond
which makes the unity of a language, so the necessity of
mutual intelligibility is the power which preserves and per-
petuates that unity.

If communication is thus the assimilating force which
averages and harmonizes the effects of discordant individual
action on language, keeping it, notwithstanding its incessant
changes, the same to all the members of the same community,
then it is clear that everything which narrows communication, and tends to the isolation of communities, favours the
separation of a language into dialects; while all that extends
communication, and strengthens the ties which bind together
the parts of a community, tends to preserve the homogeneity
of speech. Suppose a race, occupying a certain tract of
country, to possess a single tongue, which all understand
and use alike : then, so long as the race is confined within
narrow limits, however rapidly its language may yield to the
irresistible forces which produce linguistic growth, all will
learn from each, and each from all ; and, from generation to
generation, every man will understand his neighbour, whatever difficulty he might find in conversing with the spirit of
his great-grandfather, or some yet remoter ancestor. But if
the race grows in numbers, spreading itself over region after
region, sending out colonies to distant lands, its uniformity
of speech is exposed to serious danger, and can only be saved
by specially favouring circumstances and conditions. And
these conditions are yet more exclusively of an external
character than those which, as we lately saw, determine the
mode and rate of linguistic change in general : they consist
mainly in the kind and degree of culture enjoyed and the
effects which this naturally produces. In a low state of
civilization, the maintenance of community over a wide
extent of country is altogether impracticable ; the tendency

to segregation is paramount; local and clannish feeling
prevails, stifling the growth of any wider and nobler
sense of national unity and common interests; each little
tribe or section is jealous of and dreads the rest; the
struggle for existence arrays them in hostility against each
other; or, at the best, the means of constant and thorough
communication among individuals of the different parts of
the country is wanting, along with the feelings which should
impel to it. Thus all the diversifying tendencies are left to
run their course unchecked; varieties of circumstance and
experience, the subtler and more indirect influences of
climate and mode of life, the yet more undefinable agencies
which have their root in individual and national caprice,
gradually accumulate their discordant effects about separate
centres, and local varieties of speech arise, which grow into
dialects, and these into distinct and, finally, widely dissimilar
languages. The rate at which this separation will go on
depends, of course, in no small degree, upon the general
rate of change of the common speech; as the dialects can
only become different by growing apart, a sluggishness of
growth will keep them longer together—and that, not by its
direct operation alone, but also by giving the weak forces of
an imperfect and scanty communication opportunity to work
more effectively in counteraction of the others. Thus all
the influences which have already been referred to as restricting the variation of a language from generation to
generation are, as such, equally effective in checking its
variation from portion to portion of a people. But the
most important of them also contribute to the same result
in another way, by directly strengthening and extending the
bonds of community. Culture and enlightenment give a
wonderful cohesive force; they render possible a wide political unity, maintenance of the same institutions, government under the same laws; they facilitate community of
memories and traditions, and foster national feeling; they
create the wants and tastes which lead the people of different regions to mix with and aid one another, and they
furnish the means of ready and frequent intercourse: all of
which make powerfully for linguistic unity also. A tra-

ditional literature, sacred or heroic, tends effectively in the same direction. But of more account than all is a written literature, and an organized and pervading system of instruction, whereby the same expressions for thought, feeling, and experience are set as models before the eyes of all, and the most far-reaching and effective style of linguistic communication is established.

Moreover, that same necessity of mutual understanding which makes and preserves the identity of language throughout a community has power also to bring forth identity out of diversity. No necessary and indissoluble tie binds any human being to his own personal and local peculiarities of idiom, or even to his mother-tongue; habit and convenience alone make them his;. he is ever ready to give them up for others, when circumstances make it worth his while to do so. The coarse and broad-mouthed rustic whom the force of inborn character and talent brings up to a position among cultivated men, wears off the rudeness of his native dialect, and learns to speak as correctly and elegantly, perhaps, as one who has been trained from his birth after the best models. Those who come up from among the dialects of every part of Britain to seek their fortune in the metropolis acquire some one of the forms of English speech which flourish there; and, even if they themselves are unable ever to rid themselves wholly of provincialisms, their children may grow up as thorough cockneys as if their families had never lived out of hearing of Bow bells. Any one of us who goes to a foreign land and settles there, identifying himself with a community of strange speech, learns to talk with them, as well as his previously formed habits will let him, and between his descendants and theirs there will be no difference of language, however unlike they may be in hue and feature. If adventurers of various race and tongue combine themselves together in a colony and take up their abode in some wild country, their speech at once begins to undergo a process of assimilation, which sooner or later makes it one and homogeneous: how rapidly this end shall be attained, and whether some one element shall absorb the rest, or whether all shall contribute equally to the resulting dialect, must be determined by the special circumstances of the case. Of the multitudes of Germans whom emigration brings to our shores, some establish themselves together in considerable numbers : they cover with their settlements a tract in the West, or fill a quarter in some of our large towns and cities. They form, then, a kind of community of their own, in the midst of the greater community which surrounds them, having numerous points of contact with the latter, but not absorbed into its structure : there are enough speakers of English among them to furnish all the means of communication with the world about them which they need ; they are proud of their German nationality and cling to it ; they have their own schools, papers, books, preachers—and their language, though sure to yield finally to the assimilating influences which surround it, may be kept up, possibly, for generations. So also with a crowd of Irish, clustered together in a village or suburb, breeding in and in, deriving their scanty instruction from special schools under priestly care : their characteristic brogue and other peculiarities of word and phrase may have an indefinite lease of life. But, on the other hand, families of foreign nationality scattered in less numbers among us can make no effective resistance to the force which tends to identify them thoroughly with the community of English speakers, and their language is soon given up for ours.

There is evidently no limit to the scale upon which such fusion and assimilation of speech may go on. The same causes which lead an individual, or family, or group of families, to learn and use another tongue than that which they themselves or their fathers have been accustomed to speak, may be by historical circumstances made operative throughout a whole class, or over a whole region. When two communities are combined into one, there comes to be but one language where before there were two. A multiplication and strengthening of the ties which bind together the different sections of one people tends directly toward the effacement of already existing varieties of dialect, and the production of linguistic uniformity.

Such effacement and assimilation of dialectic varieties, not

less than dissimilation and the formation of new dialects, are
all the time going on in human communities, according as
conditions favour the one or the other class of effects; and a
due consideration of both is necessary, if we would comprehend the history of any tongue, or family of tongues. Let
us look at one or two examples, which shall serve to illustrate their joint and mutual workings, and to set forth
more clearly the truth of the principles we have laid down.

We will consider first the history of that one among the
prominent literary languages of the present day which has
most recently attained its position, namely the German.
From the earliest dawn of history, Germany has been filled
with a multitude of more or less discordant dialects, each
occupying its own limited territory, and no one of them
better entitled than any other to set itself up as the norm
of correct German speech.   How far back their separation
goes, it is impossible to tell ; whence, when, and how the
first Germanic tribe entered central Europe, that its tongue
might become there the mother of so many languages, crowding Germany and Scandinavia, and spreading, through England, even to the shores and prairies of a new world ; or
whether the beginnings of dialectic division were made before
the entrance of the race into its present seats—these are
secrets which will never be fully disclosed.   There were
sweeping changes in the range and character of the Germanic dialects during those ages of migration and strife
when Germany and Rome were carrying on their life and
death struggle. Whole branches of the German race, among
them some of the most renowned and mighty, as the Goths
and Vandals, wholly lost their existence as separate communities, being scattered and absorbed into other communities, and their languages also ceased to exist. Leagues
and migrations, intestine struggles and foreign conquests,
produced fusions and absorptions, extensions, contractions,
and extinctions, in manifold variety ; but without any
tendency to a general unity : and three centuries and a half
ago, when the modern German first put forth its claim to
stand as the common language of Germany, there was in
that country the same Babel of discordant speech as at the

Christian era. Since the introduction of Christianity and
the beginnings of civilization, more than one of the High-
German dialects, as they are called,.the dialects of central
and southern Germany, had been for a season the subject
of literary culture. This was the case with the idioms, in
succession, of the Alemannic, Frankish, and Bavarian divisions of the race, between the seventh and the thirteenth
centuries ; then, for a time, the Swabian dialect gained the
preëminence, and in it was produced a rich and noble legendary literature, containing precious memorials of national
heroic story, and still studied and valued wherever the German tongue is spoken. Here was a promising beginning for
a truly national language, but the conditions of the times
were not yet such as to give the movement lasting and assured
success. Three centuries later began the grand national up-
heaval of the Reformation. The writings of Luther, multiplied and armed with a hundred-fold force by the new art of
printing, penetrated to all parts of the land, and to nearly
all ranks and classes of the people, awakening everywhere a
vivid enthusiasm. The language he used was not the local
dialect of a district, but one which had already a better
claim than any other to the character of a general German
language : it was the court and official speech of the principal
kingdoms of central and southern Germany, made up of
Swabian, Austrian, and other dialectic elements.* To a language so accredited, the internal impulse of the religious
excitement and the political revolutions accompanying it,
and the external influence of the press, which brought its
literature, and especially Luther's translation of the Bible,
into every reading family, were enough to give a common
currency, a general value. It was set before the eyes of the
whole nation as the most cultivated form of German speech ;
it was acknowledged and accepted as the dialect of highest
rank, the only fitting organ of communication among the
educated and refined. From that time to the present, its
influence and power have gone on increasing. It is the
vehicle of literature and instruction everywhere. Whatever
may be the speech of the lower classes in any section, the

* See Schleicher, Deutsche Sprache, p. 107 seq.

11 *

educated, those who make up good society, speak the
literary German; their children are trained in it; nothing
else is written. The popular dialects are still as numerous
as ever, because education is not pervading and thorough
enough to extirpate them ; and their existence may be prolonged for an indefinite period ; but the literary language
exercises a powerfully repressing and assimilating effect
upon them all; it has lessened their rank and lowered their
character, by withdrawing from them in great measure the
countenance and aid of the cultivated ; it has leavened them
all with its material and its usages ; and it may finally
succeed in crowding them altogether out of use. Its sway
extends just as far as the external influences which established it reach : it is not confined to the territory occupied
by the High-German dialects, its nearest kindred ; the
people of the northern provinces also, speaking tongues of
Low-German descent, which are much more nearly related
with the Netherlandish, or even with the English, are drawn
by the ties of political, social, and religious community with
the rest of Germany to accept and use it. While, on the
other hand, political independence, aided by diversity of
social and religious usages, has given a separate existence
as a literary language to the Dutch or Netherlandish, and
yet more notably to the English, descendants of dialects
originally undistinguished among the crowd of Low-German
idioms which lined the shores of the North Sea.

The history of most other literary languages is of the
same character with that which we have just been examining. Each was, at the outset, one out of a number of kindred but more or less diverse forms of speech, and the
predominance which it came to gain over them was the result, not of its inherent merits as an instrument of thought
and means of communication, but of outward circumstances,
which made its usages worth the acquisition of a wider and
wider community. Thus the parent language of the modern
French was the vernacular speech of only a small part of
the population of France ; and it long had a rival, and
almost a superior, in the early and highly cultivated dialect
of southern France, the Provençal, or *langue d'oc ;* nor,

if the kingdom of Toulouse had maintained itself, would the latter ever have yielded to the former : but the sceptre of political supremacy over all France passed into the keeping of the northern provinces, and their speech became the rule of good usage throughout the land, while the *langue d'oc* lost by degrees its character as a cultivated dialect, and survives only in rude and insignificant provincial *patois*. The Italian was, in like manner, the popular idiom only of Tuscany, one of the innumerable local dialects which crowd and jostle one another between the Alps and Sicily, and its currency among the educated classes of the whole peninsula is the effect of literary influence and of instruction.

An illustration of a somewhat different character is afforded us by the history of the Latin, a history in many respects more remarkable than that of any other language which has ever existed. This conquering tongue—whose descendants now occupy so large and fair a part of Europe, and, along with their half-sister, the English, fill nearly all the New World, and numerous scattered tracts, coasts, and islands, on every continent and in every ocean, while its material has leavened and enriched the speech of all enlightened nations—was the vernacular idiom, not twenty-five centuries ago, of a little isolated district in middle Italy, a region which, on any map of the world not drawn upon a scale truly gigantic, one might easily cover with the end of a finger. How and when it came there, we know not; but it was one of a group of related dialects, descendants and joint representatives of an older tongue, spoken by the first immigrants, which had grown apart by the effect of the usual dissimilating processes. Remains of at least two of these sister dialects, the Oscan and the Umbrian, are still left in existence, to exercise the ingenuity of the learned, and to illustrate the ante-historic period of Italic speech. The Latin was pressed on the north by the Etruscan, and threatened from the south by the Greek, languages of much more powerful races, and the latter of them possessing a higher intrinsic character, and an infinitely superior cultivation : no one could then have dared to guess that its after career

would be so much more conspicuous than theirs. Its spread
began with the extension of Roman dominion, and was the
plainest and most unequivocal sign of the thorough and
penetrating nature of that dominion. Not content with the
loose and nominal sway which the Persian sovereign exercised over the heterogeneous parts of his vast empire, or the
yet laxer authority of the modern Mongol rulers over
their wider conquests, the Romans infused, as it were, a new
organic life into the vast body corporate of which they were
the head, and made their influence felt through its every
nerve and fibre. Italy they first subjected and Romanized.
The yoke they imposed, and riveted by their military colonies,
their laws and institutions, their culture, and their all-pene-
trating administration, was a bond of community against
which no other proved able to maintain itself; all the languages of the peninsula, from the Gaulish of the north to
the Greek of the extreme south, gave way by degrees before
the tongue of the conquering city, and Italy became a
country of one uniform speech. And yet not wholly
uniform : relics of the ancient languages maintained themselves for a long time in certain more inaccessible districts,
and their influence was doubtless to be distinctly seen in the
varying local dialects of the different parts of the peninsula
—as, indeed, traces of it are even now discoverable there.
The common speech of Italy, too, setting aside these dialectic distinctions, was not the pure polished Latin of Cicero
and Virgil, but a ruder idiom, containing already the germs
of many of the changes exhibited by the modern Italian and
the other Romanic tongues. The same process of conquest
and incorporation into the Roman community was carried
farther, upon a grand and surprising scale, into the other
countries of Europe. The Celts of Gaul, the Celts and
Iberians of Spain, gave up their own languages and adopted
that of their rulers and civilizers, not less completely than
have the Celts of Ireland, within the last few centuries,
exchanged their Irish speech for English : of Celtic words
and usages only scanty and unimportant traces are to be
found in the modern French and Spanish. The same fate
threatened Germany, had not her brave and hardy tribes

offered too stubborn a resistance to the already waning
forces of the empire ; and Britain also, had not its remote
situation and inferior value as a province caused the Roman
hold upon it to be weak, and soon abandoned. Less considerable tracts of south-eastern Europe, stretching from the
northern border of Italy to near the mouth of the Danube,
yielded to the same influence : subdued by the arms, colonized from the population, organized by the policy, civilized
by the culture, of the great city, they learned also to talk
her language, forgetting their own. Thus arose the great
and important group of the Romanic languages, as they are
called ; namely, the Italian, the French, the Spanish and
Portuguese, the Rhæto-Romanic of southern Switzerland, and
the Wallachian—each including a host of varying dialects,
all lineal descendants of the Latin, all spoken by populations
only in small part of Latin race.

We must not suppose, however, that a pure and classical
Latin was ever the popular dialect of this wide-extended
region of Europe, any more than of Italy after its first
Romanization. The same counteracting causes, acting on a
grander scale and with an intensified force, prevented correctness and homogeneity of speech. The populace got their
Latin rather from the army and its followers, the colonists
and low officials, than from educated Romans and the works
of great authors. Doubtless there was not at first such a
difference between the dialect of the highest and of the
lowest that they could not understand one another. But,
whatever it was, it rapidly became wider : while study and
the imitation of unchanging models kept the scholars and
ecclesiastics in possession of the classical Latin, only a little
barbarized by the irresistible intrusion into it of words and
constructions borrowed from vernacular use, the language of
the masses grew rapidly away from it, breaking up at the
same time into those innumerable local forms to whose existence we have already referred. There was no conserving and
assimilating influence at work among the millions who had
taken for their own the language of Rome, capable either of
binding them fast to its established usages or of keeping
their lines of linguistic growth parallel. Special disturbing

forces came in here and there. Incursions and conquests of
German tribes brought an element of Germanic speech into
the tongues alike of Spain, France, and Italy. Centuries of
Saracen domination engrafted upon the Spanish language a
notable store of words of Arabic derivation. When, at
length, the dark ages of European history were over, and
knowledge and culture were to be taken out of the exclusive
custody of the few, and made the wealth and blessing of the
many, the Latin was a dead language, much too far removed
from popular wants and sympathies to be able to serve the
needs of the new nations. Hence the rise in each separate
country, at not far from the same time, of a new national
tongue, to be the instrument and expression of the national
culture. All Romanized Europe was in the condition already
described as that of Germany prior to the advancement of the
modern German to its present position ; a chaos of varying
dialects was there ; and, in every case, external historical
circumstances determined which of them should attain a
higher value, and should subject and absorb the rest.

In all this alternate and repeated divergence and convergence of dialects there is evidently nothing which needs to be
looked upon as mysterious, or even puzzling. Such has been
the history of language from the beginning, and in all parts
of the earth. We need only the tendency of individual
language to vary, and the effect of community to check,
limit, and even reverse this tendency, in order to explain
every case that arises : the peculiar conditions of each case
must decide whether their joint action shall, on the whole,
make for homogeneity or for diversity of speech ; and the
result, in kind and in degree, will vary according to the sum
of the causes which produced it ; as the resultant motion, in
rate and direction, combines and represents all the forces,
however various and conflicting, of whose united action it is
the effect.

Thus, as has been already pointed out, when there takes
place a fusion of two communities, larger or smaller, of
varying speech, no general law can determine what shall be
the resulting dialect. When the Romans conquered Gaul,
although forming only a minority of the population, they

almost totally obliterated the Gaulish speech, putting the
Latin in its place, for they brought with them culture and
polity, art and science, learning and letters: they made it
better worth while for the Celts to learn Latin than to
adhere to their own ancient idiom. When, however, the
Germanic Franks, a few centuries later, conquered in their
turn the now Latinized Gaul, and turned it into a kingdom
of France, they adopted the language of their more numerous and more cultivated subjects, only adding a small percentage of Germanic words to its vocabulary, and perhaps
contributing an appreciable influence.toward hastening the
decay, already well in progress, of the Latin grammatical
system. The same thing happened once more, when the
Scandinavian Northmen, representing another branch of the
Germanic family, after extorting from the beaten and trembling monarchs of France the cession of one of her fairest
provinces, became the not less formidable and dreaded Normans. Although placed in seemingly favourable circumstances for conserving their linguistic independence, crowded
together as they were within comparatively narrow bounds,
and making on their own ground, of which they were
absolute masters, the majority of the population, they yet
could not resist the powerful assimilating influences which
pressed them, a horde of uncouth and unlearned barbarians,
on every side. Within a wonderfully short time, their
Norse tongue had altogether gone out of use, leaving traces
only in a few geographical names: along with French manners, French learning, and French polity, they had implicitly
adopted also French speech. Hardly was this conversion
accomplished, when they set forth to propagate their new
linguistic faith in a country occupied by dialects akin with
that which they had recently forsworn. The Angles and
Saxons, Germanic tribes, had meantime finished the task,
only begun by the Romans, of extirpating upon the largest
and best part of British ground the old Celtic speech. They
had done it in a somewhat different way, by sheer brute
force, by destroying, enslaving, or driving out the native
population, and filling all but the most inaccessible regions
of the island with their own ferocious tribesmen. Hence

the wholly insignificant remains of Celtic material to be
found among the ordinary stores of expression of our English
tongue.   Christianity and civilization found the invaders in
their new home, and an Anglo-Saxon literature grew up,
which, had circumstances continued favourable, might have
aided national unity of government, institutions, and culture
to assimilate the varying dialects of the country, producing
a national language not inferior in wealth and polish to our
present speech.   But they who take the sword shall perish
by the sword: upon the Anglo-Saxons were wreaked the
woes they had themselves earlier brought upon the Celts.
Danish and Norse invasions, during a long period, bitterly
vexed and weakened the Saxon state, and it finally sank
irrecoverably under the Norman conquest.   This time, the
collision of two diverse languages, upborne by a nearly
equal civilization—the partial superiority of that of the
Normans being more than counterbalanced by their inferiority in numbers—under the government of political
circumstances already explained, produced a result different
from any which we have thus far had occasion to notice—
namely, a truly composite language, drawing its material and
its strength in so nearly equal part from the two sources
that scholars are able to dispute whether the modern English
is more Saxon or more French.   Into the details of the
combination we cannot now stay to enter, but must pass
on to note the later dialectic history of the language,
merely directing attention to the important and familiarly
known fact that its formative apparatus—whether consisting
in inflections, affixes of derivation, or connectives and relational words—along with the most common and indispensable
part of its vocabulary, remained almost purely Saxon, so
that it is to be accounted still a Germanic dialect in structure, although furnished with stores of expression in no
small part of Romanic origin.

The fusion of Saxon and Norman elements in English
speech did not reach in equal measure all parts of the land
or all classes of the people, nor did it by any means wipe
out previously existing dialectic differences, thus furnishing
a new and strictly homogeneous speech as a starting-point

whence a new process of dialectic divergence should commence. On the contrary, Britain is still, like Germany, only in a less degree, a country full of dialects, some of whose peculiarities go back to the diversities of speech among the tribes by whom the Anglo-Saxon conquest of the island was achieved, thirteen hundred years ago, while the rest are of every date of origin, from that remote period to the present. One or two of these dialects—especially the Scottish and the Yorkshire—poetry and fiction have made somewhat familiarly known to us; others are matters of keen and curious interest to the student of language, their testimony being hardly less essential than that of the literary dialect to his comprehension of the history of English speech.

But it was impossible that, in the transfer of English to the continent of America, these local dialects should maintain themselves intact; that could only have been the result of a separate migration of parts of the local communities to which they belonged, and of the continued maintenance of their distinct identity in their new place of settlement. Such was not the character of the movement which filled this country with an English-speaking population. Old lines of local division were effaced; new ties of community were formed, embracing men of various province and rank. It was not more inevitable that the languages of the various nationalities which have contributed to our later population should disappear, swallowed up in the predominant English, than that the varying forms of English should disappear, being assimilated to that one among them which was better supported than the rest. Nor could it be doubtful which was the predominant element, to which the others would have to conform themselves. In any cultivated and lettered community, the cultivated speech, the language of letters, is the central point toward which all the rest gravitate, as they are broken up and lose their local hold. And our first settlers were in no small part from the instructed class, men of high character, capacity, and culture. They brought with them a written language and a rich literature; they read and wrote; they established schools of every grade, and

took care that each rising generation should not fall behind
its predecessor in learning. The basis, too, of equality of
rights and privileges on which they founded their society
added a powerful influence in favour of equality of speech.
As a natural and unavoidable consequence, then, of these
determining conditions, and not by reason of any virtue for
which we are to take credit to ourselves, the general language of America, through all sections of the country and
all orders of the population, became far more nearly homogeneous, and accordant with the correct standard of English
speech, than is the average language of England. And the
same influences which made it so have tended to keep it so :
the democratic character of our institutions, and the almost
universality of instruction among us, have done much to
maintain throughout our community an approximate uniformity of idiom. There was doubtless never a country
before, where, down to the very humblest classes of the
people, so many learned to read and spell out of the same
school-books, heard the same speakers, from platform, desk,
and pulpit, and read the same books and papers ; where
there was such a surging to and fro of the population, such
a mixture and intimate intercourse of all ranks and of all
regions. In short, every form of communication is more
active and more far-reaching with us than ever elsewhere ;
every assimilating influence has had unequalled freedom and
range of action. Hence, there was also never a case in
which so nearly the same language was spoken throughout
the whole mass of so vast a population as is the English now
in America. Modern civilization, with the great states it
creates, and the wide and active intercourse among men to
which it prompts and for which it affords the needed facili-
ties, is able to establish upon unoccupied soil, and then to
maintain there, community upon a scale of grandeur to
which ancient times could afford no parallel.

Nor have we failed to keep nearly even pace with our
British relations in the slow progressive development of the
common tongue : our close connection with the mother-
country, the community of culture which we have kept up
with her, our acknowledgment of her superior authority in

matters of learning and literature, have been able thus far
to restrain our respective lines of linguistic growth from
notable divergence. Though we are sundered by an ocean,
there have been invisible ties enough between us to bind us
together into one community. Yet our concordance of
speech is not perfect: British purism finds fault with even
our higher styles of discourse, oral and written, as disfigured
by Americanisms, and in both the tone and the material of
colloquial talk the differences are, of course, much more
marked. We have preserved some older words, phrases,
and meanings which their modern use discards; we have
failed as yet to adopt certain others which have sprung up
among them since the separation; we have originated yet
others which they have not accepted and ratified. Upon
all these points we are, in the abstract, precisely as much in
the right as they; but the practical question is, which of
the two is the higher authority, whose approved usage shall
be the norm of correct English speaking. We have been
content hitherto to accept the inferior position, but it is not
likely that we shall always continue so. Our increasing
numbers and our growing independence of character and
culture will give us in our own estimation an equal right, at
the least, and we shall feel more and more unwilling to yield
implicitly to British precedent; so that the time may perhaps
come when the English language in America and the English
language in Britain will exhibit a noteworthy difference of
material, form, and usage. What we have to rely upon to
counteract this separating tendency and annul its effect is
the predominating influence of the class of highest cultivation, as exerted especially through the medium of literature.
Literature is the most dignified, the most legitimate, and
the most powerful of the forces which effect the conservation
of language, and the one which acts most purely according
to its true merit, free from the adventitious aids and draw-
backs of place and time. It is through her literature that
America has begun, and must go on, to win her right to
share in the elaboration of the English speech. Love and
admiration of the same master-works in poetry, oratory,
philosophy, and science has hitherto made one community

of the two great divisions of speakers of English, and ought
to continue to unite them—and it will, we hope, do so : but
more or less completely, according as that portion of the
community which is most directly reached and effectively
guided by literature is allowed authority over the rest.

We are, however, by no means free from dialects among our
own population, although we may hope that they will long,
or always, continue to be restricted within narrow limits of
variation from the standard of correct speech, as they are at
present. The New Englander, the Westerner, the Southerner, even of the educated class, betrays his birth to a
skilled observer by the peculiarities of his language ; and
the lower we descend in the social scale, the more marked
and prominent do these peculiarities become. There is
hardly a locality in the land, of greater or less extent, which
has not some local usages, of phrase or utterance, characterizing those whose provincialism has not been rubbed off by
instruction or by intercourse with a wider public. There is
a certain degree of difference, too, of which we are all
conscious, between the written and the colloquial style :
there are words and phrases in good conversational use,
which would be called inelegant, and almost low, if met
with in books ; there are words and phrases which we employ in composition, but which would seem forced and stilted
if applied in the ordinary dealings of life. This is far from
being a difference sufficient to mark the literary English as
another dialect than that of the people ; yet it is the beginning of such a difference ; it needs no change in kind, but
only a change in degree, to make it accord with the distinction between any literary language which history offers to
our knowledge and the less cultivated dialects which have
grown up in popular usage by its side, and by which it has
been finally overthrown and supplanted.

Nothing, then, as we see, can absolutely repress dialectic
growth ; even the influences most powerfully conservative
of identity of language, working in the most effective
manner which human conditions have been found to admit,
can only succeed in indefinitely reducing its rate of progress.

It will be noticed that we have used the terms "dialect" and "language" indifferently and interchangeably, in speaking of any given tongue ; and it will also have been made plain, I trust, by the foregoing exposition how vain would be the attempt to establish a definite and essential distinction between them, or give precision to any of the other names which indicate the different degrees of diversity among related tongues. No form of speech, living or dead, of which we have any knowledge, was not or is not a dialect, in the sense of being the idiom of a limited community, among other communities of kindred but somewhat discordant idiom ; none is not truly a language, in the sense that it is the means of mutual intercourse of a distinct portion of mankind, adapted to their capacity and supplying their needs. The whole history of spoken language, in all climes and all ages, is a series of varying and successive phases ; external circumstances, often accidental, give to some of these phases a prominence and importance, a currency and permanence, to which others do not attain ; and according to their degree of importance we style them idiom, or *patois*, or dialect, or language. To a very limited extent, natural history feels the same difficulty in establishing the distinction between a " variety " and a " species : " and the difficulty would be not less pervading and insurmountable in natural than in linguistic science, if, as is the case in language, not only the species, but even the genera and higher groups of animals and plants were traceably descended from one another or from common ancestors, and passed into each other by insensible gradations. Transmutation of species in the kingdom of speech is no hypothesis, but a patent fact, one of the fundamental and determining principles of linguistic study.

LECTURE V.

Erroneous views of the relations of dialects. Dialectic variety implies
original unity. Effect of cultivation on a language. Grouping of languages by relationship. Nearer and remoter relations of the English.
Constitution of the Indo-European family. Proof of its unity. Impossibility of determining the place and time of its founders; their
culture and customs, inferred from their restored vocabulary.

HAVING previously considered in some detail the various
modes of change in language—the processes of linguistic
life, as, by an allowable figure, we termed them—we went
on at our last interview to direct our attention to the circumstances and conditions which govern the working of those
processes, giving prominence to the one or the other of them,
and quickening or retarding their joint effects. We then
proceeded to inquire into the manner in which the same
processes operate to divide any given form of speech, with
the lapse of time, into varying forms, or to convert a language into dialects. We passed in review the causes which
favour the development of dialectic differences, as well as
those which limit and oppose such development, and even
tend to bring uniformity out of diversity. They are, we
found, of two general kinds: the one, proceeding from individuals, and founded on the diversities of individual character and circumstance, tend to indefinite separation and
discordance; the other, acting in communities, and arising
from the necessity of mutual intelligence, the grand aim and
purpose of language, make for uniformity and assimilation,

sacrificing a merely personal to a more comprehensive unity, merging the individual in the society of which he is a member. Language is an institution founded in man's social nature, wrought out for the satisfaction of his social wants; and hence, while individuals are the sole ultimate agents in the formation and modification of every word and meaning of a word, it is still the community that makes and changes its language. The one is the molecular force; the other, the organic. Both, as we saw, are always at work, and the history of human tongues is a record of their combined effects; but the individual diversifying forces lie deeper down, are more internal, more inherent in the universal use of speech, and removed from the control of outward circumstances. Language, we may fairly say, tends toward diversity, but circumstances connected with its employment check, annul, and even reverse this tendency, preserving unity, or producing it where it did not before exist.

One or two recent writers upon language * have committed the very serious error of inverting the mutual relations of dialectic variety and uniformity of speech, thus turning topsy-turvy the whole history of linguistic development. Unduly impressed by the career of modern cultivated dialects, their effacement of existing dialectic differences and production of homogeneous speech throughout wide regions, and failing to recognize the nature of the forces which have made such a career possible, these authors affirm that the natural tendency of language is from diversity to uniformity; that dialects are, in the regular order of things, antecedent to language; that human speech began its existence in a state of infinite dialectic division, which has been, from the first, undergoing coalescence and reduction. It may seem hardly worth while to spend any effort in refuting an opinion

---

* I refer in particular to M. Ernest Renan, of Paris, whose peculiar views upon this subject are laid down in his General History of the Semitic Languages, and more fully in his treatise on the Origin of Language (2nd edition, Paris, 1858, ch. viii.)—a work of great ingenuity and eloquence, but one of which the linguistic philosophy is in a far higher degree constructive than inductive. Professor Max Müller, also, when treating of the Teutonic class of languages (Lectures on Language, first series, fifth lecture), appears distinctly to give in his adhesion to the same view.

of which the falsity will have been made apparent by the
exposition already given ; yet a brief additional discussion of
the point will afford us the opportunity of setting in a
clearer light one or two principles whose distinct apprehension is necessary in order to the successful prosecution of
our farther inquiries.

It will be readily admitted that the difference between
any given dialect and another of kindred stock is made up
of a multitude of separate items of difference, and consists in
their sum and combined effect : thus, for instance, words are
possessed by the one which are wanting in the other ; words
found in both are differently pronounced by each, or are used
in senses either not quite identical or very unlike ; combinations and forms belong only to one, or are corrupted and
worn down in diverse degrees by the two ; phrases occur in
the one which would be meaningless in the other.   Now the
gradual production of such differences as these is something
which we see to have been going on in language during the
whole period of its history illustrated by literary records ;
nay, which is even going on at the present day under our
own eyes.   If the Italian uses in the sense of 'truth' the
word *verità*, the Spanish *verdad*, the French *vérité*, the
English *verity*, we know very well that it is not because all
these forms were once alike current in the mouths of the
same people, till those who preferred each one of them sorted
themselves out and combined together into a separate community ; it must be because some single people formerly used
in the same sense a single word, either coincident with one
of these or nearly resembling them all, from which they have
all descended, in the ordinary course of linguistic tradition,
that always implies liability to linguistic change.   We happen
to know, indeed, in this particular case, by direct historical
evidence, what the original word was, and who were the
people that used it : it was *vēritāt* (nominative *veritas*), and
belonged to the language of Rome, the Latin : its present
varieties of form merely illustrate the usual effects of
phonetic corruption. So, too, if I say *attend!* and the Frenchman *attendez!* our words differ in pronunciation, in grammatical form (the latter having a plural ending which the

former lacks), and in sense (the French meaning 'wait!') ;
and, in all these respects save the last, both differ from the
Latin *attendite ;* yet of this both are alike the hereditary
representatives : no Roman ever said either *attend* or *attendez.* But this same reasoning we apply also in other cases,
where direct historical evidence is wanting, arriving without
hesitation or uncertainty at like conclusions. If we say *true,*
while the German says *treu,* the Dane *tro,* the Netherlander
trouw, and so on, we do not once think of doubting that it is
because we have all gotten nearly the same word, in nearly
the same sense, by uninterrupted tradition from some primitive community in which a like word had a like sense ; and
we set ourselves to discover what this word was, and what
and why have been the changes which have brought it into
its present varying forms. The discordance between our
father, the Anglo-Saxon *fæder,* the Icelandic *fadir,* the Dutch
vader, and the German *vater,* does not, any more than that
between *verity* and its analogues, compel us to assume a
time when these words existed as primitive dialectic varieties
in the same community : we regard them as the later effects
of the separation of one community into several. And when
we compare them all with the Latin *pater,* the Greek *patër,*
the Persian *peder,* the Sanskrit *pitar*—all which are but
palpable forms of the same original from which the rest have
come—our inference is still the same. Or, to recur once
more to an example which we have already had occasion to
adduce, our word *is* is the English correspondent of the
German *ist,* the Latin *est,* the Greek *esti,* the Lithuanian
esti, the Slavonian *yest',* the Persian *est,* the Sanskrit *asti.*
To the apprehension of the historical student of language,
all these are nothing more than slightly varying forms of the
same vocable : their difference is one of the innumerable
differences of detail which distinguish from one another the
languages we have named. ' We cannot, to be sure, go back
under the sure guidance of contemporary records to the
people among whom, and the time at which, the word originated : but we are just as far in this case as in those referred
to above from being driven to the conclusion that all its present representatives are equally primitive, that they consti-

tute together the state of indefinite dialectic variety in which
the expression of the third person singular of the verb *to be*
began, and that the nations, modern or ancient, in whose
languages we find them are the lineal descendants of those
groups in a former community who finally made up their
minds to prefer the one or the other of them. On the
contrary, we derive, with all the confidence belonging to a
strictly logical process of reasoning, the conclusion that the
words we are considering are later variations of a single
original, namely *asti*, and that they would have no existence
if a certain inferrible community, at an unknown period in
the past, had not put together the verbal root *as*, signifying
' existence,' and the pronoun *ti*, meaning ' that,' to form that
original.

The same reasoning is applicable to every other individual
instance of dialectic difference.   And it is so applied, in each
individual instance, even by those who maintain the priority
of dialects : such comparison and inference as we have been
illustrating constitute the method of linguistic research of the
comparative philologists, among whom they too desire to
count themselves.   Only they fail to note that the whole sum
of dialectic difference is made up of instances like these, and
that, if the latter point back, in detail, to an original unity,
the former must, in its entirety, do the same.   " As there
were families, clans, confederacies, and tribes," we are told,[*]
" before there was a nation, so there were dialects before
there was a language." The fallacy involved in this comparison, as in all the reasoning by which is supported the
view we are combating, is that it does not go back far
enough ; it begins in the middle of historic development,
instead of at its commencement.   If families, clans, and
tribes were ultimate elements in the history of humanity, if
they sprang up independently, each out of the soil on which
it stands, then the indefinite diversity of human language in
its early stages—a diversity, however, fundamental, and not
dialectic—might follow, not only as an analogical, but as a
direct historical consequence.   But, if a population of
scattered communities implies dispersion from a single point,

* Max Muller, *l.c.*

if we must follow back the fates of our race until they centre
in a limited number of families or in a single pair, which
expanded by natural increase, and scattered, forming the
little communities which later fused together into greater
ones—and who will deny that it was so?—then, also, both
by analogy and by historical necessity, it follows that that is
the true view of the relation of dialects and language to
which we have been led above: namely, that growth and
divarication of dialects accompany the spread and disconnec-
tion of communities, and that assimilation of dialects accompanies the coalescence of communities.

Prevalence of the same tongue over wide regions of the
earth's surface was, indeed, impossible in the olden time, and
human speech is now, upon the whole, tending toward a condition of less diversity with every century; but this is only
owing to the vastly increased efficiency at present of those
external influences which counteract the inherent tendency
of language to diversity. As, here in America, a single cultivated nation, of homogeneous speech, is taking the place of
a congeries of wild tribes, with their host of discordant
tongues, so, on a smaller scale, is it everywhere else : civilization and the conditions it makes are gaining upon barbarism
and its isolating influences. In the fact that Frenchmen,
Spaniards, and Italians, on entering our community, all learn
alike to say with us *verity*, there is nothing which at all goes
to prove that *verity*, *vérité*, *verdad*, and *verità* are primitive
dialectic varieties, tending toward unity; nor, in the extended
sway of the cultivated tongues of more modern periods, is
there aught which in the most distant manner favours the
theory that dialects are antecedent to uniform speech, and
that the latter everywhere grows out of the former.

It is true, again, that a certain degree of dialectic variety
is inseparable from the being of any language, at any stage
of its history. We have seen that even among ourselves,
where uniformity of speech prevails certainly not less than
elsewhere in the world, no two individuals speak absolutely
the same tongue, or would propagate absolutely the same, if
circumstances should make them the founders of independent
linguistic traditions. However small, then, may have been

the community which laid the basis of any actually existing language or family of languages, we must admit the existence of some differences between the idioms of its individual members, or families. And if we suppose such a community to be dispersed into the smallest possible fragments, and each fragment to become the progenitor of a separate community, it might be said with a kind of truth that the languages of these later communities began their history with dialectic differences already developed. The more widely extended, too, the original community before its dispersion, and the more marked the local differences, not inconsistent with mutual intelligibility, existing in its speech, the more capital, so to speak, would each portion have, on which to commence its farther accumulation of dialectic variations. But these original dialectic differences would themselves be the result of previous growth, and they would be of quite insignificant amount, as having been able to consist at the outset with unity of speech; they might be undistinguishable even by the closest analysis among the peculiarities of idiom which should have arisen later ; and it would be the grossest error to maintain either that these last were original and primitive, or that they grew out of and were caused by the first slight varieties: we should rather say, with entire truth, that the later dialects had grown by gradual divergence out of a single homogeneous language.

In an uncultured community, the value of such minor discordances of usage as may exist, and do always exist, among those who yet, as being able to communicate freely with one another, are to be regarded as speaking the same tongue, is at its maximum. The first effect of the cultivation of a language, as we style it, is to wipe out this class of differences, extending the area and perfecting the degree of linguistic uniformity. And its work is accomplished, first as last, whether the scale of variation over which its influence bears sway be less or greater, by selection, not by fusion. The varying usages of different individuals and localities are not averaged, but the usages of one part of the community are set up as a norm, to which those of the rest shall be conformed, and from which farther variation shall be

checked or altogether prevented. An element of consciousness, of reflectiveness, is introduced into the use of language ;
acknowledged imitation of certain models, deference to
authority in matters of speaking, take the place of the
former more spontaneous and careless employment of the
common means of communication, governed only by the
necessities of communication, which are always felt but not
always reasoned upon. The best speakers, those who use
words with most precision, with most fulness and force
of meaning, with most grace and art, become the teachers of
the rest. And however this influence be exerted, whether
by simple recognition of authority in those who deserve it,
or with the aid of a popular literature, handed down by
tradition, or whether it rise to grammatical and lexical culture,
to the possession of letters and learning, it is of the same
nature ; it produces its conserving and ennobling effects in
the same way. It is the counsellor and guide, not the
master, of national usage. It undertakes no wholesale reformation. It does not shear off from a language masses of
unnecessary means of expression which untaught speakers
would fain force upon it ; it finds no such materials to deal
with. Some write and speak as if the uncultivated employer
of speech were impelled to launch out indefinitely into new
words and forms, rioting in the profusion of his linguistic
creations, until grammar comes to set bounds to his prodi-
gality, and to reduce the common tongue within reasonable
dimensions. But it is by no means so easy and seductive a
thing to increase the resources of a language. We do not
look to our dictionaries and grammars to know if we may
use elements which come crowding to our lips and demanding
utterance. Linguistic growth is a slow process, extorted, as
it were, by necessity, by the exigencies of use, from the
speakers of language. The obligation resting upon each one
of making himself intelligible to his fellows, and understanding them in turn, is the check, and a sufficient one, upon individual license of production. Economy is a main element
in linguistic development ; that which is superfluous in
a dialect, not needed for practical use, falls off and dies of
itself, without waiting to be lopped away by the pruning-

knife of a grammarian. Culture chooses, from among the varieties of equivalent form, utterance, and phrase which a defective communication has allowed to spring up within the limits of the same community, those which shall be accepted as most worthy of preservation. It maintains what is good, warns against abuses, and corrects offences committed by a part against the authority of prevailing usage. A cultivated language is thus simply one whose natural growth has gone on for a certain period under the conscious and interested care of its best speakers; which has been placed in their charge, for the maintenance of a standard, for the repression of disfiguring alterations, for enrichment with expressions for higher thought and deeper knowledge; for the enforcement, in short, of their own studied usages of speech upon the less instructed and more heedless masses of a community.

It is obviously futile to attempt to draw anywhere a dividing line in the development of language—to say, these differences on the one side are the result of later linguistic growth; those, on the other side, are original, a part of the primitive variety and indefiniteness of human speech. The nature and uses of speech, and the forces which act upon it and produce its changes, cannot but have been essentially the same during all the periods of its history, amid all its changing circumstances, in all its varying phases; and there is no way in which its unknown past can be investigated, except by the careful study of its living present and its recorded past, and the extension and application to remote conditions of laws and principles deduced by that study. Like effects, as we have already had occasion to claim, imply like causes, not less in the domain of language than in that of physical science; and he who pronounces the origin and character of ancient dialects and forms of speech to be fundamentally different from those of modern dialects and forms of speech can only be compared with the geologist who should acknowledge the formation by aqueous action of recent gravel and pebble-beds, but should deny that water had anything to do with the production of ancient sandstones and conglomerates.

The continuity and similarity of the course of linguistic history in all its stages, and the competency of linguistic correspondences, wherever we find them, to prove unity of origin and community of tradition, are truths which we need to bear in mind as we proceed with our inquiries into language. If we meet in different tongues with words which are clearly the same word, notwithstanding differences of form and meaning which they may exhibit, we cannot help concluding that they are common representatives of a single original, once formed and adopted by a single community, and that from this they have come down by the ordinary and still subsisting processes of linguistic tradition, which always and everywhere involve liability to alteration in outer shape and inner content. It is true that there are found in language accidental resemblances between words of wholly different origin : of such we shall have to take more particular notice in a later lecture (the tenth) : but exceptions like these do not make void the rule ; the possibility of their occurrence only imposes upon the etymologist the necessity of greater care and circumspection in his comparisons, of studying more thoroughly the history of the words with which he has to deal. It is also true that real historical correspondences may exist between isolated words in two languages without implying the original identity of those languages, or anything more than a borrowing by the one out of the stores of expression belonging to the other. Our own tongue, for instance, aside from its wholesale composition out of the tongues of two different races, draws more or less of its material from nearly every one of the languages of Europe, and from not a few of those of Asia, Africa, and America. Yet it is evident that such borrowing has its limits, both of degree and of kind, and that it may be within the power of the linguistic student readily to distinguish its results from the effects of a genuine community of linguistic tradition.

The method by which we are to proceed in grouping and classifying the languages spoken by mankind, now and in former times, results with necessary consequence from the principles which we have laid down. We have seen that no given form of speech remains permanently the same : each

changes continually, in its structure and content, and tends
to divide, with the progress of time, into varying forms or
dialects.   No existing language, no recorded language, is
original; each is the descendant of some earlier one, from
which, perhaps, other existing or recorded languages are
equally descended.   With this easy clew to guide us, the
labyrinth of human speech is a labyrinth no longer; it is
penetrated by paths which we may securely follow.   We
have simply to group together according to their affinities the
languages known to us; connecting, first of all, those whose
totality of structure, along with what history actually teaches
us of their derivation, shows them so plainly to be forms of
the same original that even the most exaggerated scepticism
could not venture to deny their relationship; then going on
to extend our classification from the more clearly to the more
obscurely, from the more closely to the more remotely connected, until we have done the utmost which the nature of
the case permits, until analysis and deduction will carry us
no farther.   The way is plain enough at first, and even the
most careless may tread it without fear of wandering; but to
follow it to the end demands, along with much labour and
pains, no little wariness and clearness of vision.

Let us, then, turn aside for a time from pursuing the
direct course of our fundamental inquiry, "why we speak so
and so," to ask who "we" are to whom the inquiry relates;
who, along with us that acknowledge the various forms of
the English as our native speech, use languages which are,
after all, only dialectic forms of one great original mother-
tongue.

The results of such an investigation into the relationship
of the English language have been, to a certain extent, taken
for granted during our whole discussion.   This was unavoidable : we could not otherwise have talked at all of genetic
connection, or illustrated the processes of linguistic growth.
Now, however, we have to take up the subject more systematically, showing the extent to which the tie of relationship
reaches, and presenting some of the evidence which proves its
reality.

To assert that the slightly differing forms of speech which

prevail in the various parts of our own country, and even the
more noteworthy dialects found among the classes of the
population of Britain, form together only one language, is to
assert a truism : no man in his sober senses would presume
to doubt it. Let any one, however ignorant of history he
may be, go about the globe, finding on each side of the
Atlantic, and scattered from island to island, communities
who speak English, though tinged with local colouring, and
it will not enter into his mind to doubt that they were
scattered thither from some common centre, that they all
have their accordant speech by community of linguistic
tradition. A like conclusion is reached almost as directly,
if we follow back to the continent of Europe the traces of
those adventurous tribes which, as history distinctly informs
us, colonized at no very remote date the British isles, and
note what languages are still spoken upon the shores whence
they set forth on their career of conquest. The larger and
more indispensable part of English, as has been already
pointed out, finds its kindred in Germany, whence came the
Saxon and Anglian portion of our ancestry. The community
of tradition between the English and the German, Netherlandish, Swedish, Danish, and so on, is so pervading, and its
evidences are so patent to view, that no one, probably, who
has ever added a knowledge of either of the languages named
to that of his English mother-tongue has failed to be struck
by it, and to be convinced that, in their main structure and
material, the two were one speech. But his experience has
also taught him that the difference between them is far from
being inconsiderable, and that, unfortunately for him, he is by
no means able to speak and write German or Swedish,
because English, like them, is Germanic. If an American,
he will talk readily with an educated Englishman ; he will
even make shift to understand a Yorkshireman, a broad
Scotchman, or an Irishman fresh from his native bogs ; but
put him and a German together, and the two are well-nigh
as deaf and dumb to each other as if the one of them were a
Greek or a Hindu. Plainly enough, the explanation of
their difficulty is simply this : these two Germanic dialects,
originally one language and belonging to a single community,

have been now so long separated, and their independent
changes in the interval have been so great, that free and
intelligent communication is no longer possible between
those who have learned to speak them : one must have somewhat of instruction in both in order to be able to discover
the fact of their relationship.

Not all the Germanic languages, however, are allied with
the English in equal degree. The Low-German dialects, as
they are called, those which occupy the northern shores and
lowlands of the country, stand notably nearer to our tongue
than do the dialects of central and southern Germany, the
literary High-German and its next of kin. This relation is
readily and sufficiently accounted for by the circumstances
of the Germanic emigration to Britain: our ancestors came
from the shore provinces, and brought with them the forms
of speech there prevailing. And there is yet another
principal group of Germanic languages, coördinate with the
two already mentioned : it occupies the outliers of Germany
to the north, namely Denmark, Sweden and Norway, and
their remote colony of Iceland. It is usually called the
Scandinavian group. We have in our own present speech
not a few traces of its peculiar words and usages, imported
into England by those fierce Northmen—or Danes, as
English history is accustomed to style them—whose incursions during many centuries so harassed the Saxon mon-
archy.

These three groups or classes of existing dialects, the
Low-German, the High-German, and the Scandinavian, with
their numerous subdivisions, constitute, then, a well-marked
family of related languages ; although those who speak them
can only to a very limited extent understand one another,
the same sentence or paragraph could not be written in any
two of them without bringing to light such and so many
resemblances as even to a superficial examination would
appear sure proof of a genetic connection. It is past question that all the Germanic dialects are descendants and joint
representatives of a single tongue, spoken somewhere, at
some time in the past, by a single community, and that all
the differences now exhibited by them are owing to the

separation of this community, in the progress of time, into
detached and somewhat isolated portions, with the consequent
breaking up into diverging lines and currents of the common
stream of their linguistic tradition. It is even clear that, so
far as concerns the surviving dialects, the divergence was
primarily into three main branches, now represented by the
three groups of languages which have been defined above.

How it happens that our vocabulary also contains so large
a store of words that are foreign to all the other Germanic
dialects, but are shared with us by the nations of southern
Europe, was fully set forth in the last lecture. We saw that
the Normans—who, though a people of Germanic blood, had
lived long enough in France to substitute the idiom of that
country for their own forgotten tongue—imported into
England a new current of linguistic tradition, which, after a
time, mingled peacefully in the same bed with the former
one. The languages with which ours is thus brought into a
kind of relationship by marriage were seen to be the French,
the Spanish and Portuguese, the Italian, the Rhæto-Romanic,
and the Wallachian, each including a host of minor dialects.
The descent of these tongues, constituting together the
Romanic group or family, from a common mother, the Latin,
is written down in full upon the pages of history, and has
been by us already briefly reviewed.

That these two important families of human language, the
Germanic and the Romanic, are also in remoter degree
related to one another and to other ancient and modern
families, as joint branches of a yet more extensive family, is
a truth equally undeniable, although not equally obvious.
That it might be so is evident enough, according to the
principles which we have already established respecting the
life of language.   There is no limit assignable to the extent
to which the descendants of a common linguistic stock may
diverge and become separated from one another.   The question is one of fact, of evidence.   Only a careful and thorough
sifting of their linguistic material can determine how far the
ramifications of genetical relationship may bind together
languages apparently diverse.   If two kindred tongues can,
by divergent growth, come to differ from each other as much

as English and German, there is no *à priori* ground for believing that they may not come to differ as much as English and Polish, or Greek, or Hindustani. And, by approved scientific methods of linguistic research, students of language have traced out the boundaries of a grand family of human speech, embracing, along with the Germanic and Romanic groups, nearly all the other tongues of Europe, and those of no small portion of south-western Asia. We will accordingly go on first to pass in review the various branches claimed to constitute this family, and then to examine the evidence upon which the claim is founded.

Of nearest kindred with the Latin, as well as most nearly associated with it in history, is the ancient Greek, its classic compeer, but its superior in flexibility and beauty ; superior, too, as regards the genius and culture of those to whom it served as the instrument of thought ; but of far less conspicuous career, and making at the present day but an insignificant figure in the sum of human speech, being spoken only by the scanty population of Greece itself, and by the peoples, partly of Greek origin, which fill the islands and line the shores of the Ægean and Black seas.

The languages displaced by the Latin were, as we have seen, in great part Celtic. At the beginning of the historic period, the domain of the Celts included no mean portion of the soil of Europe. Britain, Gaul, a part of Spain, and the north of Italy, together with some of the provinces of central Europe, were in their possession. But the more energetic and persistent Italic and Germanic races soon began to gain ground upon them : and now, for a long succession of centuries, no Celtic tribe of any importance has maintained its integrity and independence. The Erse, or Gaelic of the Scotch Highlands, the native Irish, or Gaelic of Ireland, and the insignificant dialect of the Isle of Man, representing together the Gadhelic division of Celtic speech— and the Welsh in Wales, and the Breton or Armorican in Brittany, representatives of the other, the Cymric division, are the scanty remains of that great family of related tongues which, but little more than two thousand years ago, occupied more territory than German, Latin, and Greek combined ; and they are all, probably, on their way to extinction.

The eastern part of Europe is mainly filled by the numerous branches of another important family, the Slavic or Slavonic. Although somewhat encroached upon on the west by the Germanic, it has, upon the whole, from inconspicuous beginnings, grown steadily in consequence since its first appearance on the stage of history, and now occupies a commanding position eastward, as the vehicle of civilization to northern and central Asia. It covers most of Russia in Europe, with Poland, the eastern provinces of Austria, and the northern of Turkey. Among its principal branches are the Russian, with numerous subdivisions, the Polish, the Bohemian, the Servian, and the Bulgarian. All these are as distinctly and closely akin with one another as are the modern Germanic dialects.

A more remotely allied branch of the same family, constituting almost a family by itself, occupies a narrow territory about the great bend of the Baltic sea, from the gulf of Finland to beyond the German frontier, and comprises the Lithuanian, the Livonian or Lettish, and the Old Prussian. The latter is already extinct, and the others also appear to be going gradually out of existence, under pressure of the assimilating influence exerted upon them by the languages of the surrounding more powerful communities.

We have thus reviewed all the languages of modern Europe, excepting, first, the Albanian, which is the living representative of the ancient Illyrian, and of which the connections are doubtful (although it is likely to be yet proved to belong with the rest, as a branch of the same stock) ; secondly, the Basque, in the Pyrenees, a wholly isolated and problematical tongue ; thirdly, the Hungarian, with its relatives, the Finnish and Lappish of the extreme north, and other languages spoken by scattered tribes in northern and eastern Russia ; and finally, the Turkish and its congeners, which do but overlap slightly the south-eastern frontier. These two last groups, as we shall see hereafter (in the eighth lecture), are of a kindred that occupies no small part of northern and central Asia. But before we have gathered in all the members of the great family we are seeking to establish, we must cross the border of Europe, and enter southern Asia. Asia Minor is chiefly in the hands of Turkish tribes, who have crowded themselves in there in comparatively modern times, driving out, or subjecting and assimilating, the previous occupants. The same races stretch eastward, across the southern extremity of the Caspian sea, intervening between Europe and the countries whose speech shows affinity with that of Europe. But within, in the hilly provinces of Media and Persia, and on the great Iranian table-land, which stretches thence to the Indus, we find again abundant traces of a linguistic tradition coinciding ultimately with our own. The Persian, with all its dialects, ancient and modern, and with its outliers on the north-west and on the east—as the Armenian, the Kurdish, the Ossetic, and the Afghan—constitutes a branch of our family, the Persian or Iranian branch. And yet one step farther we are able to pursue the same tie of connection. The Iranian languages conduct us to the very borders of India : beyond those borders, in Hindustan, between the bounding walls of the Himalayas and Vindhyas, and eastward to the mouths of the Ganges, lies the easternmost branch of that grand division of human speech to which our own belongs, the Indian branch, comprising the ancient Sanskrit, with its derived and kindred languages.

The seven groups of languages at which we have thus glanced—namely, the Indian, the Persian, the Greek, the Latin, the Slavonic (including the Lithuanic), the Germanic, and the Celtic—each made up of numerous dialects and sub-dialects, are the members composing one vast and highly-important family of human speech, to which, from the names of its two extreme members, we give the title of " Indo-European." It is known also by various other designations : some style it "Japhetic," as if it appertained to the descendants of the patriarch Japhet, as the so-called " Semitic" tongues to the descendants of Shem ; " Aryan " is a yet more popular and customary name for it, but is liable to objection, as being more especially appropriate to the joint Indo-Persian branch of

the family, since it is used by them, and them alone, in designating themselves ; and a few still employ the term " Indo-
Germanic," which seems to savour of national prepossession,
since no good reason can be given why, among the western
branches, the Germanic should be singled out for representation in the general title of the family.

The languages of this whole family sustain to one another
a relation which is the same in kind with that subsisting
between the various Germanic dialects, and differs from it
only in degree.   That the signs of their relationship escape
the notice of a superficial observer—that the school-boy, or
even the college-student, when toiling over his Greek and
Latin tasks, does not suspect, and might be hard to persuade, that the classical languages and his mother-tongue
are but modified forms of the same original, is evidently no
ground for discrediting the fact.   The uninstructed English
speaker, as we have seen, finds even the nearly kindred
German as strange and unintelligible as the Turkish : both
are to him in equal degree, as he says, "all Dutch," or "all
Greek ; " and yet, a little learning enables him to find half
his native vocabulary, in a somewhat changed but still plainly
recognizable form, in the German dictionary.   A higher degree of instruction is required, in order to the discovery and
appreciation of that evidence which proves the remoter relationship of the Indo-European tongues ; a wider comparison, a
more skilled and penetrating analysis, must be applied ; but,
by its application, the conclusion is reached just as directly
and surely in the one case as in the other.   The inquirer
fully convinces himself that the correspondences in their
material and structure are too numerous, and of too intimate
a character, to be explained with any plausibility by the
supposition of accidental coincidence, or of mutual borrowing
or imitation ; that they can only be the consequence of a
common linguistic tradition.

Any complete or detailed exhibition of the evidence which
shows the original unity of the languages claimed to constitute the Indo-European family is, of course, utterly impossible within the necessary limits of these lectures ; but it
is altogether desirable that we should direct our attention to

13

at least a few samples of the correspondences from which so
important a truth is derived.   It will be allowable to do this
the more succinctly, inasmuch as the truth is one now so
well established and so generally received, and of which the
proof is already familiar to so many.   We may fairly claim,
indeed, that it is denied only by those who are ignorant of
the facts and methods of linguistic reasoning, or whose judgments are blinded by preconceived opinion.

I shall not strive after originality in my selection of
the correspondences which illustrate the common origin
of the Indo-European tongues, but shall follow the course
already many times trodden by others.   This is one which
is marked out by the circumstances of the case.   It would
be extremely easy, choosing out any two from among the
languages which we wish to compare—as the Latin and
Greek, the Greek and Sanskrit, the Latin and Russian,
the Lithuanian and German — to draw up long lists of
words common to both, out of every part of their respective
vocabularies ; especially, if we were to take the time and
pains to enter into a discussion of the laws governing their
phonetic variations, and so to point out their obscure as
well as their more obvious correspondences : and we might
thus satisfactorily prove them all related, by proving each
one related with each of the rest in succession.   When,
however, we seek for words which are clearly and palpably
identical in all or nearly all the branches of the family, we
have to resort to certain special classes, as the numerals and
the pronouns.   The reason of this it is not difficult to point
out.   For a large portion of the objects, acts, and states, of
the names for which our languages are composed, it is comparatively easy to find new designations : they offer numerous salient points for the names-giving faculty to seize upon ;
the characteristic qualities, the analogies with other things,
which suggest and call forth synonymous or nearly synonymous titles, are many.   Hence a language may originate a
variety of appellations for the same thing—as, for *horse*, we
have also the almost equivalent names *steed, nag, courser,
racer ;* and further, for the different kinds and conditions of
the same animal, the names *stallion, mare, gelding, filly, colt,*

pony, and others—and, in the breaking up of the language into dialects, one of these synonymous appellations is liable to become the prevailing one in one dialect, another in another, to the neglect and loss of all but the one selected. Or, a new name is started in a single dialect, wins currency there, and crowds out of use its predecessors. The German, for instance, has, indeed, our word *horse*, in the form *ross* (earlier *hros*), but employs it more rarely, preferring to use instead *pferd*, a word of which we know nothing. The modern Romanic tongues, too, say in the same sense *caballo*, *cheval*, etc., words coming from the Latin *caballus*, ' nag,' and they have lost almost altogether the more usual and dignified Latin term *equus*. Thus, further, the modern French name for ' shoemaker ' is *cordonnier*, literally ' worker in Cordovan leather ; ' for ' cheese,' *fromage*, properly ' pressed into a form, moulded ; ' for ' liver,' *foie*, originally ' cooked with figs '—that fruit having been, as it seems, at a certain period, the favourite garnish for dishes of liver : while the Latin appellations of these three objects have gone out of use and out of memory. But for the numerals and pronouns our languages have never shown any disposition to create a synonymy ; it was, as we may truly say, no easy task for the linguistic faculty to arrive at a suitable sign for the ideas they convey ; and, when the sign was once found, it maintained itself thenceforth in use everywhere, without danger of replacement by any other, of later coinage. Hence all the Indo-European nations, however widely they may be separated, and however discordant in manners and civilization, count with the same words, and use the same personal pronouns in individual address—the same, with the exception, of course, of the changes which phonetic corruption has wrought upon their forms.

For reasons not so easily explainable, the Indo-European languages show a hardly less noteworthy general accordance in regard to the terms by which, within the historical period, or down even to the present time, they indicate the degrees of near relationship, such as *father, mother, daughter, brother, sister*. Formed, as these words were, in the earliest period of history of the common mother-tongue, they have in nearly

13 *

all its branches escaped being superseded by expressions of later growth, although there is hardly one of them which does not here and there exhibit a modern substitute. The following table will set forth, it is believed, in a plain and apprehensible manner some of the correspondences of which we have been speaking. For the sake of placing their value in a clearer light, I add under each word its equivalents in three of the languages—namely Arabic, Turkish, and Hungarian—which, though neighbours of the Indo-European tongues, or enveloped by them, are of wholly different kindred.

English	two	three	seven	thou	me	mother	brother	daughter
Germanic								
Dutch	twee	drie	zeven		mij	moeder	broeder	dochter
Icelandic	tvö	thriu	sió	thu	mik	modhir	brodhir	dottir
High-German	zwei	drei	sieben	du	mich	mutter	bruder	tochter
Mœso-Gothic	twa	thri	sibun	thu	mik		brothar	dauhtar
Lithuanic	du	tri	septyni	tu	manen	moter	brolis	dukter
Slavonic	dwa	tri	sedmi	tu	man	mater	brat	dochy
Celtic	dau	tri	secht	tu	me	mathair	brathair	dear (?)
Latin	duo	tres	septem	tu	me	mater	frater	
Greek	dúo	treis	hepta	sü	me	meter	phrater	thugater
Persian	dwa	thri	hapta	tum	me	matar		
Sanskrit	dwa	tri	sapta	twam	me	matar	bhratar	duhitar
Arabic	ithn	thalath	sab'	anta	ana	umm	akh	bint
Turkish	iki	úch	yedi	sen	ben	ana	kardash	kiz
Hungarian	ket	harom	het	te	engem	anya	fiver	leany

I have selected, of course, for inclusion in this table, those words of the several classes represented which exhibit most clearly their actual unity of descent : in others, it would require some detailed discussion of phonetic relations to make the same unity appear. Thus, the Sanskrit *panca*, the Greek *pente*, the Latin *quinque*, and the Gothic *fimf*, all meaning ' five,' are as demonstrably the later metamorphoses of a single original word as are the varying forms of the primitive *tri*, ' three,' given above : each of their phonetic changes being supported by numerous analogies in the respective languages. The whole scheme of numeral and pronominal forms and of terms of relationship is substantially one and the same in all the tongues ranked as Indo-European.

These facts, of themselves, would go far toward proving the original unity of the languages in question. To look upon correspondences like those here given as the result of accident is wholly preposterous: no sane man would think of ascribing them to such a cause. Nor is the hypothesis of a natural and inherent bond between the sound and the sense, which would prompt language-makers in different parts of the earth to assign, independently of one another, these names to these conceptions, at all more admissible. The existence of a natural bond could be claimed with even the slightest semblance of plausibility only in the case of the pronouns and the words for 'father' and 'mother;' and there, too, the claim could be readily disposed of—if, indeed, it be not already sufficiently refuted by the words from stranger tongues which are cited in the table. Mutual borrowing, too, transfer from one tongue to another, would be equally far from furnishing an acceptable explanation. Were we dealing with two or three neighbouring dialects alone, the suggestion of such a borrowing would not be so palpably futile as in the case in hand, where the facts to be explained are found in so many tongues, covering a territory which stretches from the mouths of the Ganges to the shores of the Atlantic. A modified form of the hypothesis of mutual borrowing is put forth by some who are indisposed to admit the essential oneness of Indo-European speech. Some tribe or race, they say, of higher endowments and culture, has leavened with its material and usages the tongues of all these scattered peoples, engrafting upon their original diversity an element of agreement and unity. But this theory is just as untenable as the others which we have been reviewing. Instances of mixture of languages—resulting either from the transmission of a higher and more favoured culture, or from a somewhat equal and intimate mingling of races, or from both together—have happened during the historical period in sufficient numbers to allow the linguistic student to see plainly what are its effects upon language, and that they are very different from those which make the identity of Indo-European language. The introduction of culture and knowledge, of art and science, may bring in a vocabulary of expressions for the knowledge communicated, the conceptions taught or prompted; but it cannot touch the most intimate fund of speech, the words

significant of those ideas without whose designation no
spoken tongue would be worthy of the name.   If we could
possibly suppose that the rude ancestors of the Indo-European nations, more brutish than the Africans and Polynesians of the present day, were unable to count their fingers even
until taught by some missionary tribe which went from one
to the other, scattering these first rudiments of mathematical
knowledge, we might attribute to its influence the close
correspondence of the Indo-European numeral systems; but
then we should have farther to assume that the same teachers
instructed them how to address one another with *I* and *thou*,
and how to name the members of their own families : and
who will think of maintaining such an absurdity?   All the
preponderating influence of the Sanskrit-speaking tribes of
northern India over the ruder population of the Dekhan, to
which they gave religion, philosophy, and polity, has only
resulted in filling the tongues of the south with learned
Sanskrit, much as our own English is filled with learned
Latin and Greek.   Even that coalescence of nearly equal
populations, languages, and cultures out of which has grown
the tongue we speak, has, as was pointed out in the fourth
of these lectures, left the language of common life among
us—the nucleus of a vocabulary which the child first learns,
and every English speaker uses every day, almost every
hour—still overwhelmingly Saxon : the English is Germanic
in its fundamental structure, though built higher and de-
corated in every part with Romanic material.   So is it also
with the Persian, in its relation to the Arabic, of whose
material its more learned and artificial styles are in great
part made up ; so with the Turkish, of which the same thing
is true with regard to the Persian and Arabic.   But most of
all do these cases of the mingling of different tongues in one
language, and every other known case of a like character,
show that the grammatical system, the apparatus of inflection
and word-making, the means by which vocables, such as they
stand in their order in the dictionary, are taken out and
woven together into connected discourse, resists longest and
most obstinately any trace of intermixture, the intrusion of
foreign elements and foreign habits.   However many French

nouns and verbs were admitted to full citizenship in English
speech, they all had to give up in this respect their former
nationality : every one of them was declined or conjugated
after Germanic models. Such a thing as a language with a
mixed grammatical apparatus has never come under the
cognizance of linguistic students : it would be to them a
monstrosity ; it seems an impossibility. Now the Indo-
European languages are full of the plainest and most unequivocal correspondences of grammatical structure ; they
show abundant traces of a common system of word-formation,
of declension, of conjugation, however disguised by the corruptions and overlaid by the new developments of a later time :
and these traces are, above all others, the most irrefutable
evidences of the substantial unity of their linguistic tradition.
We will notice but a single specimen of this kind of evidences,
the most striking one, perhaps, which Indo-European grammar has to exhibit. This is the ordinary declension of the
verb, in its three persons singular and plural. In drawing
out the comparison, we cannot start, as before, from the
English, because, as has been shown in a previous lecture
(the third), the English has lost its ancient apparatus of
personal endings : we must represent the whole Germanic
branch by its oldest member, the Mœso-Gothic. The table
is as follows : *

English	'I have'	'thou hast'	'he has'	'we have'	'ye have'	'they have'
Mœso-Gothic	haba	habai-s	habai-th	haba-m	habai-th	haba-nd
Mod Persian	-m		-d	-m	-d	-nd
Celtic	-m		-d	-m	-d	-t
Lithuanic	-mi	-si	-ti	-me	-te	-ti
Slavonic	-mi	-si	-ti	-mu	-te	-nti
Latin	habeo	habe-s	habe-t	habe-mus	habe-tis	habe-nt
Greek	-mi	-si	-ti	-mes	-te	-nti
Sanskrit	-mi	-si	-ti	-masi	-tha	-nti

Fundamental and far-reaching as are the correspondences,

* Owing to the difficulty of finding a single verb which shall present the
endings in all the different languages, the verb *to have* has been selected, and
given in full in the two languages in which it occurs, the terminations alone
being elsewhere written. These are not in all cases the most usual endings
of conjugation, but such as are found in verbs, or in dialects, which have
preserved more faithfully their primitive forms.

of material and of form, which have thus been brought forward, it is not necessary that we insist upon their competency, alone and unaided, to prove the Indo-European languages only later dialectic forms of a single original tongue. Their convincing force lies in the fact that they are selected instances, examples chosen from among a host of others, which abound in every part of the grammar and vocabulary of all the languages in question, now so plain as to strike the eye of even the hasty student, now so hidden under later peculiar growth as to be only with difficulty traceable by the acute and practised linguistic analyst. He who would know them better may find them in such works as the Comparative Grammars of Bopp and Schleicher and the Greek Etymologies of Curtius. An impartial examination of them must persuade even the most sceptical that these tongues exhibit resemblances which can be accounted for only on the supposition of a prevailing identity of linguistic tradition, such as belongs to the common descendants of one and the same mother-tongue. On the other hand, all their differences, great and widely sundering as these confessedly are, can be fully explained by the prolonged operation of the same causes which have broken up the Latin into the modern Romanic dialects, or the original Germanic tongue into its various existing forms, and which have converted the Anglo-Saxon of a thousand years ago into our present English. Besides its natural divergent growth, the original Indo-European tongue has doubtless been in some degree diversified by intermixture here and there with languages of other descent; but there is no reason for believing that this has been an element of any considerable importance in its history of development. At some period, then, in the past, and in some limited region of Europe or Asia, lived a tribe from whose imperfect dialect have descended all those rich and cultivated tongues now spoken and written by the teeming millions of Europe and of some of the fairest parts of Asia.

To know when and where this tribe lived and formed its language is unfortunately beyond our power. It is, indeed, often assumed and asserted that the original Indo-European home was in the north-eastern part of the Iranian plateau, near the Hindu-Koh mountains; but so definite a determination possesses not the slightest shadow of authority or value. We really know next to nothing of the last movements which have brought any branch of the family into its present place of abode ; even these lie beyond the reach of the very hoariest traditions which have come down to us. The daylight of recorded history dawns first upon the easternmost, the Indo-Persian or Aryan, branch. The time is probably not far from two thousand years before Christ. We there see the Sanskrit-speaking tribes but just across the threshold of India, working their way over the river-valleys and intervening sand-plains of its north-western province, the Penjab, toward the great fertile territory, watered by the Ganges and its tributaries, of which they are soon to become the masters ; and we know that India, at least, is not the first home, but one of the latest conquests, of the family. The epoch, however, early as it appears to us, is far from the beginning of Indo-European migrations ; the general separation of the branches had taken place long before : and who shall say which of them has wandered widest, in the search after a permanent dwelling-place ? The joint home of Indians and Persians was doubtless in north-eastern Iran, the scene of the oldest Persian religious and heroic legend and tradition ; but there is no evidence whatever to prove that they were the aborigines of that region, and that all migration had been westward from thence.* Greek history and tradition also penetrate a little way into the second thousand years before Christ; but the Greeks are then already in quiet possession of that little peninsula, with the neighbouring islands and Asiatic shores, whence the glory of their genius afterward irradiated the world ; and, for aught that they are able to tell us of their origin, they might have sprung out of the ground there—born, according to their own story, of the stones which Deucalion and Pyrrha threw

---

* Some authorities incline to regard the geographical reminiscences of the Zend-avesta (in the first chapter of the Vendidad) as indicating the course of the joint Aryan migration from the original family home; but the claim appears to me so wholly baseless, and even preposterous, that I find it difficult to understand how any man should seriously put it forward.

behind them. The Latin race first appears as an insignificant handful in central Italy, crowded by other communities, in part of kindred blood; but no legend told us respecting its entrance into the Italian peninsula is of the very smallest historical value. Roman historians first bring to our knowledge the Celts and Germans. The former are already beginning to shrink and waste away within their ancient limits before the aggressions of the surrounding races : Celtic tales of the migrations westward which brought them into their European seats are but lying legends, mere echoes of their later knowledge of the countries and nations to the eastward. Germany is, from the first, the home of the Germans : they are a seething mass; south-eastward as well as southwestward rove their restless hordes, disturbing for centuries the peace of the civilized world; they leave their traces in every country of middle Europe, from the Volga to the Pillars of Hercules; but whence and when they came into Germany, we ask in vain. Last to appear upon the historic stage are the Slavonians, in nearly their present abodes : a less enterprising, but a stubborn and persistent race, whose lately acquired civilization has only within a short time begun to be aggressive. Of its own origin, it has nothing at all to say.

But if history and tradition thus refuse to aid us in searching for the Indo-European home, neither do the indications of language point us with anything like definiteness or certainty to its locality. The tongues of the easternmost branches, the Persian and Indian, do, indeed, exhibit the least departure from that form of speech which a general comparison of all the dialects shows to have been the primitive one ; but this is very far from proving the peoples who speak them to have remained nearest to their primitive seats. Migration does not necessarily lead to rapidity of linguistic changes, nor does permanence of location always imply persistency of linguistic type. Thus—to refer only to two or three striking facts among the languages of this family—the Greek has preserved much more than the Armenian of that material and structure which were of earliest Indo-European development, notwithstanding the more oriental position of

the latter; of all the existing tongues of the whole great
family, the Lithuanian, on the Baltic, retains by far the most
antique aspect ; and, among the Germanic dialects, the
speech of Iceland, the latest Germanic colony, is least varied
from their common type. All that primitiveness of form, in
respect both to language and institutions, which characterizes
the Aryan branch of the family—and especially the Indian
member of the branch, in its oldest period, represented to us
in the Vedas—would be fully and satisfactorily accounted
for, without denying them a long history and wide migration,
by attributing to them an exceptionally conservative disposition—such a disposition as so markedly distinguishes the
Indian above the Persian people since their separation, making
the former, in a vastly higher degree than the latter, the
model and illustration of earliest Indo-European antiquity.

Nor, again, are the inter-connections of the different
branches, so far as yet made out, of a nature to cast much
light upon the history of their wanderings. That the separation of Indian and Persian is latest of all is, it is true,
universally admitted. Nearly all agree, moreover, in allowing
a like special relationship of the Greek and Latin, although
its comparative remoteness, and the loss of intermediate
forms, make the question one of decidedly greater doubt and
difficulty. Beyond this, nothing is at present firmly established. The honour of a later and closer alliance with the
Aryan or Indo-Persian branch has been confidently claimed
for the classical or Greco-Latin, for the Slavonic, and for the
Germanic, respectively. Within no long time past, a German scholar of high rank * has attempted to lay out a scheme
of relationship for all the branches of the family. He assumes
that the original stock parted first into a northern and a
southern grand division : the northern included what afterward became the Germanic and the Slavo-Lithuanic branches,
the latter of them dividing yet later into Slavonic and
Lithuanic ; the southern was broken up first into an Aryan
and a southern European group, which respectively under-

* Professor August Schleicher, of Jena · his views may be found drawn
out in full in the preface to his interesting work on the German language
(Die Deutsche Sprache, Stuttgart, 1860).

went farther separation, the one into Persian and Indian, the
other into Greek and Italo-Celtic: while the Italic, of which
the Latin is the chief, and the Celtic, were the last to begin
their independent history, being still more closely related
than the Latin and the Greek. The feature of this arrangement which is most calculated to repel rather than attract
assent is the position assigned to the Celtic languages.
Few scholars are ready to allow that these tongues, in which
the original and distinctive features of Indo-European speech
are most of all hidden under the manifold effects of decay
and new growth, whose Indo-European character was therefore the last of all to be recognized, and whose separation
from the common stock has been generally looked upon as
the commencement of its dispersions, are to be regarded as
the nearest kindred of the Latin—although no one who re-
members how greatly the rates of linguistic change vary
among different peoples and under different circumstances
will venture to pronounce the connection impossible. The
time has not yet come for a full settlement of these controverted points; the means of their solution are, however,
doubtless contained in the linguistic facts which lie within our
reach, and a more thorough study and closer comparison will
one day bring them to light, and may perhaps at the same time
illustrate the course and order of those grand movements which
have brought the various races of the family into their present
seats.   But that such or any other evidences will ever direct
our gaze to the precise region whence the movements had
their first start is in the very highest degree unlikely: and
in the mean time it is better candidly to confess our ignorance than to try to hold with confidence an opinion resting
upon grounds altogether insufficient and untenable. At any
rate, we ought fully to acknowledge that linguistic science,
as such, does not presume to decide whether the Indo-
European home was in Europe or in Asia: the utmost that
she does is to set up certain faint and general probabilities,
which, combined with the natural conditions of soil and
climate, the traditions of other races, and the direction of
the grand movements of population in later times, point to

the East rather than the West as the starting-point of migration.

If the question of place must thus be left unsettled, that of time is not less uncertain. The geologist makes hitherto but lame and blundering work of establishing an absolute chronology for even the latest alterations of the earth-crust; and the student of language is compelled to found his estimates upon data not less scanty and questionable. The strata of human speech laid down in past ages have suffered most sweeping and irrestorable denudation, and their rate of growth during our present period is too greatly varying to furnish us any safe standard of general application. But to set a date lower than three thousand years before Christ for the dispersion of the Indo-European family would doubtless be altogether inadmissible; and the event is most likely to have taken place far earlier. Late discoveries are showing us that the antiquity of the human race upon the earth must be much greater than has been generally supposed. Vistas of wonderful interest are opened here, down which we can only catch glimpses; but the comparative brevity of the period covered by human records must make us modest about claiming that we shall ever understand much about ultimate beginnings, the first origin of races.

As regards, however, the grade of civilization and mode of life of the Indo-European mother-tribe before its separation into branches, the study of language is in condition to give us more definite and trustworthy information. It is evidently within our power to restore, to a certain extent, the original vocabulary of the tribe, out of the later vocabularies of the different branches. These are composed of words of every age, from the most recent to the most primitive. As the principal features of grammatical structure were struck out before the dispersion, and are yet traceable by the comparative philologist amid the host of newer formations which surround them, so was it also with the developed material of speech, with the names for such objects, and acts, and processes, and products, as the community had already found occasion, and acquired power, to express: they constituted

the linguistic patrimony with which each branch commenced
its separate history, and may still be seen among the stores
of more recent acquisition. Any word which is found in the
possession of all or nearly all the branches is, unless there be
special reasons to the contrary, to be plausibly regarded as
having formed part of their common inheritance from the
time of their unity. A vocabulary constructed of words
thus hunted out can be, indeed, but an imperfect one, since
no one can tell what proportion of the primitive tongue may
have become altogether lost, or changed by phonetic corruption past possibility of recognition, in the later dialects of so
many branches that its true character is no longer discoverable : but, if the list be drawn up with due skill and care,
it may be depended upon as far as it goes. And as, from the
stock of words composing any existing or recorded language,
we can directly draw important conclusions respecting the
knowledge, circumstances, and manners of the people who
speak it, so we can do the same thing with the fragment of
Indo-European speech which we shall have thus set up. It
is obvious, too, that the results of such an investigation
must be more satisfactory, the more primitive and unlettered
the people respecting which it is made, the more exclusively
native in origin and restricted in scope their civilization. A
language like our own is an immense encyclopedia, as it
were, in which are laid away the cognitions and experiences
of a whole world, and of numerous generations ; it is as many-
sided, as cosmopolitan, as hard to grasp and interpret in
detail, as is our culture ; while the tongue of a rude and
isolated tribe—like the Fuegians, the Fijians, the Eskimos
—would be a comparatively plain and legible portraiture of
its condition and character.

Some of the main results of the investigation made by
means of language into the primitive state of that tribe which
spoke the mother-tongue of the Indo-European family have
been long since drawn out, and are already become the
commonplaces of ethnological science. The subject is far
from being yet exhausted, and we may look forward to much
greater confidence of conclusion and definiteness of detail,
when all the languages of the family shall have been more

thoroughly compared and analyzed, and especially when the establishment of a true scheme of degrees of relationship among the branches shall reduce the doubt now thrown over the primitiveness of a term by its absence from the languages of some among them.

By this kind of research, then, it is found that the primitive tribe which spoke the mother-tongue of the Indo-European family was not nomadic alone, but had settled habitations, even towns and fortified places, and addicted itself in part to the rearing of cattle, in part to the cultivation of the earth. It possessed our chief domestic animals—the horse, the ox, the sheep, the goat, and the swine, besides the dog: the bear and the wolf were foes that ravaged its flocks; the mouse and fly were already its domestic pests. The region it inhabited was a varied one, not bordering upon the ocean. The season whose name has been most persistent is the winter. Barley, and perhaps also wheat, was raised for food, and converted into meal. Mead was prepared from honey, as a cheering and inebriating drink. The use of certain metals was known; whether iron was one of them admits of question. The art of weaving was practised; wool and hemp, and possibly flax, being the materials employed. Of other branches of domestic industry, little that is definite can be said; but those already mentioned imply a variety of others as coordinate or auxiliary to them. The weapons of offence and defence were those which are usual among primitive peoples, the sword, spear, bow, and shield. Boats were manufactured, and moved by oars. Of extended and elaborate political organization no traces are discoverable: the people was doubtless a congeries of petty tribes, under chiefs and leaders, rather than kings, and with institutions of a patriarchal cast, among which the reduction to servitude of prisoners taken in war appears not to have been wanting. The structure and relations of the family are more clearly seen; names of its members, even to the second and third degrees of consanguinity and affinity, were already fixed, and were significant of affectionate regard and trustful interdependence. That woman was looked down upon, as a being in capacity and dignity inferior to man, we find no indication whatever. The art of numeration was learned, at least up to a hundred ; there is no general Indo-European word for ' thousand.' Some of the stars were noticed and named : the moon was the chief measurer of time. The religion was polytheistic, a worship of the personified powers of nature. Its rites, whatever they were, were practised without the aid of a priesthood.

Such, in briefest possible description, was the simple people from whom appear to have descended those mighty nations who have now long been the leaders of the world's civilization. Of their classification, their importance in history, and the value of their languages to linguistic science, we shall treat further in the next lecture.

LECTURE VI.

Languages and literatures of the Germanic, Slavonic, Lithuanic, Celtic,
Italic, Greek, Iranian, and Indian branches of Indo-European speech.
Interest of the family and its study; historical importance of the Indo-
European races; their languages the basis of linguistic science.
Method of linguistic research. Comparative philology. Errors of
linguistic method or its application.

OUR consideration of the processes of linguistic growth,
and of their effects upon the condition of language and the
rise of discordant tongues, was brought to a close in the
preceding lecture with a brief discussion of certain erroneous views respecting original dialectic variety, and the
influence exerted upon it by literary and grammatical cultivation. We then looked to see how and how far the principles which we had established could be applied to explain
the seemingly infinite confusion of tongues now prevailing
upon the earth, and to facilitate their classification and
reduction to order. This led us to a recognition of our own
language as one of a group of nearly related dialects, the
Germanic group; and, on inquiring farther, we found that
this was itself a member of a wider family, embracing nearly
all the tongues of Europe, with a part of those of Asia, and
divided into seven principal branches: namely, the Indian,
the Iranian, the Greek, the Latin, the Germanic, the
Slavonic (including the Lithuanic, sometimes reckoned as a
separate branch), and the Celtic. We called it the Indo-
European family. At some place and time, which we were
obliged to confess ourselves unable to determine with any

14

even tolerable degree of confidence—but more probably in
Asia, and certainly not less than three thousand years before
Christ—and in a condition of civilization respecting which
the evidence of language furnished us valuable hints, some
single community had spoken a single tongue, from which
all these others were descended, in accordance with the
universal laws of linguistic tradition, by processes which are
still active in every part of human speech. And now, waiving for a while the question whether it may not be possible
to regard the great Indo-European family itself as only a
member of a yet vaster family, including all or nearly all the
languages of the human race, we have, in the present lecture,
to review more in detail its constitution, to note the period
and locality of its constituent members, to glance at the special
historical importance attaching to them and to the peoples
who speak them, to set forth their value as the fundamental material of linguistic science, and to examine anew
and more systematically the general method of linguistic
research, as established upon their study.

We may best commence our survey of the varieties of
Indo-European speech with our own branch, the Germanic.
Its existing dialects, as has been already pointed out, are
divided into three groups or sub-branches : 1, the Low-German, occupying northern Germany and the Netherlands,
with their colony Britain, and with the numerous and
widely-scattered modern colonies of Britain ; 2, the High-
German, in central and southern Germany ; 3, the Scandinavian, in Denmark, Sweden, Norway, and Iceland. Of the
Low-German group, the English is by far the most important
member ; its eventful history, illustrated at every step by
valuable literary documents, we trace back, through Middle
English (A.D. 1350-1550), Old English (A.D. 1250-1350), and
Semi-Saxon (A.D. 1150-1250), to the Anglo-Saxon, which
reaches into the seventh century of our era, possessing an antiquity exceeded by only one other Germanic dialect. Its
earliest monuments, in their style and metre, and at least one
of them, the Beowulf, in subject and substance also, carry us
back to the pre-Christian period of Germanic history. We
cannot delay here to enter into any detailed examination

of the character and changes of English speech, interesting
and instructive as such a task would be ; save so far as they
have been and may hereafter be brought in by way of illustration of general linguistic laws, they must be left to more
special treatises.*

Next of kin with the Anglo-Saxon, or oldest form of English, are the ancient Frisian, of the northern sea-coast of
Germany, which had, in the fourteenth century and later,
a literature of its own, of juridical content, composed in
an idiom of form little less antique than Old High-German,
notwithstanding its comparatively modern date — and the
Old Saxon, the principal language of northern Germany between the Rhine and the Elbe, represented to us by but
a single work, the *Heliand* or ' Savior,' a poetical life of
Christ, probably of the ninth century.   Both Saxon and
Frisian have been almost wholly crowded out of cultivated
use in modern times, as was explained in a former lecture
(see p. 164), by the overpowering influence of the High
German, and their domain has also been encroached upon by
other dialects of the same kindred, so that they survive
at present only as insignificant popular *patois*.   Nothing but
the political independence of Holland has saved its peculiar
speech from the same fate : the literary cultivation of the
Netherlandish or Dutch can be traced back to the thirteenth
century, although dating chiefly from the sixteenth, the era
of the country's terrible struggle against the political tyranny
of Spain.   The Flemish, the closely allied idiom of Flanders,
has its own separate records, of about the same antiquity,
but is now nearly extinct.

The history of High-German speech was succinctly
sketched in connection with our inquiries into the rise and
extension of literary dialects.   It falls into three periods.
The first period is that of the Old High-German (*Althoch-
deutsch*), from the eighth to the twelfth century ; its monuments are tolerably abundant, but, with trifling exceptions, of
Christian origin and religious content : they represent three

* See the works of Marsh, Craik, and others ; and especially, for a clear and
succinct view of the history and connections of English speech, with grammatical analyses and illustrative specimens, the work of Professor Hadley,
already once referred to, on p. 84.

principal sub-dialects, the Frankish, the Alemannic and
Swabian, and the Bavarian and Austrian. The second
period, that of the Middle High-German (*Mittelhochdeutsch*),
covers about four centuries, beginning with the twelfth and
ending with the fifteenth ; its ruling dialect is the Swabian ;
and its rich literature hands down to us valuable productions
of the poetical fancy of the times, in the lyric verses of the
Minnesingers, and precious memorials of ancient German
national tradition, in the heroic legends (*Heldensagen*). The
foremost work of the latter class, the Lay of the Nibelungen
(*Nibelungenlied*), is one of the noblest epics which any country has produced, in any age of the world. Of the language
and literature of the New High-German period, from early
in the sixteenth century to our own times—the " German "
language and literature, as we are accustomed to call it—
there is no need that I speak more particularly.

The third subdivision of the Germanic branch is the
Scandinavian. Its earliest monuments come to us from Iceland, that far-off and inhospitable island of volcanoes, boiling
springs, and ice-fields, which, settled in the ninth century by
refugees from Norway, long continued a free colony, a home
of literary culture and legendary song. Christianity, more
tolerant there than elsewhere on Germanic soil, did not sweep
from existence the records of ancient religion and customs.
The two Eddas, gathered or preserved to us from the twelfth
and thirteenth centuries, are, in virtue of their tone and
content, by far the most primitive works in the whole circle
of the Germanic literatures, documents of priceless value for
the antiquity of the Germanic race. Their language also,
though of so much more recent date than the oldest Anglo-
Saxon and High-German, is not exceeded by either in respect
to the primitiveness of its phonetic and grammatical form.
Nor has it greatly changed during the six or seven centuries
which have elapsed since the compilation of the Eddas. The
modern Icelandic is still, among all the existing Germanic
tongues, the one that has preserved and possesses the most
of that original structure which once belonged to them all
alike. Three other dialects, the Norwegian, the Swedish,
and the Danish, constitute along with it the Scandinavian

group, and are languages of literary culture. They are not
direct descendants of the "Old Norse" tongue, as the ancient
Icelandic is usually called : the Norwegian comes nearest to
being so ; the others represent more ancient dialectic divisions of Scandinavian speech.

How many other Germanic branches, originally coördinate
with the three we have described, once had existence, but
have become extinct in later times, by the extinction of the
communities who spoke them, we have not, nor shall we ever
have, any means of knowing. But of one such, at least,
most precious remains have escaped the general destruction
of the nationality to which it belonged. One portion of
the western division of the great and famous Gothic nation
crossed the lower Danube, some time in the early part of the
fourth century, and settled in the Roman province of Mœsia,
as subjects of the empire and as Christians. For them,
their bishop and leader, Ulfilas, later in the same century,
made a translation into their own vernacular of nearly the
whole Bible, writing it in an alphabet of his own devising,
founded on the Greek. Five hundred years afterward, the
Gothic was everywhere an extinct tongue ; but considerable
portions of the Gothic Scriptures—namely, a part of the
Gospels, Paul's epistles nearly complete, and fragments of
the Old Testament—are happily still preserved, in a single
manuscript of the fifth century, now at Upsala, in Sweden.
Scanty as these relics may be, they are of inestimable value
in illustrating the history of the whole Germanic branch of
Indo-European language, and bridging over the distance
which separates it from the other branches. For, as in time,
so still more notably in material and structure, their idiom
is much the most ancient of all the varied forms of Germanic
speech : it is not, indeed, the mother of the rest, nor of any
among them ; but it is their eldest sister, and fully entitled
to claim the place of head of their family.

The Slavonian branch—to which, on account of its local
vicinity, as well as its probable nearer relationship, to the
Germanic, we next turn our attention—need not occupy us
long. It is of much less interest to us, because of its greater
remoteness from our race and from our knowledge, its inferior

214 THE SLAVONIC BRANCH. [LECT.

historical importance and literary value, and its more modern
appearance.* The oldest of its dialects in date, and, in nearly
all respects, the most primitive in form, is the language of
the ancient Bulgarians, into which their apostle Cyril translated the Scriptures, now just about a thousand years ago.
It is a curious coincidence that our knowledge of both Germanic and Slavonic speech thus begins, like that of many a
rude and hitherto unlettered dialect in the hands of missionaries at the present day, with a Bible version, and at nearly
the same geographical locality; the kingdom of the Bulgarians
having followed that of the Goths on the southern bank of
the lower Danube. But this ancient idiom—from which the
modern Bulgarian differs greatly, having changed with
unusual rapidity in the interval—is more commonly called the
Old Slavonic, or the Church Slavic, having been adopted by
a large part of the Slavonian races as their sacred language,
and being still employed as such, within the ecclesiastical
limits of the Greek Church. It belongs to what is known as
the south-eastern section of the Slavonic branch. By far the
most important of the other languages in the same section is
the Russian, in its two divisions, the Russian proper and the
Little-Russian, or Ruthenian. The Russian is in our day a
literary language of considerable importance; its forms are
traceable, in scanty documents, back into the eleventh century.
In its cultivated development, it has been strongly influenced
by the Church Slavonic. The south-eastern section further
includes the Servian, with its closely related dialect, the
Kroatian, and the Slovenian of Carinthia and Styria.
Specimens of these tongues are as old as the tenth, or even
the ninth, century. The Servian has an interesting modern
literature of popular songs.

To the other section, the western, belong the Polish, the
Bohemian with the related Moravian and Slovakian, the
upper and lower Sorbian, and the Polabian, on the Elbe. Of
these, the Bohemian is the oldest, having monuments probably
of the tenth century. Polish literature begins in the four-

---

* In sketching the relations of the Slavonic languages, I follow the
authority of Professor August Schleicher, in the Beitrage zur Vergleichenden
Sprachforschung, vol. i., p. 1 *seq*.

teenth century, since, down to that time, the cultivated of the nation had written wholly in Latin. The others can show nothing older than the sixteenth century, and are of little consequence in any aspect.

The Lithuanic or Lettic group of dialects is sometimes treated as a subdivision of the Slavonic, and sometimes—perhaps with better reason—as a separate branch, coördinate with the other, although very closely related to it. It is of very slight historical or literary importance : ·its interest lies chiefly in the fact that, under the operation of causes in its history which are yet unexplained and probably unexplainable, it has preserved many of the original forms of Indo-European speech in a more uncorrupted condition than any other known dialect of the whole family which is not as much as two thousand years older. It is composed of only three dialects, one of which, the Old Prussian, the original language of the inhabitants of north-eastern Prussia, has been extinct for two hundred years, crowded out of existence by the Low-German, and leaving behind, as its only monument, a brief catechism. The other two, the Lithuanian and the Lettish, or Livonian, are still spoken by a million or two of people in the Russian and Prussian provinces bordering on the Baltic, but seem destined to give way helplessly before the encroachments of the German and Russian, and to share one day the fate of their sister-dialect. The oldest Lithuanian document dates from the middle of the sixteenth century. The southern or High Lithuanian is of most antique form ; the Low Lithuanian, and yet more notably the Lettish to the north, show a less remarkable conservation of ancient material.

The Celtic languages, as was pointed out in the last lecture, have been well-nigh extinguished by the Romanic and Germanic tongues, and now only lurk in the remotest and most inaccessible corners of the wide territory which they once occupied in Europe. The Scotch Highlands, the wildest parts of Ireland, the Isle of Man, the mountains of Wales, the rough glens of Cornwall, and the land lying nearest to Cornwall across the British Channel, the promontory of Brittany, are the only regions where, for many centuries past, Celtic speech has been heard. The Cornish, too, has become extinct within the memory of the present generation ; the Irish is rapidly on its way to the same fate ; the Gaelic will not survive the complete taming and civilization of the Highlands ; the French is likely to crowd out the *patois* of the Breton peasant ; and it is greatly to be doubted whether even the Welsh people, passionate as is the attachment with which at present they cling to their peculiar speech, will continue always to refuse the advantages that would accrue to them from its relinquishment, and a more thorough fusion with the greater community of speakers of English to which they form an adjunct. There has never been a homogeneous, independent, and cultivated Celtic state, capable of protecting its idiom from the encroachment of other tongues ; and only such protection, now unattainable, can, as it seems, save Celtic speech from utter extinction.

There is no small difficulty in treating satisfactorily the documents which illustrate the history of the Celtic languages, owing to the prevalence of a peculiar and strongly-marked linguistic disease, well known among philologists as " Celtomania," which has been very apt to attack students of the subject—especially such as were of Celtic extraction, but in some degree foreigners also—leading them wildly to exaggerate the antiquity and importance of the Celtic civilization, language, and literature. We have had Celtic set up as the most primitive and uncorrupted of tongues, spoken by generations long anterior to the oldest worthies whom history, sacred or profane, recognizes, and furnishing the only sure foundation to universal etymology ; we have had ancient inscriptions and difficult texts, of the most diverse origin and distant locality, explained out of Celtic into high-sounding phrases, of true Ossianic ring ; we have had the obscure words of various languages traced to Celtic roots, provided with genealogies from an Irish or Welsh ancestor—and much more of the same sort. Sober and unprejudiced inquiry cuts down these claims to greatly reduced, though still respectable, dimensions.

So completely were the Gaulish dialects of northern Italy, France, and Spain wiped out by the Latin, so few traces of

them are left to us, either in the later idioms of the Latin or
in fragments of writings, inscriptions, and coins, that it is
still a matter of doubt and question among Celtic scholars to
which of the known divisions of Celtic speech, the Gadhelic
or the Cymric, they belonged, or whether they did not constitute a third division, coördinate with these. Aside from
the exceedingly scanty and obscure Gallic epigraphical
monuments, and the few single words preserved in classic
authors, the earliest records, both of Irish and Welsh speech,
are glosses, or interlinear and marginal versions and comments, written by Celtic scholars upon manuscripts which
they were studying, in old times when Wales and Ireland,
especially the latter, were centres of a lively literary and
Christian activity. Of these glosses, the Irish are by far the
most abundant, and afford a tolerably distinct idea of what
the language was at about the end of the eighth century.
There is also an independent literary work, a life of Saint
Patrick, which is supposed to belong to the beginning of the
ninth century. The other principal Gadhelic dialect, the
Scotch Gaelic, presents us a few songs that claim to be of the
sixteenth century. The Ossianic poems, which excited such
attention a hundred years ago, and whose genuineness and
value have been the subject of so lively discussion, are probably built upon only a narrow foundation of real Gaelic
tradition.

   In the Cymric division, the Welsh glosses, just referred
to, are the oldest monuments of definite date. Though
hardly, if at all, less ancient than the Irish, coming down
from somewhere between the eighth and the tenth centuries,
they are very much more scanty in amount, hardly sufficient
to do more than disprove the supposed antiquity of the
earliest monuments of the language that possess a proper
literary character. For long centuries past, the Welsh bards
have sung in spirit-stirring strains the glories and the woes
of their race ; and it is claimed that during much more than
a thousand years, or ever since the sixth century, the era of
Saxon invasion and conquest, some of their songs have been
handed down from generation to generation, by a careful
and uninterrupted tradition. And the claim is probably well

founded : only it is also pretty certain that, as they have
been handed down, they have been modernized in diction,
so that, in their present form, they represent to us the
Welsh language of a time not much preceding the date of
the oldest manuscripts, or of the twelfth to the fourteenth
centuries. The later Welsh literature, as well as the Irish,
is abundant in quantity. The Cornish, also, has a tolerably
copious literature of not far from the same age ; its earliest
monument, a Latin-Cornish vocabulary, may be as old as the
twelfth century. The language of Brittany, the Armorican
—which is so closely allied with the two last-mentioned that
it cannot well be regarded as a remnant and representative
of the Celtic dialects of Gaul, but must rather belong to
colonists or fugitives from Britain—is recorded in one or
two brief works going back to the fourteenth century, or
even farther.

We come next to the Romanic branch, as we have called
it when briefly noticing its history at an earlier point in our
discussions. Of the languages which compose it, and whose
separate currents of linguistic tradition we trace backward
until they converge and meet in the Latin, two, the Rhæto-
Romanic in southern Switzerland and at the head of the
Adriatic, and the Wallachian of the northern provinces of
Turkey, have no literature of any antiquity or independent
value. The other five—the Italian, French, Provençal,
Spanish, and Portuguese—all emerged out of the condition
of vulgar *patois*, and began to take on the character of
national cultivated languages, at not far from the same time,
or in the eleventh, twelfth, and thirteenth centuries. There
are fragments of French texts dating from the tenth century,
but the early French literature, abundant and various, and,
in its romances, attaining a wonderfully sudden and general
popularity throughout cultivated Europe, belongs to the
twelfth and thirteenth centuries. The Provençal poetry,
consisting of the songs of the *troubadours*, whose chief
activity was displayed at the court of Toulouse, in southernmost France, was wholly lyrical in form, and amatory or
satirical in content : it finished its brilliant but brief career,
of about three hundred years, in the fourteenth century. The

culture of Italian begins at the court of Frederic II., about
A.D. 1200, and within a century and a half of that time lived,
sang, and narrated the three greatest writers of Italy—Dante
(ob. 1321), Petrarch (ob. 1374), and Boccaccio (ob. 1375).
The Spanish heroic legend commences in the twelfth century;
and there are monuments of Portuguese speech of about
the same time.   Among these languages, the French is that
which has undergone most change during the historical
period; the oldest French and Provençal form a kind of
middle term between the modern language and the ancient
Latin, illustrating the transition from the latter to the
former.

But if we have called the branch of Indo-European speech
to which these tongues belong the Romanic, we have done so
out of regard to its later history and present constitution,
and not altogether properly.   To the student of Indo-
European philology, these are the recent branchings of a
single known stock, the Latin; to trace their development
is a task of the highest interest, a whole linguistic school in
itself; they furnish rich and abundant illustration of all the
processes of linguistic growth: but, as regards any direct
bearing upon the history of Indo-European speech, they have
value only through the Latin, their common parent.   The
remoter relations of the Latin itself receive light from various
sources.   In its familiar classic form, it represents to us the
speech of the learned and educated Romans of a century or
two before the Christian era; it is somewhat refined by
literary culture from the diction of the oldest authors whose
works have come down to us, in fragments or entire—as
Livius Andronicus, Plautus, Terence—and is far more notably
changed from the language of earlier Roman times—as is
shown by the yet extant monuments, like the inscription on
the Duilian column (about B.C. 260), that on the sarcophagus
of a founder of the Scipio family (a little older than the last
mentioned), and especially the Salian hymn and song of the
fratres arvales, of yet earlier but uncertain date, in which
the best Latin scholar would find himself wholly at fault
without the traditional interpretation which is handed down
along with them: in these monuments is preserved to us

many an antique form, giving valuable hints respecting the grammatical and phonetic development of the language. Their evidence is supplemented in a very important manner by that of other kindred Italian dialects. The Oscan or Opican of southern Italy was the language of the Samnites and their allies, from whose hands Rome wrung after a severe and often doubtful struggle the dominion of the peninsula: it was not disused as the official speech of some of the southern provinces until less than a hundred years before Christ; and coins and inscriptions dating from the two or three preceding centuries still teach us something of its structure and character. The Umbrian, the tongue of north-eastern Italy, is yet more fully represented to us by the Euguvine tablets, inscribed with the prayers and ceremonial rules of a fraternity of priests, and supposed to be as old as the third and fourth centuries before our era. Of the Volscian dialect, also, and the Sabine or Sabellian—the former being more akin with the Umbrian, the latter with the Latin—some exceedingly scanty relics have been discovered. The interpretation and comprehension of all these —resting, as it does, solely upon comparison with the Latin and other more distantly related tongues—is at present, and is likely always to remain, incomplete and doubtful; but they are of essential importance, both in explaining some of the peculiarities of the Latin, and in fixing its position as one of a group of kindred dialects occupying the greater portion of the Italian peninsula, and hence most suitably to be denominated the Italic group. The theory that the Latin was produced by a mixture of somewhat discordant elements —of Roman, Sabine, and Oscan; or of these and Etruscan —brought together by historical circumstances, and finally fused into homogeneousness, is one which belonged to a former stage of linguistic science, and is now rejected as uncalled-for and groundless. Yet more untenable, and wanting even a semblance of foundation, is the derivation of Latin from Greek, a favourite dogma of times not long past, but at present abandoned by every comparative philologist whose opinion is of the slightest value.

In the Greek language, we reach an antiquity in the

recorded history of Indo-European speech considerably higher than we have anywhere else attained. The exact date of its earliest monuments, the grand and unrivalled poems of Homer, the Iliad and Odyssey, cannot, it is true, be determined ; but they go back, doubtless, to near the beginning of the thousand years before Christ's birth. From the different parts of Greece, too, as of Italy, we have received records of dialects that subsisted side by side through all the earlier periods of the country's history, until at length (about B.C. 300) the political importance and superior literature of Athens made her idiom, the later Attic, the common language of cultivated Greeks everywhere. The earlier Attic is found first in the writings of the great dramatists, beginning about five centuries before Christ : it is more nearly akin with the earlier Ionic of Homer and Hesiod (before 700 B.C.), and the later Ionic of Herodotus (about 400 B.C.), than with the Doric of Alcman, Pindar, and Theocritus (600-250 B.C.), or the Æolic of Alcæus and Sappho (about 600 B.C.). The differences of the Greek dialects are quite insignificant as compared with those of the Italic, yet they are of no small service to the historical student of the Greek language, since each brings to his knowledge some elements less corrupted and modernized than are to be found in the others, or in the later common tongue.

The modern Greek has also its dialects, respecting which little is known in detail ; and it has, besides, its common tongue, the Romaic (as it is ordinarily styled), spoken and written by all the educated Greeks of the present day. This Romaic is very much less altered from the ancient classic language, as spoken by Plato and Demosthenes, than are the modern Romanic languages from the speech of Virgil and Cicero. The difference of the two is even so slight that a party in Greece are now engaged in making the somewhat pedantic and utopian effort to eliminate it altogether, to make the turbulent population of the present petty and insignificant kingdom talk and write as did their heroic forefathers, when, though feeble in numbers, they were the foremost community of the world. Small result is to be looked for from this experiment ; should it prove successful, it will be the first time that such a thing has been accomplished in all the history of language.

Of the Asiatic branches of our family, the one which lies nearest us, the Iranian, or Persian, may first engage our attention. Its oldest monuments of well-determined date are the inscriptions—cut on the surface of immense walls of living rock, in the so-called cuneiform characters—by which the Achæmenidan sovereigns of Persia, Darius, Xerxes, and their successors, made imperishable record for posterity of their names and deeds. Fifty years ago, these inscriptions were an unsolved and apparently insoluble enigma; now, by a miracle of human ingenuity and patience, not without the aid of a combination of favouring circumstances wholly impossible at any earlier period, almost every word and every character is fully laid open to our comprehension, and they have been made to yield results of great value both to linguistic and to national history. The oldest of them come from a time about five centuries before Christ, and their extent is sufficient to give us a very distinct idea of the language of those Persians against whom the Greeks so long fought, first for independence, then for empire.

Of about the same age, and even, probably, in part considerably older, are the sacred Scriptures of the religion established by Zoroaster (in his own tongue, *Zarathustra*)— the book called the Avesta, or Zend-Avesta. The dialect in which these writings are composed goes usually by the name of the Zend; it is also styled the Avestan, and sometimes the Old Bactrian, from the country Bactria, the north-easternmost region of the great Iranian territory, which is supposed to have been its specific locality. They have been preserved to us by the Parsis of western India, who fled thither from their native country after its reduction under Mohammedan vassalage in the seventh century of our era, and who have ever since faithfully maintained, under Hindu and British protection, the rites of the Magian faith, the pure worship of Ormuzd (*Ahura-Mazda*, 'the mighty spirit') through the symbol of fire. The Avesta shows two dialects, a younger and an older; some of its hymns and prayers possibly go back to the time of Zoroaster himself—whatever that may

have been : it was doubtless more than a thousand years, at
least, before Christ—but the bulk of the work is considerably
later. Accompanying the Avesta is a version of it, made for
the use of the priests, in another and much more modern
Iranian dialect, the Pehlevi or Huzvaresh, supposed to have
been the literary language of the westernmost provinces of
Iran at a period some centuries later than the Christian era,
and much mixed with materials derived from the Semitic
tongues lying next westward, across the border. A few inscriptions and legends of coins, of the early Sassanian
monarchs (after A.D. 226), furnish further specimens of the
same or a nearly kindred dialect.

The general body of religious literature belonging to the
Parsis of India contains tolerably copious documents of a
somewhat younger and much purer Iranian dialect, usually
styled the Parsi (sometimes also the Pazend). It comes,
without much question, from a more eastern locality than
the Pehlevi, and from a time nearly approaching that of the
Mohammedan conquest.   Finally, after the conquest, and
when Persia was thoroughly made over into a province of
the Moslem empire, arises, in the tenth century, the modern
Persian, and becomes during several centuries, and even to
our own day, the vehicle of an abundant and admirable
literature, rich in every department, in poetry, fiction, history,
philosophy, science.   Its first great work, and almost or
quite the greatest it has to offer us, is the Shah-Nameh,
' Book of Kings,' of Firdusi (ob. 1020), a true national epic,
grand in extent, noble in style, varied in contents, in which
is summed up and related at length the history of the land,
traditional, legendary, and mythological, as it lay in the
minds of the generation by whom was revived the ancient
independence and glory of the Persian nationality. For the
impoverishment of its grammar by the loss of ancient forms,
the modern Persian is almost comparable with the English.
It is more nearly related to the language of the Achæmenidan inscriptions than to that of the Avesta, although not
the lineal descendant and representative of either.   In its
later literary use, it is greatly disfigured by the unlimited
introduction of words from the Arabic vocabulary.

There are several other languages, in regions bordering on or included within the Iranian territory, which stand in such relations with those we have been describing as to be ranked in the same class, although their Iranian attributes are greatly obscured by the changes which have passed upon them since their separation from the principal stock. By far the most important of these is the Armenian, with an abundant literature going back to the fifth century, the era of the Christianization of the Armenian people. Others are the Ossetic, in the Caucasus; the Kurdish, the dialect of the wild mountaineers of the border lands between Persia, Turkey, and Russia; and the Afghan or Pushto, which in very recent times has enjoyed a certain degree of literary cultivation.

We come, finally, to that member of our family which has lived its life within the borders of India. Not all the numerous dialects which fill this immense peninsula, between the impassable wall of the Himalayas and the Indian ocean, own kindred with the Indo-European tongues, but only those of its northern portion, of Hindustan proper, ranging from the Indus to the mouths of the Ganges, together with a certain extent of the sea-coast and its neighbourhood stretching southward on either side. The central mountainous region and the table-lands of the Dekhan yet belong to the aboriginal tribes, who in the north were crowded out or subjugated, at a period lying only just beyond the ken of recorded history, by the Indo-European races, as they intruded themselves through the avenue, the passes on the north-western frontier, by which the conquerors of India have in all ages found entrance. The principal modern dialects of our kindred are the Hindi, Bengali, and Mahratta, each with various subdivisions, and each with a literature of its own, running back only a few centuries. The Hindustani, or Urdu, is a form of the Hindi which grew up in the camps (*úrdú*) of the Mohammedan conquerors of India, since the eleventh century, as medium of communication between them and the subject population of central Hindustan, more corrupted in form, and filled with Persian and Arabic words —being thus, as it were, the English of India: it has enjoyed more literary cultivation than any other of the recent dialects,

and is the *lingua franca*, the official language and means of
general intercourse, throughout nearly the whole peninsula.
The tongue of the roving Gypsies all over Europe, though
everywhere strongly tinged with the local idiom of the region
of their wanderings, is in its main structure and material a
modern Hindu *patois :* the Gypsies are exiles from India.

Next older than the languages we have mentioned are the
Prakrit and the Pali, represented by a literature and inscriptions which come to us in part from before the Christian era.
The Pali is the sacred language of the Buddhist religion in
the countries lying eastward and south-eastward from India.
The Prakrit dialects are chiefly preserved in the Sanskrit
dramas, where the unlearned characters, the women, servants,
and the like, talk Prakrit—just as, in a modern German
theatre, one may hear the lower personages talk the dialects
of their own districts, while the higher employ the literary
German, the common speech of the educated throughout the
country.

The virtual mother of all these dialects is the Sanskrit.
For the last twenty-five centuries, at least, the Sanskrit has
been no longer a proper vernacular language, but kept artificially in life, as the sacred dialect of Brahmanism and the
cultivated tongue of literature and learning ; thus occupying
a position closely analogous with that held by the Latin
since the decline of the western empire, as the language of
Roman Catholicism, and the means of communication among
the learned of all Europe. It is still taught in the schools
of the Brahmanic priesthood, used in the ceremonies of their
religion, and spoken and written by their foremost scholars
—although, like the Latin in more recent times, much
shaken in its sway by the uprise of the modern cultivated
dialects, and the decadence of the religion with whose uses it
is identified. We possess it in two somewhat varying forms,
the classical Sanskrit, and the older idiom of the so-called
Vedas, the Bible of the Hindu faith. The former is more
altered, by elaborate and long-continued literary and grammatical training, from the condition of a true vernacular, than
is almost any other known literary language. Partly for
this reason, and partly because, at the time of its establish-

15

ment and fixation as the learned tongue of all Aryan India,
it must have been one among a number of somewhat differing local varieties of Aryan speech, whose differences form a
part of the discordance of the later dialects, I have called it
above rather their virtual than their actual progenitor : it
represents very closely the primitive stock out of which they
have all grown, by varying internal development, and by
varying influence and admixture of foreign tongues. When
and where it was at first a spoken dialect, is out of our
power to determine ; but it cannot well be regarded as of
less age than the earliest Greek records ; and it is probably
older by centuries. It possesses a most abundant literature,
in nearly every department save history ; its religious and
ethical poetry, its epics, its lyric flights, its dramas, its systems of philosophy and grammar, have been found worthy of
high admiration and of profound study by Western scholars ;
they have even been ranked by some, though very unjustly,
as superior to the masterpieces of the Greek and Latin
literatures. To fix the chronology of its separate works is a
task of the extremest difficulty ; but some of them, even in
their present form, and the substance of many others, certainly come from a time considerably anterior to the Christian era.

The Vedic dialect is yet more ancient ; the earliest portions of the oldest collection, the Rig-Veda ('Veda of hymns'),
must, it is believed, date from nearly or quite two thousand
years before Christ. The considerations from which this age
is deduced for them are of a general and inexact character,
yet tolerably clear in their indications. Thus, for example,
the hymns of the Vedas were chiefly composed on the banks
of the Indus and its tributaries, when the great valley of the
Ganges was as yet unknown to the Aryan immigrants ; and
they present the elephant as still a wondered-at and little-
known animal : while the earliest tidings of India which we
have from without show us great kingdoms on the Ganges,
and the elephant reduced to the service of man, both in war
and in peace. Buddhism, too, which is well known to have
preceded by several centuries the birth of Christ, was a revolt against the oppressive domination of the Brahmanic

hierarchy; and in the Vedas are to be seen only the germs of Brahmanism, not yet developed : no hierarchy, no system of castes, no vestige of the doctrine of transmigration. The conclusions drawn from a study of the internal history and connection of the different classes of works composing the sacred literature of India—which follow one another, in a close succession of expositions, rules, and comments, from a time not much later than that of the more recent hymns down to the historical period—point also to the same age. The Vedas are thus by not less than a thousand years the earliest documents for the history of Indo-European language—for the history, moreover, of Indo-European conditions and institutions. The civil constitution, the religious rites, the mythologic fancies, the manners and customs, which they depict, have a peculiarly original and primitive aspect, seeming to exhibit a far nearer likeness to what once belonged to the whole Indo-European family than is any-where else to be attained. The Vedas appear rather like an Indo-European than an Indian record; they are the pro-perty rather of the whole family than of a single branch.

Much of the same character appertains to the classical Sanskrit : it is both earlier in chronologic period and more primitive in internal character than any other language of the whole great family. Its peculiar value lies in its special conservation of primitive material and forms, in the transpar-ency of its structure, in its degree of freedom from the cor-rupting and disguising effects of phonetic change, from obliteration of original meaning and application. We must beware of supposing that at all points, in every item of structure, it is the superior of the other Indo-European tongues, or that it constitutes an infallible norm by which their material is to be judged ; on the contrary, each of the other branches here and there excels it, offering some re-mains of early Indo-European speech which it has lost ; but to it must be freely conceded the merit of having retained, out of the common stock, more than any one among them, almost more than they all. Exaggerated and unfounded claims are often put forward in its behalf by those who do not fully understand the true sources of its value : its alphabet, though rich and very harmoniously developed, does not cover more than about two-thirds of our English system of spoken sounds ; as an instrument of the expression of thought it has very serious and conspicuous defects, being inferior—especially in its handling of the verb (the soul of the sentence), in a loose and bald syntactical arrangement, and in an excessive use of compounds—not only to the Greek, but to almost every other cultivated Indo-European tongue ; nor (as has been already hinted) can its literature sustain a moment's comparison with those of the classical languages. It is to be prized chiefly as a historical document, casting inestimable light upon the earliest development of the common speech of the Indo-European family, and the relations of its members. Had all its literature besides perished, leaving us only a grammar of its forms and a dictionary of its material, it would still in a great measure retain this character; were but a fragment of one of its texts saved, as has been the case with the Mœso-Gothic, it would still vindicate its right to a place at the head of all the languages of the family. It may easily be appreciated, then, what an impulse to the historical study of language, then just struggling into existence by the comparison of the tongues of Europe, was given by the discovery and investigation of this new dialect, having a structure that so invited and facilitated historic analysis, and even presented by the native grammatical science in an analyzed condition, with roots, themes, and affixes carefully separated, distinctly catalogued, and defined in meaning and office. In all researches into the beginnings of Indo-European speech, the genesis of roots and forms, its assistance is indispensable, and its authority of greatest weight. It often has been and still is wrongly estimated and misapplied by incautious or ill-instructed investigators ; it is sometimes treated as if it were the mother of the Indo-European dialects, as the Latin of the modern Romanic tongues, instead of merely their eldest sister, like the Mœso-Gothic among the Germanic languages ; it is unduly brought in to aid the inter-comparison of dialects of a single branch, and its peculiar developments, its special laws of euphony or construction, are sought to be forced upon

them; the facts it presents are erroneously accepted as ultimate, cutting off further inquiry; portions of its existing
material which are of modern growth, or the artificial productions of Hindu scholasticism, are perversely used as
of avail for Indo-European etymology : and such abuse has
naturally provoked from some scholars a distrust of its
genuine claims to regard : but, stripping off all exaggerations,
and making all due allowances, the Sanskrit is still the main-
stay of Indo-European philology; it gave the science a rapid
development which nothing else could have given; it imparted to its conclusions a fulness and certainty which would
have been otherwise unattainable.

Such is the constitution of the grand division of human
speech to which our own language belongs.   That its limits
have been everywhere traced with entire exactness cannot,
of course, be claimed ; other existing dialects may yet make
good their claim to be included in it—and it is beyond all
reasonable question that, as many of its sub-branches have
perished without leaving a record, so various of its branches,
fully coördinate with those we have reviewed, must have
met a like fate.   We may now proceed to glance briefly at
some of the grounds of the preëminent importance with which
it is invested.

One source of the special interest which we feel in the
study of Indo-European language lies in the fact that our
own tongue is one of its branches.   In the moral and intellectual world, not less than in the physical, everything cannot
but appear larger in our eyes according as it is nearer to us.
This would be a valid consideration with any race upon
earth, since, for each, its own means of communication and
instrument of thought is also the record of its past history,
and must be its agency of future improvement in culture,
and therefore calls for more study in order to its fuller comprehension, and its development and elevation, than should be
given to any other tongue, of however superior intrinsic value.
But we are further justified in our somewhat exclusive interest
by the position which our languages, and the races which speak
them, hold among other languages and races.   It is true,
as was claimed at the outset of these lectures, that linguistic

science, as a branch of human history, aims at universality,
and finds the tongues of the humblest tribes as essential to
her completeness as those of the most cultivated and gifted
nations ; but it is also true that, mindful of proportion, she
passes more lightly over the one, to give her longer and
more engrossed attention to the other. While the weal
and woe of every individual that ever lived goes to make up
the sum of human interests, with which our human nature
both justifies and demands our sympathy, we cannot but lin-
ger longest and with keenest participation over the fortunes
of those who have played a great part among their fellows,
whose deeds and words have had a wide and deep-reaching
influence. And this is, in a very marked degree, the
character of the Indo-European race. Its first entrance as
an actor into what we are accustomed to call universal history, or that drama of action and influence whose *denouement*
is the culture of the modern European nations, was in the
far East, in the Persian empire of Cyrus and his successors.
This founded itself upon the ruins and relics of more ancient
empires and cultures, belonging to other peoples, in part
Semitic, in part of obscurer kindred. For the Indo-Europeans were, of all the great civilizing and governing races,
the last to commence their career. Not only in Mesopotamia, but also in Egypt and China, the light of knowledge
burned brightly, and great deeds were done, whereof the
world will never lose the memory, while the tribes of our
kindred were wandering savages, or weak and insignificant
communities, struggling for existence. The Persian empire,
in its conquering march westward, was first checked by one
of these humble communities, the little jarring confederation
of Greek states and cities, destined to become, notwithstanding its scanty numbers, the real founder of Indo-European
preëminence. Greece, enriching itself with elements drawn
from the decaying institutions of older races, assimilated
them, and made them lively and life-giving, with an energy
of genius unrivalled elsewhere in the annals of the world.
The wider the range of our historical study, the more are we
penetrated with the transcendent ability of the Greek race.
In art, literature, and science, it has been what the Hebrew

race has been in religion, and its influence has been hardly less unlimited, in space and in time. It seemed at one period, as is well known, that Greece would succeed to the imperial throne of Persia, subjecting the civilized world to her sway; but the prospect lasted but for a moment : the sceptre of universal dominion slipped from the hands of Alexander's successors, and soon passed over into the keeping of another and younger branch of the same family. Rome, appropriating the fruits of Greek culture, and adding an organizing and assimilating force peculiarly her own, went forth to give laws to all nations, and to impose upon them a unity of civilization and of social and political institutions. And if Christianity was of Semitic birth, Greeks and Romans gave it universality. Rejected by the race which should have especially cherished it, it was taken up and propagated by the Indo-Europeans, and added a new unity, a religious one, to the forces by which Rome bound together the interests and fates of mankind.

Now came the turn of yet another branch, the Germanic. This had, indeed, only the subordinate part to play of aiding in the downfall of the old order of things, and preparing the way for a new and more vigorous growth. Its tribes ravaged Europe from east to west, and even to the farthest southern coasts, giving ruling class and monarch to nearly every country of the continent. But centuries of weakness and confusion were the first result of this great up-turning, and it even appeared for a time as if the dominion of the world were destined to be usurped by another race. The Semites, inspired with the furious zeal of a new religion, Mohammedanism, broke from their deserts and overran the fairest parts of Asia and Africa ; and their conquering hosts entered Europe at either extremity, establishing themselves firmly, and pushing forward to take possession of the rest. They recoiled, at last, before the reviving might of the superior race, and the last and grandest era of Indo-European supremacy began, the era in the midst of which we now live. For the past few centuries, the European nations have stood foremost, without a rival, in the world's history.

They are the enlightened and the enlighteners of mankind. They alone are extending the sphere of human knowledge, investigating the nature of matter and of mind, and tracing out their exhibition in the past history and present condition of the earth and its inhabitants. They alone have a surplus stock of intelligent energy, which is constantly pushing beyond its old boundaries, and spurns all limit to its action. The network of their activity embraces the globe ; their ships are in every sea between the poles, for exploration, for trade, or for conquest ; the weaker races are learning their civilization, falling under their authority, or perishing off the face of the land, from inherent inability to stand before them. They have appropriated, and converted into outlying provinces of their race and culture, the twin world of the West, and the insular continent of the south-eastern seas, while their lesser colonies dot the whole surface of the inhabitable globe. They have inherited from its ancient possessors the sceptre of universal dominion, over a world vastly enlarged beyond that to which were limited the knowledge and the power of former times : and they are worthy to wield it, since their sway brings, upon the whole, physical well-being, knowledge, morality, and religion to those over whom it is extended.

All that speciality of interest, then, which cleaves to historical investigations respecting the origin, the earliest conditions, the migrations, the mutual intercourse and influence, and the intercourse with outside races, of that division of mankind which has shown itself as the most gifted, as possessing the highest character and fulfilling the noblest destiny, among all who have peopled the earth since the first dawn of time, belongs, of right and of necessity, to Indo-European philology.

It may, indeed, be urged that this is an interest lying somewhat apart from the strict domain of linguistic science, whose prime concern is with speech itself, not with the characters or acts of those who speak. Yet, as was pointed out in our first lecture, the study of language is not introspective merely ; they would unduly narrow its sphere and restrict its scope who should limit it to the examination of linguistic facts : these are so inextricably intertwined with historical facts, so dependent upon and developed out of them, that the two cannot be separated in consideration and treatment ; one chief department of the value of the science lies in its capacity to throw light upon the history of human races. The importance of the Indo-European races in history is, then, legitimately to be included among the titles of Indo-European philology to the first attention of the linguistic scholar. Moreover, since the relation between the capacity of a race and the character of the tongue originated and elaborated by that race is a direct and necessary one, it could not but be the case that the speech of the most eminently and harmoniously endowed part of mankind should itself be of highest character and most harmonious development, and so the most worthy object of study, in its structure and its relations to mind and thought. And this advantage also, as we shall see more plainly hereafter, is in fact found to belong to Indo-European language : in the classification of all human speech it takes, unchallenged, the foremost rank.

But these considerations, weighty as they are, do not fully explain the specially intimate bond subsisting between general linguistic science and the study of Indo-European speech. Not only did the establishment of the unity of that family, and the determination of the relations of its members, constitute the most brilliant achievement of the new science ; they were also its foundation ; it began with the recognition of these truths, and has developed with their elaboration. The reason is not difficult to discover : Indo-European language alone furnished such a grand body of related facts as the science needed for a sure basis. Its dialects have a range, in the variety of their forms and in the length of the period of development covered by them, which is sought elsewhere in vain. They illustrate the processes of linguistic growth upon an unrivalled scale, and from a primitive era to which we can make but an imperfect approach among the other languages of mankind. Portions of the Chinese literature, it is true, are nearly or quite as old as anything Indo-European, and the Chinese language,

as will be shown later, is in some respects more primitive
in its structure than any other human tongue; but what it
was at the beginning, that it has ever since remained, a
solitary example of a language almost destitute of a history.
Egypt has records to show of an age surpassing that of any
other known monuments of human speech; but they are of
scanty and enigmatical content, and the Egyptian tongue
also stands comparatively alone, without descendants, and
almost without relatives.   The Semitic languages come
nearest to offering a worthy parallel; but they, too, fall far
short of it.   The earliest Hebrew documents are not greatly
exceeded in antiquity by any others, and the Hebrew with
its related dialects, ancient and modern, fills up a linguistic
scheme of no small wealth; yet Semitic variety is, after all,
but poor and scanty as compared with Indo-European;
Semitic language possesses a toughness and rigidity of structure which has made its history vastly less full of instructive
change; and its beginnings are of unsurpassed obscurity.
The Semitic languages are rather a group of closely kindred
dialects than a family of widely varied branches: their
whole yield to linguistic science is hardly more than might
be won from a single subdivision of Indo-European speech,
like the Germanic or Romanic.   None of the other great
races into which mankind is divided cover with their dialects,
to any noteworthy extent, time as well as space; for the
most part, we know nothing more respecting their speech
than is to be read in its present living forms.   Now it is so
obvious as hardly to require to be pointed out, that a science
whose method is prevailingly historical, which seeks to arrive at an understanding of the nature, office, and source
of language by studying its gradual growth, by tracing out
the changes it has undergone in passing from generation to
generation, from race to race, must depend for the sound-
ness of its methods and the sureness of its results upon the
fulness of illustration of these historical changes furnished
by the material of its investigations.   It is true that the
student's historical researches are not wholly baffled by the
absence of older dialects, with whose forms he may compare
those of more modern date.   Something of the development

of every language is indicated in its own structure with
sufficient clearness to be read by analytic study.   Yet more
is to be traced out by means of the comparison of kindred
contemporaneous dialects ; for, in their descent from their
common ancestor, it can hardly be that each one will not
have preserved some portion of the primitive material
which the others have lost.   Thus—to illustrate briefly by
reference to one or two of our former examples—the identity of our suffix *ly*, in such words as *godly* and *truly*, with
the adjective *like* might perhaps have been conjectured from
the English alone ; and it is made virtually certain by comparison with the modern German (*göttlich, treulich*) or
Netherlandish (*goddelijk, waarlijk*) ; it does not absolutely
need a reference to older dialects, like the Anglo-Saxon or
Gothic, for its establishment.   Again, not only the Sanskrit
and other ancient languages exhibit the full form *asmi*,
whence comes our *I am*, but the same is also to be found
almost unaltered in the present Lithuanian *esmi*.   But,
even if philological skill and acumen had led the student of
Germanic language to the conjecture that *I loved* is originally *I love-did*, it must ever have remained a conjecture
only, a mere plausible hypothesis, but for the accident which
caused the preservation to our day of the fragment of manuscript containing a part of Bishop Ulfilas's Gothic Bible.
And a host of points in the structure of the tongues of our
Germanic branch which still remain obscure would, as we
know, be cleared up, had we in our possession relics of them
at a yet earlier stage of their separate growth.   The extent
to which the history of a body of languages may be penetrated by the comparison of contemporary dialects alone will,
of course, vary greatly in different cases ; depending, in the
first place, upon the number, variety, and degree of relation
of the dialects, and, in the second place, upon their joint
and several measure of conservation of ancient forms : but
it is also evident that the results thus arrived at for modern
tongues will be, upon the whole, both scanty and dubious,
compared with those obtained by comparing them with
ancient dialects of the same stock.   Occasionally, within the
narrow limits of a single branch or group, the student

enjoys the advantage of access to the parent tongue itself, from which the more recent idioms are almost bodily derived : thus, for example, our possession of the Latin gives to our readings of the history of the Romanic tongues, our determination of the laws which have governed their growth, a vastly higher degree of definiteness and certainty than we could reach if we only knew that such a parent tongue must have existed, and had to restore its forms by careful comparison and deduction. Next in value to this is the advantage of commanding a rich body of older and younger dialects of the same lineage, wherein the common speech is beheld at nearer and remoter distances from its source, so that we can discover the direction of its currents, and fill out with less of uncertainty those parts of their network of which the record is obliterated. This secondary advantage we enjoy in the Germanic, the Persian, the Indian branches of Indo-European speech ; and, among the grander divisions of human language, we enjoy it to an extent elsewhere unapproached in the Indo-European family, that immense and varied body of allied forms of speech, whose lines of historic development are seen to cover a period of between three and four thousand years, as they converge toward a meeting in a yet remoter past.

Herein lies the sufficient explanation of that intimate connection, that almost coincidence, which we have noticed between the development of Indo-European comparative philology and that of the general science of language. In order to comprehend human language in every part, the student would wish to have its whole growth, in all its divisions and subdivisions, through all its phases, laid before him for inspection in full authentic documents. Since, however, anything like this is impossible, he has done the best that lay within his power : he has thrown himself into that department of speech which had the largest share of its history thus illustrated, and by studying that has tried to learn how to deal with the yet more scanty and fragmentary materials presented him in other departments. Here could be formed the desired nucleus of a science ; here the general laws of linguistic life could be discovered ; here could be worked

out those methods and processes which, with such modifications as the varying circumstances rendered necessary,
should be applied in the investigation of other types of
language also. The foundation was broad enough to build
up a shapely and many-sided edifice upon. Yet the study
of Indo-European language is not the science of language.
Such is the diversity in unity of human speech that exclusive attention to any one of its types could only give us
partial and false views of its nature and history. Endlessly
as the dialects of our family appear to differ from one
another, they have a distinct common character, which is
brought to our apprehension only when we compare them
with those of other stock ; they are far from exhausting the
variety of expression which the human mind is capable of
devising for its thought ; the linguist who trains himself in
them alone will be liable to narrowness of vision, and will
stumble when he comes to walk in other fields. We claim
only that their inner character and outer circumstances
combine to give them the first place in the regard of the
linguistic scholar ; that their investigation will constitute in
the future, as it has done in the past, a chief object of his
study ; and that their complete elucidation is both the most
attainable and the most desirable and rewarding object proposed to itself by linguistic science.

The general method of linguistic research has already been
variously set forth and illustrated, in an incidental way ; but
a summary recapitulation of its principles, with fuller reference to the grounds on which they are founded, will not be
amiss at this point in our progress. The end sought by the
scientific investigator of language, it will be remembered, is
not a mere apprehension and exposition, however full and
systematic, of the phenomena of a language, or of all human
speech—of its words, its forms, its rules, its usages : that is
work for grammarians and lexicographers. He strives to
discover the *why* of everything : why these words, these
affixes, have such and such meanings ; why usage is thus,
and not otherwise ; why so many and such words and forms,
and they only, are found in a given tongue—and so on, in
ever farther-reaching inquiry, back even to the question,

why we speak at all. And since it appears that every existing or recorded dialect, and every word composing it, is
the altered successor, altered in both form and meaning, of
some other and earlier one; since all known language has
been made what it is, out of something more original, by
action proceeding from the minds of those who have used
it, its examination must be conducted historically, like that
of any other institution which has had a historic growth and
development. All human speech has been during long ages
modified, was even perhaps in the first place produced, by
human capacities, as impelled by human necessities and
governed by human circumstances; it has become what
these influences by their gradual action have made it: it, on
the one hand, is to be understood only as their product;
they, on the other hand, are to be read in the effects which
they have wrought upon it. To trace out the transformations of language, following it backward through its successive stages even to its very beginnings, if we can reach so
far; to infer from the changes which it is undergoing and
has undergone the nature and way of action of the forces
which govern it; from these and from the observed character of its beginnings to arrive at a comprehension of its
origin—such are the inquiries which occupy the attention
of the linguistic scholar, and which must guide him to his
ultimate conclusions respecting the nature of speech as an
instrumentality of communication and of thought, and its
value as a means of human progress.

And as in its general character, so also in its details, the
process of investigation is historical. We have already
seen (lecture second, p. 54) that the whole structure of
our science rests upon the study of individual words; the
labours of the etymologist must precede and prepare the
way for everything that is to follow. But every etymological question is strictly a historical one; it concerns the
steps of a historical process, as shown by historical evidences; it implies a judgment of the value of testimony, and a
recognition of the truth fairly deducible therefrom. What
is proved respecting the origin and changes of each particular word by all the evidence within reach, is the etymolo-

gist's ever-recurring inquiry. To answer it successfully,
he needs a combination of many qualities; he must be, in
fact, a whole court in himself : the acuteness, perseverance,
and enterprise of the advocate must be his, to gather every
particle of testimony, every analogy, every decision, bearing
upon the case in hand ; he must play the part of the opposing counsel, in carefully sifting the collected evidence,
testing the character and disinterestedness of the witnesses,
cross-examining them to expose their blunders and inconsistencies ; he must have, above all, the learning and candour of
the judge, that he may sum up and give judgment impar-
tially, neither denying the right which is fairly established,
nor allowing that which rests on uncertain allegation and
insufficient proof. In short, the same gifts and habits of
mind which make the successful historian of events are
wanted also to make the successful historian of words.

The ill-repute in which etymology and those who follow
it are held in common opinion is a telling indication of the
difficulty attending its practice. The uncertainty and arbitrariness of its prevailing methods, the absurdity of its
results, have been the theme of many a cutting and well-
directed gibe. It has in all ages been a tempting occupation to curious minds, and always a slippery one. An
incalculable amount of human ingenuity has been wasted
in its false pursuit. Men eminent for acuteness and sound
judgment in other departments of intellectual labour have
in this been guilty of folly unaccountable. It has been
often remarked that the Greeks and Romans, when once
engaged in an etymological inquiry, seem to have taken leave
of their common sense. Great as were the advantages
offered by the Sanskrit language to its native analysts, in
the regularity of its structure and the small proportion of
obscure words which it contained, they stumbled continually
as soon as they left the plain track of the commonest and
clearest derivations, and their religious, philosophical, and
grammatical books are filled with word-genealogies as fanciful and unsound as those of the classic writers. In no one
respect does the linguistic science of the present day show
its radical superiority to that of former times more clearly

than in the style and method of its etymologies : upon these, indeed, is its superiority directly founded.

The grand means, now, of modern etymological research is the extensive comparison of kindred forms. How this should be so appears clearly enough from what has been already taught respecting the growth of dialects and the genetical connections of languages. If spoken tongues stood apart from one another, each a separate and isolated entity, they would afford no scope for the comparative method. As such entities the ancient philology regarded them ; or, if their relationship was in some cases recognized, it was wrongly apprehended and perversely applied—as when, for instance, the Latin was looked upon as derived from the Greek, and its words were sought to be etymologized out of the Greek lexicon, as corrupted forms of Greek vocables. In the view of the present science, while each existing dialect is the descendant of an older tongue, so other existing dialects are equally descendants of the same tongue. All have kept a part, and lost a part, of the material of their common inheritance ; all have preserved portions of it in a comparatively unchanged form, while they have altered other portions perhaps past recognition. But, while thus agreed in the general fact and the general methods of change, they differ indefinitely from one another in the details of the changes effected. Each has saved something which others have lost, or kept in pristine purity what they have obscured or overlaid: or else, from their variously modified forms can be deduced with confidence the original whence these severally diverged. Every word, then, in whose examination the linguistic scholar engages, is to be first set alongside its correspondents or analogues in other related languages, that its history may be read aright. Thus the deficiencies of the evidence which each member of a connected group of dialects contains respecting its own genesis and growth are made up, in greater or less degree, by the rest, and historical results are reached having a greatly increased fulness and certainty. The establishment of a grand family of related languages, like the Indo-European, makes each member contribute, either immediately or mediately, to the elucidation of every other.

The great prominence in the new science of language of this comparative method gave that science its familiar title of " comparative philology," a title which is not yet lost in popular usage, although now fully outgrown and antiquated. It designated very suitably the early growing phase of linguistic study, that of the gathering and sifting of material, the elaboration of methods, the establishment of rules, the deduction of first general results; it still properly designates the process by which the study is extended and perfected; but to call the whole science any longer " comparative philology " is not less inappropriate than to call the science of zoölogy " comparative anatomy," or botanical science the " comparison of plants."

But the comparative method, as we must not fail to notice, is no security against loose and false etymologizing; it is not less liable to abuse than any other good thing. If it is to be made fruitful of results for the advancement of science, it must not be wielded arbitrarily and wildly; it must have its fixed rules of application. Some appear to imagine that, in order to earn the title of " comparative philologist," they have but to take some given language and run with it into all the ends of the earth, collating its material and forms with those of any other tongue they may please to select. But that which makes the value of comparison — namely, genetical relationship — also determines the way in which it shall be rendered valuable. We compare in order to bring to light resemblances which have their ground and explanation in a real historical identity of origin. We must proceed, then, as in any other genealogical inquiry, by tracing the different lines of descent backward from step to step toward their points of convergence. The work of comparison is begun between the tongues most nearly related, and is gradually extended to those whose connection is more and more remote. We first set up, for example, a group like the Germanic, and by the study of its internal relations learn to comprehend its latest history, dis-

16

tinguishing and setting apart all that is the result of independent growth and change among its dialects, recognizing what in it is original, and therefore fair subject of comparison with the results of a like process performed upon the other branches of the same family. It needs not, indeed, that the restoration of primitive Germanic speech should be made complete before any farther step is taken; there are correspondences so conspicuous and palpable running through all the varieties of Indo-European speech, that, the unity of the family having been once established, they are at a glance seen and accepted at their true value. But only a small part of the analogies of two more distantly related languages are of this character, and their recognition will be made both complete and trustworthy in proportion as the nearer congeners of each language are first subjected to comparison. If English were the only existing Germanic tongue, we could still compare it with Attic Greek, and point out a host of coincidences which would prove their common origin ; but, as things are, to conduct our investigation in this way, leaving out of sight the related dialects on each side, would be most unsound and unphilological; it would render us liable to waste no small share of our effort upon those parts of English which are peculiar, of latest growth, and can have no genetic connection whatever with aught in the Greek : it would expose us, on the one hand, to make false identifications (as between our *whole* and the Greek *holos*, ' entire ') ; and, on the other hand, to find diversity where the help of older dialectic forms on both sides would show striking resemblance. What analogy, for instance, do we discern between our *bear*, in *they bear*, and Greek *pherousi ?* but comparison of the other Germanic dialects allows us to trace *bear* directly back to a Germanic form *berand*, and Doric Greek gives us *pheronti*, from which comes *pherousi* by one of the regular euphonic rules of the language ; the law of permutation of mutes in the Germanic languages (see above, p. 97) exhibits *b* as the regular correspondent in Low German dialects to the original aspirate *ph ;* and the historical identity of the two words compared, in root and termination, is thus put beyond the reach of cavil.

Yet more contrary to sound method would it be, for example, to compare directly English, Portuguese, Persian, and Bengali, four of the latest and most altered representatives of the four great branches of Indo-European speech to which they severally belong. Nothing, or almost nothing, that is peculiar to the Bengali as compared with the Sanskrit, to the Persian as compared with the ancient Avestan and Achæmenidan dialects, to the Portuguese as compared with the Latin, can be historically connected with what belongs to English or any other Germanic tongue. Their ties of mutual relationship run backward through those older representatives of the branches, and are to be sought and traced there.

But worst of all is the drawing out of alleged correspondences, and the fabrication of etymologies, between such languages as the English — or, indeed, any Indo-European dialect—on the one hand, and the Hebrew, or the Finnish, or the Chinese, on the other. Each of these last is the fully recognized member of a well-established family of languages, distinct from the Indo-European. If there be genetic relation between either of them and an Indo-European language, it must lie back of the whole grammatical development of their respective families, and can only be brought to light by the reduction of each, though means of the most penetrating and exhaustive study of the dialects confessedly akin with it, to its primitive form, as cleared of all the growth and change wrought upon it by ages of separation. There may be scores, or hundreds, of apparent resemblances between them, but these are worthless as signs of relationship until an investigation not less profound than we have indicated shall show that they are not merely superficial and delusive.

Let it not be supposed that we are reasoning in a vicious circle, in thus requiring that two languages shall have been proved related before the correspondences which are to show their relationship shall be accepted as real. We are only setting forth the essentially cumulative nature of the evidences of linguistic connection. The first processes of comparison by which it is sought to establish the position and relations of a new language are tentative merely. No sound linguist

is unmindful of the two opposing possibilities which interfere
with the certainty of his conclusions : first, that seeming
coincidences may turn out accidental and illusory only ;
second, that beneath apparent discordance may be hidden
genetic identity. With every new analogy which his researches bring to view, his confidence in the genuineness
and historic value of those already found is increased. And
when, examining each separate fact in all the light that he
can cast upon it, from sources near and distant, he has at
length fully satisfied himself that two.tongues are fundamentally related, their whole mutual aspect is thereby modified ; he becomes expectant of signs of relationship · everywhere, and looks for them in phenomena which would not
otherwise attract his attention for a moment. When, on
the contrary, an orderly and thorough examination, proceeding from the nearer to the remoter degrees of connection,
has demonstrated the position of two languages in two
diverse families, the weight of historic probability is shifted
to the other scale, and makes directly against the interpretation of their surface resemblances as the effect of anything
but accident or borrowing.

The new etymological science differs from the old, not in
the character of the results which it is willing to admit, but
in the character of the evidence on which it is willing to admit
them. It will even derive *lucus*, 'grove,' from *non lucendo*,
'its not shining there,' if only historical proof of the
derivation be furnished. It finds no difficulty in recognizing
as identical two words like the French *évêque* and the English *bishop*, which have not a single sound or letter in common ; for each is readily traceable back to the Greek
episkopos.* But it does not draw thence the conclusion
that, in this or in any other pair of languages, two words
meaning the same thing may, whatever their seeming discordance, be assumed to be one, or are likely to be proved

---

* *Evêque*, earlier *evesque*, *evesc*, represents the syllables *episk*, while *bishop*,
earlier *biskop*, represents the syllables *piskop*   Each has saved, and still accents, the accented syllable of the original ; but the French, whose words are
prevailingly accented on their final syllables, has dropped off all that followed
it ; while the Germanic tongues, accenting more usually the penult in words
of this structure, has retained the succeeding syllable.

one : it waits for the demonstration in each separate case. The claim made in our third lecture, that, in the history of linguistic changes, any given sound may pass over into any other, any given meaning become modified to its opposite, or to something apparently totally unconnected with it, may seem to take away from etymology all reliable basis ; but it is not so ; for the same researches which establish this claim show also the difference between those facile changes which may be looked for everywhere, and the exceptional ones which only direct and convincing evidence can force us to accept as actual in any language ; they teach us to study the laws of transition of each separate language as part of its idiosyncrasy, and to refrain from applying remote and doubtful analogies in the settlement of difficult questions.

In short, the modern science of language imposes upon all who pursue it thoroughness and caution. It requires that every case be examined in all its bearings. It refuses to accept results not founded on an exhaustive treatment of all the attainable evidence. It furnishes no instruments of research which may not be turned to false uses, and made to yield false results, in careless and unskilful hands. It supplies nothing which can take the place of sound learning and critical judgment. Even those who are most familiar with its methods may make lamentable failures when they come to apply them to a language of which they have only superficial knowledge,* or which they compare directly with some distant tongue, regardless of its relations in its own family, and of its history as determined by comparison with these. A scholar profoundly versed in the comparative philology of some special group of languages, and whom we gladly suffer to instruct us as to their development, may have nothing to say that is worth our listening to, when he would fain trace their remoter connections with groups of which he knows little or nothing. Notwithstanding the

---

* Thus, as a striking example and warning, hardly a more utter caricature of the comparative method is to be met with than that given by Bopp, the great founder and author of the method, himself, in the papers in which he attempts to prove the Malay-Polynesian and the Caucasian languages entitled to a place in the Indo-European family.

immense progress which the study of language has made during the past few years, the world is still full of hasty generalizers, who would rather skim wide and difficult conclusions off the surface of half-examined facts than wait to gather them as the fruits of slow and laborious research. The greater part of the rubbish which is even now heaping up in the path of our science, encumbering its progress, comes from the neglect of these simple principles: that no man is qualified to compare fruitfully two languages or groups who is not deeply grounded in the knowledge of both, and that no language can be fruitfully compared with others which stand, or are presumed to stand, in a more distant relationship with it, until it has been first compared with its own next of kin.

We see, it may be farther remarked, upon how narrow and imperfect a basis those comparative philologists build who are content with a facile setting side by side of words; whose materials are simple vocabularies, longer or shorter, of terms representing common ideas. There was a period in the history of linguistic science when this was the true method of investigation, and it still continues to be useful in certain departments of the field of research. It is the first experimental process; it determines the nearest and most obvious groupings, and prepares the way for more penetrating study. Travellers, explorers, in regions exhibiting great diversity of idiom and destitute of literary records—like our western wilds, or the vast plains of inner Africa—do essential service by gathering and supplying such material, anything better being rendered inaccessible by lack of leisure, opportunity, or practice. But it must be regarded as provisional and introductory, acceptable only because the best that is to be had. Genetic correspondences in limited lists of words, however skilfully selected, are apt to be conspicuous only when the tongues they represent are of near kindred; and even then they may be in no small measure obscured or counterbalanced by discordances, so that deeper and closer study is needed, in order to bring out satisfactorily to view the fact and degree of relationship. Penetration of the secrets of linguistic structure and growth, dis-

covery of correspondences which lie out of the reach of
careless and uninstructed eyes, rejection of deceptive resemblances which have no historical foundation—these are
the most important part of the linguistic student's work.
Surface collation without genetic analysis, as far-reaching as
the attainable evidence allows, is but a travesty of the
methods of comparative philology.

Another not infrequent misapprehension of etymologic
study consists in limiting its sphere of action to a tracing
out of the correspondences of words. This is, indeed, as we
have called it, the fundamental stage, on the solidity of
which depends the security of all the rest of the structure ;
but it is only that. Comparative etymology, like chemistry,
runs into an infinity of detail, in which the mind of the student is sometimes entangled, and his effort engrossed; it
has its special rules and methods, which admit within certain
limits of being mechanically applied, by one ignorant or
heedless of their true ground and meaning. Many a man
is a skilful and successful hunter of verbal connections whose
views of linguistic science are of the crudest and most imperfect character. Not only does he thus miss what ought
to be his highest reward, the recognition of those wide
relations and great truths to which his study of words should
conduct him, but his whole work lacks its proper basis, and
is liable to prove weak at any point. The history of words
is inextricably bound up with that of human thought and
life and action, and cannot be read without it. We fully
understand no word till we comprehend the motives and
conditions that called it forth and determined its form. The
word *money*, for example, is not explained when we have
marshalled the whole array of its correspondents in all European tongues, and traced them up to their source in the
Latin *moneta* : all the historical circumstances which have
caused a term once limited to an obscure city to be current
now in the mouths of such immense communities ; the wants
and devices of civilization and commerce which have created
the thing designated by the word and made it what it is;
the outward circumstances and mental associations which, by
successive changes, have worked out the name from a root

signifying 'to think;' the structure of organ, and the habits
of utterance—in themselves and in their origin—which have
metamorphosed *monéta* into *móney* :—all this, and more,
is necessary to the linguistic scholar's perfect mastery of
this single term.   There is no limit to the extent to which
the roots of being of almost every word ramify thus through
the whole structure of the tongue to which it belongs, or
even of many tongues, and through the history of the people
who speak them : if we are left in most cases to come far
short of the full knowledge which we crave, we at least
should not fail to crave it, and to grasp after all of it that
lies within our reach.

We have been regarding linguistic comparison as what it
primarily and essentially is, the effective means of determining genetical relationship, and investigating the historical development of languages.   But we must guard against leaving
the impression that languages can be compared for no other
purposes than these.   In those wide generalizations wherein
we regard speech as a human faculty, and its phenomena as
illustrating the nature of mind, the processes of thought,
the progress of culture, it is often not less important to put
side by side that which in spoken language is analogous in
office but discordant in origin than that which is accordant
in both.   The variety of human expression is well-nigh infinite, and no part of it ought to escape the notice of the
linguistic student.   The comparative method, if only it be
begun and carried on aright—if the different objects of the
genetic and the analogic comparison be kept steadily in
view, and their results not confounded with one another—
need not be restricted in its application, until, starting from
any centre, it shall have comprehended the whole circle of
human speech.

LECTURE VII.

Beginnings of Indo-European language. Actuality of linguistic analysis.
Roots, pronominal and verbal; their character as the historical
germs of our language; development of inflective speech from them.
Production of declensional, conjugational, and derivative apparatus,
and of the parts of speech. Relation of synthetic and analytic
forms. General character and course of inflective development.

THE last two lectures have given us a view of the Indo-
European family of languages. We have glanced at the
principal dialects, ancient and modern, of which it is composed, noticing their exceeding variety and the high antiquity of some among them—the unequalled sweep, of time
and of historic development together, which they include
and cover. The family has been shown to be of preëminent
importance and interest to the linguistic student, because
the peoples to whom it belongs have taken during the past
two thousand years or more a leading or even the foremost
part in the world's history, because it includes the noblest
and most perfect instruments of human thought and expression, and because upon its study is mainly founded the
present science of language. We examined, in a general
way, the method pursued in its investigation—namely, a
genetic analysis, effected chiefly by the aid of a widely extended comparison of the kindred forms of related dialects
(whence the science gets its familiar name of "comparative
philology")—and noted briefly some of the misapprehensions and misapplications to which this was liable. At
present, before going on to survey the other great families

of language, and to consider the relation in which they
stand to the Indo-European, we have to pause long enough
to look at the main facts in the history of growth of the
latter—of our own form of speech, using the word " our "
in the widest sense to which we have as yet extended it.
This we do, partly on account of the intrinsic interest of
the subject, and partly because the results thus won will be
found valuable, and even almost indispensable, in the course
of our farther inquiries.

The history of Indo-European language has been more
carefully read, and is now more thoroughly understood, than
that of any other of the grand divisions of human speech.
Not that our knowledge of it is by any means complete, or
is not marked even by great and numerous deficiencies and
obscurities : owing in no small part to the obliteration of
needed evidence, and hence irreparable ; but in part also
to incomplete comparison and analysis of the material yet
preserved, and therefore still admitting and sure ere long to
receive amendment.   Such deficiencies, however, are more
concerned with matters of minor detail, and less with facts
and principles of fundamental consequence, here than elsewhere.   Hence the mode of development of language in
general, even from its first commencement, can in no other
way be so well exemplified as by tracing its special history
in this single family.

Our first inquiry concerns the primitive stage of Indo-
European language, its historical beginnings.

The general processes of linguistic growth and change, as
they have for long ages past been going on in all the dialects
of our kindred, were set forth and illustrated with some detail in the early part of our discussions respecting language
(in the second and third lectures).   We there saw that, in
order to provide new thought and knowledge with its appropriate signs, and to repair the waste occasioned by the
loss of words from use and memory, and the constant wearing out of forms, new combinations were made out of old
materials, words of independent significance reduced to the
position and value of modifying appendages to other words,
and meanings variously altered and transferred.   These

processes may, for aught we can see, work on during an indefinite period in the future, with never-ending evolution
out of each given form of speech of another slightly differing from it; even until every now existing dialect shall have
divided into numerous descendants, and each of these shall
have varied so far from its ancestor that their kindred shall
be scarcely, or not at all, discoverable. Have we, now, any
good reason to believe that they have not worked on thus
indefinitely in the past also, with a kaleidoscopic resolution
of old forms and combination of new, changing the aspect of
language without altering its character as a structure? Or,
are we able to find distinct traces of a condition of· speech
·which may be called primitive in comparison with that in
which it at present exists ?

This question admits an affirmative answer. The present
structure of language has its beginnings, from which we are
not yet so far removed that they may not be clearly seen.
Our historical analysis does not end at last in mere obscurity ; it brings us to the recognition of elements which we
must regard as, if not the actual first utterances of men,
at least the germs out of which their later speech has been
developed. It sets before our view a stage of expression
essentially different from any of those we now behold among
the branches of our family, and serving as their common
foundation.

It must be premised that this belief rests entirely upon
our faith in the actuality of our analytical processes, as
being merely a retracing of the steps of a previous synthesis
—in the universal truth of the doctrine that the elements
into which we separate words are those by the putting
together of which those words were at first made up. The
grounds upon which such a faith reposes were pretty distinctly set forth in the second lecture (p. 66), but the importance of the subject will justify us in a recapitulation of
the argument there presented.

No one can possibly suppose that we should ever have
come to call our morning meal *breakfast*, if there had not
already existed in our language the two independent words
break and *fast*; any more than that we should say *telegraph-*

wire, hickory-pole, campaign-document, gun-boat, without previous possession of the simple words of which are formed these modern compounds. *Fearful* and *fearless,* in like manner, imply the existence beforehand of the noun *fear,* and of the adjectives *full* and *loose,* or their older equivalents, which have assumed, with reference to that noun, the quality of suffixes. Nor should we have any adverbial suffix *ly,* if we had not earlier had the adjective *like,* nor any preterits in *d* (as *I love-d*), but for the fact that our Germanic ancestors owned an imperfect corresponding to our *did,* which they added to their new verbs to express past action. Any one, I think, will allow that elements distinguishable by word-analysis which can thus be identified with independent words are thereby proved to have been themselves once in possession of an independent *status* in the language, and to have been actually reduced by combination to the form and office with which our analysis finds them endowed. But farther, few or none will be found to question that all those formative elements which belong to the Germanic languages alone, of which no traces are to be discovered in any other of the branches of the Indo-European family, which constitute the peculiar patrimony of some or all of the dialects of our branch, must have been gained by the latter since their separation from the common stock, and in the same way with the rest, even though we can no longer demonstrate the origin of each affix. With the disguising and effacing effects of the processes of linguistic change fully present to our apprehensions, we shall not venture to conclude that those cases in which our historical researches fail to give us the genesis of both the elements of a compound form are fundamentally different from those in which it fully succeeds in doing so. The difference lies, not in the cases themselves, but in our attitude toward them ; in our accidental possession of information as to the history of the one, and our lack of it as to that of the other. This reasoning, however, obviously applies not to Germanic speech alone ; it is equally legitimate and cogent in reference to all Indo-European language. We cannot refuse to believe that the whole history of this family of languages has been, in its

grand essential features, the same ; that their structure is
homogeneous throughout. There is no reason whatever for
our assuming that the later composite forms are made up,
and not the earlier ; that the later suffixes are elaborated
out of independent elements, and not the earlier. So far
back as we can trace the history of language, the forces
which have been efficient in producing its changes, and the
general outlines of their modes of operation, have been the
same ; and we are justified in concluding, we are even compelled to infer, that they have been the same from the outset. There is no way of investigating the first hidden steps
of any continuous historical process, except by carefully
studying the later recorded steps, and cautiously applying
the analogies thence deduced. So the geologist studies the
forces which are now altering by slow degrees the form
and aspect of the earth's crust, wearing down the rocks here,
depositing beds of sand and pebbles there, pouring out
floods of lava over certain regions, raising or lowering the
line of coast along certain seas ; and he applies the results
of his observations with confidence to the explanation of
phenomena dating from a time to which men's imaginations,
even, can hardly reach. The legitimacy of the analogical
reasoning is not less undeniable in the one case than in the
other. You may as well try to persuade the student of the
earth's structure that the coal-bearing rocks lie in parallel
layers, of alternating materials, simply because it pleased
God to make them so when he created the earth ; or that
the impressions of leaves, the stems and trunks of trees, the
casts of animal remains, shells and bones, which they contain, the ripple and rain-marks which are seen upon them,
are to be regarded as the sports of nature, mere arbitrary
characteristics of the formation, uninterpretable as signs of
its history—as to persuade the student of language that
the indications of composition and growth which he discovers
in the very oldest recorded speech, not less than in the
latest, are only illusory, and that his comprehension of
linguistic development must therefore be limited to the
strictly historical period of the life of language. It is no
prepossession, then, nor à *priori* theory, but a true logical

necessity, a sound induction from observed facts, which brings us to the conclusion that all linguistic elements possessing distinct meaning and office, variously combined and employed for the uses of expression, are originally independent entities, having a separate existence before they entered into mutual combination.

In the light of these considerations let us examine a single word in our language, the word *irrevocability*. It comes to us from the Latin, where it had the form *irrevocabilitas* (genitive -*tatis*). It is clearly made by the addition of *ty* (*tas, tatis*) to a previously existing *irrevocable* (*irrevocabili-s*), just as we now form a new abstract noun from any given adjective by adding *ness :* for example, *doughfacedness.* Again, *revocable* (*revocabilis*) preceded *irrevocable,* as *dutiful* preceded *undutiful.* Further, if there had been no verb *to revoke* (*revocare*), there would have been no adjective *revocable,* any more than *lovable* without the verb *to love.* Yet once more : although we in English have the syllable *voke* only in composition with prefixes, as *revoke, evoke, invòke, provoke,* yet in Latin, as the verb *vocare,* ' to call,' it is, of course, older than any of these its derivatives, as *stand* is older than *understand* and *withstand.* Thus far our way is perfectly clear. But while, in our language, *voke* appears as a simple syllable, uncombined with suffixes, this is only by the comparatively recent effect of the wearing-out processes, formerly illustrated (in the third lecture) ; in the more original Latin, it is invariably associated with formative elements, which compose with its forms like *vocare,* ' to call,' *vocat,* ' he calls,' *vocabar,* 'I was called ;' or, in substantive uses, *vocs* (*vox*), ' a calling, a voice,' *vocum,* ' of voices ;' and so on. There is nothing, so far as concerns the formative elements themselves, to distinguish this last class of cases from the others, before analyzed ; each suffix has its distinct meaning and office, and is applied in a whole class of analogous words ; and some of them, at least, are traceable back to the independent words out of which they grew. The only difference is that here, if we cut off the formative elements, we have left, not a word, actually employed as such in any ancient language of our family, but a significant syllable, expressing the general and indeterminate idea of 'calling,' and found to occur in connected speech only when limited and defined by the suffixes which are attached to it. This is not, however, a peculiarity which can exempt the words so formed from a like treatment, leading to like conclusions, with the rest ; we must still trust in the reality of our analysis ; and especially, when we consider such forms as the Sanskrit *vak-mi, vak-shi, vak-ti,* where the *mi, shi,* and *ti* are recognizable pronouns, making compounds which mean clearly ' call-I,' ' call-thou,' ' call-he,' we cannot doubt that the element *voc (vak)* had also once an independent *status*, that it was a word, a part of spoken speech, and that the various forms which contain it were really produced by the addition of other elements to it, and their fusion together into a single word, in the same manner in which we have fused *truth* and *full* into *truthful, truth* and *loose* into *truthless, true* and *like* into *truly*.

The same conclusion may be stated in more general terms, as follows. The whole body of suffixes, of formative endings, is divided into two principal classes : first, primary, or such as form derivatives directly from roots ; second, secondary, or such as form derivatives from other derivatives, from themes containing already a formative element. But the difference between these two classes is in their use and application, not in their character and origin. No insignificant portion of each is traceable back to independent words, and the presumption alike for each is that in all its parts it was produced in the same manner. If, then, we believe that the themes to which the secondary endings are appended were historical entities, words employed in actual speech before their further composition, we must believe the same respecting the roots to which are added the primary endings : these are not less historical than the others.

The conclusion is one of no small consequence. Elements like *voc*, each composing a single syllable, and containing no traceable sign of a formative element, resisting all our attempts at reduction to a simpler form, are what we arrive at as the final results of our analysis of the Indo-European vocabulary ; every word of which this is made up—save those whose history is obscure, and cannot be read far back toward its beginning—is found to contain a monosyllabic root as its central significant portion, along with certain other accessory portions, syllables or remnants of syllables, whose office it is to define and direct the radical idea. The roots are never found in practical use in their naked form; they are (or, as has been repeatedly explained, have once been) always clothed with suffixes, or with suffixes and prefixes; yet they are no mere abstractions, dissected out by the grammarian's knife from the midst of organisms of which they were ultimate and integral portions; they are rather the nuclei of gradual accretions, parts about which other parts gathered to compose orderly and membered wholes; germs, we may call them, out of which has developed the intricate structure of later speech. And the recognition of them in this character is an acknowledgment that Indo-European language, with all its fulness and inflective suppleness, is descended from an original monosyllabic tongue; that our ancestors talked with one another in single syllables, indicative of the ideas of prime importance, but wanting all designation of their relations; and that out of these, by processes not differing in their nature from those which are still in operation in our own tongue, was elaborated the marvellous and varied structure of all the Indo-European dialects.

Such is, in fact, the belief which the students of language have reached, and now hold with full confidence. New and strange but a few years ago, it commands at present the assent of nearly all comparative philologists, and is fast becoming a matter of universal opinion. Since, however, it is still doubted and opposed by a few even among linguistic scholars, and is doubtless more or less unfamiliar and startling to a considerable part of any educated community, it will be proper that we combine with our examination of it some notice and refutation of the arguments by which it is assailed.

It is surely unnecessary, in the first place, to protest against any one's taking umbrage at this theory of a primitive monosyllabic stage of Indo-European language out of regard for the honour and dignity of our remote ancestors. The linguist is making a historical inquiry into the conditions of that branch of the human family to which we belong, and should no more be shocked at finding them talking in single syllables than dwelling in caves and huts of branches, or clad in leaves and skins. To require, indeed, for man's credit that he should have been sent upon the earth with a fully developed language miraculously placed in his mouth, with lists of nouns, verbs, and adverbs stored away in his memory, to be drawn upon at will, is not more reasonable than to require that the first human beings should have been born in full suits of clothes, and with neat cottages, not destitute of well-stocked larders, ready built over their heads. It surely is most of all to the honour of human nature that man should have been able, on so humble a foundation, to build up this wondrous fabric of speech ; and also, as we may already say, that he should have been allowed to do so is more in accordance with the general plan of the Creator, who has endowed him with high capacities, and left him to work them out to their natural and intended results.

Nor, again, will any one venture to object that it would have been impossible to make so imperfect and rudimentary a language answer any tolerable purpose as a means of expression and communication—any one, at least, who knows aught of the present condition of language among the other races of the globe. One tongue, the Chinese—as we shall see more particularly farther on (in the ninth lecture)—has never advanced out of its primitive monosyllabic stage ; its words remain even to the present day simple radical syllables, closely resembling the Indo-European roots, formless, not in themselves parts of speech, but made such only by their combination into sentences, where the connection and the evident requirements of the sense show in what signification and relation each is used. Yet this scanty and crippled language has served all the needs of a highly cultivated and literary people for thousands of years.

After these few words of reply to one or two of the difficulties which sometimes suggest themselves at first blush to

17

those before whom is brought the view we are defending, we will next proceed to examine in more detail the original monosyllabism of Indo-European language, and see of what character it was.

The roots of our family of languages are divided into two distinct classes: those ultimately indicative of position merely, and those significant of action or quality. The former class are called demonstrative or pronominal roots; the latter class are styled predicative or verbal roots.

The pronominal roots are subjective in their character; they have nothing to do with the inherent qualities of objects, but mark them simply in their relation to the speaker, and primarily their local relation; they give the distinction between the *this* and the *that*, the nearer and the remoter object of attention, myself here, you there, and the third person or thing yonder, present or absent. By their nature, they are not severally and permanently attachable to certain objects or classes of objects, nor are they limited in their application; each of them may designate any and every thing, according to the varying relation sustained by the latter to the person or thing with reference to which it is contemplated. Only one thing can be called the *sun;* only certain objects are *white;* but there is nothing which may not be *I*, and *you*, and *it*, alternately, as the point from which it is viewed changes. In this universality of their application, as dependent upon relative situation merely, and in the consequent capacity of each of them to designate any object which has its own specific name besides, and so, in a manner, to stand for and represent that other name, lies the essential character of the pronouns.* From the pronominal roots come most directly the demonstrative pronouns, of which the personal are individualized forms, and the interrogatives; from these are developed secondarily the possessives and relatives, and the various other subordinate classes. They also generate adverbs of position and of direction. To examine in detail the forms they take, and the variations of

* Their Hindu title, *sarvanâman,* 'name for everything, universal designation,' is therefore more directly and fundamentally characteristic than the one we give them, *pronoun,* 'standing for a name.'

the fundamental distinction between *this* and *that* which they
are applied to express, would lead us too far. So much as
this may be pointed out : those beginning with *m* are especially employed to denote the subject, the *ego*, ' me myself ; '
those with *t* and *n* are used more demonstratively, and those
with *k* interrogatively. They are few in number, hardly
counting a dozen all together, including some which are probably variants of the same original. They are of the simplest
phonetic structure, consisting either of a pure vowel, like *a*
or *i*, or of a vowel combined with a single preceding consonant, forming an open syllable, which is the easiest that the
organs of articulation can be called upon to utter : instances
are *ma, na, ta, tu, ka*.

The roots of the other class, those of action or quality,
are very much more numerous, being reckoned by hundreds ;
and they are of more complicated structure, illustrating every
variety of the syllable, from the pure single vowel to the
vowel preceded or followed, or both, by one consonant,
or even by more than one. They are of objective import,
designating the properties and activities inherent in natural
objects—and prevailingly those that are of a sensible phenomenal character, such as modes of motion and physical
exertion, of sound, and so forth. Let us notice a few instances of roots which are shown to have belonged to the
original language of our family by being still met with in all
or nearly all of its branches.   Such are *i* and *ga*, denoting
simple motion ; *ak*, swift motion ; *stā*, standing ; *ās* and *sad*,
sitting ; *kī*, lying ; *pad*, walking ; *vas*, staying ; *sak*, following ; *vart*, turning ; *sarp*, creeping ; *pat*, flying ; *plu*, flowing ;
ad, eating ; *pā*, drinking ; *an*, blowing ; *vid*, seeing ; *klu*,
hearing ; *vak*, speaking ; *dhā*, putting ; *dā*, giving ; *labh*,
taking ; *garbh*, holding ; *dik*, pointing out ; *bhar*, bearing ;
kar, making ; *tan*, stretching ; *skid* and *dal*, dividing ; *bandh*,
binding ; *star*, strewing ; *par*, filling ; *mar*, rubbing ; *bhā*,
shining ; *bhū*, growing, etc., etc.

In endeavouring to apprehend the significance of these
roots, we must divest their ideas of the definite forms of
conception which we are accustomed to attach to them :
each represents its own meaning in nakedness, in an indeter-

minate condition from which it is equally ready to take on
the semblance of verb or of noun. We may rudely illustrate
their quality by comparing them with such a word in our own
language as *love*, which, by the wearing off of the formative
elements with which it was once clothed, has reverted to the
condition of a bare root, and which must therefore now be
placed in such connection, or so pregnantly and significantly
uttered, as to indicate to the intelligent and sympathizing
listener in what sense it is meant and is to be understood
—whether as verb, in " I *love*," or as substantive, in "my
love," or as virtual adjective, in " *love*-letter."

The inquiry, which might naturally enough be raised at
this point, how the radical syllables of which we are treating
were themselves originated, and whether there be any
natural and necessary connection between them, or any of
them, and the ideas which they represent, such as either
necessitated or at least recommended the allotment of the
particular sign to the particular conception, we must pass
by for the present, having now to do only with that for
which direct evidence is to be found in language itself, with
the historically traceable beginnings of Indo-European
speech ; this question, with its various dependent questions
of a more theoretical and recondite nature, is reserved for consideration at a later time (in the eleventh lecture).

It deserves to be renewedly urged that, in this account
of the primitive stage of Indo-European language, there is
nothing which is not the result of strict and careful induction from the facts recorded in the dialects of the different
members of the family. No one's theory as to what the
beginnings of language must have been, or might naturally
have been expected to be, has had anything to do with
shaping it. It has been a matter of much controversy
among linguistic theorizers what parts of speech language
began with ; whether nouns or verbs were the first words ;
but I am not aware that any acute thinker ever devised,
upon *à priori* grounds, a theory at all closely agreeing with
the account of the matter of which omparative philology
soon arrived through her historical researches. That the
first traceable linguistic entities are not names of concrete

objects, but designate actions, motions, phenomenal conditions, is a truth resting on authority that overrides all
preconceived theories and subjective opinions.   How far and
why it is accordant with what a sound theory, founded on
our general knowledge of human nature and human speech,
would teach, and is therefore entitled to be accepted as a
satisfactory explanation of the way in which men began to
talk, we shall inquire in the lecture devoted to such subjects.

Thus is it, also, as regards the division of the roots into
two classes, pronominal and verbal: this division is so
clearly read in the facts of language that its acceptance
cannot be resisted.   Some are loth to admit it, and strive
to find a higher unity in which it shall disappear, the two
classes falling together into one ; or to show how the pronominal may be relics of verbal roots, worn down by
linguistic usage to such brief form and unsubstantial significance ; but their efforts must at least be accounted altogether unsuccessful hitherto, and it is very questionable
whether they are called for, or likely ever to meet with
success.   As regards the purposes of our present inquiry,
the double classification is certainly primitive and absolute ;
back to the very earliest period of which linguistic analysis
gives us any knowledge, roots verbal and roots pronominal
are to be recognized as of wholly independent substance,
character, and office.

But, it may very properly be asked, how do we know that
the roots which we have set up, and the others like them,
are really ultimate and original ? why may they not be the
results of yet more ancient processes of linguistic change—
like *love* and *lie*, and so many others, which have been repeatedly cited, and shown to have taken in our language the
place of earlier complicated forms, such as *lagamasi* and
laganti ? how should they be proved different from our word
count, for example, which we treat like an original root, expanding it by means of suffixes into various forms—as he
counts, they *counted, counting, counter, countable*—while yet
it is only a modern derivative from a Latin compound verb
containing a preposition, namely *computare*, 'to think together, combine in thought,' got through the medium of the

French *compter* (where the *p* is still written, though not
pronounced)—in fact, the same word as the evidently made-
up *compute?* Of apparent monosyllabic verbal roots like
this, which are readily proved by a little historical study to
be of polysyllabic origin, or to contain the relics of formative processes, our language contains no small number :
other instances are *preach* from *pre-dicare*, *vend* from *venum-
dare*, *blame* from Greek *blas-phēmein ; don* and *doff* from *do
on* and *do off; learn*, of which the *n* is a passive ending,
added to *lere*, 'teach,' whence comes *lore*, 'doctrine ;' *to
throng*, a denominative from the noun *throng*, which is
derived from *thring* (Anglo-Saxon *thringan*), 'press,' lost in
our modern use (as if we were to lose *sing*, and substitute
for it *to song*, from the derived noun *song*) ; *to blast*, a like
denominative from *blast*, a derivative from *blæsan*, 'to blow,
blare ;' and so on.   Such are to be found also abundantly
in other languages, modern and ancient ; why not as well
among the alleged Indo-European roots ?   Now there can
be no question whatever that such additions to the stock
of verbal expression have been produced at every period of
the growth of language, not only throughout its recorded
career, but also in times beyond the reach of historic analysis.   There is not a known dialect of our family which does
not exhibit a greater or less number of seeming roots peculiar to itself ; and of these the chief part may be proved, or
are to be assumed, to be of secondary origin, and not at all
entitled to lay claim to the character of relics from the original stock, lost by the sister dialects.   Even the Sanskrit,
upon which we have mainly to rely for our restoration of
Indo-European roots, possesses not a few which are such
only in seeming, which are of special Aryan or Indian
growth, and valueless for the construction of general Indo-
European etymologies.   And, yet farther, among those very
radical syllables whose presence in the tongues of all the
branches proves them a possession of the original community before its dispersion, there are some which show the
clearest signs of secondary formation.   As a single example,
let us take the root *man*, 'think' (in Latin *me-min-i, mon-
eo, mens ;* Greek *men-os, man-tis ;* Lithuanian *men-ù ;* Mœso-

Gothic *man*, German *mein-en*, our *I mean*) : distinct analogies lead us to see in it a development—probably through a
derivative noun, of which it is the denominative—of the
older root *mā*, meaning either ' to make ' or ' to measure ; '
a designation for the mental process having been won by
figuratively regarding it as a mental manufacture or production, or else as an ideal mensuration of the object of thought,
a passing from point to point of it, in estimation of its
dimension and quality. Some linguistic scholars go much
farther than others in their attempts at analyzing the Indo-
European roots, and referring them to more primitive elements ; all the methods of secondary origin which we have
illustrated above have been sought for and thought to be
recognized among them; and there are those who are unwilling to believe that any absolutely original root can have
ended otherwise than in a vowel, or begun with more than
a single consonant, and who therefore regard all radical
syllables not conforming with their norm as the product of
composition or fusion with formative elements. We need
not here enter into the question as to the justice of these
extreme views, or a criticism of the work of the root-
analysts ; we are compelled at any rate to concede that the
results of growth are to be seen among even the earliest
traceable historical roots ; that we must be cautious how we
claim ultimateness for any given radical syllable, unless we
can succeed in establishing an ultimate and necessary tie
between it and the idea it represents ; and that the search
after the absolutely original in human speech is a task of
the most obscure and recondite character.

   But these concessions do not impair our claim that the
inflective structure of Indo-European speech is built up
upon a historical foundation of monosyllabic roots. If the
particular roots to which our analysis brings us are not in
all cases the products of our ancestors' first attempts at
articulation, they are at any rate of the same kind with
these, and represent to us the incipient stage of speech. If
in every dissyllable whose history we can trace we recognize
a compound structure, if in every nominal and verbal form
we find a formative element which gives it character as

noun or verb, then we must believe that the germs out of
which our language grew were not more complicated than
single syllables, and that they possessed no distinct character as nouns or verbs, but were equally convertible into both.
Our researches are only pointed a step farther back, without
a change of method or result. That in these roots we
approach very near to, if we do not quite touch, the actual
beginnings of speech, is proved by other considerations. In
order to bring into any language new apparent roots, and
give them mobility by clothing them with inflections, a
system of inflections must have been already elaborated by
use with other roots in other forms. We cannot apply our
d as sign of the imperfect tense to form such words as *I
electrified, I telegraphed*, until we have worked down our
preterit *did*, in substance and meaning, to such a mere formative element. And when we have traced the suffix back
until we find it identical with the independent word out of
which it grew, we know that we are close upon the beginning of its use, and have before us virtually that condition
of the language in which its combinations were first made.
So also with the adverbial suffix *ly*, when we have followed
it up to *lîce*, a case of the adjective *lîc*, 'like.' Now, in
connection with the roots of which examples have been given
above, we see in actual process of elaboration the general
system of Indo-European inflection, the most ancient,
fundamental, and indispensable part of our grammatical
apparatus ; and we infer that these roots and their like are
the foundation of our speech, the primitive material out of
which its high and complicated fabric has been reared. It
is not possible to regard them as the worn-down relics of a
previous career of inflective development. The English, it
is true, has been long tending, through the excessive prevalence of the wearing-out processes, toward a state of flec-
tionless monosyllabism ; but such a monosyllabism, where the
grammatical categories are fully distinguished, where relational words and connectives abound, where every vocable
inherits the character which the former possession of inflection has given it, where groups of related terms are applied
to related uses, is a very different thing from a primitive

monosyllabism like that to which the linguistic analyst is
conducted by his researches among the earliest representatives of Indo-European language; and he finds no more
difficulty in distinguishing the one from the other, and
recognizing the true character of each, than does the geologist in distinguishing a primitive crystalline formation from
a conglomerate, composed of well-worn pebbles, of diverse
origin and composition, and containing fragments of earlier
and later fossils. If the English were strictly reduced to
its words of one syllable, it would still contain an abundant
repertory of developed parts of speech, expressing every
variety of idea, and illustrating a rich phonetic system.
The Indo-European roots are not parts of speech, but of
indeterminate character, ready to be shaped into nouns and
verbs by the aid of affixes ; they are limited in signification
to a single class of ideas, the physical or sensual, the phenomenal, out of which the intellectual and moral develop
themselves by still traceable processes; and in them is
represented a system of articulated sounds of great simplicity.   It will be not uninstructive to set down here, for
comparison with the spoken alphabet of our modern English, already given (see p. 91), that scanty scheme of articulations, containing but three vowels and twelve consonants,
which alone is discoverable in the earliest Indo-European
language ; it is as follows :

	a		
i		u	} Vowels.
	l,r		Semivowel.
	n	m	Nasals.
h*			Aspiration.
	s		Sibilant.
g	d	b	} Mutes.
k	t	p	

---

* The aspiration is not found as a separate letter, but only in close combination with the mutes, forming the aspirated mutes *gh, dh, bh*, and (probably
by later development) *kh, th, ph*. These aspirates, though historically they
are independent and important members of the system of spoken sounds, I
have not given separately in the scheme, because phonetically they are compound, containing the aspiration as a distinctly audible element following
the mute.

These are the sounds which are distinguished from one
another by the most marked differences, which our organs
most readily utter, and which are most universally found in
human speech : all others are of later origin, having grown
out of these in the course of the phonetic changes which
words necessarily undergo, as they pass from one generation's keeping to another's. Our race has learned, as we
may truly express it, by long ages of practice, of both mouth
and ear, what the child now learns, by imitation and instruction, in a few months or years : namely, to add to its
first easy utterances others more nicely differentiated, and
produced by a greater effort of the organs. In like manner, starting from the mere rudiments of expression in
radical monosyllables, the tribes of our family have acquired,
through centuries and thousands of years of effort, the distinction and designation of innumerable shades of meaning,
the recognition and representation of a rich variety of
relations, in the later wealth of their inflective tongues—
resources which, being once won, the child learns to wield
dexterously even before he is full grown. It will be our
next task to review the steps by which our language advanced out of its primitive monosyllabic stage, by which it
acquired the character of inflective speech. To follow out
the whole process in detail would be to construct in full
the comparative grammar and history of the Indo-European
dialects—a task vastly too great for us to grapple with here ;
we can only direct our attention to some of the principal
and characteristic features of the development.

The first beginning of polysyllabism seems to have been
made by compounding together roots of the two classes
already described, pronominal and verbal. Thus were produced true forms, in which the indeterminate radical idea
received a definite significance and application. The addition, for example, to the verbal root *vak*, ' speaking,' of
pronominal elements *mi, si, ti* (these are the earliest historically traceable forms of the endings : they were probably
yet earlier *ma, sa, ta*), in which ideas of the nearer and
remoter relation, of the first, second, and third persons, were
already distinguished, produced combinations *vakmi, vaksi,*

vakti, to which usage assigned the meaning 'I here speak,' 'thou there speakest,' 'he yonder speaks,' laying in them the idea of predication or assertion, the essential characteristic which makes a verb instead of a noun, just as we put the same into the ambiguous element, *love,* when we say *I love.* Other pronominal elements, mainly of compound form, indicating plurality of subject, made in like manner the three persons of the plural: they were *masi* (*ma-si,* 'I-thou,' i.e. 'we'), *tasi* (*ta-si,* 'he-thou,' i.e. 'ye'), and *anti* (of more doubtful genesis). A dual number of the same three persons was likewise added; but the earliest form and derivation of its endings cannot be satisfactorily made out. Thus was produced the first verbal tense, the simplest and most immediate of all derivative forms from roots. The various shapes which its endings have assumed in the later languages of the family have already more than once been referred to, in the way of illustration of the processes of linguistic growth: our *th* or *s,* in *he goeth* or *goes,* still distinctly represents the *ti* of the third person singular; and in *am* we have a solitary relic of the *mi* of the first. Doubtless the tense was employed at the outset as general predicative form, being neither past, present, nor future, but all of them combined, and doing duty as either, according as circumstances required, and as sense and connection explained; destitute, in short, of any temporal or modal character; but other verbal forms by degrees grew out of it, or allied themselves with it, assuming the designation of other modifications of predicative meaning, and leaving to it the office of an indicative present. The prefixion of a pronominal adverb, *a* or *ā,* the so-called "augment," pointing to a 'there' or 'then' as one of the conditions of the action signified, produced a distinctively past or preterit tense. Although only very scanty and somewhat dubious traces of such an augment-preterit (aorist or imperfect) are found in any languages of the family beside the Aryan and the Greek, it is looked upon as an original formation, once shared by them all. Again, the repetition of the root, either complete, or by "reduplication," as we term it, the repetition of its initial part, was made to indicate symboli-

cally the completion of the action signified by the root, and
furnished another past tense, a perfect: for example, from
the root *dā*, 'give,' Sanskrit *dadāu*, Greek *dedōka*, Latin
dedi; from *dhā*, 'put, make,' Greek *tetheika*, Old High-
German *tēta*, Anglo-Saxon *dide*, our *did*. This reduplicated
perfect, as is well known, is a regular part of the scheme of
Greek conjugation; in the Latin, not a few of the oldest
verbs show the same, in full, or in more or less distinct
traces; the Mœso-Gothic has preserved it in a considerable
number of verbs (for example, in *haihald*, 'held,' from *haldan*,
'hold;' *saislep*, 'slept,' from *slepan*, 'sleep'); in the other
Germanic dialects it is nearly confined to the single word
did, already quoted. Moods were added by degrees : a
conjunctive, having for its sign a union-vowel, *a*, interposed
between root and endings, and bearing perhaps a symbolical
meaning; and an optative, of which the sign is *i* or *ia* in the
same position, best explained as a verbal root, meaning
' wish, desire.' From this optative descends the " subjunctive " of all the Germanic dialects. The earliest future
appears to have been made by compounding with the root
the already developed optative of the verb ' to be,' *as-yā-mi;*
for ' I shall call,' then, the language literally said ' I may be
calling' (*vak-s-yā-mi*). Of primitive growth, too, was a reflexive or " middle " voice, characterized by an extension of
the personal endings, which is most plausibly explained as a
repetition of them, once as subject and once as object : thus,
vak-mai, for *vak-ma-mi*, ' call-I-me,' i.e. ' I call myself: ' it
was also soon employed in a passive sense, ' I am called '—
as reflexives, of various age and form, have repeatedly been
so employed, or have been converted into distinct passives,
in the history of Indo-European language.* Other secondary forms of the verb, as intensives, desideratives, causa-
tives, were created by various modifications of the root,
or compositions with other roots; yet such verbal derivatives have played only a subordinate part in the develop-

---

* The Latin passive, for instance, is of reflexive origin, as is that of the
Scandinavian Germanic dialects. Among modern European tongues, the
Italian is especially noticeable for its familiar use of reflexive phrases in a
passive sense . thus, *si dice*, ' it says itself,' for ' it is said.'

ment of the languages of our family, and need not be dwelt
upon here.   Of more consequence is the frequent formation
of a special theme for the present tense, to which was then
added a corresponding imperfect, made by means of the
augment.   This was accomplished in various ways: either
by vowel-increment (as in Greek *leipō*, from *lip*, 'leave '),
by reduplication (as in Greek *dadāmi*, from *dā*: the repetition of the root doubtless indicated repetition or continuity
of the action), or by the addition or even insertion of formative elements (as in Greek *deiknumi* from *dik*, 'point out,'
Sanskrit *yunajmi* from *yuj*, 'join;' Greek *gignōscō*, Latin
gnosco, from *gnā*, 'know '); these last are, at least in part,
noun-suffixes, and the forms they make are by origin de-
nominatives.

Of this system of primitive verbal forms, produced before
the separation of the family into branches, almost every
branch has abandoned some part, while each has also new
forms of its own to show, originated partly for supplying the
place of that which was lost, partly in order to fill up the
scheme to greater richness, and capacity of nicer and more
varied expression.   The Greek verb is, among them all, the
most copious in its wealth, the most subtle and expressive
in its distinctions: it has lost hardly anything that was
original, and has created a host of new forms, some of which
greatly tax the ingenuity of the comparative philologist who
would explain their genesis.   The Latin follows not very
far behind, having made up its considerable losses, and supplied some new uses, by combinations of secondary growth:
such are its imperfect in *bam*, its future in *bo*, and its derivative perfects in *ui* and *si*, in all of which are seen the
results of composition with the roots of the substantive
verb.   Both these are greatly superior to the Sanskrit, in
copiousness of forms, and in preciseness of their application.
The Germanic verb was reduced at one period almost to the
extreme of poverty, having saved only the ancient present,
which was used also in the sense of a future, and a preterit,
the modern representative of the original reduplicated perfect; each of the two tenses having also its subjunctive
mood.   The existing dialects of the branch have supplied a

host of new expressions for tense and mood by the extensive
employment of auxiliaries, which, in their way, afford an admirable analytic substitute for the old synthetic forms.   To
trace out and describe in full the history of the Indo-
European verb, in these and in the other branches of the
family, showing the contractions and expansions which
it has undergone, down even to such recent additions as the
future of the Romanic tongues, and our own preterit in *d*
(the reason and method of whose creation have been explained above, in the third lecture), would be a most interesting and instructive task ; but it is one which we may not
venture here to undertake.

To follow back to its very beginnings the genesis of nouns,
and of the forms of nouns, is much more difficult than to
explain the origin of verbal forms.   Some nouns—of which
the Latin *vox* (*voc-s*), 'a calling, a voice,' and *rex* (*reg-s*),
'one ruling, a king,' are as familiar examples as any within
our reach—are produced directly from the roots, by the addition of a different system of inflectional endings ; the idea
of substantiation or impersonation of the action expressed
by the root being arbitrarily laid in them by usage, as was
the idea of predication in the forms of the verb.   The two
words we have instanced may be taken as typical examples
of the two classes of derivatives coming most immediately
and naturally from the root : the one indicating the action
itself, the other, either adjectively or substantively, the
actor ; the one being of the nature of an infinitive, or abstract verbal noun, the other of a participle, or verbal adjective, easily convertible into an appellative.   Even such
derivatives, however, as implying a greater modification of
the radical idea than is exhibited by the simplest verbal
forms, appear to have been from the first mainly made by
means of formative elements, suffixes of derivation, comparable with those which belong to the moods and tenses, and
the secondary conjugations of the verb.   Precisely what
these suffixes were, in their origin and primitive substance,
and what were the steps of the process by which they lost
their independence, and acquired their peculiar value as
modifying elements, it is not in most cases feasible to tell.

But they were obviously in great part of pronominal origin,
and in the acts of linguistic usage which stamped upon
them their distinctive value there is much which would
seem abrupt, arbitrary, or even perhaps inconceivable, to one
who has not been taught by extensive studies among various
tongues how violent and seemingly far-fetched are the mutations and transfers to which the material of linguistic structure is often submitted—on how remote an analogy, how
obscure a suggestion, a needed name or form is sometimes
founded.   Verbal roots, as well as pronominal, were certainly also pressed early into the same service : composition
of root with root, of derived form with form, the formation
of derivative from derivative, went on actively, producing in
sufficient variety the means of limitation and individualiza-
tion of the indeterminate radical idea, of its reduction
to appellative condition, so as to be made capable of designating by suitable names the various beings, substances, acts,
states, and qualities, observed both in the world of matter
and in that of mind.

This class of derivatives from roots was provided with
another, a movable, set of suffixes, which we call case-endings, terminations of declension.   Where, as in the case of
our two examples *vox* and *rex*, the theme of declension was
coincident with the verbal root, the declensional endings
themselves were sufficient to mark the distinction of noun
from verb, without the aid of a suffix of derivation.   They
formed a large and complicated system, and were charged
with the designation of various relations.   In the first place,
they indicated case, or the kind of relation sustained by the
noun to which they were appended to the principal action of
the sentence in which it was used, whether as subject, as direct object, or as indirect object with implication of meanings
which we express by means of prepositions, such as *with, from,
in, of.* Of cases thus distinguished there were seven.   Three
of them distinctly indicated local relations : the ablative (of
which the earliest traceable form has *t* or *d* for its ending :
thus, Sanskrit *aҫvāt*, Old Latin *equod*, 'from a horse')
denoted the relation expressed by *from ;* the locative (with
the ending *i*), that expressed by *in ;* the instrumental (with

the ending *ā*), that expressed by *with*, or *by*—the idea of
adjacency or accompaniment passing naturally into that of
means, instrument, or cause. Two cases, the dative and
genitive, designated relations of a less physical character :
the former (with the ending *ai*) we should render by *for* before the noun ; the latter (its ending is *asya* or *as*) expressed
general pertinence or possession. Then the accusative (with
the sign *m*) assumed the office of indicating the directest
dependent relation, that which even with us is expressed
without the aid of a preposition—the objective—as well as
that most immediate relation of motion which we signify by
to. The nominative, finally, has also its ending, *s*, in the
presence of which is strikingly exhibited the tendency of
the earliest Indo-European language to make every vocable
a true form, to give to every theme, in every relation, a sign
of its mode of application, a formative element. Besides
these seven proper cases, the vocative or interjectional case,
the form of address, also makes a part of the scheme of declension ; it has no distinctive ending, but is identical with
the theme or the nominative case, or is only phonetically
altered from them.

The declensional endings which we have instanced are
those of the singular number. To explain their origin in
any such way as shows us their precise value as independent
elements, and the nature of the act of transfer by which they
were made signs of case-relations, is not practicable. Pronominal elements are distinctly traceable in most of them,
and may have assumed something of a prepositional force
before their combination. The genitive affix is very likely
to have been at the first, like many genitive affixes of later
date in the history of the Indo-European languages, one
properly forming a derivative adjective : and it is not impossible that the dative ending was of the same nature.

There are many existing tongues which have for the
plurals of their nouns precisely the same case-endings as for
the singular, only adding them along with a special pluralizing suffix. The attempt has been made* to find such a

---

* By Professor Schleicher, in his Compendium of Indo-European Comparative Grammar.

plural-suffix also among the plural endings of our earliest nouns, but with only faint and doubtful success; if these are actually of composite derivation, the marks of their composition are hidden almost beyond hope of discovery. We must be content to say for the present, at least, that the suffixes of declension indicate by their differences the distinctions of number as well as of case. And, among the nouns as well as the verbs of the primitive language, not only a plural, but also a dual, was distinguished from the singular by its appropriate endings, which are of not less problematical derivation, and, in the earliest condition of speech that we can trace, much fewer in number, being limited to three.

One other distinction, that of gender, was partially dependent for its designation upon the case-endings. We have already (in the third lecture) had occasion to refer to the universal classification of objects named, by the earliest language-makers of our family, according to gender, as masculine, feminine, or neuter—a classification only partially depending upon the actual possession of sexual qualities, and exhibiting, in the modern dialects which have retained it, an aspect of almost utter and hopeless arbitrariness. Nor, as was before remarked, is it possible even in the oldest Indo-European tongues to trace and point out otherwise than most dimly and imperfectly the analogies, apparent or fanciful, which have determined the grammatical gender of the different words and classes of words : such is the difficulty and obscurity of the subject that we must avoid here entering into any details respecting it. It appears that, in the first place, from the masculine, as the fundamental form, certain words were distinguished as possessed of feminine qualities, and marked by a difference of derivative ending, often consisting in a prolongation of the final vowel of the ending; while to all the derivatives formed by certain endings like qualities were attributed. The distinction was doubtless made in the beginning by the endings of derivation alone, those of case having no share in it; but it passed over to some extent into those of case also, the feminine here again showing a tendency to broader and fuller forms.

18

The separation of neuter from masculine was both later in
origin and less substantially marked, having little to do with
suffixes of derivation, and extending through only a small
part of the declensional endings (it is mainly limited to the
nominative and accusative).

This system of Indo-European declension has suffered not
less change in the history of the various branches of the
family than has that of conjugational inflection. The dual
number was long ago given up, as of insignificant practical
value, by most of the branches : the oldest Aryan dialects
exhibit it most fully; it also makes some figure in ancient
Greek ; but even the most antique Germanic tongues have
a dual only in the personal pronouns of the first and second
persons ; and the Latin shows but the faintest traces of it
(in the peculiar nominative and accusative endings of *duo*,
'two,' and *ambo*, ' both '). As regards, again, the cases, the
complete scheme only appears in the Indian and Persian ;
and even there the process of its reduction has begun, by
the fusion, in one or another number, and in one or another
class of words, of two cases into one—that is to say, the
loss of the one as a distinct form, and the transference
of its functions to another. In the oldest known condition
of the classic tongues, this process has gone yet farther ; in
Latin, the locative and instrumental are thus fused with the
dative and ablative ; and in Greek, the genitive and ablative have been also compressed into one. The oldest
Germanic dialects have nominative, accusative, genitive, and
dative ; with traces of the instrumental, which the later
tongues have lost. But the modern development of the
prepositions, and their rise to importance as independent
indicators of the relations formerly expressed by the case-
endings, has brought with it a yet more sweeping abandonment of the latter. We, in English, have saved a single
oblique case, the ancient genitive, so restricting its use at
the same time as to make a simple " possessive " of it—and
further, among the pronouns, an accusative or " objective "
(*me*, *us*, etc., and *whom*) ; in the Romanic languages, the
noun has become wholly stripped of case-inflection. In
what manner we have rid ourselves of the distinctions of

grammatical gender has been shown in a previous lecture
(the third) : we still keep up a linguistic distinction of
natural gender by the use of our generic pronouns of the
third person, *he*, *she*, and *it;* the modern Persian has
abandoned even that, and the consideration of sex no longer
enters into it in any way, save in the vocabulary, in the use
of such words as *son* and *daughter*, *bull* and *cow*. Of the
other modern tongues of the family, some, like these two,
have eliminated from their grammatical systems the distinctions of gender ; some, like the French, have reduced the
three genders to two, by effacing the differences of masculine and neuter ; but the larger part, like the German, still
faithfully adhere to the inherited distinction of masculine,
feminine, and neuter, so long ago established.

The ancient Indo-European language made no difference,
as regarded declension, between its two classes of nouns,
nouns substantive and nouns adjective.   In their genesis,
the two are but one ; the same suffixes, to no small extent,
form both ; each passes by the most easy and natural transfer
into the other ; whether a given word indicating the possession of quality should be used attributively or predicatively,
or as an appellative, was a question of subordinate consequence.   The pronouns, also, both substantive and adjective, were inflected by a declension mainly corresponding,
although marked by some peculiarities, and tending earlier
to irregular forms.

With conjugation and declension, the subject of grammatical structure is, in fact, as good as exhausted : everything in language is originally either verb or noun.   To the
other parts of speech, then, which have been developed out
of these, we shall need to give but a brief consideration.

Adverbs, the most ancient and necessary class of indeclin-
able words, or particles, are by origin, in the earliest stage
of language as in the latest, forms of declension, cases of
substantives, or adjectives, or pronouns.   We have seen
already how our adverbs in *ly* were elaborated out of former
oblique cases (instrumentals) of adjectives in *líc* ('like ') ;
so also the usual adverbial ending *ment* of the Romanic
languages is the Latin ablative *mente*, ' with mind ' (thus,

18 *

French *bonnement*, 'kindly,' is *bonâ mente*, 'with kind intent') ; the *ōs* which forms Greek adverbs (for example, *kakōs*, 'ill,' from *kakos*, ' bad') is the original ablative case-ending : and we are doubtless to infer that both the general classes of adverbs, made by means of apparent adverbial suffixes, and the more irregular and obscure single words, of kindred meaning and office, which we trace in the earliest vocabulary of the family, are of like derivation. Those parts of speech which we call prepositions were originally such, not in our present understanding of the term, but according to its etymological signification ; they were adverbial prefixes to the verb, serving to point out more clearly the direction of the verbal action ; it was only later, and by degrees, that they detached themselves from the verb, and came to belong to the noun, furthering the disappearance of its case-endings, and assuming their office. The earliest of them, as was to be expected from their designation of direction, trace their origin chiefly to pronominal roots ; but in part, also, they come from verbal. Conjunctions, connectives of sentences, are almost altogether of comparatively late growth ; the earliest style was too simple to call for their use : we have seen examples already (in the third lecture) of the mode in which they were arrived at, by attenuation of the meaning of words possessing by origin a more full and definite significance. Other products of a like attenuation, made generally at a decidedly modern date, are the articles : the definite article always growing out of a demonstrative pronoun ; the indefinite, out of the numeral *one*.

The interjections, finally, however expressive and pregnant with meaning they may be, are not in a proper sense parts of speech ; they do not connect themselves with other words, and enter into the construction of sentences ; they are either the direct outbursts of feeling, like *oh ! ah !* or else, like *st ! sh !* mere " vocal gestures," immediate intimations of will—in both cases alike, substitutes for more elaborate and distinct expression. They require, however, to be referred to here, not merely for the sake of completeness, but also because many words come to be employed only interjectionally which were once full parts of speech; even a whole phrase being, as it were, reduced to a single pregnantly uttered exclamation: examples are *alas!* that is, *O me lasso*, 'oh weary me!' *zounds!* 'I swear by *God's wounds*,' *dear me!* that is, *dio mio*, 'my God!' and many others.

Such are, compendiously and briefly stated, the steps by which Indo-European language was developed out of monosyllabic weakness into the wealth and fertility of inflective speech. At what rate they went on, how rapid was the growth after its first inception, we know not, and we can hardly hope ever to know. The conditions of that primitive period, and the degree in which they might have been able to quicken the now sluggish processes of word-combination and formation, are so much beyond our ken that even our conjectures respecting them have—at least as yet—too little value to be worth recording. What may have been the numbers of the community which laid the foundation of all the Indo-European tongues, and what its relation to other then existing communities, are also points hitherto involved in the deepest obscurity. But we know that, before the separation, whether simultaneous or successive, of this community into the parts which afterward became founders of the different tongues of Europe and south-western Asia, the principal part of the linguistic development had already taken place— enough for its traces to remain ineffaceable, even to the present day, in the speech of all the modern representatives of the family: the inflective character of Indo-European language, the main distinctions of its parts of speech, its methods of word-formation and inflection, were elaborated and definitely established.

But, though we cannot pretend to fix the length of time required for this process of growth, in terms of centuries or of thousands of years, we can at least see clearly that it must have gone on in a slow and gradual manner, and occupied no brief period. Such is the nature of the forces by which all change in language has been shown to be effected, that anything like a linguistic revolution, a rapid and sweeping modification of linguistic structure, is wholly impossible—and most especially, a revolution of a construct-

ive character, building up a fabric of words and forms.
Every item of the difference by which a given dialect is distinguished from its ancestor, or from another dialect having
the same ancestry, is the work of a gradual change of usage
made by the members of a community in the speech which
they were every day employing as their means of mutual
communication, and which, if too rapidly altered, would not
answer the purposes of communication. It takes time for
even that easiest of changes, a phonetic corruption or abbreviation, to win the assent of a community, and become
established as the law of their speech : it takes decades, and
even generations, or centuries, for an independent word
to run through the series of modifications in form and meaning which are necessary to its conversion into a formative element. That the case was otherwise at the very beginning,
we have not the least reason for believing. The opinion of
those who hold that the whole structure of a language was
produced "at a single stroke" is absolutely opposed to all
the known facts of linguistic history ; it has no inductive
basis whatever ; it rests upon arbitrary assumption, and
is supported by à priori reasoning. There must have been
a period of some duration—and, for aught we know, it may
have been of very long duration—when the first speakers of
our language talked together in their scanty dialect of formless monosyllables. The first forms, developed words containing a formal as well as a radical element, cannot have
come into existence otherwise than by slow degrees, worked
out by the unconscious exercise of that ingenuity in the
adaptation of means to ends, of that sense for symmetry, for
finished, even artistic, production, which have ever been
qualities especially characterizing our division of the human
race. Every form thus elaborated led the way to others : it
helped to determine a tendency, to establish an analogy,
which facilitated their further production. A protracted
career of formal development was run during that primitive
period of Indo-European history which preceded the dispersion of the branches : words and forms were multiplied
until even a maximum of synthetic complexity, of fullness of
inflective wealth, had been reached, from which there has

been in later times, upon the whole, a gradual descent and impoverishment.

Here we must pause a little, to consider an objection urged by some linguistic scholars of rank and reputation against the truth of the views we have been defending, as to the primitive monosyllabism of Indo-European language, and its gradual emergence out of that condition—an objection which has more apparent legitimacy and force than any of those hitherto noticed. It is this. In ascending the current of historical development of the languages of our family, say the objectors, instead of approaching a monosyllabic condition, we seem to recede farther and farther from it. The older dialects are more polysyllabic than the later : where our ancestors used long and complicated forms, we are content with brief ones, or we have replaced them with phrases composed of independent words. Thus, to recur once more to a former example, for an earlier *lagamasi* we say *we lie;* thus, again, for the Latin *fuisset*, the French says simply *fût*, while we express its meaning by four distinct words, *he might have been*. Modern languages are full of verbal forms of this latter class, which substitute syntactical for substantial combinations. The relations of case, too, formerly signified only by means of declensional endings, have lost by degrees this mode of expression, and have come to be indicated by prepositions, independent words. This is what is well known as the "analytical" tendency in linguistic growth. Our own English tongue exhibits its effects in the highest known degree, having reduced near half the vocabulary it possesses to a monosyllabic form, and got rid of almost all its inflections, so that it expresses grammatical relations chiefly by relational words, auxiliaries and connectives : but it is only an extreme example of the results of a movement generally perceptible in modern speech. If, then, during the period when we can watch their growth step by step, languages have become less synthetic, words less polysyllabic, must we not suppose that it was always so ; that human speech began with highly complicated forms, which from the very first have been undergoing reduction to simpler and briefer shape ?

This is, as we have confessed, a plausible argument, but it is at the same time a thoroughly unsound and superficial one. It skims the surface of linguistic phenomena, without penetrating to the causes which produce them. It might pass muster, and be allowed to determine our opinions, if the analytical tendency alone had been active since our knowledge of language began; if we had seen old forms worn out, but no new forms made; if we had seen words put side by side to furnish analytic combinations, but no elements fused together into synthetic union. But we know by actual experience how both synthetic and analytic forms are produced, and what are the influences and circumstances which favour the production of the one rather than of the other. The constructive as well as the destructive forces in language admit of illustration, and have been by us illustrated, with modern as well as with ancient examples. Both have been active together, during all the ages through which we can follow linguistic growth. There have never been forms which were not undergoing continual modification and mutilation, under the influence of the already recognized tendencies to forget the genesis of a word in its later application, and then to reduce it to a shape adapted to more convenient utterance; there was also never a time when reparation was not making for this waste in part by the fresh development of true forms out of old materials. Nor has the tendency been everywhere and in all respects downward, toward poverty of synthetic forms, throughout the historic period. If the Greek and Latin system of declension is scantier than that of the original language of the family, their system of conjugation, especially the Greek, is decidedly richer, filled up with synthetic forms of secondary growth; the modern Romanic tongues have lost something of this wealth, but they have also added something to it, and their verb, leaving out of view its compound tenses, will bear favourable comparison with that which was the common inheritance of the branches. Some of the modern dialects of India, on the other hand, having once lost, in the ordinary course of phonetic corruption, the ancient case-terminations of the Sanskrit, have replaced them by a new scheme, not

less full and complete than its predecessor. The Russian of
the present day possesses in some respects a capacity of
synthetic development hardly, if at all, excelled by that of any
ancient tongue. For example, it takes the two independent
words *bez Boga*, ' without God,' and fuses them into a theme
from which it draws a whole list of derivatives. Thus, first,
by adding an adjective suffix, it gets the adjective *bezbozhnïï*,
' godless ; ' a new suffix appended to this makes a noun,
bezbozhnik, ' a godless person, an atheist ; ' the noun gives
birth to a denominative verb, *bezbozhnichat*, ' to be an atheist;'
from this verb, again, come a number of derivatives, giving
to the verbal idea the form of adjective, agent, act, and
so on : the abstract is *bezbozhnichestvo*, ' the condition of
being an atheist ; ' while, once more, a new verb is made
from this abstract, namely *bezbozhnichestvovat*, literally ' to be
in the condition of being a godless person.' A more intricate synthetic form than this could not easily be found in
Greek, Latin, or Sanskrit ; but it is no rare or exceptional
case in the language from which we have extracted it ;
it rather represents, by a striking instance, the general character of Russian word-formation and derivation.

It is obviously futile, then, to talk of an uninterrupted
and universal reduction of the resources of synthetic expression among the languages of the Indo-European family, or
to allow ourselves to be forced by an alleged pervading
tendency toward analytic forms into accepting synthesis, inflective richness, as the ultimate condition of the primitive
tongue from which they are descended. If certain among
them have replaced one or another part of their synthetic
structure by analytic forms, if some—as the Germanic
family in general, and, above all, the English—have taken on
a prevailingly analytic character, these are facts which we
are to seek to explain by a careful study of the circumstances
and tendencies which have governed their respective development. If, moreover, as has been conceded, the general bent
has for a long time been toward a diminution of synthesis
and a predominance of analytic expressions, another question,
of wider scope, is presented us for solution ; but the form
in which it offers itself is this : why should the forces which

produce synthetic combinations have reached their height of
activity during the ante-historic period of growth, and have
been gradually gained upon later, at varying rates in different communities, by those of another order? We do not
in the least feel impelled to doubt the historic reality of the
earliest combinations, their parallelism, in character and
origin, with those which we see springing up in modern
times. That we now say analytically *I did love*, or *deal*, or
lead is no ground for questioning that our ancestors said
compositely *I love-did, deal-did, lead-did*, and then worked
them down into the true synthetic forms *I loved, dealt, led*.
The cause which produced the different nature of the two
equivalent expressions *I loved* and *I did love*, composed, as
they are, of identical elements, was a difference in habit of
the language at the periods when they were respectively
generated. Any language can do what it is in the habit of
doing. We can turn almost any substantive in our vocabulary into a *quasi* adjective—saying *a gold watch, a grass
slope, a church mouse*, and so on—because, through the intermediate step of loose compounds like *goldsmith, grasshopper,
churchman*, we have acquired the habit of looking upon our
substantives as convertible to adjective uses without alteration and without ceremony. Neither the Frenchman nor
the German can do the same thing, simply because his
speech presents no analogies for such a procedure. We, on
the other hand, like the French, have lost the power to form
compounds with anything like the facility possessed by the
ancient tongue from which ours is descended and by some
of its modern representatives, as the German ; not because
they would not be intelligible if we formed them, but because,
under the operation of traceable circumstances in our linguistic history, we have grown out of the habit of so combining our words, and into the habit of merely collocating
them, with or without connectives. Now we have only to
apply this principle upon a wider scale, and under other
conditions of language, in order to find, as I think, a sufficient answer to the question which is engaging our attention. When once, after we know not how long a period of
expectation and tentative effort, the formation of words by

synthesis had begun in the primitive Indo-European language, and had been found so fruitful of the means of varied and distinct expression, it became the habit of the language. The more numerous the new forms thus produced, the greater was the facility of producing more, because the material of speech was present to the minds of its speakers as endowed with that capacity of combination and fusion of which the results in every part of its structure were so apparent. But the edifice after a time became, as it were, complete; a sufficient working-apparatus of declensional, conjugational, and derivative endings was elaborated to answer the purposes of an inflective tongue; fewer and rarer additions were called for, as occasional supplements of the scheme, or substitutes for lost forms. Thus began a period in which the formative processes were more and more exclusively an inheritance from the past, less and less of recent acquisition; and as the origin of forms was lost sight of, obscured by the altering processes of phonetic corruption, it became more and more difficult to originate new ones, because fewer analogies of such forms were present to the apprehension of the language-makers, as incentives and guides to their action. On the other hand, the expansion of the whole vocabulary to wealth of resources, to the possession of varied and precise phraseology, furnished a notably increased facility of indicating ideas and relations by descriptive phrases, by groups of independent words. This mode of expression, then, always more or less used along with the other, began to gain ground upon it, and, of course, helped to deaden the vitality of the latter, and to render it yet more incapable of extended action. That tendency to the conscious and reflective use of speech which comes in with the growth of culture especially, and which has already been repeatedly pointed out as one of the main checks upon all the processes of linguistic change, cast its influence in the same direction; since the ability to change the meaning and application of words, even to the degree of reducing them to the expression of formal relations, is a much more fundamental and indefeasible property of speech than the ability to combine and fuse them bodily together. Then, when peculiar circumstances in the history of a language have arisen, to cause the rapid and general decay and effacement of ancient forms, as in our language and the Romanic, the process of formative composition, though never wholly extinct, has been found too inactive to repair the losses; they have been made up by syntactical collocation, and the language has taken on a prevailingly analytic character.

These considerations and such as these, I am persuaded, furnish a satisfactory explanation of the preponderating tendency to the use of analytic forms exhibited by modern languages; as they also account for the greatly varying degree in which the tendency exhibits itself. But even should they be found insufficient, this would only throw open for a renewed investigation the question respecting the ground of the tendency; the general facts in the history of earliest development of our languages would still remain sure, beyond the reach of cavil, since they are established by evidence which cannot be gainsaid, contained in the structure of the most ancient forms. We are compelled to believe that the formative processes which we see going on, in decreasing abundance, in the historically recorded ages of linguistic life, are continuations and repetitions of the same constructive acts by which has been built up the whole homogeneous structure of inflective speech.

One more theoretic objection to the doctrine of a primitive Indo-European monosyllabism we may take the time to notice, more on account of the respectability of its source than for any cogency which it in itself possesses. M. Renan, namely,* asserts that this doctrine is the product of a mistaken habit of mind, taught us by the artificial scholastic methods of philosophizing, and leading us to regard simplicity as, in the order of time, anterior to complexity; while, in fact, the human mind does not begin with analysis; its first acts being, on the contrary, complex, obscure, synthetic, containing all the parts, indistinctly heaped together. To this claim respecting the character of the mental act we may safely yield a hearty assent; but, instead of inferring

* In his work on the Origin of Language, seventh chapter.

from it that "the idea *expressed itself* at the beginning with
its whole array of determinatives and in a perfect unity,"
and that hence, "in the history of languages, synthesis is
primitive, and analysis, far from being the natural form of
the human mind, is only the slow result of its development,"
we shall be conducted to a precisely contrary conclusion.
The synthetic forms which we are asked to regard as original
have not the character of something indistinctly heaped
together; they contain the clear and express designation of
the radical idea and of its important relations ; they represent by a linguistic synthesis the results of a mental analysis.
The idea is, indeed, *conceived* in unity, involving all its aspects and relations ; but these cannot be separately *expressed*
until the mind has separated them, until practice in the
use of language has enabled it to distinguish them, and to
mark each by an appropriate sign. In *amabor*, the (Latin)
word cited as an example of synthesis, are contained precisely
the same designations as in the equivalent English analytic
phrase, '*I shall be loved:* ' *ama* expresses 'loving ; ' *bo* unites
future-sign and ending designating the first person ; and the
r is the sign of passivity. Who can possibly maintain that
a system of such forms, gathered about a root, exhibits the
results of experience, of developed acuteness, in thought and
speech, any less clearly than the analytic forms of our English conjugation ? The two are only different methods of
expressing the same "array of determinatives." The first
synthetic mental act, on the contrary, is truly represented
by the bare root : there all is, indeed, confused and indis-
crete. The earliest radical words, when first uttered, stood
for entire sentences, expressed judgments, as undeniably as the
fully elaborated phrases which we now employ, giving every
necessary relation its proper designation. It is thus that,
even at present, children begin to talk ; a radical word or
two means in their mouths a whole sentence : *up* signifies
' take me up into your lap ; ' *go walk*, ' I want to go out to
walk,' or ' I went to walk,' or various other things, which
the circumstances sufficiently explain ; but forms, inflections,
connectives, signs of tense and mode and condition, they do
not learn to use until later, when their minds have acquired

power to separate the indistinct cognition into its parts.
M. Renan, in short, has made a very strange confusion of
analytic style of expression with mental analysis : all expression of relations, whether by means that we call synthetic or
analytic, is the result and evidence of analysis ; and his own
thesis respecting the complexity in obscurity of unpractised
and uninstructed thought, brings us directly to a recognition
of the radical stage of Indo-European language as the necessary historical basis of its inflective development.

This development, it may be remarked in conclusion, has
been gradual and steadily progressive, being governed in
both its synthetic and analytic phases by the same causes
which universally regulate linguistic growth, and which have
been here repeatedly set forth or referred to : namely, on the
one hand, the traditional influence of the stores of expression already worked out and handed down, consisting in the
education given by them to thought, and the constraining
force exerted by their analogies ; and, on the other hand,
the changing character and capacity, the varying circumstances and needs, of the community of speakers, during the
different periods of their history.   It has experienced no
grand revolution, no sudden shift of direction, no pervading
change of tendency.   There is no cleft, as is sometimes
assumed, parting ancient tongues from modern, justifying the
recognition of different forces, the admission of different
possibilities, in the one and in the other.   Nor are we to
regard the energies of a community as absorbed in the work
of language-making more at one period than at another.
Language-making is always done unconsciously and by the
way, as it were : it is one of the incidents of social life, an
accompaniment and result of intellectual activity, not an
end toward which effort is directed, nor a task in whose performance is expended force which might have been otherwise employed.   The doctrine that a race first constructs its
language, and then, and not till then, is ready to commence
its historic career, is as purely fanciful as anything in the
whole great chapter of à priori theorizings about speech.
No living language ever ceases to be constructed, or is less
rapidly built upon in ages of historic activity : only the style

of the fabric is, even more than the rate, determined by external circumstances. It is because the very earliest epochs of recorded history are still far distant from the beginnings of Indo-European language, as of human language generally, that we find its peculiar structure completely developed when it is first discovered by our researches. We have fully acknowledged the powerful influence exerted by culture over the growth of language : but neither the accident of position and accessibility to other nations that at a certain time brings a race forward into the light of record, and makes it begin to be an actor or a factor in the historic drama, nor its more gradual and independent advance to conspicuousness in virtue of acquired civilization and political power, can have any direct effect whatever upon its speech. The more thorough we are in our study of the living and recent forms of human language, the more rigorous in applying the deductions thence drawn to the forms current in ante-historic periods, the more cautious about admitting forces and effects in unknown ages whereof the known afford us no example or criterion, so much the more sound and trustworthy will be the conclusions at which we shall arrive. It is but a shallow philology, as it is a shallow geology, which explains past changes by catastrophes and cataclysms.

We have now long enough given our almost exclusive attention to the language of the Indo-European race, and, in the next two lectures, shall proceed to define the boundaries and sketch the characters, as well as we may, of the other grand divisions of human speech.

LECTURE VIII.

Families of languages, how established. Characteristic features of Indo-
European language. Semitic family : its constitution, historic value,
literatures, and linguistic character. Relation of Semitic to Indo-
European language. Scythian or Altaic family : its five branches :
their history, literatures, and character. Unity of the family somewhat doubtful.

WE have now taken a survey of the most important
phenomena of language and of linguistic growth, as they
are illustrated in the forms of speech peculiar to the Indo-
European family. We have seen in what scanty beginnings
our own tongue and those related to it had their origin, and
what, in brief, were the steps by which they advanced from
the weakness and barrenness of radical monosyllabism to the
rich completeness of inflective speech. These matters were
brought to light in the course of the regular prosecution of
our fundamental inquiry, " why *we* speak as we do," it
having been made to appear that our English linguistic
tradition had been, during a protracted and most important
period, one with that of all the other members of the family
mentioned. But now, considering the possibility that the
Indo-European family may be found, after all, only a constituent group in some yet vaster family—or even, supposing
that possibility to be disproved, considering the impropriety
of our so circumscribing our interests and our sympathies
as to understand by the " we " of our question anything
less than the whole human race—it becomes our duty next
to pass in review the other great linguistic families which

the science of language has established, and to see wherein they agree with that which has hitherto absorbed the chief share of our attention, and wherein they differ from it. Moreover, it is clear that we should not appreciate the peculiar character of the mode of communication and expression belonging to our family, we should not even know that it had a distinctive character of its own, that the problem of speech was not solved in an identical manner by all parts of the human race, if we did not look to see how the other families have constructed the fabric of their language. We shall, accordingly, devote the present lecture and the one next following to such an examination; making it, of course, much more brief and cursory than has been our examination of Indo-European language.

There was the more reason why we should draw out with some fullness of detail the recognized history of development of the language which has been most deeply studied and is most thoroughly understood by linguistic scholars, inasmuch as some of the main results thereby won have a universal value. Much of that which has been demonstrated to be true respecting Indo-European speech is to be accepted as true respecting all human speech. Not that its historical analysis has been everywhere made so complete as to yield in each case with independent certainty the same results which the study of this one family has yielded. But nothing has been found which is of force to prove the history of language otherwise than, in its most fundamental features, the same throughout the globe; while much has been elicited which favours its homogeneousness: enough, indeed, when taken in connection with the theoretical probabilities of the case, to make the conclusion a sufficiently certain one, that all the varied and complicated forms of speech which now fill the earth have been wrought into their present shape by a like process of gradual development; that all designation of relations is the result of growth; that formative elements have been universally elaborated out of independent words; that the historical germs of language everywhere are of the nature of those simple elements which we have called roots; moreover, that roots have generally, if

19

not without exception, been of the two classes described in the last lecture, pronominal and verbal ; and that, in the earliest stages of growth, forms have been produced especially by the combination of roots of the two classes, the verbal root furnishing the central and substantial idea, the pronominal indicating its modifications and relations.

Linguistic families, now, as at present constituted, are made up of those languages which have traceably had at least a part of their historical development in common ; which have grown together out of the original radical or monosyllabic stage ; which exhibit in their grammatical structure signs, still discoverable by linguistic analysis, of having descended, by the ordinary course of linguistic tradition, from a common ancestor.   We shall see hereafter (in the tenth lecture), indeed, that the science of language does not and cannot deny the possible correspondence of some or all of the families in their ultimate elements, a correspondence anterior to all grammatical development ; but neither does she at present assert that correspondence.   She has carried her classification no farther than her collected material, and her methods of sober and cautious induction from its study, have justified her in doing ; she has stopped grouping where her facts have failed her, where evidences of common descent have become too slight and vague to be longer depended upon : and the limit of her power is now, and is likely ever to be, determined by coincidences of grammatical structure.   The boundaries of every great family, again, are likely to be somewhat dubious ; there can hardly fail to be branches which either parted so early from the general stock, or have, owing to peculiar circumstances in their history, varied so rapidly and fundamentally since they left it, that the tokens of their origin have become effaced almost or quite beyond recognition.   There was a time when the Celtic languages were thus regarded as of doubtful affinity, until a more penetrating study of their material and structure brought to light abundant and unequivocal evidence of their Indo-European descent.   The Albanian, the modern representative of the ancient Illyrian, spoken by the fierce and lawless race which inhabits the mountains of

north-western Greece, is still in the same position; linguistic
scholars are divided in opinion as to whether it is yet proved
to be Indo-European, though with a growing preponderance
upon the affirmative side. Examples of excessive and effacing
differentiation are not wanting in existing speech. There
are now spoken among barbarous peoples in different parts
of the world—as on some of the islands of the Pacific,
among the African tribes, and the aborigines of this continent—dialects in which the processes of linguistic change,
the destruction and reconstruction of words and forms, are
going on at a rate so abnormally rapid, that a dialect, it is
said, becomes unintelligible in a generation or two ; and in a
few centuries all material trace of affinity between idioms of
common descent may become blotted out.   Such exceptional
cases do not take away the value of the genetic method of
investigation, nor derogate from the general certainty of its
results in the classification of languages.   But they do cause
the introduction, cautiously and to a limited extent, of
another indication of probable relationship : namely, concordance in the general method of solution of the linguistic
problem.   It is found that the great families of related
languages differ from one another, not only in the linguistic
material which they employ, in the combinations of sounds
out of which, back to the remotest traceable beginning, they
make their radical and formative elements, and designate
given meanings and relations, but also, and often to no small
degree, in their way of managing their material ; in their
apprehension of the relations of ideas which are to be expressed by the combination of elements, and in the method
in which they apply the resources they possess to the
expression of relations : they differ in the style, as well as
the substance, of their grammatical structure.   It is evident
that the style may be so peculiar and characteristic as to
constitute valid evidence of family relationship, even where
the substance has been altered by variation and substitution
till it presents no trustworthy coincidences.   We shall have
occasion to note and examine, farther on, some of the cases
in which reliance is placed upon morphological correspondences, as they are called, upon correspondences of structural

19 *

form; and also to refer to the morphological classifications
of human languages which are founded upon them—classifications which mainly coincide with genetic, but also more or
less combine and overlap them.

The main characteristic features of the structure of Indo-
European language are readily enough deducible from the
exposition given in the preceding lecture. It generates its
forms by the intimate combination of elements originally independent; in this respect agreeing with nearly all other
known tongues. In its combinations, moreover, the formative element is almost invariably added after the radical,
forming a suffix; the only noteworthy exceptions are the
augment of the primitive preterit tense of the verb, the
negative prefix (our *un*, *in*, in *unthankful*, *incapable*, and the
like), and the more separable elements which we call prepositions (in *intend, pretend, extend, distend,* and so forth) : and
here, too, its usage is paralleled by that of the majority of
spoken languages throughout the world. A more distinctive
characteristic of Indo-European language is the peculiar
aptitude which it possesses for closely combining its radical
and formal elements, for losing sight of their separate individuality, and applying their combination as independent
conventional sign of the object indicated. It disembarrasses
itself of useless reminiscences of the former *status* and
quality of its elements, fuses them completely together, and
exposes the result, as one whole, to the action of all the
wearing and altering processes of linguistic life. In different
constituents of the dialects of our family, in different dialects, and in different stages of their history, this tendency
is seen exhibited in very different degree. In our own
tongue, for instance, in such words as *fully, thankfully, un-
thankfulness,* the combined elements are held distinctly
apart, and are present in their separate substance and office
to the mind of any one who reflects a moment upon the
words; on the other hand, in *ken* and *can*, in *sit* and *set*, in
man and *men*, in *lead* and *led*, in *sing, sang, sung,* and *song,*
in *bind, bound, band,* and *bond,* and other like cases, the
fusion has gone to its utmost extent: various combinations
of subordinate elements with the roots of these words have

caused the development of the roots themselves into varying phonetic forms ; and these have then been applied, at first to support, and afterwards to replace, the primitive means of grammatical expression : an internal flection has come in upon and supplanted the original aggregation. All Indo-European forms are originally of the kind here first illustrated, mere agglutinations of independent elements, whereof a part are reduced to a subordinate value and formal significance ; but they tend, in a marked degree, to pass over into the other kind, indicating formal relations by internal change in the root or theme, instead of by external additions alone.

This tendency is generally regarded as constituting the highest characteristic of the Indo-European dialects, as making them properly *inflective ;* and languages possessing in this sense an inflective character are reckoned to stand at the head of all the forms of human speech. Some, however, are inclined to claim a more original and fundamental importance for the process of internal change in the history of the tongues of our family, to regard a capacity of significant variation of vowel as inherent in their roots, and bearing a regular and conspicuous part in even the earliest steps of their development. The evidence upon which this claim is founded I cannot but regard as altogether insufficient to sustain it. Wherever, in the most ancient as well as the more modern processes of word-formation and inflection, we find internal changes of the root, they are, I am persuaded, of secondary growth, inorganic ; they are called out ultimately by phonetic causes, not originated for the purpose of marking variation of meaning, though sometimes seized and applied to that purpose. To prove the element of internal flection one of prime value in the growth of Indo-European language, it would be necessary to show that the variation of vowel had a distinctly assignable office in the primitive production of words ; that it regularly distinguished from one another certain parts of speech, certain classes of derivatives, certain forms of declension or conjugation ; that it formed guiding analogies, which could be and actually were imitated continuously in the further processes of word-making. But this is far from being the case ; on the con-

trary, the phenomena bear everywhere an irregular and
sporadic character : the change of vowel in the oldest derivatives is only an accompaniment of derivation by means
of suffixes ; it has no constant significance ; it acquires
significance only at second hand, in the manner of a result,
not a cause ; and it remains everywhere as barren of formative force as in the Germanic verbs (where, as was shown
in the third lecture, its infecundity led to the construction
of a new scheme of conjugation), or as in our irregular
plurals like *men* and *feet*, from *man* and *foot*. Only, therefore,
so far as it is regarded as an effect and sign of thorough integration of elements, of complete unity of designation, can
we accept internal change as an exponent of the superiority
of Indo-European speech.

But the peculiarities belonging to the character of our
family of languages will be more clearly apprehensible when
we shall have taken a survey of the other principal forms of
human speech, to which, accordingly, after these necessary
introductory remarks, we now turn.   We shall take up the
families in an order partly geographical, and partly based
upon a consideration of their respective importance.

On both these grounds, there can be no question as to
which group of languages, outside of the Indo-European
domain, ought first to receive our attention.   It is evidently
that one which includes as its principal branches the Hebrew,
the Syriac, and the Arabic.   From the names of its two extreme members, it is sometimes styled the Syro-Arabian family;
but its usual and familiar designation is Semitic or Shemitic,
derived from the name of the patriarch Shem, son of Noah,
who in Genesis is made the ancestor of most of the nations
that speak its dialects.   It is a very distinctly marked group,
and, though occupying but a limited tract in the south-
western corner of Asia, with some of the adjacent parts
of Africa, is of the highest consequence, by reason of the
conspicuous part which the race to which it belongs has
played in the history of the world.   This is too well known
to require to be referred to here otherwise than in the
briefest manner.

The Phenicians, inhabiting Tyre, Sidon, and the adjacent

parts of the Mediterranean coast, and speaking a dialect so
nearly akin with the Hebrew that its scanty remains are
read with no great difficulty by the aid of that language,
have been wont to be accounted as the first to give the race
prominence in general history. The part which they played
was of the most honourable and useful character. Their
commercial enterprise widely extended the limits of geographical knowledge, and bound together distant peoples by the
ties of mutual helpfulness ; their colonies opened to civilization the countries bordering the Mediterranean, and prepared
the way for the extension of Greek and Roman culture. A
significant indication of the far-reaching and beneficent
nature of their activity is to be seen in the fact that a large
portion of the world's alphabets, including many of those
which have the widest range, and have been used by the
most cultivated nations, come from the Phenician alphabet
as their ultimate source. To great political importance the
Phenicians never attained, except in their most flourishing
colony, Carthage, which, as we well know, disputed for a time
with the Romans the empire of the world.

But it must not fail to be noticed that, even before the
rise of the Phenician world-commerce, there were great
Semitic empires in Mesopotamia, that country where the idea
of universal empire appears to have had its origin and its first
realization, and where some of the earliest germs of world-
civilization, sprang up and were nursed. The mixture of
nationalities and of cultures which contended in that arena
for the mastery during tens of centuries, until the Indo-
European Persians subjected all beneath their sway, is most
intricate, and as yet only partially understood : the knowledge of its intricacy, and the hopeful means of its final solution, were given together, but a few years since, in the discovery and decipherment of the monuments of Nineveh and
Babylon, of the records known as "cuneiform," from the
shape of the characters in which they are written. These
records are abundant, and of various content, consisting
not in inscriptions alone, but in whole libraries of annals
and works of science and literature, stamped upon tablets
and cylinders of burnt clay ; but their examination is as yet

too incomplete, and the results drawn from it too fragmentary and uncertain, to allow of our taking any detailed notice
of them here; the questions which they affect are still
under judgment, and only the very few who have made profound and original studies among the monuments can venture
to speak respecting them with authority. It is enough for
us to note that the Semitic race was prominent, and during
a long period preëminent, in Mesopotamia, and that a highly
important part of its history, and of the history of Semitic
language, is coming to light as the fruit of cuneiform studies.

During all this time there was enacting—behind a screen,
as it were—a part of Semitic history which was to prove of
incomparably greater importance to the world than Phenician commerce or Babylonian empire. The little people of
the Hebrews was politically a most insignificant item in the
sum of human affairs; but its religion, made universal by
Christ, has become the mightiest element in human history;
its wonderful ancient literature is the work which all enlightened nations of the present day unite in calling Bible,
that is, 'the book;' its language is even now more studied
than any other outside the pale of Indo-European speech.

And yet once more, in comparatively modern times, long
after Mesopotamian empire, and Phenician commerce, and
Carthaginian lust of conquest, and Jewish temple-worship,
had passed away for ever, extinguished in the extinction of
those several nationalities, a new branch of the Semitic race,
which till then had slumbered in inaction and insignificance
in the deserts of Arabia, awoke all at once to the call of
a great religious teacher, Mohammed, burst its limits, overwhelmed Asia, Africa, and no small part of Europe, and
flowered out suddenly and brilliantly in science, art, and
philosophy, attaining a combined political and literary
eminence to which no Semitic people had made before any
approach, and threatening to wrench the leadership of
human destiny from the keeping of the enfeebled races of
Europe. Finally, corrupted within, and foiled and broken
without, it sank again into comparative obscurity; and with
it went down, probably for ever, the star of Semitic glory
and importance in the external history of the world; al-

though half mankind still own the sway of Semitic religious
ideas and institutions.

The Semitic dialects are divided into three principal
branches : the northern, comprehending the idioms of Syria
and Assyria, and usually called the Aramaic; the central, or
Canaanitic, composed of the Hebrew and Phenician, with the
Punic; and the southern, or Arabic, including, besides the
proper or literary Arabic and the dialects most closely akin
with it, the Himyaritic in the south-western region of the
peninsula, and the outliers of the latter in Africa, the literary
Ethiopic or Geëz, the Amharic, and other Abyssinian dialects.
Passing over the Mesopotamian records, as of an age and
character not yet fully established, the Hebrew literature is
by far the oldest which the family has to show, and, as is
known to every one, ranks among the oldest in the world.
From a time anterior, doubtless, to that of Moses, the works
of the Hebrew annalists, poets, and prophets cover the whole
period of Jewish history until some four centuries before
Christ, when the Hebrew had ceased to exist as a vernacular
language, and was replaced by the Chaldee or Aramaic, the
dialect of Syria. But it has never ceased to be read,
written, and even to some extent spoken, by the learned,
from that time until now—especially since the revival of its
use, and the purification of its style, among the scattered
Jewish populations of Europe, following upon the expulsion
of the Jews from Spain in the twelfth century. Of the
degraded and mixed Hebrew used as the learned dialect of
the Rabbins, not far from the beginning of our era, the
Mishna is the most important monument. The Samaritan
is another impure dialect of the Hebrew, so permeated with
Aramaic elements as to be a kind of medium between
Hebrew and Aramaic. Its oldest monument, a version of
the Pentateuch, is referred to the first century of our era.
It seems at present to be on the point of extinction.

Phenicia has left us no literature. The coffin of one of
the kings of Sidon, found but a few years since, presents in
its detailed inscription a fuller view of the Phenician tongue
than is derivable from all its other known records, taken
together. A few inscriptions, and a mutilated and obscure

fragment in a play of the Roman poet Plautus, whereof the scene is laid in Carthage, are the only relics left us of the idiom of that queenly city.

The earliest records of Aramaic speech are the so-called Chaldee passages found in some of the later books of the Hebrew Bible (a single verse in Jeremiah, and longer passages in Esdras and Daniel). Other products of the literary use by the Jews of the same language are the Targums, or paraphrases of Scripture, dating from about the time of Christ, and the Talmuds, of the fourth and fifth centuries. But in the second century, with the translation of the whole Bible into the language of Syria (usually called the Peshito version), begins an important Christian Syriac literature, of which considerable portions are still preserved to us. It flourished especially between the fourth and ninth centuries. Besides the valuable historical information, touching the early ages of the Christian church, which it records, it played an important part in transmitting to the Arabs the literature, science, and philosophy of the Greeks. Its career was brought to a close, and even the Syriac idiom itself nearly crowded out of existence, by the rise and rapid extension of the Arabic, in the centuries after Mohammed. But the ancient Syriac is still the sacred dialect of the feeble bodies of Christians in Asia which represent the Syriac church ; and its modern representatives, much corrupted in form and of mixed material, are even now spoken by a few scattered communities. With one of these communities, the Nestorians of Orumiah and its vicinity—scanty remains of a sect which once sent its missionaries into the remotest regions of Asia, into India, Mongolia, and China—the labours of American missionaries have lately made our public well acquainted. A modern Syriac literature is growing up once more under their auspices.

Besides these two Aramaic literatures, the one Jewish and the other Christian, it is believed that there has existed another, of native origin and of character more truly national; but it is now lost, doubtless beyond recovery. Traditions of ancient Chaldean learning attach themselves to the name Nabatean, and one or two curious books have been recently brought to light out of the Arabic literature, claiming to be versions of Nabatean works of a very high antiquity : but they are generally regarded as literary impostures, containing only a scanty, if an appreciable, element of what is genuine and ancient. In the practices and traditions of the Mendaites and Sabians are also seen traces of an indigenous Chaldean culture.

The oldest monuments belonging to the southern or Arabian branch of Semitic speech are the inscriptions discovered in the south-western corner of the great peninsula. They represent a language very different from the classical Arabic, as the character and civilization of the Sabeans and Himyarites, from whom they come, appear to have been very unlike those of the Arabs of the desert. Their exact period is hitherto unknown. Language and civilization have alike been almost wholly supplanted, since the rise of Islamism, by the conquering Arabic, only obscure relics of them being left in the Ehkili and other existing idioms of the south. Most nearly akin with the Himyaritic is the speech of the neighbouring region of Africa, which was unquestionably peopled from southern Arabia, by emigration across the Red Sea. The ancient tongue of Abyssinia, the Ethiopic or Geëz, has a literature, wholly of Christian origin and content, coming down from the fourth century of our era : its earliest monument is a version of the Bible. As a cultivated and current language, it has been gradually crowded out of use during the past six centuries by the Amharic, another dialect of the same stock, but of a more corrupt and barbarous character.

Immensely superior in value to all the other Semitic literatures, excepting the Hebrew, although latest in date of them all, is that which is written in the Arabic tongue. Its beginning is nearly contemporaneous with the rise of the Arab people to historical importance : the Koran, collected and written down, about the middle of the seventh century, from the records and traditions of Mohammed's revelations, is its starting-point. Only a few poems, of no great length, belong to an age somewhat earlier ; and the inscriptions of Sinai and of Petra, which go back nearly to, or even somewhat beyond, the Christian era, give scanty representation of dialects nearly kindred. That which we call the Arabic was, anterior to Mohammed, the spoken dialect of the tribes occupying the central part of the country ; that is to say, of that part of the population which was of purest Semitic blood, and less affected than any other, in language, manners, and institutions, by disturbing foreign influences. As a natural consequence of the political and religious revolution by which Islamism became the religion, first of Arabia, then of so large a portion of Asia and Africa, this dialect has had a career almost comparable with that of the Latin. It has extinguished nearly all the other dialects of the Semitic family within their ancient limits ; it has spread over Egypt and the whole northern coast of Africa ; the language of Spain, and yet more the Hindustani of central India, have borrowed abundantly of its material ; the modern literary Persian and Turkish have their vocabularies made up almost more of Arabic words than of those of native growth. Of the wonderfully rich and various Arabic literature, of the part it played in the preservation and transmission of classical learning to modern times, of the treasures of information it contains respecting the history and geography of the Orient, it is not necessary here to speak ; the theme belongs to literary, not to linguistic, history. We turn to a consideration of the chief peculiarities of Semitic language.

The Semitic type of speech is called inflective, like the Indo-European, and philologists are accustomed to allow the title to no other languages than these two. We must beware, however, of supposing that this inclusion in one morphological class implies any genetic relationship between the families, or is to be regarded as even suggesting the probability of their common descent. There is between them, on the contrary, only such a resemblance as is due to a correspondence of natural endowments in the language-making races. Semitic inflection is so totally diverse from Indo-European inflection, that the historical transition from the one to the other, or from a common original to both, is of a difficulty which cannot be exceeded. The Semitic tongues possess in many respects a more peculiar and isolated

character than any others which exist. Their most fundamental characteristic is the triliterality of their roots. With
rare and insignificant exceptions, every Semitic verbal root
—the pronominal roots are not subject to the same law—
contains just three consonants, no more and no less. Moreover, it is composed of consonants alone. That is to say :
whereas, in the Indo-European and other tongues, the
radical vowel is as essential a part of the root as any other,
even though more liable than the consonants to phonetic
alteration, in the Semitic, on the other hand, the vocalization
of the radical consonants is almost solely a means of grammatical flexion.   Only the consonants of the root are
radical or significant elements ; the vowels are formative or
relational.   Thus, for example, the three consonants *q-t-l*
form a root (Arabic) which conveys the idea of 'killing : '
then *qatala* means 'he killed;' *qutila*, 'he was killed; '
qutilū, 'they were killed; ' *uqtul*, 'kill;' *qātil*, 'killing; '
iqtāl, 'causing to kill;' *qatl*, 'murder;' *qitl*, 'enemy;'
qutl, 'murderous;' and so on.   Along with this internal
flection is found the use of external formative elements, both
suffixes and prefixes, and also, to a limited extent, infixes, or
inserted letters or syllables ; yet they are but little relied on,
and play only a subordinate part, as compared with their
analogues in the languages of other races ; the main portion
of the needed inflection is provided for by means of the
varying vocalization of the root, and what remains for
affixes to do is comparatively trifling.   The aggregation of
affix upon affix, the formation of derivative from derivative,
so usual with us (it was illustrated in a former lecture by
such examples as *inapplicabilities* and *untruthfully*), is a
thing almost unknown in the domain of Semitic speech.
This truly Procrustean uniformity of the Semitic roots, and
this capacity of significant internal change, separate the
languages to which they belong by a wide and almost
impassable gulf from all others spoken by the human race.
So far as we can discover, the varying vocalization of the roots
in these languages is an ultimate fact, and directly and
organically indicative of a variation of meaning : it is not,
like the occasional phenomena of a somewhat similar char-

acter presented by the Indo-European languages, a distinction originally euphonic, and afterwards made significant.
We can point out the influences which have made *men* the
plural of *man*, *led* the preterit of *lead ;* we can trace back
set and *sang* to forms in which their distinction from *sit* and
sing was conveyed by formative elements added from without
to the root; but no historical researches bring the Semitic
scholar to, or even perceptibly toward, any such explanation
of the forms he is studying. Now and then a kind of
symbolism is pretty distinctly traceable : the weaker vowels
i and *u* sometimes convey by their use an intimation of less
active or transitive meaning, as compared with the strong
full *a :* thus, the *act* of 'killing' is expressed by *qatala*, but
the *conditions* of 'being sorry,' of 'being beautiful,' by
'hazina, 'hasuna ; and especially, every active verb, like *qatala*,
has its corresponding passive *qutila*. But such considerations can explain only a small portion of the derivatives from
Semitic roots ; the genesis of the rest is an unsolved
problem, of extremest difficulty. The triplicity of radical
consonants is an equally primitive characteristic of all the
Semitic tongues, yet there are not wanting certain apparent
indications that it is the result of historical development.
To make out the required number of three, some roots contain the same consonant doubled ; in others, one of the three
is a weak or servile letter, hardly more than a hiatus, or it is
a semivowel which seems to have been developed out of an
original vowel ; further, there are groups of roots of somewhat kindred signification which agree in two of their consonants, so that the third is plausibly conjectured to be an
introduced letter, having the effect to differentiate a general
meaning once conveyed by the other two alone. Guided by
such signs, and urged on by the presumed necessity in theory
for regarding triliterality as not absolutely original, scholars
have repeatedly made the attempt to reduce these roots to
an earlier and simpler condition, out of which they should be
accounted a historic growth—but hitherto with only indifferent success ; we are yet far from attaining any satisfactory
understanding of the beginnings of Semitic speech. It is
suggested with much plausibility that the universality of the

three root-letters may be due to the inorganic and arbitrary
extension of an analogy which had by some means become a
dominant one; and that, in attaining their present form,
the roots have prevailingly passed through the condition of
derivative nouns. The Semitic verbal forms show many
signs of a more immediate and proximate development out
of forms of nouns than is to be traced in the structure of
the Indo-European verb. *

In no small part of its structure, the Semitic verb differs
very strikingly from the Indo-European. It distinguishes,
indeed, the same three numbers, singular, dual, and plural,
and the same persons, first, second, and third, and its personal endings are to a considerable extent formed in the
same manner, by adding pronominal elements to the verbal
root. But in the second and third persons it makes a
farther distinction of the gender of the subject: thus,
qatalat, 'she killed,' is different from *qatala*, 'he killed.'
What is of much more consequence is that its representation of the important element of time is quite diverse from
ours. The antithesis of past, present, and future, which
seems to us so fundamental and necessary, the Semitic mind
has ignored, setting up but two tenses, whose separate uses
are to no small extent interchangeable and difficult of
distinct definition, but whereof the one denotes chiefly completed action, the other incomplete; each of them admitting
of employment, in different circumstances, as past, present,
or future. The perfect or preterit is the more original, and
its persons are formed by appended pronominal endings; the
imperfect (sometimes called future) has the terminations of
number belonging to a noun, and indicates person and
gender by prefixes: thus, the three masculine persons in the
singular are *aqtulu, taqtulu,* and *yaqtulu;* the third, masculine and feminine, dual, are *yaqtulāni* and *taqtulāni;* plural,
yaqtulūna and *yaqtulna.* To the imperfect belongs a subjunctive and imperative, and one or two other less common
quasi-modal forms. But of the wealth of modal expression
into which our own verb has always tended to develop, in a

---

* See A. Schleicher, in the Transactions of the Saxon Academy (Leipsic,
1865), vol. iv. (of the phil-historical series), p. 514 sq.

synthetic or an analytic way, that of the Semites has
generated very little; its proneness is rather to the multiplication of such distinctions as are called conjugational,
to the characterizing of the verbal action as in its nature
transitive, causal, intensive, iterative, conative, reflexive, or
the like: thus, *qatala* meaning 'he killed,' *qattala* means
'he killed with violence, massacred;' *qātala*, 'he tried to
kill;' *aqtala*, 'he caused to kill;' *inqatala*, 'he killed himself;' and so on.   Each Arabic verb has theoretically fifteen
such conjugations; and near a dozen of them, each with its
own passive, are in tolerably frequent and familiar use ; in
the other dialects, the scheme is less completely filled out.
Verbal nouns and adjectives, or infinitives and participles,
belong likewise to every conjugation.

In their nouns, the Semites distinguish only two genders,
masculine and feminine.   They have, of course, the same
three numbers here as in the verb.   Distinctions of case,
however, are almost entirely deficient; only the Arabic
makes a scanty separation of nominative and accusative, or
of nominative, genitive, and accusative; and opinions still
differ as to whether this is to be regarded as a separate
acquisition made by the Arabic alone, or as an original
possession of the whole family, lost by the other branches:
the latter is probably the correcter view.

The simple copula, the verb *to be*, is generally wanting in
the Semitic languages : for " the man is good " they say,
" the man good " (often with a form of the adjective which
indicates that it is used predicatively, rather than attributively), or " the man, he good."   They are poor in connectives and particles ; and this, with the deficiency of modal
forms in the verb, gives to their syntax a peculiar character
of simplicity and baldness : the Semite strings his assertions
together, just putting one after the other, with an *and* or a
but interposed, where the Indo-European twines his into a
harmoniously proportioned and many-membered period.
The same stiffness and rigidity which these languages show
in respect to word-development appears also in their development of signification.   While it is characteristic of our
mode of speech that we use such words as *comprehend, under-*

stand, forgive, as if they originally and always meant just
what we employ them to express—not giving a thought to
the metaphor, often striking, or even startling, which they
contain—in the Semitic, the metaphor usually shows plainly
through, and cannot be lost sight of. The language of the
Semite, then, is rather pictorial, forcible, vivid, than adapted
to calm and reasoning philosophy.

The various dialects of this family stand in a very close
relationship with one another, hardly presenting such differences even as are found within the limits of a single branch
of the Indo-European family: they are to one another like
German, Dutch, and Swedish, for example, rather than like
German, Welsh, and Persian. This fact, however, does not
at all prove their separation to have taken place at a later
period than that of the Indo-European branches ; for, during
its whole recorded history, Semitic speech has shown itself
far less variable, less liable to phonetic change and corruption, less fertile of new words and forms, of new themes and
apparent roots, than our own. And the reasons, at least in
part, are not difficult to discover. Each Semitic word, as a
general rule, presents distinctly to the consciousness of him
who employs it its three radical consonants, with its complement of vowels, each one of which has a recognized part to
play in determining the significance of the word, and cannot
be altered, or exchanged for another, without violating a
governing analogy, without defacing its intelligibility. The
genesis of new forms, moreover, is rendered well-nigh impossible by the fact that such a thing as a Semitic compound
is almost totally unknown : the habit of the language, from
its earliest period, has forbidden that combination of independent elements which is the first step toward their fusion
into a form. Hence everything in Semitic speech wears an
aspect of peculiar rigidity and persistence. In its primitive
development—as development we cannot but believe it to
have been, however little comprehensible by us—it assumed
so marked and individual a type that it has since been comparatively exempt from variation. In no other family of
human speech would it be possible that the most antique
and original of its dialects, the fullest in its forms, the most

20

uncorrupted in its phonetic structure, the most faithful representative of the ideal type inherent in them all, should be the youngest of their number. But such is the character of the classical Arabic, whose earliest literary monuments are from fifteen to twenty centuries later than those of the Hebrew and Assyrian. There is reason, however, it should be remarked, to suspect that the Hebrew as we have it does not in all points truly represent the language of the earliest period of Hebrew history, that it has both partaken of the modernization of the popular tongue, and suffered some distortion in the hands of the grammarians from whom we receive it. The spoken vernaculars of the present day, while they exhibit something of the same character as the modern Indo-European dialects, in the abbreviation of words, the loss of inflectional forms, and the obscuration of etymological relations, yet do so in a much less degree. The modern Syriac of Orumiah has decidedly more of the aspect of a European analytic language than any other existing dialect of its family, and even more than, a few years ago, Semitic scholars were willing to believe possible. But its predecessor, the ancient Syriac, had been itself distinguished by like peculiarities among the contemporaneous and older dialects ; having felt, perhaps, the modifying influence of the strange peoples and cultures by which Syria was shut in, invaded, and more than once subdued.

It may be hoped that wider and deeper study will succeed one day in casting additional light upon the difficulties of Semitic linguistic history. The dialect which is now in process of construction out of the recently discovered cuneiform monuments is claimed to possess some peculiar characteristics, yet it appears to be too decidedly accordant with the rest in its general structure to play other than a subordinate part, by farther illustrating that part of the course of development with which we are already more or less familiar. It is confidently claimed, however, by some linguistic scholars (although as confidently denied by others), that the ancient tongue of Egypt, and a considerable group of the languages of northern Africa, have traces, still distinctly visible, of a far remoter connection with this family,

a connection anterior to the full elaboration of the fundamental peculiarities of Semitic language which we have been
considering. If this claim shall be established by maturer
investigation, there will be reason to look for important
revelations as the result of comparisons made between the
two classes. The often-asserted relationship between the
beginnings of Indo-European and of Semitic speech does
not at present offer any appreciable promise of valuable light
to be thrown upon their joint and respective history. It
must be evident, I think, from the foregoing exposition, that
the whole fabric and style of these two families of language
is so discordant, that any theory which assumes their joint
development out of the radical stage, the common growth of
their grammatical systems, is wholly excluded. If correspondence there be between them, it must lie in their roots,
and it must have existed before the special working-over of
the Semitic roots into their present form. It will be time,
then, to talk of the signs of Indo-European and Semitic
unity when the earliest process of Semitic growth is better
understood, its effects distinguished from the yet earlier
material upon which they were wrought. Against so deep
and pervading a discordance, the surface analogies hitherto
brought to light have no convincing weight. The identification is a very alluring theme : the near agreement of the
peoples speaking these two classes of languages in respect to
physical structure and mental capacity, their position as the
two great white races, joint leaders in the world's history,
taken in connection with their geographical neighbourhood
and an apparent agreement between the traditions held by
some nations of each touching their earliest homes and fates,
are inducements which have spurred on many a linguist to
search for verbal and radical coincidences in the tongues of
both, and to regard with a degree of credence such as he
appeared to find—while, nevertheless, if the same coincidences were found to exist, along with the same differences,
between our languages and those of some congeries of Polynesian or African tribes, they would at once be dismissed as
of no value or account. To claim, then, that the common
descent of Indo-European and Semitic races has been proved

by the evidence of their speech is totally unjustifiable ; the
utmost which can be asserted is that language affords
certain indications, of doubtful value, which, taken along
with certain other ethnological considerations, also of questionable pertinency, furnish ground for suspecting an ultimate relationship. The question, in short, is not yet ripe
for settlement. Whether the better comprehension of the
history of Semitic speech which further research may give
will enable us to determine it with confidence, need not
here be considered : while such a result is certainly not to
be expected with confidence, it may perhaps be looked for
with hope.

To discuss the Semitic character, and to show how in its
striking features it accords with Semitic speech, would be a
most interesting task, but lies aside from the proper course
of our inquiries. Through the might of their religious ideas,
this people have governed, and will continue to govern, the
civilized world ; but in other respects, in that gradual working-out of ethnic endowment and capacity which constitutes
the history of a race, they have shown themselves decidedly
inferior to the other great ruling family, and their forms of
speech undeniably partake of this inferiority. The time is
long past when reverence for the Hebrew Scriptures as the
Book of books could carry with it the corollary that the
Hebrew tongue was the most perfect and the oldest of all
known languages, and even the mother of the rest : it is now
fully recognized as merely one in a contracted and very
peculiar group of sister dialects, crowded together in a corner
of Asia and the adjacent parts of Africa, possessing striking
excellences, but also marked with striking defects, and not
yet proved genetically connected with any other existing
group.

The family of languages to which we have next to direct
our attention is one of much wider geographical range, and
more varied linguistic character. As usually constructed, it
covers with its branches the whole northern portion of the
eastern continent, through both Europe and Asia, together
with the greater part of central Asia, and portions of Asiatic
and European territory lying still further south. It is

known by many different names : some call it the Altaic, or
the Ural-Altaic, family, from the chains of mountains which
are supposed to have served as centres of dispersion to
its tribes ; others style it, from one or other of its principal
branches, the Mongolian, or the Tataric ; the appellation
Turanian has also won great currency within no long time,
owing to its adoption by one or two very conspicuous authorities in linguistic ethnology, although recommended
neither by its derivation nor its original application (we
shall speak more particularly of both later) ; Scythian,
finally, is a title which it has sometimes received, taken from
the name by which the Greeks knew the wild nomad races of
the extreme north-east, which were doubtless in part, at
least, of this kindred—and the designation Scythian we will
here employ, as, upon the whole, though far from being unexceptionable, best answering our purpose.

Five principal branches compose the family. The first of
them, the Ugrian, or Finno-Hungarian, is almost wholly European in its position and known history. It includes the
language of the Laplanders, the race highest in latitude, but
lowest in stature and in developed capacity, of any in Europe ; that of the Finns in north-western Russia, with related
dialects in Esthonia and Livonia; those of several tribes, of no
great numbers or consequence, stretching from the southern
Ural mountains toward the interior of Russia and down the
Volga—as the Permians, Siryanians, Wotiaks, Cheremisses,
and Mordwins ; and the tongue of the Hungarians or Magyars, far in the south, with those of their kindred, the
Ostiaks and Woguls, in and beyond the central chain of the
Ural—which was the region whence the rude ancestors of
the brave and noble race who now people Hungary fought
their way down to the Danube, within the historical period,
or hardly a thousand years ago.

The second branch is the Samoyedic, nearest akin with the
Ugrian, yet apparently independent of it. It occupies the
territory along the northern coast of Europe and Asia, from
the White Sea across the lower Yenisei, and almost to the
Lena, one of the most barren and inhospitable tracts of the
whole continent ; while some of its dialects are spoken in the

mountains to the south, about the head waters of the Yenisei—
probably indicating the region whence the Samoyed tribes were
driven, or wandered, northward, following the river-courses,
and spreading out upon the shores of the northern ocean.
What is known of them and their speech is mainly the fruit
of the devoted labours of the intrepid traveller Castrén. The
Samoyed dialects are destitute of literary cultivation and of
records, and the wild people who speak them are without interest or consequence, in the present or the past, save simply
as human beings. No other branch of the family has so
little to recommend it to our notice.

The third branch includes the languages spoken by the
Turkish tribes, a race which has played a part in modern
history not altogether insignificant. Their earliest wanderings and conquests are doubtfully read in the annals of the
Chinese empire, and their long struggles with the Iranian
peoples in their border-lands are conspicuous themes of Persian heroic tradition. It was in the ninth and tenth centuries that they finally broke forth from their dreary abodes
on the great plateau of central Asia; falling upon the
eastern provinces of the already decaying Mohammedan
caliphate, they hastened its downfall and divided its inheritance; and their victorious arms were carried steadily westward, until, in the middle of the fifteenth century, they were
masters of Constantinople and of all that was left of the
Greek empire; nor was their progress toward the heart of
Europe checked but by the most heroic and long-continued
efforts on the part of Magyars, Germans, and Slavonians.
Their modern history, and their present precarious position
upon the border of Europe, are too well known to call for
more than an allusion. The subdivisions of the branch are
numerous, and they cover a territory of very wide extent,
reaching from the eastern edge of the Austrian dominions,
through Asia Minor, Tatary, and Chinese Tatary, to beyond
the centre of the Asiatic continent, while their outliers are
found even along the Lena, to its mouth, in northernmost
Siberia. They are classed together in three principal groups:
first, the northern, of which the Kirghiz, Bashkir, and Yakut
are the most important members; they occupy (with the

exception of the Yakut in the extreme north-east) southern
Siberia and Tatary, between the Volga and the Yenisei;
second, the south-eastern, including the Uigurs, Usbeks,
Turkomans, etc., and ranging from the southern Caspian,
eastward to the middle of the great plateau; third, the
western, stretching through northern Persia, the Caucasus,
the Crimea, and Asia Minor, to the Bosphorus, and scattered
in patches amid the varied populations which fill the European
dominions of the Sultan.   This division, however, is rather
geographical than linguistic : the nearer mutual relations of
the different dialects are still, in great part, to be determined.   They compose together a very distinct body of
nearly kindred forms of speech, not differing from one
another in anything like the same degree as the Ugrian languages.   It is even claimed, although with questionable truth,
that a Yakut of the Lena and a man of the lower orders
at Constantinople could still make shift to communicate together.
    The fourth branch of Scythian language is the Mongolian.
The Mongols, in the twelfth and thirteenth centuries, ran a
wonderful career of conquest, overwhelming nearly all the
monarchies of Asia, and reducing even the eastern countries
of Europe to subjection.   The Mongol emperor Kublai
Khan, reigning from the borders of Germany to the coasts
of south-eastern Asia, with his capital in China, the most
populous and at that time well-nigh the most enlightened
country of the earth, governed such a realm as the world
never saw, before or since.   But the unwieldy mass fell in
pieces almost as rapidly as it had been brought together.
The horribly devastating wars by which Mongol dominion
was established were neither attended nor followed by any
compensating benefits : they were a tempest of barbarian
fury, to be thought of only with a shudder, and with gratitude for its brevity.   The Mongols themselves were but the
leaders in the movement, which was in great part executed
by hordes of Turkish descent.   A Mongol dynasty held possession of the Chinese throne for a century, until expelled,
about A.D. 1365, by a successful revolt of the native race.
At present, the still powerful remains of this once so re-

doubtable people are living in quiet and insignificance, as
dependents of the Chinese empire. Their territory is
bounded in the south by the Tibetan frontier, and extends
thence eastward to the border of China, northward to lake
Dzaisang, north-eastward to beyond lake Baikal, and to the
edge of Manchuria, including the upper waters of the Lena
and the Amoor. Their scattered fragments, too, are left in
almost every country westward to the Volga, and a considerable colony of them are to be found upon both sides of the
Volga, to some distance above its mouth. The Khalkas,
Kalmucks, and Buriats are the most notable of their tribes.

The fifth and last branch is called the Tungusic. It occupies a broad tract of north-eastern Asia, from the frontier
of China on the north to the Arctic Ocean, and from the
neighbourhood of the Yenisei almost to Kamchatka. Its
most conspicuous dialect, the Manchu, belongs to tribes
which have established a claim upon the attention of the
world by their conquest of China a little more than two centuries ago (A.D. 1644). In wielding the forces of that
mighty empire, they long displayed a consummate ability ;
but their administration, attacked at once by foreign encroachment and domestic revolt, has now for some time been
marked with fatal weakness : Scythian power seems at present not less decadent in the extreme East than in the
West. This is not the first time that Tungusian races have
built up their power upon a Chinese foundation. The
powerful dynasties of Khitan and Kin, from the beginning
of the tenth century to near the middle of the thirteenth,
held a great part of northern China in subjection, though
not to the entire subversion of the empire : like the modern
Manchus, they adopted and perpetuated the Chinese institutions and culture. The realm of the Kin was one of the
many which went down before the Mongolian onset. The
Manchus call by the name Orochon, ‘reindeer-possessors,’
all Tungusian tribes excepting their own : respecting their
mutual relations little is known in detail : they are depend-
ences partly of the Chinese empire, partly of the Russian.

The brief survey of the history of the Scythian races with
which we have thus accompanied our statement of their di-

visions is sufficient to set forth clearly the subordinate part
they have played in human affairs. War and devastation
have been the sphere in which their activity has chiefly
manifested itself. Some of them have shown for a time no
mean capacity in governing and managing their conquests.
But they have had no aptitude for helping the advance of
civilization, and but little, in general, even for appropriating
the knowledge and culture of their subjects or their neighbours. The Manchus have written their language during
some centuries past; but they have nothing which deserves
the name of a national literature ; their books are translations or servile imitations of Chinese works. The Mongol
literature goes back to the thirteenth century, the period
when the race rose to importance in history, but is almost
equally scanty. The Mongol alphabet was the original of
the present Manchu, and, in its turn, was derived from that
of the Uigur Turks; the latter, again, goes back to the
Syriac, having been brought into central Asia by Nestorian
missionaries. The Uigurs, the easternmost members of the
family of Turkish tribes, seem to have been the first among
them to acquire and use the art of writing : their alphabet
is said to be mentioned in Chinese annals of the fifth century, and their reputation for learning won them consideration and high employment even down to the era of the
Mongolian outbreak ; but they, their civilization, and their
literature have since passed so nearly out of existence that
it has even been possible to raise the question whether they
were, in fact, of Turkish kindred and speech. Very scanty
fragments of what are supposed to have been their literary
productions, of uncertain age, are still preserved to us. The
general conversion of the Turkish tribes to Mohammedanism led to the crowding out of their ancient alphabet by the
Arabic. From the south-eastern division of the same
branch, generally called the Jagataic, or Oriental Turkish,
we have a literature of some value, dating from the fifteenth
and sixteenth centuries, but not continued later : its most
important work is the autobiography of the emperor Baber,
that extraordinary man who early in the sixteenth century
conquered India, founding there the Mogul dynasty, the final

extinction of which we have ourselves witnessed within the past few years. The westernmost Turkish race, the conquerors of Constantinople, usually known by the distinctive name of Osmanlis, or Ottomans (both words are corruptions of the name of their leader, Othman), have a very rich and abundant literature, covering the whole period from the rise of the race to power in the fourteenth century down to our own time. It is, however, of only secondary interest, as being founded on Persian and Arabic models, and containing little that is distinctively national in style and spirit. The learned dialect, too, in which it is written, is crowded full of Persian and Arabic words, often to the nearly total exclusion of native Turkish material. In the Finno-Hungarian branch of the family, finally, there is the same paucity of literary records. In Hungary, after its conversion to Roman Christianity (about A.D. 1000), Latin was for a long time the almost exclusive medium of learned communication and composition. The Reformation, in the sixteenth century, favoured the uprising of a national literature, in the vernacular tongue ; but Austrian policy checked and thwarted its development ; and a renewed start, taken about the beginning of the present century, was baffled when the remains of Hungarian liberty were trampled out in 1849. Finnish written literature is still more recent, but boasts at least one work of a high order of interest, of a wholly native and original stamp : the Kalevala, composed of half-mythical, half-legendary songs, which have been handed down by tradition, apparently for many centuries, from generation to generation of the Finnish people. No other Ugrian race possesses a literature.

It is claimed of late, however, by those who are engaged in constructing linguistic, ethnological, and political history out of the just disentombed records of Assyrian culture and art, that sufficient evidence is found to compel the belief that neither Indo-Europeans nor Semites, but some third race, were the first occupants and owners of the soil, and laid the foundation of the culture which was adopted and developed there by the other races, as they later, one after another, succeeded to the supremacy ; and some maintain further that the language of this race shows it to have been Scythian, a member of the westernmost, or Finno-Hungarian, branch of the family. By others the Scythian character of the dialect is explicitly denied. The discussion is at present in the hands of too few persons, and those too little versed in Scythian philology, to admit of a definite and satisfactory conclusion ; and meanwhile we are justified in regarding with extreme incredulity any theory which puts Scythian races in the position of originators of an independent civilization, and teachers of Semites and Indo-Europeans. Such a position is wholly inconsistent with what is known of their history elsewhere, and would constitute a real anomaly in ethnology ; while we are not authorized utterly to deny its possibility, we certainly have the right to demand full and unequivocal evidence before we yield it our belief. The fact—if fact it be—is of a revolutionary character, and must fight its way to acknowledgment.

The linguistic tie, now, which binds together the widely scattered branches of this great family, is a somewhat loose and feeble one, consisting less in the traceable correspondence of material and forms, the possession of the same roots and the same inflections, than in a correspondence of the style of structure, of the modes of apprehension and expression of grammatical relations. Each great branch forms by itself a group as distinct as is, for instance, the Germanic or the Slavonic in our own family ; but there is no such palpable and unmistakable evidence of kinship between Ugrian, Turkish, Mongol, and Manchu, as between German, Russian, Greek, and Sanskrit. It is, to no small extent, those who know least in detail respecting the languages of the family who are most ready to assert and defend their historical connection : and, on the other hand, Castrén, himself a Finn, and whose long and devoted labours have taught us more respecting them than has been brought to light by any other man, ventures* to assert with confidence only the demonstrable linguistic relationship of Ugrian, Samoyed, and Turkish, and regards the inclusion of Mongol and Man-

* Ethnological Lectures respecting the Altaic Races (St Petersburg, 1857), p. 94.

chu within the same circle as still questionable. But even
between the three former, the material evidence is but weak
and scanty, as compared with that presented in the Indo-
European idioms, of which specimens were given above, in
the fifth lecture; no investigator has ever been able to
draw up tables of pervading correspondences in the Scythian tongues, which should at once illustrate and prove
their genetic unity. It is possible, of course, that the races
who speak these tongues may have been separated longer
than the Indo-European, enough longer for a more sweeping
effacement of the evidence of their common descent; or,
again, that the lack of those remains of dialects of great
antiquity which so aid our researches into the history of our
own family of speech is what prevents our recognition of the
links that bind the Scythian languages into one. It may be,
too, that these have possessed as much more variable and
mobile a character than the Indo-European forms of speech
as the latter than the Semitic: this, indeed, has been repeatedly assumed to be true, and even defended by theoretical
and à priori arguments; but I am not aware that it has ever
been established by proper linguistic evidence and reasoning,
and it is strongly opposed by the coherence of the several
branches, and the near accordance of the dialects composing
them. And, were either or both of these possible explana-
tions of the discordances of the Scythian tongues proved
true, they would by no means settle the question in favour
of the unity of the family; they would simply forbid us to
maintain too dogmatically that the tongues were not and could
not be related as members of one family; before consenting
positively to regard them as thus related, we should still be
entitled to demand tangible evidences; if not correspondences of material, then at least definite and distinctive correspondences of form. And, as already intimated, a morphological resemblance is the ground on which the claim
of Scythian unity is chiefly founded; their fundamental
common characteristic is that they follow what is styled an
agglutinative type of structure. That is to say, the elements
out of which their words are formed are loosely put together,
instead of being closely compacted, or fused into one; they

are aggregated, rather than integrated ; the root or theme is
held apart from the affixes, and these from one another, with
a distinct apprehension of their separate individuality. As
Professor Müller well expresses it, while Indo-European
language, in putting two roots together to compose a form,
sinks the individuality of both, the Scythian sinks that of
but one, the suffix. The process is not, in its first stages,
diverse in the two families, since every Indo-European form
began with being a mere collocation, and, in a large proportion of cases, the root maintains to the end its integrity of
form and meaning : the difference is one of degree rather
than of kind; of the extension and effect, rather than the
essential nature, of a mode of formation : and yet, it is a
palpable and an important difference, when we compare the
general structure of two languages, one out of each family.
    The simple possession in common of an agglutinative cha-
racter, as thus defined, would certainly be a very insufficient
indication of the common parentage of the Scythian tongues ;
mere absence of inflection would be a characteristic far too
general and indeterminate to prove anything respecting
them. They do, however, present some striking points of
agreement in the style and manner of their agglutination,
such as might supplement and powerfully aid the convincing
force of a body of material correspondences which should be
found wanting in desired fullness. The most important of
these structural accordances are as follows.
    In the Scythian languages, derivation by prefixes is un-
known ; the radical syllable always stands at the head of the
word, followed by the formative elements. The root, too, to
whatever extent it may receive the accretion of suffixes,
itself remains pure and unchanged, neither fused with them,
nor euphonically affected by them : throughout the whole
body of its derivatives, it has one unvarying and easily recognized form. It would appear, however, on theoretical
grounds, that this fundamental characteristic, of the inviola-
bility of the Scythian roots, must be admitted with some
grains of allowance : since, if root be kept absolutely separate from ending, and changeless, we should, on the one
hand, look for a much closer coincidence of roots than we

actually find between the different dialects ; and, on the other hand, the grand means of development of new words and roots would be cut off, and linguistic growth almost stifled. While, then, in general the root receives no modification from the endings, the latter, on the contrary, are modified by the root, in a way which constitutes the most striking phonetic peculiarity of the family. The vowels, namely, are divided into two classes, heavy (*a, o, u,* etc.), and light (*e, i, ü,* etc.), or guttural and palatal ; and, in the suffixes, only vowels of the same class with that of the root, or with that of the last syllable of the root, if there be more than one, are allowed to occur. Hence, every suffix has two forms, one with light vowel and one with heavy, either of which is used, as circumstances may require. Thus, in Turkish, from *baba,* ' father,' comes *baba-lar-um-dan,* ' from our fathers,' with heavy vowels ; but from *dedeh,* ' grandfather,' with light vowels, comes *dede-ler-in-den,* ' from their grandfathers ' ; *al,* ' to take,' makes *almak, alma, alajak,* while *sev,* ' to love,' makes *sevmek, sevme, sevejek :* or, in Hungarian, *yuh-asz-nak,* means, ' to the shepherd,' but *kert-esz-nek,* ' to the gardener.' This is usually called the " law of harmonic sequence 'of vowels : " it takes somewhat different forms in the different branches, and exhibits niceties and intricacies of harmonic equipoise into which it is unnecessary here to enter : it is most elaborately developed and most strictly obeyed in the Turkish dialects.

One or two important general characteristics of the languages of the family are the natural and direct results of this agglutinative method, which attributes to each suffix a distinct form and office, and in which a true feeling for the unity of words does not forbid an excessive accumulation of separate formative elements in the same vocable. In the first place, varieties and irregularities of conjugation and declension are almost unknown in Scythian grammar: all verbs, all nouns, are inflected upon the same unvarying model ; every grammatical relation has its own sign, by which it is under all circumstances denoted. In the second place, a host of more or less complicated forms are derivable by inflectional processes from one root or theme. An

instance is the word *baba-lar-um-dan*, given above, which
contains the possessive *um*, signifying 'our,' besides the
plural ending *lar* and the ablative case-affix *dan*. The
Turkish verbs exemplify the same peculiarity in a much
more striking manner : thus, by appending to the root one
or more than one of half-a-dozen modifying elements, expressing passivity, reflexiveness, reciprocity, causation, nega-
tion, and impossibility, we may form an almost indefinite
number of themes of conjugation, each possessing the complete scheme of temporal and modal forms : examples are,
from the root *sev*, 'love,' *sev-ish-dir-mek*, 'to cause to love
one another,' *sev-ish-dir-il-eme-mek*, 'not to be capable of
being made to love one another,' and so on.

Of the more ordinary inflectional apparatus, analogous
with that of the tongues of our own family, some of the
Scythian languages possess an abundant store : the Finnish
has a regular scheme of fifteen cases for its nouns ; the
Hungarian, one of more than twenty. Their plurals are
formed by a separate pluralizing suffix (in Turkish, *ler* or
lar, as seen above), to which then the same case-endings are
added as to the simple theme in the singular. No distinction of grammatical gender is marked. Verbal forms are
produced, as with us, by personal endings, of pronominal
origin. These are of two kinds, personal and possessive,
and are appended respectively to conjugational themes having
a participial and an infinitival significance, to names of the
actor and of the action. Thus, from Turkish *dog-mak*,
'to strike,' through the present participle *dogur*, 'striking,'
comes the present *dogur-um*, 'striking-I,' i.e., 'I strike ; '
the preterit is *dogd-um*, 'act-of-striking-mine,' i.e., 'I have
struck ; ' the third person is the simple theme, without suffix,
as *dogur*, 'he strikes,' *dogdi*, 'he has struck ; ' and the addition to these of the common plural suffix of declension
makes the third persons plural, *dogur-lar*, 'they strike,'
dogdi-ler, 'they have struck'—literally, 'strikers,' 'strikings.'
Such verbal forms are, then, essentially nouns, taken in a
predicative sense ; the radical idea has been made a noun of,
in order to be employed as a verb ; and so much of the
nominal form and character still cleaves to them, that it must

be conceded that the Scythian tongues have not clearly apprehended and fully worked out the distinction of these two fundamental parts of speech. Their conjugation, however, such as it is, is rich in temporal and modal distinctions. The root appears in its naked form as second person singular imperative.

Connectives and relational words are nearly unknown in the languages of this family. Where we should employ a clause, they set a case-form of a noun : for example, "while we were going" is rendered in Turkish by *git-diy-imiz-de*, ' in our act of going (wenting).' By means of gerundives and possessives, the different members of a period are twined together into a single intricate or lumbering statement, having the principal verb regularly at the end, and the determining word followed by the determined, often producing an inverted construction which seems very strange to our apprehension.

It must not fail to be observed that the different branches of this family are not a little discordant as regards the degree of their agglutinative development. The Ugrian dialects, especially the Hungarian and Finnish, are the highest in rank, being almost entitled to be reckoned as inflective. The eastern branches, the Mongolian and Tungusian, are in every way poorer and scantier, and the Manchu even verges upon monosyllabic stiffness, not having, for example, so much as a distinction of number and person in its predicative or verbally employed words. The Turkish, in rank as in geographical position, holds a middle place.

Whether the morphological correspondences thus set forth, along with others less conspicuous, which have been found to exist between Ugrian, Samoyed, Turkish, Mongol, and Tungusic languages, are of themselves sufficient to prove these languages genetically allied, branches of one original stock, may be regarded as still an open question. A wider induction, a more thorough grasp and comprehension of the resemblances and differences of all human speech, is probably needed ere linguistic science shall be justified in pronouncing a confident decision of a question so recondite. Whether, again, coincidences in the actual material of the

same tongues have been brought out in sufficient number, or
of a sufficiently unequivocal character, to constitute, along
with these correspondences of form, such an argument in
favour of the unity of the family as may be deemed satisfactory and accepted, is also a matter for doubt. It is safest
to regard the classification at present as a provisional one,
and to leave to future researches its establishment or its
overthrow. The separate investigation and mutual comparison of many of the dialects is as yet only very imperfectly made, or even hardly commenced : further and more
penetrating study may strengthen and render indissoluble the
tie that is already claimed to bind together the eastern and
western branches ; but it may also show their connection to
be merely imaginary.

LECTURE IX.

Uncertainties of genetic classification of languages. "Turanian" family. Dravidian group. North-eastern Asiatic. Monosyllabic tongues: Chinese, Farther Indian, Tibetan, etc. Malay-Polynesian and Melanesian families. Egyptian language and its asserted kindred : Hamitic family. Languages of southern and central Africa. Languages of America : problem of derivation of American races. Isolated tongues . Basque, Caucasian, etc.

IN the last lecture, we began a survey of the general dividing lines of human speech, an enumeration and description of the families into which linguistic science has combined the languages thus far brought under her notice. We had time, however, to examine but two of these families, comprehending the tongues of the two great white races which have taken or are taking, after our own, the most conspicuous parts in the history of mankind: they were, on the one hand, the Semitic, a little group of closely related dialects in the south-western corner of Asia, counting as its principal members the Hebrew, Arabic, and Syriac ; and, on the other hand, the Scythian, an immense aggregation of greatly varying forms of speech, occupying with its five principal branches—the Ugrian, Samoyedic, Turkish, Mongolian, and Tungusic—a very large, but, in part, a not very valuable, portion of the combined continent of Asia and Europe. We have now to complete our work by passing in cursory review the remaining families. The task may be found, as I cannot help fearing, a somewhat tedious one—consisting, as it must do, to no small extent, in going over a catalogue of unknown or unfamiliar names, belonging to races and tongues that stand far off from our interests; but, if its result shall be to give us a comprehensive view of the grand outlines, geographical and structural, of human speech, our hour will not have been spent unprofitably.

It must be borne in mind from the outset that the best classification of human languages now attainable is neither exhaustive, nor equally certain and reliable in all its parts. While nearly the whole field has been explored, it has not been explored everywhere with equal minuteness and care, nor by equally trustworthy investigators. In language, as in geography, there are few extensive regions which need any longer be marked "unknown;" yet there are many of which only the most general features have been determined: and that, perhaps, in part by inference, in part upon information which may turn out incorrect. It may be said in general that, where travellers' reports, or mere vocabularies, have alone been accessible as the ground of classification, the results reached are of superficial character and provisional value. No family of languages can have either its internal or its external relations well established, until its material has been submitted to analysis, the genesis and mode of construction of its forms traced out, and its laws of phonetic change deduced from an examination and comparison of all the accessible phenomena—until, in short, its vital processes are comprehended, in their past history and their present workings. To accomplish this for all existing and recorded human speech will be a slow and laborious task; and, for a long time to come, we must expect that the limits of families will be more or less altered, that languages now separated will come to be classed together, and even that some of those now connected will be sundered. It is not alone true that penetrating study often brings to light resemblances between two languages which escape a superficial examination; it also sometimes shows the illusiveness of others which at first sight appeared to be valid evidences of relationship. In a preliminary comparison, chance coincidences are liable to be overvalued. Moreover, the first tentative groupings are wont to be made by the more sanguine and enterprising class

of philologists. The "personal equation," as the astro-
nomers call it, the allowance for difference of temperament,
endowment, and skill, has to be applied, certainly not less
rigorously, in estimating the observations and deductions of
linguistic scholars than those of the labourers in other
sciences. There is, on the one hand, the class of facile and
anticipative investigators, whose minds are most impressed
by apparent resemblances; who delight in construction, in
establishing connections, in grouping together extensive
classes, in forming grand and striking hypotheses; who are
never willing to say "I do not know:" and, on the other
hand, there is the class of less ardent and more phlegmatic
students, who look beneath superficial resemblances to pro-
founder differences; who call always for more proof; who
are ever ready to confess ignorance, and to hold their judgment in suspense; who refuse their assent to engaging
theories, allowing it to be wrung from them only by cogent
and convincing evidence. Each class has its advantages:
the one furnishes the better explorers, the other the sounder
critics; the one is the more numerous and the more popular,
the other is the safer and the more strictly scientific.

A notable exemplification of this temperamental difference
of authorities is furnished us in connection with one of the
families of which we have already treated. We saw reason,
in the last lecture, to regard with some doubt the genetic
relationship claimed to exist between the five great branches
of the Scythian family, as being founded too little on actual
correspondence of linguistic materials demonstrably derived
from a common source, and too much on mere analogies of
linguistic structure—analogies, too, which were able to consist with such important differences as separate the jejune
dialect of the Manchus from the rich and almost inflective
languages of the Finns and Hungarians. We could not
pronounce it certain that the family will be able to maintain
its integrity in the light of a more thorough and comprehensive investigation. But, on the other hand, we were unable
to deny that it may succeed in doing so; and farther, it
is altogether possible that recognizable evidences of ultimate

connection with the family may be found among other Asiatic tongues, as yet unclassed. Now some linguistic scholars, of no little note and authority, have ventured to give to these possibilities the value of established and unquestionable facts. They have set up an enormous family, which they have styled the " Turanian ; " they have allotted to it the agglutinative structure as its distinctive characteristic, and have made it include nearly all known tongues save the Indo-European and Semitic, not in Asia alone, but through the oceanic islands and over the continent of America. Such sweeping and wholesale conglomeration (for we can hardly call it classification), at the present stage of progress of linguistic research, is wholly unscientific, and of no authority or value. It represents only a want of detailed knowledge, and a readiness to give way to loose and unscrupulous theorizing, on the part of its authors, who are, at the very best, anticipators of the result of scientific inquiry — who are even already proved in part its contradictors : for it is long since shown that many of the alleged " Turanian " dialects are hardly less fundamentally different in their structure from the typical languages of the family than is the Greek or the Hebrew. That the inventors of the name Turanian have associated it with such a baseless classification is sufficient reason why it should be strictly rejected from the terminology of linguistic science. Nor has it in virtue of its derivation any peculiar claim to our acceptance. It is borrowed from the legendary history of the Persian or Iranian race, as represented to us chiefly by the Shah-Nameh, or ' Book of Kings,' of Firdusi. There Irej and Tur are two of the three brothers from whom spring the races of mankind ; and the tribes of Iran and Turan, their descendants—namely, the native Persians and their neighbours upon the north-east, probably of Turkish kindred— are represented as engaged in incessant warfare upon the frontier of their respective territory. Why we should adopt a term so local in its original application, out of a cycle of legends with which so few of us are familiar, as the name of a race which is claimed to extend from the north-western

border of Europe eastward across continent and ocean, widening as it goes, till it spreads along the whole western Atlan-
tic shore, cannot easily be made to appear. There are especially two groups of Asiatic languages,
which have been confidently claimed, and with some show of
reason, to belong to the Scythian family. Of these, the first
is that occupying the southern portion of the peninsula of
India, and commonly called the Tamulian or Dravidian
group or family. We have already seen (in the fifth and
sixth lectures) that the Sanskrit speaking tribes, of Indo-
European race, forced their way into India through the
passes on its north-western frontier, almost within the historic period ; and that they there took exclusive possession
only of the northern portion of the country, including especially the vast plains and valleys of Hindustan proper, with
a tract of the sea-coast stretching southward on either hand ;
dispossessing so far, by reduction to servitude or by expulsion, the more aboriginal inhabitants, but leaving to their
former owners the hilly and elevated southern region, the
Dekhan, as well as the yet less accessible heights and slopes
of the Himalaya chain in the north. Throughout nearly the
whole Dekhan, these older races still form the predominant
population, and speak and write their own languages. Chief
among the latter are the Tamil, occupying the south-eastern
extremity of the peninsula, along with most of the island of
Ceylon ; the Telinga or Telugu, spoken over a yet more
extensive region lying north of this ; the Canarese, extending from the interior border of the Tamil and Telugu westward almost to the coast ; the Malayâlam or Malabar, covering a narrow strip of the south-western coast, from Cape
Comorin northwards ; and the Tulu, filling a still more
restricted area to the north of the Malayâlam. All these
are cultivated tongues, and possess written literatures, of
greater or less extent and antiquity ; that of the Tamil is
the most important and the oldest, parts of it appearing to
date back as far as to the eighth or ninth century of our
era ; nothing in Telugu is earlier than the twelfth. The
Dravidian races, however, have derived their religion, their
polity, and their culture, from the superior race to the north

of them, the Hindus ; their alphabets are of Hindu descent ; their philosophical and scientific terms are borrowed from the rich stores of the Sanskrit ; their literary works are in no small part translations or imitations of Sanskrit authors. There are other tribes in the peninsula, of less numbers and importance, wholly uncultivated, and in part of savage manners and mode of life. Some of these—as the Tudas of the Nilagiri hills, the Kotas of the same neighbourhood, and the wild Gonds and Khonds of the hilly country of Gondwana—are proved by their language to be akin with the Dravidian peoples ; * others—as the Kols, Suras, and Santals —appear to be of entirely diverse race and speech ; relics, perhaps, of a yet more ancient Indian population, which occupied the soil before the incursion of the Dravidians, and was driven out by these, as they, in their turn, by the Indo-Europeans.   Once more, outside the borders of India proper, in the neighbouring country of Beluchistan (the ancient Gedrosia), there is found a people, the Brahuîs, whose tongue, though filled with words of Hindu origin, is claimed to exhibit unequivocal traces of a Dravidian basis.

The Dravidian languages are not only, like the Scythian, of a generally agglutinate character, but their style of agglutinative structure is sufficiently accordant with that of the Scythian tongues to permit of their being ranked in the same family, provided that material evidence of the relationship, of a sufficiently distinct and unequivocal character, shall also be discovered.   That such has been already found out and set forth, is not to be believed.   The investigation has not yet been undertaken by any scholar profoundly versed in the languages of both families, nor has the comparative grammar of the Scythian dialects reached results which can be applied in conducting it and in arriving at a determinate decision.   That an outlying branch of the Scythian race once stretched down through western and southern Iran into the Indian peninsula is at present only an attractive and plausible theory, which may yet be established

---

* This is the opinion of Caldwell, from whose excellent Comparative Grammar of the Dravidian Languages (London, 1856) are mainly derived the materials for this account of the family.

by comparison of languages, when this comparison shall have been made with sufficient knowledge and sufficient caution.

The other group referred to, as having been sometimes claimed to exhibit traces of relationship with the Scythian family, is composed of the languages which occupy the peninsulas and islands of the extreme north-eastern part of the Asiatic continent. Their character and relations constitute a very obscure and difficult problem in linguistic ethnology : whether they make up a group in any other than a geographical sense, whether they are not isolated and independent tongues, is at present exceedingly doubtful. Their linguistic tie, if there be one, is yet to be established.

By far the most conspicuous and important member of the group is the Japanese. It is wholly confined to the islands forming the empire of Japan (and into the northernmost of these, Yesso, it is a recent intrusion ; the chief population of the island is Kurilian), and has no representatives or near kindred upon the main-land. So lively attention has been directed to it of late, since the re-opening of the empire to Europeans—its grammars, dictionaries, conversation-books, and the like, are multiplying so rapidly in European languages, and are leading to so much discussion of its linguistic character, that we may hope to see its position ere long definitely established. It has recently been repeatedly and confidently asserted to be " of the Turanian family ; " but this is a phrase of so wholly dubious meaning that we cannot tell what it is worth : we shall be obliged to hold our judgments suspended until the general relations of the northeastern Asiatic languages are better settled. The language is polysyllabic and agglutinative in character, possessing some of the features of construction which also characterize the Scythian tongues. It is of a simple phonetic structure (its syllables being almost always composed of a single consonant with following vowel), and fluent and easy of utterance. Besides the ordinary spoken dialect, there is another, older and more primitive, used as the medium of certain styles of composition : it is called the Yamato. Much, too, of the learned literature of the Japanese is written in Chinese. Their culture and letters come from China, being

introduced, it is believed, in the third century of our era:
the annals of the empire, however, claim to go back to a
much higher antiquity, even to a time some centuries before
Christ.   It was unfortunate for an inflected tongue like the
Japanese to be obliged to resort to China for an alphabet;
and although a thoroughly practical and convenient set of
characters, of syllabic value, easy to write and to read, was
at one time devised, being made out of parts of Chinese
ideographs, it is of very restricted use; and the mode of
writing generally employed for literary texts is one of the
most detestable in the world, and the greatest existing obstacle to the acquirement of the language.

The dialect of the Loo-Choo islands is nearly akin with the
Japanese.

The peninsula of Corea, lying in close proximity to
the empire of Japan, is occupied by a language between
which and the Japanese, though they are not so dissimilar in
structure that they might not be members of one family, no
material evidences of relationship have been traced and
pointed out.   The Corean also possesses some literary cultivation, derived from China; but of both language and literature only the scantiest knowledge has reached the West.

Along the coast of Asia north of Corea, and also upon the
island of Saghalien or Karafto, and through the Kurile chain
of islands, which stretch from Yesso northward to the extremity of the peninsula of Kamchatka, dwells another race,
that of the Ainos or Kurilians.   They are hairy savages,
who live by hunting and fishing, but are distinguished by
nobility of bearing and gentleness of manners.   Their speech
has been sometimes pronounced radically akin with the
Japanese, but, apparently, without any sufficient reason.   A
few of their popular songs have been written down by
strangers.

The peninsula of Kamchatka itself belongs to yet another
wild race, the Kamchadales; and to the north of these lie the
nearly related peoples of the Koriaks and Chukchi, between
whom and the American races a connection has been sus-
pected, but not satisfactorily proved.   The Namollos, who
occupy the very extremity of the continent, next to Beh-

ring's straits, are pretty certainly related with the Eskimos of the northern shores of the opposite continent, and thus appear to be emigrants out of America into Asia.

Between the races we have mentioned and the Yakuts of the Lena, that far outlying branch of the Turkish family, finally, live the Yukagiris, another isolated and widely spread people, not proved by their language to be akin with any of their neighbours.

It was the more necessary to glance at the intricate and ill understood linguistic relations of this part of the Asiatic continent, because our eyes naturally turn curiously in that direction, when we inquire whence and how our own American continent obtained the aboriginal population which we have been dispossessing. It is evident that much remains to be done upon the Asiatic side of the straits before the linguistic scholar can be ready for a comparison which shall show with what race of the Old World, if with any, the races of the New are allied in speech.

The south-eastern portion of Asia is occupied by peoples whose tongues form together a single class or family. They fill China and Farther India, and some of the neighbouring parts of the central Asiatic plateau. The distinctive common characteristic of these tongues is that they are monosyllabic. Of all human dialects, they represent most nearly what, as we have already seen reason for concluding, was the primitive stage of the agglutinative and inflective forms of speech ; they have never begun that fusion of elements once independently significant into compound forms which has been the principal item in the history of development of all other tongues. The Chinese words, for example, are still to no small extent roots, representing ideas in crude and undefined form, and equally convertible by use into noun, verb, or adverb. Thus, *ta* contains the radical idea of ' being great,' and may, as a substantive, mean ' greatness ; ' as an adjective, ' great ; ' as a verb, either ' to be great,' or ' to make great, to magnify ; ' as an adverb, ' greatly : ' the value which it is to have as actually employed, in any given case, is determined partly by its position in the phrase, and partly by the requirements of the sense, as gathered from the complex of ideas which the sentence presents. We have already had occasion to remark (in the seventh lecture) that somewhat the same thing may be said of many English words; we took *love* as an instance of one which is now either verb or noun, having lost by phonetic abbreviation the formative elements which once distinguished it as the one and as the other. It is a very customary thing with us, too, to take a word which is properly one part of speech, and convert it into various others without changing its shape : for example, *better* is primarily an adjective, as in " a *better* man than I;" but we employ it in connections which make of it an adverb, as in "he loves party *better* than country;" or a noun, as when we speak of yielding to our *betters*, or getting the *better* of a bad habit; or, finally, a verb, as in "they *better* their condition." Such analogies, however, do not explain the form and the variety of application of the words composing the Chinese and its kindred languages. Of the former possession of formative elements these words show no signs, either phonetic or significant; they have never been made distinct parts of speech in the sense in which ours have been and are so. How different is the state of monosyllabism which precedes inflection from that which follows it in consequence of the wearing off of inflective elements, may be in some measure seen by comparing a Chinese sentence with its English equivalent. The Chinese runs, as nearly as we can represent it, thus : " King speak : Sage! not far thousand mile and come; also will have use gain me realm, hey ? " which means, 'the king spoke : O sage! since thou dost not count a thousand miles far to come (that is, hast taken the pains to come hither from a great distance), wilt thou not, too, have brought some thing for the weal of my realm ? ' *

While all the languages of the region we have described thus agree in type, in morphological character, they show a great and astonishing diversity of material; only scanty correspondences of form and meaning are found in their vocabularies; and hence, the nature and degree of their mutual

* This example is taken from Schleicher's Languages of Europe in Systematic Review (Bonn, 1850), p. 51.

relationship are still obscure.   But the structural accordance
is here, evidently, a pretty sure sign of common descent.
If monosyllabic tongues were of frequent occurrence among
human races, if, for instance, we met with one group of them
in China, another in Africa, and another in America, we
should have no right to infer that they were all genetically
related ; for it is, beyond all question, hypothetically possible
that different divisions of mankind should be characterized
by a kindred inaptitude for linguistic development.   When,
however, we find the known languages of this type clustered
together in one corner of a single continent, we cannot well
resist the conviction that they are all dialects of one original
tongue, and that their differences, however great these may
be, are the result of discordant historic growth.

Infinitely the most important member of the monosyllabic
group or family is the Chinese : its history is exceeded in
interest by that of very few other known tongues.   Its
earliest literary records (some of the odes of the Shi-King,
'Book of Songs') claim to go back to nearly two thousand
years before Christ, and the annals and traditions of the
race reach some centuries farther, so that Chinese antiquity
almost exceeds in hoariness both Semitic and Indo-European.
China, indeed, in the primitiveness and persistency of its
language, its arts, and its polity, is one of the most remarkable and exceptional phenomena which the story of our race
presents.   It has maintained substantially the same speech
and the same institutions, by uninterrupted transmission
from generation to generation upon the same soil, all the
way down to our own times from a period in the past at
which every Indo-European people of which we know aught
was but a roving tribe of barbarians.   Elsewhere, change has
been the dominating principle ; in China, permanency.   Nor
has this permanency been quietism and stagnation.   China has
had, down even to modern times, no insignificant share of
activity and progress, though always within certain limits,
and never of a radical and revolutionary character.   She has
been one of the very few great centres of culture and enlightenment which the world has known ; and her culture
has been not less original in its beginnings, and almost more

independent of foreign aid in its development, than any other. She has been the mother of arts, sciences, and letters, to the races on every side of her; and the world at large she has affected not a little, mainly through the material products of her ingenuity and industry. Repeatedly subjected to foreign domination, she has always vanquished her conquerors, compelling them implicitly to adopt her civilization, and respect and maintain her institutions. That she now at last seems to have become in a measure superannuated and effete, and to be nearing her downfall, under the combined pressure of overcrowded population, a detested foreign yoke and internal rebellion against it, and the disorganizing interference of Western powers, may be true; but it does not become us to regard otherwise than with compassion the final decay of a culture which, taking into account the length of its duration and the number of individuals affected by it, has perhaps spread as much light and made as much happiness as any other that ever existed.

The representative man of China is Confucius, who lived in the sixth century before Christ. He is no religious teacher, but an ethical and political philosopher. In him the wisdom of the olden time, the national apprehension of the meaning and duties of life, found its highest expression, which has been accepted as authoritative by all succeeding ages. He determined how much of the ancient literature should be saved from oblivion: his excerpts from it, historical and poetical, together with his own writings, and the works of his pupils, in which are handed down his own instructions in public and private virtue, form nearly the whole of the Five King and the Four Books, the national classics, the earliest and most revered portion of the national literature. Their continuation and elaboration have engaged no insignificant part of the literary activity of following generations. But, aside from this, almost every department of mental productiveness is represented in China by hosts of works, ancient and modern : in history, in biography, in geography and ethnology, in jurisprudence, in the grammar and lexicography especially of their own tongue, in natural history and science, in art and industry, in the various branches of belles-lettres, as poetry, romance, the drama, the Chinese have produced in abundance what, tried even by our own standard, is worthy of high respect and admiration. No race, certainly, outside the Indo-European and Semitic families, nor many races even of those families, can show a literature of equal value with the Chinese.

Not very much requires to be said in explanation of the structure and history of a language so simple—a language which might be said to have no grammatical structure, which possesses neither inflections nor parts of speech, and which has changed less in four thousand years than most others in four hundred, or than many another in a single century. So restricted, in the first place, is its phonetical system, that its whole vocabulary, in the general cultivated dialect (which has lost the power of uttering final mutes, still preserved and distinctly sounded in some of the popular *patois*), is composed of only about four hundred and fifty different vocables, combinations of sounds : these, however, are converted into not far from three times that number of distinct words by means of the tones of utterance, which in Chinese, as in some other languages of similarly scanty resources, are pressed into the service of the vocabulary, instead of being left, as with us, to the department of rhetoric and elocution. As a necessary consequence, the several words have a much greater range of signification than in more richly endowed tongues ; each seems to unite in itself the offices of many distinct words, the tie of connection between its significations being no longer traceable. External development, the formation of derivative words to bear the variety of derived meanings into which every root tends to branch out, is here almost or quite unknown : internal, significant development has been obliged to do the whole work of linguistic growth. Of course, then, not only the grammatical form, but also the radical significance, is often left to be pointed out by the connection. And here, again, the Chinese finds its nearest parallel, among inflected tongues, in the numerous homonyms (words identical in sound but different in meaning) of our own English : for example, in our three different *meet's* (*meet, mete,* and *meat*), and *bear's* (*bear,* verb, *bear,* noun,

and *bare*, adjective), and *found's* (*found* from *find, found,*
' establish,' and *found*, ' cast '), and other the like.   In the
written language, much of this ambiguity is avoided, since
each Chinese character represents a word with regard, not to
its phonetic form alone, but to its meaning also * — whence
comes the strange anomaly that a language composed of but
a thousand or two of words is written with an alphabet containing tens of thousands of different signs. The literary style
is thus enabled to unite with sufficient intelligibility a wonderful degree of conciseness, to combine brevity and precision
to a degree elsewhere unapproached. The spoken language is
much more wordy, using, to secure the mutual understanding
of speaker and hearer, various devices, which here and there
approach very near to agglutination, although they always
stop short of it.   To no small extent, the Chinese is in practical use a language of groups of monosyllabic roots rather
than of isolated monosyllables: a host of conceptions which
we signify by single words, it denotes by a collocation of
several words : thus, ' virtue ' is represented by four cardinal
virtues, *faith-piety-temperance-justice ;* ' parent ' by *father-
mother ;* exceedingly often, two nearly synonymous words are
put together to express their common meaning, like *way-path*,
for 'way' (such a collocation being mainly a device for suggesting to the mind the one signification in which two words, each
of various meaning, agree with one another) ; very often, again,
a " classifier," or word denoting the class in which a vocable is used, is appended to it, as when we say *maple-tree*,
whale-fish, for *maple* and *whale* (many of these classifiers are
of very peculiar sense and application) ; certain words,
further, are virtual signs of parts of speech, as those meaning
' get,' ' come,' ' go,' added to verbs ; ' place,' making nouns
from verbs and adjectives ; a relative particle, pointing out
the attributive relation ; objective particles, indicating
an instrumental, locative, dative case ; pluralizing words,
meaning originally ' number, crowd, heap ; ' a diminutive
sign, the word for ' child ; ' and so on. There has been
here not a little of that attenuation and integration of

* See the twelfth lecture, where this peculiarity of the Chinese mode of
writing will be more fully explained.

meaning by which in our own language we have found
so many relational words and phrases; but there is no
fusion, no close combination, even, of elements; these are
simply placed side by side, without losing their separate individuality. There is no reason assignable why a truly agglutinative stage might not possibly grow out of a condition
of things like this; and it is claimed by some that, in certain
of the popular dialects (which differ notably from the *kwan-
hwa*, the common dialect of the lettered classes), agglutination, to a limited extent, is actually reached.

While thus the Chinese is, in certain respects of fundamental importance, the most rudimentary and scanty of all
known languages, the one least fitted to become a satisfactory
means of expression of human thought, it is not without its
compensations. The power which the human mind has over
its instruments, and independent of their imperfections, is
strikingly illustrated by the history of this form of speech,
which has successfully answered all the purposes of a cultivated, reflecting, studious, and ingenious people throughout a
career of unequalled duration; which has been put to far
higher and more varied uses than most of the multitude of
highly organized dialects spoken among men—dialects rich
in flexibility, adaptiveness, and power of expansion, but poor
in the mental poverty and weakness of those who should
wield them. In the domain of language, as in some departments of art and industry, no race has been comparable with
the Chinese for capacity to accomplish wonderful things with
rude and uncouth instruments.

The principal nations of Farther India are the Annamese
or Cochin-Chinese, the Siamese, and the Burmese; tribes of
inferior numbers, civilization, and importance are the Kwanto,
Cambodians, Peguans, Karens, and others. Annamese culture is of Chinese origin; the races of Siam and Burmah
emerge from obscurity as they receive knowledge, letters,
and religion (Buddhism) together from India. Their languages are, like the Chinese, monosyllabic and isolating; but
they are as much inferior to that tongue in distinctness of
construction and precision of expression as the people that
speak them have shown themselves to be inferior to the

inhabitants of China in mental activity and reach. Of indicative words, substitutes for the formative elements of more highly developed languages, they make an extended use. Such auxiliary and limiting words are in Siamese always put before, in Burmese always after, the principal root. To the same general class of tongues, yet with sundry variations of type, even sometimes appearing to overstep the boundary which divides mere collocation from actual agglutination of elements, are deemed to belong the exceedingly numerous and not less discordant dialects which crowd the mountain valleys on both sides of the great range of the Himalayas, and that part of the plateau of central Asia which lies next north of the range. The linguistic student is lost, as yet, in the infinity of details presented by these dialects, and is unable to classify them satisfactorily. Most of them are known only by partial vocabularies, lists of words gathered by enterprising collectors,* no penetrating investigation and clear exposition of their structure and laws of growth having yet been made. It were useless to detail here the names of the wild tribes to which they belong, or set forth the groupings which have been provisionally established among them. The only one which possesses any historical or literary importance is the Tibetan. Tibet was one of the early conquests of Buddhism, and has long been a chief centre of that religion. It has an immense Buddhist literature, in great part translated from the Sanskrit, and written in a character derived from that in which the Sanskrit is written. Though strictly a monosyllabic language, the Tibetan exhibits some very peculiar and problematical features—in its written but now unpronounced prefixes, and a kind of inflective internal change appearing in many of its words—which are a subject of much controversy among comparative philologists.

With the next great family, the Malay-Polynesian, or Oceanic, we shall not need to delay long. Those who speak its dialects fill nearly all the islands from the coasts of Asia southward and eastward, from Madagascar to the Sandwich

* Among these, Rev. N. Brown and Mr. B. H. Hodgson have especially distinguished themselves.

group and Easter Island, from New Zealand to Formosa. A few of those which are found nearest to Farther India possess alphabets and scanty literatures, coming chiefly from the introduction among them of religion and culture from India; but the Malay has adopted the Arabic alphabet. Considering how widely they are scattered, there prevails among these languages a notable degree of correspondence of material as well as of structure, and their coherence as a family is unquestionable; but the work of marking out subordinate groups, and determining degrees of relationship, is as yet but partially accomplished for them. Missionaries, American and English, have played and are playing an important part in laying them open to knowledge, as well as in introducing knowledge among those who speak them.

The Polynesian languages, especially those of the eastern division, are of simpler phonetic form than any others spoken by human races: their alphabets contain not more than ten consonants, often as few as seven, and their allowed combinations of sounds are restricted to open syllables, composed of a vowel alone, or of a vowel preceded by a single consonant; of combined consonants, or final consonants, they know nothing. They are polysyllabic, but hardly less destitute of forms than the monosyllabic tongues. Their roots, if we may call them so, or the most primitive elements which our imperfect historical analysis enables us to trace, are more often dissyllabic, but of indeterminate value as parts of speech: they may be employed, without change, as verb, substantive, adjective, or even preposition. All inflection is wanting: gender, case, number, tense, mode, person, have no formal distinctions; pronouns, indicative particles, prepositions, and the like, constitute the whole grammar, making parts of speech and pointing out their relations. Moreover, anything which can properly be styled a verb is possessed by none of these languages; their so-called verbs are really only nouns taken predicatively. Thus, to express ' he has a white jacket on,' the Dayak says literally "he with-jacket with-white," or " he jackety whitey." * As a means of development of signification, the repetition or reduplication of a root is very

* Steinthal, Charakteristik etc., page 165.

frequently resorted to ; prefixes and suffixes, especially the former, are also applied to the same purpose. Only the personal pronouns have a peculiar kind of variation by number, produced by composition and fusion with the numerals : in this way are often distinguished not only a singular, dual, and plural, but also a tri-al, denoting three : and the numbers other than singular of the first person have a double form, according as the *we* is meant to include or to exclude the person addressed.

The races to whom belong the dialects we have thus characterized are of a brown colour. But these do not make up the whole population of the Pacific island-world. The groups of little islands lying to the east of New Guinea —the New Hebrides, the Solomon's islands, New Caledonia, and others—are inhabited by a black race, having frizzled or woolly hair, yet showing no other signs of relationship with the natives of Africa. Men of like physical characteristics are found to occupy the greater part of New Guinea, and more or less of the other islands lying westward, as far as the Andaman group, in the Bay of Bengal. They are known by various names, as Negritos, Papuans, Melanesians. Some of their languages have been recently brought by missionary effort to the knowledge of linguistic scholars, and help to prove the race distinct from the Polynesian. In point of material, a wide diversity exists among the dialects of the different tribes ; they exhibit almost the extreme of linguistic discordance ; each little island has its own idiom, unintelligible to all its neighbours, and sometimes the separate districts of the same islet are unable to communicate together. Yet, so far as they have been examined, distinct traces of a common origin have been found ; and in general plan of structure they agree not only among themselves, but also, in a marked degree, with the Polynesian tongues, so that they are perhaps to be regarded as ultimately coinciding with the latter in origin.[*]

The aboriginal inhabitants of Australia and of parts of the neighbouring islands are by some set down as a distinct

---

[*] See Von der Gabelentz, Die Melanesischen Sprachen, etc., in vol. viii. (1861) of the Memoirs of the Saxon Society of Sciences.

race, the Alforas : our knowledge of their speech is not
sufficient for us to determine with confidence their linguistic
position.

The rank in the scale of languages generally assigned
to the ancient Egyptian (with its successor, the modern
Coptic), its often alleged connection with the Semitic, and the
antiquity and importance of the culture to which it served as
instrument, would have justified us in treating it next after
the Indo-European and Semitic ; but it seemed more convenient to traverse the whole joint continent of Europe and
Asia, before crossing into Africa.   The chronology of
Egyptian history is still a subject of not a little controversy ;
but it cannot be reasonably doubted that the very earliest
written monuments of human thought are found in the valley
of the Nile, as well as the most ancient and most gigantic
works of human art.   There was wisdom in Egypt, accumulated and handed down through a long succession of generations, for Moses, the founder of the Hebrew state, to become
learned in ; and Herodotus, the " father of history," as we
are accustomed to style him, found Egypt, when he visited
it, already entered upon its period of dotage and decay.   It
was a strange country : one narrow line of brilliant green
(but spreading fan-like at its northern extremity), traced by
the periodical overflow of a single branchless and sourceless
river through the great desert which sweeps from the Atlantic
coast to the very border of India ; so populous and so fertile
as to furnish a surplusage of labour, for the execution of
architectural works of a solidity and grandeur elsewhere
unknown, and which the absolute dryness of the climate has
permitted to come down to us in unequalled preservation.
On these monuments, within and without, the record-loving
Egyptians depicted and described the events of their national
and personal history, the course and occupations of their
daily lives, their offerings, prayers, and praises, the scenes of
their public worship and of the administration of their state,
their expeditions and conquests.   Their language has thus
stood for ages plainly written before the eyes of the world,
inviting readers ; but the key to the characters in which it
was inscribed, the sacred hieroglyphics, had been lost almost

since the beginning of the Christian era ; until, in our own
century, it has been recovered by the zeal and industry of a
few devoted men, among whose names that of Champollion
stands foremost.   The reconstruction of the ancient
Egyptian tongue, though by no means complete, is sufficiently
advanced to allow us to see quite clearly its general character.   It was but an older form of the modern Coptic.
The Coptic has itself gone out of existence within the past
three or four centuries, extinguished by the Arabic ; but we
possess a tolerably abundant Christian Coptic literature,
representing two or three slightly different dialects, written
in an alphabetic character chiefly adapted from the Greek,
and dating back to the early centuries of our era.   The
differences are comparatively slight between the old Egyptian
of the hieroglyphical monuments and the later Coptic, for the
exceedingly simple structure of the language has saved it from
the active operation of linguistic change.   A transitional
step, too, between the one and the other is set before us in
the series of records, mostly in papyrus rolls, which are called
hieratic and demotic, from the characters in which they are
written, modified forms of the hieroglyphs, adapted to a more
popular use : these records come from the last five or six
centuries preceding our era, and represent, doubtless, the
popular speech of the period.

A number of other African dialects are claimed to exhibit
affinities of material and structure with the language of
Egypt.   They fall * into three groups : the Ethiopian or
Abyssinian, of which the Galla is at present the most important member ; the Libyan or Berber, extending over a
wide region of northern Africa, from Egypt to the Atlantic
ocean ; and the Hottentot, embracing the dialects of the
degraded tribes of Hottentots and Bushmen at the far
southern extremity of the continent : these last have been but
recently recognized as showing signs of probable relationship
with the rest.   The family, as thus made up, is styled the
Hamitic (by a name correlative to Semitic and Japhetic) :
its constitution and relations, however, are still matters of

* I follow here the classification of Lepsius, given in the second edition of
his Standard Alphabet (London and Berlin, 1863), at p. 303.

no little difference of opinion among linguistic scholars, and can be fully established only by continued research.

The Egyptian was a language of the utmost simplicity, or even poverty, of grammatical structure. Its roots—which, in their condition as made known to us, are prevailingly, though not uniformly, monosyllabic—are also its words; neither noun nor verb, nor any other part of speech, has a characteristic form, or can be traced back to a simpler radical element, from which it comes by the addition of a formative element. Some roots, as in Chinese, are either verb, substantive, or adjective—thus, *ankh*, 'live, life, alive,' *sekhi*, 'write, a writing, writer'—others are only verbs or only nouns. A word used as substantive is generally marked by a prefixed article, which is often closely combined with it, but yet is not a part of it; it has no declension, the objective uses being indicated by prepositions. The personal inflection of the verb is made by means of suffixed pronominal endings, also loosely attached, and capable of being omitted in the third person when a noun is expressed as subject of the verb. Mode and tense are, to a certain limited extent, signified by prefixed auxiliary words. But these pronominal endings, which, when added to the verb, indicate the subject (sometimes also the object), have likewise a possessive value, when appended to nouns: thus, *ran-i* is either 'I name' or 'my name;' it is literally, doubtless, 'naming-mine,' applied in a substantive or a verbal sense according to the requirements of the particular case: that is to say, there is no essential distinction formally made between a noun and a verb. In the singular number of both articles and pronominal suffixes, as also in the pronouns, there is made a separation of gender, as masculine or feminine. This is a highly important feature in the structure of Hamitic speech, and the one which gives it its best claim to the title of form-language. So far as it goes, it puts the tongues of the family into one grand class along with the Indo-European and the Semitic: these three families alone have made a subjective classification of all objects of knowledge and of thought as masculine and feminine, and given it expression in their speech. But, by its general character, the Egyptian is far enough

from being entitled to rank with the Indo-European and
Semitic languages, being, rather, but a single step above the
Chinese : in many of its constructions it is quite as bald as
the latter, and sometimes even less clear and free from
ambiguity.

The Egyptian pronouns present some striking analogies
with the Semitic, and from this fact has been drawn by many
linguistic scholars the confident conclusion that the two
families are ultimately related, the Egyptian being a relic of
the Semitic as the latter was before its development into the
peculiar form which it now wears, and which was described
in the last lecture. Considering, however, the exceeding
structural difference between them, and the high improba-
bility that any genuine correspondences of so special a character should have survived that thorough working-over
which could alone have made Semitic speech out of anything
like Egyptian, the conclusion must be pronounced, at the
least, a venturesome one. Semitic affinities have been not
less confidently, and with perhaps more show of reason,
claimed for the Libyan and Abyssinian branches of the so-
called Hamitic family. Only continued investigation, and
more definite establishment of the criteria of genetic relationship, can determine what part of these alleged correspondences are real, and of force to show community of descent,
and what part are fancied, or accidental, or the result of
borrowing out of one language into another.

To enter in any detail into the labyrinths of African language and ethnography is not essential to our present
purpose, and will not be here undertaken. As a consequence
of the extraordinary activity of missionary enterprise and of
geographical exploration and discovery in Africa within a few
years past, much curiosity and study has been directed
towards African dialects ; a great mass of material has been
collected, and its examination has been carried far enough to
give us at least a general idea of the distribution of races in
that quarter of the world. A vast deal, however, still remains
to be done, before the almost innumerable and rapidly changing dialects of all these wild tribes shall be brought to our
knowledge, combined into classes and groups, and under-

stood in their resemblances and differences of material and structure.

Apart from the dialects already mentioned, as belonging to the Hamitic or the Semitic family, the best established and most widely extended group of African languages is that one which fills nearly the whole southern part of the continent, from a few degrees north of the equator to the Cape of Good Hope. It is variously called the Bantu, the Chuana, or the Zingian family; or, by a simple geographical title, the South-African. The material as well as structural coincidences between its numerous members are fully sufficient to prove its unity. Its subdivisions, and the separate dialects composing them, need not here be rehearsed.* None of these dialects has any other culture than that which it has received under missionary auspices in the most recent period. They are all of an agglutinative character, forming words of many syllables, and, in a certain way, they are rich enough in forms, and in the capacity of indicating different shades of meaning and relation. Their most marked peculiarity is their extensive use of pronominal prefixes to the nouns; these are numerous—in some languages, as many as sixteen —and distinguish the number and generic class of the nouns to which they are attached. Thus, in Zulu, we have *um-fana,* 'boy,' *aba-fana,* 'boys;' *in-komo,* 'cow,' *izin-komo,* 'cows;' *ili-zwi,* 'word,' *ama-zwi,* 'words,' and so on.† But farther, these same prefixes, or characteristic parts of them, enter into the formation of the adjectives, the possessive and relative pronouns, and the personal pronouns employed as subject or object of the verbs, agreeing with or referring to the nouns to which they respectively belong: for example, *aba-fana b-ami aba-kulu, ba tanda,* 'my large boys, they love;' but *izin-komo z-ami izin-kulu, zi tanda,* 'my large cows, they love.' Thus is produced a kind of alliterative congruence, like the rhyming one often sees in Latin, as *vir-o optim-o maxim-o, femin-æ optim-æ maxim-æ.* Of inflection by cases

---

* See Lepsius's General Table of Languages, already referred to; and Dr. Bleek's Catalogue of Sir George Grey's Library, at Capetown, 1858.

† Our examples are taken from Rev. L. Grout's "Zulu-Land" (Philadelphia, 1864), chap. xiv.

the South-African noun has hardly any; the case-relations
are indicated by prefixed prepositions. Nor is there a personal inflection of the verbs, except by means of prefixed
pronouns. Mode and tense are signified chiefly by auxiliary
words, also standing before the main root; but in part by
derivative forms of the root, made by suffixes: thus, *tandile*,
'loved,' from *tanda*, 'love;' and like suffixes form derivative
conjugations of the root, in number and in variety comparable with those which, as was shown in the last lecture, come
from the Turkish verb: examples are *bonisa*, 'show,' *bonela*,
'see for,' *bonana*, 'see each other,' *bonisana*, 'show each
other,' *bonwa*, 'be seen,' etc., etc., from *bona*, 'see.' Except
in the interjectional forms, the vocative and second person
imperative, every verb and noun in these languages appears
in connected speech clothed with a pronominal prefix; so
that a prefix seems as essential a part of one of their words
as does a suffix of an Indo-European word, in the older
dialects of the family.

A very peculiar feature of the phonetic structure of some
of the best-known South-African languages, especially of the
Kafir branch (including the Zulu), is the use, as consonants,
of the sounds called *clicks*, made by separating the tongue
sharply from the roof of the mouth, with accompanying suc-
tion—sounds which we employ only in talking to horses or
in amusing babies. As many as four of these clicks form in
some dialects a regular part of the consonantal system, each
being subject to variation by utterance simultaneously with
other sounds, guttural or nasal. It is not a little remarkable that the clicks also abound in the tongues of that isolated branch of the Hamitic family, the Hottentot and
Bushman, which is shut in among the South-African dialects:
indeed, they are conjectured to be of Hottentot origin, and
caught by the other tribes by imitation, since they are found
only in those members of the different South-African
branches which are neighbours of the Hottentots.

Upon the western coast of the continent, the languages of
the family of which we are treating extend as far as into the
territory of Sierra Leone; but they are much intermingled
at the north with other tongues of a different kindred. A

broad band across the continent at its widest part, from Cape
Verde on the north nearly to the equator on the south, and
eastward to the upper waters of the Nile, is filled with dialects not reckoned as South-African, although possessing a
structure in many respects accordant with that which we
have just described. Conspicuous among them are the
Fulah or Fellatah, the Mandingo, and the tongues of Bornu
and Darfur. How far they admit of being grouped together
as a single family, and what may be the value of their general
structural correspondence with the other great African
family, must be left for future researches to determine.
One of them, the Vei, has an alphabet of its own, of native
invention.

Throughout nearly the whole of northern and central
Africa, Arabic influence has for some time past been rapidly
spreading, carrying with it a certain degree of civilization,
the Mohammedan religion, the Koran, and some knowledge
and use of the Arabic language. It is only in this quarter
of the world that Semitic faith and speech still continue
aggressive.

There remains for consideration, of the recognized great
families of human language, only that one which occupies the
continent of North and South America. Of this, also, we
must renounce all attempt at detailed treatment; it is a theme
too vast and complicated to be dealt with otherwise than
very summarily within our necessary limits. The conditions
of the linguistic problem presented by the American languages are exceedingly perplexing, for the same reason as
those presented by the Polynesian and African dialects, and
in a yet higher degree. The number, variety, and changeableness of the different tongues is wonderful. Dialectic
division is carried to its extreme among them ; the isolating
and diversifying tendencies have had full course, with little
counteraction from the conserving and assimilating forces.
The continent seems ever to have been peopled by a congeries of petty tribes, incessantly at warfare, or standing off
from one another in jealous and suspicious seclusion. Certain striking exceptions, it is true, are present to the mind of
every one. Mexico, Central America, and Peru, at the time

of the Spanish discovery and conquest, were the seat of
empires possessing an organized system of government, with
national creeds and institutions, with modes of writing and
styles of architecture, and other appliances of a considerably
developed culture, of indigenous origin. Such relics, too,
as the great mounds which are scattered so widely through
our western country, and the ancient workings upon the
veins and ledges of native copper along the southern shore
of Lake Superior, show that other large portions of the
northern continent had not always been in the same savage
condition as that in which our ancestors found them. Yet
these were exceptions only, not changing the general rule ;
and there is reason to believe that, as the civilization of the
Mississippi valley had been extinguished by the incursion
and conquest of more barbarous tribes, so a similar fate was
threatening that of the southern peoples : that, in fact,
American culture was on its way to destruction even without European interference, as European culture for a time
had seemed to be, during the Dark Ages which attended the
downfall of the Roman empire. If the differentiation of
American language has been thus unchecked by the influence
of culture, it has been also favoured by the influence of the
variety of climate and mode of life. While the other great
families occupy, for the most part, one region or one zone,
the American tribes have been exposed to all the difference
of circumstances which can find place between the Arctic
and the Antarctic oceans, amid ice-fields, mountains, valleys,
on dry table-lands and in reeking river-basins, along shores
of every clime. Moreover, these languages have shown
themselves to possess a peculiar mobility and changeableness
of material. There are groups of kindred tribes whose
separation is known to be of not very long standing, but in
whose speech the correspondences are almost overwhelmed
and hidden from sight by the discordances which have sprung
up. In more than one tongue it has been remarked that
books of instruction prepared by missionaries have become
antiquated and almost unintelligible in three or four generations. Add to all this, that our knowledge of the family begins in the most recent period, less than four hundred years

ago ; that, though it has been since penetrated and pressed
on every side by cultivated nations, the efforts made to collect
and preserve information respecting it have been only spas-
modic and fragmentary ; that it is almost wholly destitute of
literature, and even of traditions of any authority and value ;
and that great numbers of its constituent members have
perished, in the wasting away of the tribes by mutual warfare, by pestilence and famine, and by the encroachments of
more powerful races—and it will be clearly seen that the
comprehensive comparative study of American languages is
beset with very great difficulties.

Yet it is the confident opinion of linguistic scholars that a
fundamental unity lies at the base of all these infinitely varying forms of speech ; that they may be, and probably are, all
descended from a single parent language.* For, whatever
their differences of material, there is a single type or plan
upon which their forms are developed and their constructions
made, from the Arctic Ocean to Cape Horn ; and one sufficiently peculiar and distinctive to constitute a genuine indication of relationship. This type is called the incorporative
or polysynthetic. It tends to the excessive and abnormal
agglomeration of distinct significant elements in its .words ;
whereby, on the one hand, cumbrous compounds are formed
as the names of objects, and a character of tedious and time-
wasting polysyllabism is given to the language—see, for
example, the three to ten-syllabled numeral and pronominal
words of our western Indian tongues ; or the Mexican name
for ' goat,' *kwa-kwauh tentsone,* literally ' head-tree (horn)-
lip-hair (beard),' or ' the horned and bearded one '—and, on
the other hand, and what is of yet more importance, an
unwieldy aggregation, verbal or *quasi*-verbal, is substituted

---

* I make no account here of isolated dialects of an exceptional character,
like the Otomi in central Mexico, which is asserted to be a monosyllabic language ; nor of others which may exhibit the characteristic features of American speech so faintly, or in such a modified form, as to be hardly recognizable
by their structure as American : it remains yet to be determined whether
such seeming exceptions do or do not admit of explanation as the result of
special historical development. Nor, of course, is the possibility denied that
fuller knowledge will bring to light tongues radically and irreconcilably discordant from the general type.

for the phrase or sentence, with its distinct and balanced members. Thus, the Mexican says " I-flesh-eat," as a single word, compounded of three elements; or if, for emphasis, the object is left to stand separate, it is at least first represented by a pronoun in the verbal compound: as, " I-it-eat, the flesh ; " or " I-it-him-give, the bread, my son," for " I give my son the bread."

The incorporative type is not wholly peculiar to the languages of our continent. A trace of it (in the insertion, among the verbal forms, of an objective as well as a subjective pronominal ending) is found even in one of the Ugrian dialects of the Scythian family, the Hungarian; and the Basque, of which we shall presently speak more particularly, exhibits it in a very notable measure. It is found, too, in considerably varying degree and style of development in the different branches of the American family. But its general effect is still such that the linguist is able to claim that the languages to which it belongs are, in virtue of their structure, akin with one another, and distinguished from all other known tongues.

Not only do the subjective and objective pronouns thus enter into the substance of the verb, but also a great variety of modifiers of the verbal action, adverbs, in the form of particles and fragments of words; thus, almost everything which helps to make expression forms a part of verbal conjugation, and the verbal paradigm becomes well-nigh interminable. An extreme instance of excessive synthesis is afforded in the Cherokee word-phrase *wi-ni-taw-ti-ge-gi-na-li-skaw-lung-ta-naw-ne-li-ti-se-sti*, ' they will by that time have nearly finished granting [favours] from a distance to thee and me.' *

Other common traits, which help to strengthen our conclusion that these languages are ultimately related, are not wanting. Such are, for example, the habit of combining words by fragments, by one or two representative syllables ; the direct conversion of nouns, substantive and adjective, into verbs, and their conjugation as such ; peculiarities of

* A. Gallatin in Archæologia Americana, vol. ii. (Cambridge, 1836), p. 201.

generic distinction—many languages dividing animate from
inanimate beings (somewhat as we do by the use of *who* and
what), with arbitrary and fanciful details of classification,
like those exhibited by the Indo-European languages in their
separation of masculine and feminine ; the possession of a
very peculiar scheme for denoting the degrees of family
relationship ; and so on.

As regards their material constitution, their assignment of
certain sounds to represent certain ideas, our Indian dialects
show, as already remarked, a very great discordance. It has
been claimed that there are not less than a hundred languages or groups upon the continent, between whose words
are discoverable no correspondences which might not be sufficiently explained as the result of accident. Doubtless a
more thorough and sharpsighted investigation, a more penetrating linguistic analysis and comparison—though, under
existing circumstances, any even distant approximation to
the actual beginning may be hopeless—would considerably
reduce this number ; yet there might still remain as many
unconnected groups as are to be found in all Europe and
Asia. It is needless to undertake here an enumeration of
the divisions of Indian speech : we will but notice a few of
the most important groups occupying our own portion of
the continent.

In the extreme north, along the whole shore of the Arctic
ocean, are the Eskimo dialects, with which is nearly allied the
Greenlandish. Below them is spread out, on the west, the
great Athapaskan group. On the east, and as far south as
the line of Tennessee and North Carolina, stretches the immense region occupied by the numerous dialects of the
Algonquin or Delaware stock; within it, however, is enclosed
the distinct branch of Iroquois languages. Our south-eastern states were in possession of the Florida group, comprising the Creek, Choctaw, and Cherokee. The great nation of
the Sioux or Dakotas gives its name to the branch which occupied the Missouri valley and parts of the lower Mississippi.
Another wide-spread sub-family, including the Shoshonee and
Comanche, ranged from the shores of Texas north-westward
to the borders of California and the territory of the Atha-

paskas; and the Pacific coast was occupied by a medley of tribes. Mexico and Central America, finally, were the home of a great variety of tongues, that of the cultivated Aztecs, with its kindred, having the widest range.

The linguistic condition of America, and the state of our knowledge respecting it, being such as we have here seen, it is evident how futile must be at present any attempt to prove by the evidence of language the peopling of the continent from Asia, or from any other part of the world outside. We have already noticed that a relationship is asserted to exist between the Eskimo branch of American language and a dialect or two in the extreme north-east of Asia; but the fact that it is a specifically Eskimo relationship is sufficient to prove its worthlessness as a help to the explanation of the origin of American language in general, and to make it probable that the communication there has been from America to Asia, and not the contrary. To enter upon a bare and direct comparison of modern American with modern Asiatic dialects, for the purpose of discovering signs of genetic connection between them, would be a proceeding utterly at variance with all the principles of linguistic science, and could lead to no results possessing any significance or value. One might as well compare together the English, the modern Syriac, and the Hungarian, in order to determine the ultimate relationship of the Indo-European, Semitic, and Scythian families. Sound method (as was pointed out in the sixth lecture) requires that we study each dialect, group, branch, and family by itself, before we venture to examine and pronounce upon its more distant connections. What we have to do at present, then, is simply to learn all that we possibly can of the Indian languages themselves; to settle their internal relations, elicit their laws of growth, reconstruct their older forms, and ascend toward their original condition as far as the material within our reach, and the state in which it is presented, will allow; if our studies shall at length put us in a position to deal with the question of their Asiatic derivation, we will rejoice at it. I do not myself expect that valuable light will ever be shed upon the subject by linguistic evidence: others may be more sanguine; but all must at any rate agree that, as things are, the subject is in no position to be taken up and discussed with profit. The absurd theories which have been advanced and gravely defended by men of learning and acuteness respecting the origin of the Indian races are hardly worth even a passing reference. The culture of the more advanced communities has been irrefragably proved to be derived from Egypt, Phenicia, India, and nearly every other anciently civilized country of the Old World: the whole history of migration of the tribes themselves has been traced in detail over Behring's Straits, through the islands of the Pacific, and across the Atlantic; they have been identified with the Canaanites, whom Joshua and the Israelites exterminated; and, worst of all, with the ten Israelitish tribes deported from their own country by the sovereigns of Mesopotamia! When men sit down with minds crammed with scattering items of historical information, abounding prejudices, and teeming fancies, to the solution of questions respecting whose conditions they know nothing, there is no folly which they are not prepared to commit.

Our national duty and honour are peculiarly concerned in this matter of the study of aboriginal American languages, as the most fertile and important branch of American archæology. Europeans accuse us, with too much reason, of indifference and inefficiency with regard to preserving memorials of the races whom we have dispossessed and are dispossessing, and to promoting a thorough comprehension of their history. Indian scholars, and associations which devote themselves to gathering together and making public linguistic and other archæological materials for construction of the proper ethnology of the continent, are far rarer than they should be among us. Not a literary institution in our country has among its teachers one whose business it is to investigate the languages of our aboriginal populations, and to acquire and diffuse true knowledge respecting them and their history.* So much the more reason have we to be grateful to the few who are endeavouring to make up our de-

---

* This reproach, at least, is about to be removed, by the establishment of a chair of American archæology at Cambridge.

ficiencies by self-prompted study, and especially to those
self-denying men who, under circumstances of no small difficulty, are or have been devoting themselves to the work of
collecting and giving to the world original materials. The
Smithsonian Institution has recently taken upon itself the
office of encouraging, guiding, and giving effect to the
labours of collectors, under special advantages derived from
its relation to the Government, with laudable zeal, and with
the best promise of valuable results. No department of inquiry, certainly, within the circle of the historical sciences,
has a stronger claim upon the attention of such a national
institution ; and it becomes all Americans to countenance
and aid its efforts by every means in their power.

Before closing this cursory and imperfect survey of the
varieties of human language, we have to glance at one or
two dialects or groups of dialects which have hitherto resisted all attempts at classification. Most noteworthy
among these is the Basque, spoken in a little district of the
Pyrenees, on both sides of the border between France and
Spain, enveloping the angle of the Bay of Biscay, between
Bayonne and Balbao. The Basques are well identified as
descended from the primitive Iberian population which is
supposed to have filled the Spanish peninsula before the intrusion of the Celts : their stubborn and persistent character
and the inaccessibility of their mountain retreats have
enabled their native idiom successfully to resist the assimilating influences exercised by successive Celtic, Roman, and
Gothic conquest and domination. It stands, so far as is yet
known, alone among the languages of mankind ; kindred has
been sought and even claimed for it in every direction, but
to no good purpose. It is, then, naturally enough conjectured to be a sole surviving remnant of the speech of an aboriginal race, peopling some part of Europe before the
immigration of the Indo-European tribes, perhaps before
that of the Scythian ; and the possibility that it may be so
invests it with an unusual degree of interest. Its structure
is exceedingly peculiar, intricate, and difficult of analysis.
As we have already had occasion to notice, it possesses much
more striking analogies with the aboriginal languages of

23

America than with any others that are known : like them, it
is highly polysynthetic, incorporating into its verbal forms a
host of pronominal relations which are elsewhere expressed
by independent words ; like them, also, it compounds words
together by representative fragments. But it does not
show the same tendency to fuse the whole sentence into a
verb ; its nouns have an inflection which is much more
Scythian than American in type ; and there are other differences which distinctly enough discourage the conjecture that
it can be historically akin with the tongues of this continent.
Some other among the various populations of southern Europe, treated by the ancients as of strange tongue and lineage, and which have now totally disappeared, may possibly
have been akin with the Basques : such questions are covered with a darkness which we cannot hope ever to see dis-
pelled.

In Italy are still found the relics of one of these isolated
and perished peoples, the Etruscans. They were a race of
much higher culture than the Basques, and their neighbourhood to Rome, and their resulting influence, peaceful and
warlike, upon her growing polity and developing history,
give them a historical importance to which the Iberian race
can lay no claim. Inscriptions in their language, written in
legible characters, and in some instances of assured meaning, are preserved to our day ; yet its linguistic character
and connections are an unsolved and probably insoluble
problem. Every few years, some one of those philologists
whose judgments are easily taken captive by a few superficial correspondences claims to have proved its relationship
with some known family, and thus to have determined the
ethnological position of the race that spoke it ; but his arguments and conclusions are soon set aside as of no more value
than others already offered and rejected.

Again, there is found in the mountain-range of the Caucasus a little knot of idioms which have hitherto baffled the
efforts of linguistic scholars to connect them with other
known forms of speech. Their principal groups are four :
the Georgian and the Circassian stretch along the southern
and northern shores respectively of the eastern extremity of

the Black Sea, and through the mountains nearly to the Caspian; the Lesghian borders the Caspian; and the Mitsjeghian lies between it and the Circassian. The Georgian possesses a peculiar alphabet and a literature; but the whole group, except as it presents a problem for the solution of the linguistic ethnographer, has no special importance.

The Albanian or Skipetar, the modern representative of the ancient Illyrian, has already been spoken of as doubtfully classifiable with the Indo-European languages. If its connection with them shall not finally be made out to the satisfaction of the learned, it, too, will have to be numbered among the isolated and problematical tongues.

One more Asiatic dialect may be worth a moment's notice: the Yenisean, occupying a tract of country along the middle course of the Yenisei, with traces in the mountains about the head waters of that river; it belongs to the feeble and scanty remnant of a people which is lost in the midst of Scythian tribes, and apparently destined to be ere long absorbed by them, but which is proved to be of different race by its wholly discordant language.

The number of such isolated tongues is, of course, liable to be increased as we come to know more thoroughly the linguistic condition of regions of the world which are as yet only partially explored. There is a possibility that many types of speech, once spread over wide domains, may exist at present only in scanty fragments, as well as that some may have disappeared altogether, leaving not even a trace behind.

LECTURE X.

Classification of languages. Morphological classifications; their defects. Schleicher's morphological notation. Classification by general rank. Superior value of genetic division. Bearing of linguistic science on ethnology. Comparative advantages and disadvantages of linguistic and physical evidence of race. Indo-European language and race mainly coincident. Difficulty of the ethnological problem. Inability of language to prove either unity or variety of human species. Accidental correspondences; futility of root comparisons.

OUR inquiries into the history and relations of human languages have last brought us to a review and brief examination of their groupings into families, so far as yet accomplished by the labours of linguistic students. The families may be briefly recapitulated as follows. First in rank and importance is the Indo-European, filling nearly the whole of central and southern Europe, together with no inconsiderable portion of south-western Asia, and with colonies in every quarter of the globe; it includes the languages of nearly all the modern, and of some of the most important of the ancient, civilized and civilizing races. Next is the Semitic, of prominence in the world's history second only to the Indo-European, having its station in Arabia and the neighbouring regions of Asia and Africa. Then follows the loosely aggregated family of the Scythian dialects, as we chose to term them, ranging from Norway almost to Behring's Straits, and occupying a good part of central Asia also, with outliers in southern Europe (Hungary and Turkey), and possibly in southernmost Asia (the Dekhan, or peninsula of India). Further, the south-eastern Asiatic or monosyllabic family, in China and Farther India, and countries adjacent to these ; the Malay-Polynesian and Melanesian, scattered over the numberless islands of the Pacific and Indian Oceans; the Hamitic, composed of the Egyptian and its congeners, chiefly in northern Africa; the South-African, filling Africa about and below the equator; and the American, covering with its greatly varied forms our western continent, from the Arctic Ocean to the Antarctic. Besides these great families, we took note of several isolated languages or lesser groups, of doubtful or wholly unknown relationship : as those in extreme north-eastern Asia, in the Caucasian mountains, in central Africa; as the Basque in the Pyrenees, the Albanian in north-western Greece, the Yenisean in Siberia, and the extinct Etruscan in northern Italy.

The scheme of classification, as thus drawn out, was a genetical one, founded on actual historical relationship. Each family or group was intended to be made up of those tongues which there is found sufficient reason to regard as kindred dialects, as common descendants of the same original. We were obliged, however, to confess that our classification had not everywhere the same value, as the evidences of relationship were not of an equally unequivocal character in all the families, or else had been thus far incompletely gathered in and examined. Where, as in the case of Indo-European and Semitic speech, we find structural accordance combined with identity of material, as traced out and determined by long-continued and penetrating study on the part of many investigators, there the unity of the families is placed beyond the reach of reasonable doubt. But it is unfortunately true that these two are the only groups of wide extent and first-rate importance respecting which the linguistic student can speak with such fulness of confidence ; everywhere else, there is either some present deficiency of information, which time may or may not remove, or the conditions are such that our belief in the genetic relationship must rest upon the more questionable ground of correspondence in structural development. We may by no means deny that morphological accordance is capable of rising to such a value as should

make it a sufficient and convincing evidence of genetic
unity; but it is evidently of a less direct and unmistakable
character than material identity, and requires for its estimation a wider range of knowledge, a more acute insight, and a
more cautious judgment. If two languages agree in the
very material of which their words and apparatus of grammatical inflection are composed, to a degree beyond what
can possibly be regarded as the effect of accident or of
borrowing, the conclusion that they are akin is inevitable;
nothing but community of linguistic tradition can explain
such phenomena: but agreement in the style only in which
words are composed and thought expressed admits of being
attributed to causes other than historical—to equality of
mental endowment, of intellectual force and training. We
may look hopefully forward to the time when linguistic
science shall have reached such a pitch of perfection, shall
have so thoroughly mastered the infinitely varied phenomena
of universal human language and traced out their causes,
that she shall be able to separate with certainty the effects
of ethnic capacity from those of transmitted habit: but that
time has certainly not yet come; and, as the value of morphological accordances as evidence of genetic connection has
hitherto been repeatedly overrated, so it will long, and
always in unskilful or incautious hands, be peculiarly liable
to a like mistreatment.

We have already had occasion to refer to and describe
some of the principal structural peculiarities which are illustrated in the variety of human tongues; but it will be worth
while here to bestow a few words farther upon them, and
upon the systems of morphological classification to which
they have served as foundation.

The languages of mankind have been divided into two
grand classes, the monosyllabic (otherwise called isolating,
or radical) and the polysyllabic (or inflectional). To the
former belong the tongues of China and Farther India, with
their relatives in the same quarter of Asia, and perhaps one
or two idioms in other parts of the world. In them there is a
formal identity of root and word; none of their vocables are
made up of radical and formative elements, the one giving

the principal idea, the other indicating its limitation, application, or relation; they possess no formally distinguished parts of speech. Usage may assign to some of their roots the offices which in inflectional tongues are filled by inflective endings, suffixes or prefixes; it may also stamp some as adjectives, others as nouns, as pronouns, as verbs, and so on: yet means of this sort can only partially supply their lack of the resources possessed by more happily developed languages; categories undistinguished in expression are but imperfectly, if at all, distinguished in apprehension; thought is but brokenly represented and feebly aided by its instrument. To the latter, or inflectional class, belong all the other languages of the world, which, whatever and however great their differences, have at least this in common, that their signs of category and relation are not always separate words, but parts of other words, that their vocables are, to some extent, made up of at least two elements, the one radical, the other formative. There can be, it is evident, no more fundamental difference in linguistic structure than this. And yet, it is not an absolute and determinate one. It lies in the nature of the case that, as the inflectional languages have grown out of a monosyllabic and non-inflecting stage, there should be certain tongues, as there are in other tongues certain forms, which stand so closely upon the line of division between the two stages, that it is hard to tell whether they are the one thing or the other. In our own tongue, there is no definite division-line to be drawn anywhere in the series of steps that conducts from a mere collocation to a pure form-word—from *house floor* to *house-top*, from *tear-filled* to *tearful*, from *godlike* to *godly*; and, in like manner, it is often a matter of doubt, in languages of low development, where isolation ends and where a loose agglutination begins. Thus, even the Chinese, the purest type of the isolating structure, is by some regarded as, in its colloquial forms, and yet more in some of its dialects, a language of compounded words; and the possession of one or two real formative elements has been claimed for the Burmese; while the Himalaya is likely to furnish dialects whose character, as isolated or agglutinative, will be much disputed.

But the main objection to the classification we are considering is not so much its want of absolute distinctness (a defect incident to all classification, in every department of science) as its one-sidedness : it is too much like the proverbial lover's division of the world into two parts, that where the beloved object is and that where she is not : it leaves almost all human tongues in one huge class together. Accordingly a much more popular and current system distinguishes three primary orders, separating the mass of inflectional languages into such as are agglutinative, or attach their formative elements somewhat loosely to a root which is not liable to variation ; and such as are inflective, or unite more thoroughly their radical and formative elements, and make internal changes of the root itself bear their part, either primarily or secondarily, in the expression of grammatical relations. The distinction between these three orders is well expressed by Professor Max Müller in the following terms :—

" 1. Roots may be used as words, each root preserving its full independence.

" 2. Two roots may be joined together to form words, and in these compounds one root may lose its independence.

" 3. Two roots may be joined together to form words, and in these compounds both roots may lose their independence."*

No better scheme of division, of a simple and comprehensive character, has yet been devised than this, and it is likely to maintain itself long in use. It faithfully represents, in the main, three successive stages in the history of language, three ascending grades of linguistic development. But its value must not be overrated, nor its defects passed without notice. In the first place, it does not include all the possible and actually realized varieties in the mode of formation of words. It leaves altogether out of account that internal change of vowels which, as was shown in the eighth lecture, is the characteristic and principal means of grammatical inflection in the Semitic tongues. The distinctions of *qatala*, ' he killed,' *qutila*, ' he was killed,' *qattala*, ' he massacred,'

* Lectures, first series, eighth lecture.

qātala, 'he tried to kill,' *aqtala*, 'he caused to kill,' and the like, are not explainable by any composition of roots and loss of their independence, even though the somewhat analogous differences of *man* and *men*, *lead* and *led*, *sing* and *sang*, *sit* and *set*, do admit of such explanation. In the second place, it is liable to something of the same reproach of one-sidedness which lies against the former, the double method of classification. It puts into a separate class, as inflective languages, only two families, the Indo-European and the Semitic : these are, to be sure, of wide extent and unapproached importance ; yet the mass of spoken tongues is still left in one immense and heterogeneous body. And finally, a yet more fundamental objection to the scheme is this heterogeneity, which characterizes not its middle class alone, but its highest also. It classes Indo-European and Semitic speech together, as morphologically alike, while yet their structural discordance is vastly greater than that which separates Indo-European from many of the agglutinative tongues—in some respects, even greater than that which separates Indo-European from the generality of agglutinative and from the isolating tongues. Not only are the higher Scythian dialects, as the Finnish and Hungarian, almost inflective, and inflective upon a plan which is sufficiently analogous with the Indo-European, but, from a theoretical point of view (however the case may be historically), Chinese, Scythian, and Indo-European are so many steps in one line and direction of progress, differing in degree but not in kind : Semitic speech, on the other hand, if it started originally from the same or a like centre, has reached an equally distant point in a wholly different direction. The two inflective families may lie upon the same circumference, but they are separated by the whole length of the diameter, being twice as far from one another as is either from the indifferent middle. A less fundamental discordance, perhaps, but an equal variety of structure, belongs to those tongues which are classed together as agglutinative. The order includes such extremes in degree of agglutination as the barren and almost isolating Manchu or Egyptian, on the one hand, and, on the other, the exuberantly aggregative

Turkish and the often excessively agglomerative American or
Basque ; it includes such differences in the mode of agglutination as are presented by the Scythian, which makes its
combinations solely by suffixes, and the Malay or South-
African, which form theirs mainly by prefixes. Here, again,
it may be made a question whether the morphological
relationship of Scythian and Indo-European be not closer
than that of Scythian and Malay. The principle which
divides the two former is, it is true, reasonably to be regarded
as of a higher order than that which divides the two latter;
yet it is more teleological than morphological; it concerns
rather the end attained than the means of attainment. The
reach and value, too, of the distinctively inflective principle,
as developed in Indo-European language, is, as I cannot but
think, not infrequently overrated. In no small part of the
material of our own tongue, for example, the root or theme
maintains its own form and distinction from the affixes, and
these their distinction from one another, not less completely
than is the case in Scythian. All the derivatives of *love*, as
love-d, lov-ing, lov-er, love-ly ; the derivatives of *true*, as *tru-ly,
tru-th, tru-th-ful, tru-th-ful-ly, un-tru-th-ful-ly*—these, and the
host of formations like them, are strictly agglutinative in
type : but we do not recognize in them any inferiority as
means of expression to those derivatives in which the radical
part has undergone a more marked fusion, or disguising
change. *Loved* from *love* is as good a preterit as *led* from
lead, or *sang* from *sing ; truth* from *true* is as good an abstract
as *length* from *long*, or *filth* from *foul ;* nor is the Latin
lædo-r, ' I am hurt,' from *lædo*, ' I hurt,' inferior to the
nearly equivalent Arabic *qutila*, from *qatala*. The claim
might plausibly enough be set up that the unity which the
Scythian gives to its derivative words by making the vowels
of their suffixes sympathize with that of the principal or
radical element, is at least as valuable, in itself considered, as
the capacity of an Indo-European root to be phonetically
affected by the ending that is attached to it—a subjection of
the superior to the inferior element. Not that the actual
working-out of the latter principle in the tongues of our
family has not produced results of higher value than the

former has led to; but this may be owing in great measure
to the way in which the two have been handled respectively.
The immensely comprehensive order of agglutinative languages is sometimes reduced a little by setting apart from it
a polysynthetic or incorporative class, composed of the
Basque and the American family. This, however, is rather
a subdivision of one of the members of the triple system than
the establishment of a new, a quadruple, scheme of classification.

Professor Müller* seeks to find a support and explanation
of the threefold division of human language which we are
now considering by paralleling it with the threefold condition of human society, as patriarchal, nomadic, and political. Monosyllabic or "family languages" are in place,
according to him, among the members of a family, whose intimacy, and full knowledge of one another's dispositions and
thoughts, make it possible for each to understand the other
upon the briefest and most imperfect hints. Agglutinative
or "nomadic languages" are required by the circumstances
of a wandering and unsettled life ; the constantly separating
and reassembling tribes could not keep up a mutual intelligence if they did not maintain the integrity of the radical
elements of their speech. Inflective or "state languages"
are rendered possible by a regulated and stable condition of
society, where uninterrupted intercourse and constant tradition facilitate mutual comprehension, notwithstanding the
fusion and integration of root and affix. The comparison is
ingenious and entertaining, but it is too little favoured by
either linguistic philosophy or linguistic history to be entitled to any other praise. It would fain introduce into the
processes of linguistic life an element of reflective anticipation, of prevision and deliberate provision, which is altogether
foreign to them. That wandering tribes should, in view of
their scanty intercourse, their frequent partings to be followed by possible meetings, conclude that they ought to
keep their roots unmodified, is quite inconceivable ; nor is it

* In his Letter on the Classification of the Turanian Languages, p. 21
seq. : see also his Lectures, first series.

easy to see what purpose the resolution should serve, if the
endings are at the same time to be suffered to vary so
rapidly that mutual unintelligibility is soon brought about.
In every uncultivated community, the language is left to take
care of itself; it becomes what the exigencies of practical
use make it, not what a forecasting view of future possibilities leads its speakers to think that it might with advantage
be made to be: let two tribes be parted from one another,
and neither has any regard to the welfare of its fellow in
shaping its own daily speech. In point of fact, moreover,
Indo-European languages were inflective, were "state languages," long before the tribes had formed states — while
many of them were as nomadic in their habits as the wildest
of the so-called Turanian tribes. And to denominate the
immense and highly-organized Chinese empire a mere exaggerated family, and account for the peculiarities of its speech
by reference to the conditions of a family, is fanciful in the
extreme. No nomenclature founded on such unsubstantial
considerations has a good claim to the acceptance of linguistic scholars; and the one in question has, it is believed,
won no general currency.

A very noteworthy attempt has been made within a short
time by Professor Schleicher, of Jena, * to give greater fulness and precision to the morphological classification and
description of language, by a more thorough analysis, and a
kind of algebraic notation, of morphological characteristics.
A pure root, used as a word without variation of form or
addition of formative elements, he denotes by a capital letter,
as A: a connected sentence expressed by a series of such
elements, as is sometimes the case in Chinese, he would represent by $A\ B\ C$, and so on. Such a sentence we may
rudely illustrate by an English phrase like *fish like water*,
in which each word is a simple root or theme, without formal designation of relations.† A root which, while retain-

---

* See his paper, "Contribution to the Morphology of Language," in the
Memoirs of the Academy of St. Petersburg, vol. i., No. 7 (1859); also, the
Introduction to his work, the "German Language" (Stuttgart, 1860), p. 11 seq.

† Of course, the parallel is to be regarded as only an imperfect one:
though these three words are to our apprehension primitives, they are far

ing its substantial independence, is so modified in signification and restricted in application as to form an auxiliary or adjunct to another root (which was shown in the last lecture to be a frequent phenomenon in the isolating languages), is marked by an accented letter, as A' : thus, in the English, *shall like* would be represented by $A' + A$; *shall have put*, by $A' + B'$ $+ A$: the interposed sign of addition indicating the closeness of relation between the elements. The position of the accented letters in the formula would point out whether the auxiliaries are placed after the main word, as in Burmese, or before it, as in Siamese, or on either or both sides, as sometimes in Chinese.

If, now, the formative element is combined with the radical into a single word, it is indicated by a small letter, which is put before or after the capital which stands for the root, according to the actual position of the elements in combination. Thus, if we represent *true* by A, *untrue* would be aA ; *truly* or *truth* would be Aq ; *untruly*, aAb; *untruthfully*, $aAbcd$; and so on. Expressions of this kind belong to the agglutinative type of structure ; and they are, it is plain, capable of very considerable variation, so as to be made to denote the various kinds and degrees of agglutination. It is possible, for example, to distinguish the endings of inflection from those of derivation, or elements of pronominal from those of predicative origin, by the use of a different series of letters (as the Greek) to indicate one of the classes : thus, *truths* might be Aaa, but *truthful* Aab ; *babalarumdan*, in Turkish (see above, p. 318), might be $Aa\beta\gamma$, but *sevishdirilememek*, $Aabcdef$. An adroit use of such means of distinction might enable one even to set forth with sufficient clearness the peculiarities and intricacies of polysynthetic tongues.

from being ultimate roots; they all either contain formative elements added to such a root, or have possessed and lost them ; each is, to be sure, employable as noun, adjective, or verb, without change of form, yet not, like Chinese roots, in virtue of an original indefiniteness of meaning, but as one distinct part of speech is in our usage convertible directly into others ; nor can it be said that, even as they stand, they are altogether formless : for each is defined in certain relations by the absence of formative elements which it would otherwise exhibit : *water* is shown to be singular by lacking an *s*, *fish* and *like* to be plural by the absence of *s* from *like*.

Again, an inflective change of the root itself for the expression of grammatical relations is denotable by exponents attached to the root-symbol. Thus, *man* being A, *men* would be A^a; *men's*, $A^a a$; *sang*, *sung*, *song*, from *sing*, would be denoted by A^a, A^b, A^c; *spoken*, from *speak*, would be $A^a a$; its German counterpart, *gesprochen*, $a A^a b$. And in the Semitic tongues, where the root never appears without a vocalization which is formal and significant, the constant radical emblem would be A^a.*

Compounds, finally, would be expressed in this method by putting side by side the symbols expressive of their separate members, the capital letters with their modifications and adjuncts. *House-top* would be AB; *songwriter*, $A^a Ba$; and so on.

It is unnecessary to explain with any more of detail Professor Schleicher's system of morphological notation, or to spend many words in pointing out its convenience and value. It may evidently be made a means of apprehending distinctly, and setting forth clearly, the main structural features of any language. It will not, indeed, enable us to put in a brief and compact form of statement the whole morphological character of every spoken tongue. Most tongues admit no small variety of formations; each must be judged by its prevailing modes of formation, by the average of highest and lowest modes, by their respective frequency of application, and the purposes they are made to serve. It does not help us to a simple and facile scale and classification of all the dialects of mankind; but this is to be imputed to

* Professor Schleicher, indeed, adopts this emblem as that of the Indo-European root also, since he holds the view, briefly stated and controverted above (in the eighth lecture, p. 293), that the radicals of our family were originally liable to a regular variation, of symbolic significance, for purposes of grammatical expression. I regard it, on the contrary, as the weak point in his system, as applied by himself, that it does not distinguish an internal flection like the Semitic—which, so far as we can trace its history, is ultimate and original, and which continues in full force, in old material and in new formations, through the whole history of the languages—from one like the Indo-European, which is rather secondary and accidental, constantly arising in new cases under the influence of phonetic circumstances, but never winning a pervading force, and in many members of the family hardly taking on anywhere a regular form and office, as significant of relations.

it as a merit, not as a fault : it thus fairly represents the
exceeding variety of languages, the complexity of the characteristics which distinguish them, and their incapacity of
separation into a few sharply defined classes.

No single trait or class of traits, however fundamental
may be its importance, can be admitted as a definite criterion
by which the character of a language shall be judged, and its
rank determined. We saw reason above to challenge the
absolute superiority of the inflective principle, strongly as it
may indicate a valuable tendency in language-making. Certainly it is wholly conceivable that some language of the
agglutinative class may decidedly surpass in strength and
suppleness, in adaptedness to its use as the instrument and
aid of thought, some other language or languages of the inflective class. Not morphological character alone is to be
taken account of ; for not every race of equal mental endowment has originated and shaped a language, any more than
an art, of equivalent formal merit. Some one needed item
of capacity was wanting, and the product remains unartistic ;
or the work of the earliest period, which has determined the
grand features of the whole after-development, was un-
adroitly performed ; the first generations left to their successors a body of constraining usages and misguiding
analogies, the influence of which is not to be shaken off ; and
the mental power of the race is shown by the skill and force
with which it wields an imperfect instrument. Many a
tongue thus stands higher, or lower, in virtue of the sum of
its qualities, than its morphological character would naturally
indicate. The Chinese is one of the most striking instances
of such a discordance ; though so nearly formless, in a morphological sense, it is nevertheless placed by Wilhelm von
Humboldt and Steinthal * in their higher class of " form
languages," along with the Indo-European and Semitic, as
being a not unsuitable incorporation of clear logical thought ;
as, though not distinctly indicating relations and categories,
yet not cumbering their conception, their mental apprehension, by material adjuncts which weaken and confuse the
thought.

* See the latter's Charakteristik etc., pp. 70, 327.

But further, apart from this whole matter of morphological form, of grammatical structure, of the indication, expressed
or implied, of relations, another department contributes
essentially to our estimate of the value of a language:
namely, its material content, or what is signified by its
words. The universe, with all its objects and their qualities,
is put before the language-makers to be comprehended and
expressed, and the different races, and tribes, and communities, have solved the problem after a very different fashion.
Names-giving implies not merely the distinction of individual
things, but, no less, classification and analysis, in every kind,
and of every degree of subtlety. There are conceptions,
and classes of conceptions, of so obvious and practical character, that their designations are to be found in every language that exists or ever has existed: there are hosts of
others which one community, or many, or the most, have
never reached. Does a given tongue show that the race
which speaks it has devoted its exclusive attention to the
more trivial matters in the world without and within us, or
has it apprehended higher things? Has it, for example, so
studied and noted the aspects of nature that it can describe
them in terms of picturesque power? Has it distinguished
with intellectual acuteness and spiritual insight the powers
and operations of our internal nature, our mind and soul, so
that it can discuss psychological questions with significance
and precision? Any dialect, isolating or inflective, monosyllabic or polysynthetic, may be raised or lowered in the
scale of languages by the characteristics which such inquiries
bring to light. In these, too, there is the widest diversity,
depending on original capacity, on acquired information and
civilization, and on variety of external circumstance and condition—a diversity among different branches of the same
race, different periods of the same history, and, where culture
and education introduce their separating influences, between
different classes of the same community. Our earliest
inquiries (in the first three lectures) into the processes of
linguistic growth showed us that the changes which bring
about this diversity, the accretions to the vocabulary of a
tongue, the deepening of the meaning of its words, are the

easiest of all to make, the most pervading and irrepressible in their action, throughout every period of its existence. Here, then, more than in any other department, it is practicable for later generations to amend and complete the work of earlier ; and yet, such is the power of linguistic habit that, even here, original infelicities sometimes adhere to a language during its whole development.

To make out a satisfactory scheme of arrangement for all human tongues upon the ground of their comparative value, accordingly, will be a task of extreme difficulty, and one of the last results reached by linguistic science. It will require a degree of penetration into the inmost secrets of structure and usage, an acuteness of perception and freedom from prejudice in estimating merits of diverse character, and a breadth and reach of learning, which will be found attainable only by a few master-minds.   Great play is here afforded for subjective views, for inherited prepossessions, for sway of mental habits.   Who of us can be trusted fairly to compare the advantages of his own and of any other language ?

There can be no question that, of all the modes of classification with which linguistic scholars have had to do, the one of first and most fundamental importance is the genetical, or that which groups together, and holds apart from others, languages giving evidence of derivation from the same original.   It underlies and furnishes the foundation of all the remaining modes.   There can be no tie between any two dialects so strong as that of a common descent.   Every great family has a structural character of its own, whereby, whatever may be the varying development of its members, it is made a unit, and more or less strikingly distinguished from the rest.   Whatever other criterion we may apply is analogous in its character and bearings with the distinction of apetalous, monopetalous, and polypetalous, or of monogynous, digynous, etc., or of exogenous and endogenous, or of phenogamous and cryptogamous, in the science of botany— all of them possessing real importance in different degrees, variously crossing one another, and marking out certain general divisions; while the arrangement of linguistic families corresponds with the division of plants into natural orders, founded upon a consideration of the whole complicate structure of the things classified, contemplating the sum of their characteristic qualities; fixing, therefore, their position in the vast kingdom of nature of which they are members, and determining the names by which they shall be called. The genetical classification is the ultimate historical fact which the historical method of linguistic study directly aims at establishing. With its establishment are bound up those more general historical results, for the ethnological history of mankind, which form so conspicuous a part of the interest of our science.

To subjects connected with this department of interest, the bearing of linguistic science on ethnology, we have next to turn our attention, occupying with them the remainder of the present lecture.

One of the first considerations which will be apt to strike the notice of any one who reviews our classification of human races according to the relationship of their languages, is its non-agreement with the current divisions based on physical characteristics. The physicists, indeed, are far from having yet arrived at accordance in their own schemes of classification, and the utter insufficiency of that old familiar distinction of Caucasian, Mongol, Malay, African, and American, established by Blumenbach, and probably learned by most of us at school, is now fully recognized. But it does not seem practicable to lay down any system of physical races which shall agree with any possible scheme of linguistic races. Indo-European, Semitic, Scythian, and Caucasian tongues are spoken by men whom the naturalist would not separate from one another as of widely diverse stock; and, on the other hand, Scythian dialects of close and indubitable relationship are in the mouths of peoples who differ as widely in form and feature as Hungarians and Lapps; while not less discordance of physical type is to be found among the speakers of various dialects belonging to more than one of the other great linguistic families.

Such facts as these call up the question, as one of high practical consequence, respecting the comparative value of linguistic and of physical evidence of race, and how their

seeming discrepancy is to be reconciled. Some method of
bringing about a reconciliation between them must evidently
be sought and found. For neither linguistic nor physical
ethnology is a science of classification merely ; both claim to
be historical also. Both are working toward the same end :
namely, a tracing out of the actual connection and genealogical history of human races ; and, though each must
follow its own methods, without undue interference from
without, they cannot labour independently, careless each of
the other's results. To point out the mode of reconciliation,
to remove the difficulties which lie in the way of harmonious
agreement between the two departments of ethnological
science, I shall not here make the least pretence ; such a
result can be attained only when the principles and conclusions of both are advanced and perfected far beyond their
present point. All that we can attempt to do is to notice
certain general considerations bearing upon the subject, and
requiring not to be lost from sight by either party ; and
especially, to point out the limitations and imperfections of
both physical and linguistic evidence, and how necessary it
is that each should modestly solicit and frankly acknowledge
the aid of the other.

How language proves anything concerning race, and what
it does and does not prove, was brought clearly to light in
the course of our earliest inquiries into its nature and
history. What we then learned respecting the mode of
acquisition and transmission of each man's, and each community's, "native tongue" was sufficient to show us the total
error of two somewhat different, and yet fundamentally
accordant, views of language, which have been put forth and
defended by certain authorities—the one, that speech is to
man what his song is to the bird, what their roar, growl,
bellow are to lions, bears, oxen ; and that resemblances of
dialect therefore no more indicate actual genetic connection
among different tribes of men than resemblances of uttered
tone indicate the common descent of various species of
thrushes, or of bears, inhabiting different parts of the world :
the other, that language is the immediate and necessary product of physical organization, and varies as this varies ; that

an Englishman, a Frenchman, and a Chinaman talk unlike
one another because their brains and organs of articulation
are unlike; and that all Englishmen talk alike, as do all
Frenchmen, or all Chinamen, because, in consequence of
their living amid similar physical conditions, and their inheritance of a common race-type, their nervous and muscular
systems minutely correspond. And doctrines akin with
these are more or less distinctly and consciously implied in
the views of those who hold that language is beyond the
reach of the free-agency of men, and can be neither made
nor changed by human effort. All who think thus virtually
deny the existence of such a thing as linguistic science, or
reduce it to the position of a subordinate branch of physiology: speech becomes a purely physical characteristic, one
among the many which by their common presence make up
man, and by their differences distinguish the different
varieties of men; and it would be for the physicist to determine, here, as in the case of other physical characteristics,
how far its joint possession indicated specific unity, or how
far its diversities of kind indicated specific variety. All
these false theories are brushed away at once by our recognition of the fact that we do not produce our speech from
within, but acquire it from without ourselves; that we
neither make nor inherit the words we use, whether of our
native tongue or of any other, but learn them from our
instructors.

But from this it also follows that no individual's speech
directly and necessarily marks his descent; it only shows in
what community he grew up. Language is no infallible
sign of race, but only its probable indication, and an indication of which the probability is exposed to very serious draw-
backs. For it is evident that those who taught us to speak,
of whose means of expression we learned to avail ourselves,
need not have been of our own kith and kin. Not only
may individuals, families, groups of families, of almost every
race on earth, be, as at present in America, turned into and
absorbed by one great community, and made to adopt its
speech, but a strange tongue may be learned by whole tribes
and nations of those who, like our negroes, are brought

away from their native homes, or, like the Irish, have lived long under a foreign yoke, or, like the Celts of ancient Gaul and Spain, have received laws, civilization, and religion from another and a superior race. Languages unnumbered and innumerable have disappeared from off the face of the earth since the beginning of human history; but only in part by reason of the utter annihilation of the individuals who had spoken them; more often, doubtless, by their dispersion, and incorporation with other communities, of other speech. Everywhere, too, where the confines of different forms of speech meet, there goes on more or less of mixture between them, or of effacement of the one by the other. Yet, on the other hand, mixture of language is not necessary proof of mixture of race. We can trace the genesis of a very large part of our own vocabulary to the banks of the Tiber, but hardly the faintest appreciable portion of our ancestry is Roman. We obtained our Latin words in the most strangely roundabout way : they were brought us by certain Germanic adventurers, the Normans, who had learned them from a mixed people, the French, chiefly of Celtic blood; and these, again, had derived them from another heterogeneous compound of Italican races, among whom the Latin tribe was numerically but a feeble element.

Of such nature are the difficulties in the way of our inferring the race-connections of an individual or of a community with certainty from the relations of the language which either speaks. They are of undeniable force and importance, and must be borne constantly in mind by every one who is pursuing investigations, and laying down conclusions, in linguistic ethnology. They drive him to seek after some other concurrent test of descent, which shall serve to check and control his own results; and they make him court and welcome the aid of the physicist, as well as of the archæologist and the historian.

But, notwithstanding this, their consequence, and their power to invalidate linguistic evidence, must not be overrated. They concern, after all, what in the grand sum of human history are the exceptions to a general rule. It still remains true that, upon the whole, language is a tolerably

sure indication of race. Since the dawn of time, those
among whom individuals were born, of whom they learned
how to express their mental acts, have been usually of their
own blood. Nor do these difficulties place linguistic evidence
at any marked disadvantage as compared with physical.
They are, to no small extent, merely the effect, on the side of
language, of the grand fact which comes in constantly to
interfere with ethnological investigations of every kind :
namely, that human races do not maintain themselves in
purity, that men of different descent are all the time mingling, mixing their blood, and crossing all their race-characteristics. Fusion and replacement of languages are impossible, except when men of different native speech are brought
together as members of the same community, so that there
takes place more or less of an accompanying fusion of races
also ; and then the resulting language stands at least a
chance of being a more faithful and intelligible witness of
the mixture than the resulting physical type. That the
modern French people, for example, is made up of a congeries
of Celtic, Germanic, and Italican elements is to a certain
extent—although only the aid of recorded history enables us
fully to interpret the evidences—testified by the considerable body of Celtic and Germanic words mixed with the
Latin elements of the French language ; but no physicist
could ever have derived the same conclusion from a study of
the French type of structure. The physicists claim that there
may be a considerable infusion of the blood of one race into
that of another, without perceptible modification of the
latter's race-type ; the intruded element, if not continuously
supplied afresh, is overwhelmed and assimilated by the other
and predominant one, and disappears : that is to say, as we
may interpret the claim, its peculiarities are so diluted by
constant remixture that they become at last inappreciable.
In any such case, then, traces discoverable in the language
may point out what there is no other means of ascertaining.
It is true that, on the other hand, the spread and propaga-
tion of a language may greatly exceed that of the race to
which it originally belonged, and that the weaker numerical
element in a composite community may be the one whose

dialect becomes the common tongue of all. Thus the Latin
swept away the primitive tongues of a great part of southern
and central Europe, and has become mingled with the speech
of all civilized nations, in the Old world and the New. But
we are not rashly to infer that such things have happened
over and over again in the history of the world. We have
rather to inquire what influences make possible a career like
that of the Latin, what lends the predominant and assimilating force to a single element where many are combined.
And, as was pointed out in the fourth lecture, we shall find
that only superior culture and the possession of a literature
can give to any tongue such great extensibility. The Persians, the Mongols, have at one period and another exercised
sway over an empire not less extensive than the Roman, but
their languages were never spread far beyond the limits of
the peoples to which they properly belonged. The German
tribes, too, conquered in succession nearly every kingdom of
Europe; but it was only in order to lose themselves and
their dialects together, almost undiscoverably, in the communities and languages into which they entered. Nay, even
the wide-spread Greek colonies, with the superiority of
Greek culture to aid them, were not able to make the Greek
the tongue of many nations. There was an organizing and
assimilating force in Roman dominion which the world has
nowhere else seen equalled. And if the career of the Arabic
furnishes something like a parallel to that of the Latin, it is
due, not to the sword of Islam, but to the book, and to the
doctrine and polity which the book enjoined and the sword
imposed. Since, then, such movements must be connected
with culture and literature, they cannot but leave their
record in written history, and find there their explanation.
Nor could there occur in every region or in every period
such an inpouring and assimilation of nationalities as is now
going on among us; it is only possible under the conditions
of civilized life in the nineteenth century, and the historical
conditions which have been created here. The wild and
uncultivated races of the earth generally are simply maintaining themselves by growth from generation to generation,
taking in no immigrants, sending out no emigrants. Culture

makes an astonishing difference in the circumstances and
fates of those portions of mankind over which its influence
is extended, and it would be the height of folly to transfer
to barbarous races and uncivilized periods of human history
analogies and conclusions drawn from the history of cultivated nations and tongues. The farther we go back into the
night of the past, the greater is the probability that the
limits of race and speech approximately coincide, and that
mixture of either is accompanied by that of the other.

And if, in certain circumstances, a race may change its
tongue, while yet retaining in its physical structure evidence
of its descent, a race may also undergo a modification of
physical type, and still offer in its speech plain indications
of its real kindred. If the talk of our coloured citizens does
not show that they were brought from Africa, neither do the
shape and bearing of the Magyars show that they came from
beyond the Ural, nor those of the Osmanli Turks that their
cousins are the nomads of the inhospitable plateau of central
Asia. This is the grand drawback to the cogency of physical
evidence of race, and it fully counterbalances those which
affect the cogency of linguistic evidence, rendering the aid
of the linguist as necessary to the physical ethnologist as is
the latter's to the linguistic ethnologist. Physical science
is as yet far from having determined the kind, the rate, and
the amount of modification which external conditions, as climate and mode of life, can introduce into a race-type ; but
that, within certain undefined limits, their influence is very
powerful, is fully acknowledged. There is, to be sure, a
party among zoölogists and ethnologists who insist much
upon the dogma of "fixity of type," and assert that all human races are original; but the general tendency of scientific opinion is in the other direction, toward the fuller
admission of variability of species. The first naturalists are
still, and more than ever, willing to admit that all the differences now existing among human races may be the effects
of variation from a single type, and that it is at least not
necessary to resort to the hypothesis of different origins in
order to explain them. In the fact that Egyptian monuments of more than three thousand years' antiquity show us

human varieties, and canine varieties, bearing the same characteristics as at the present day, there is nothing to disturb
this conclusion; for, on the one hand, a period of three
thousand years is coming to be regarded as not including a
very large part of man's existence on the earth; and, on the
other hand, such a fact only proves the persistency which a
type may possess when fully developed, and is of very doubtful avail to show the originality of the type. Something
analogous is to be seen in language. The speech of our rude
Germanic ancestors of the same remote period, had we authentic record of it, would beyond question be found to have
possessed already a general character clearly identifying it
with Germanic tongues still existing, and sharply sundering
it from Greek, from Slavonic, from Celtic, and all the other
Indo-European branches; yet we do not doubt that the
Germanic type of speech is a derived, a secondary one. In
settling all these controverted points, in distinguishing between original diversity and subsequent variation, in establishing a test and scale for the possibilities and the rate of
physical change, the physical ethnologist will need all the
assistance which historical investigations of every kind can
furnish him; and the greater part must come to him from
the student of language.

As the Indo-European family of language is that one of
which the unity, accompanying a not inconsiderable variety
of physical type in the peoples who speak its dialects,
is most firmly established, and as therefore it may naturally be regarded as furnishing a prominent illustration of
the bearing of linguistic conditions on physical inquiries
into the history of man, it is perhaps worth our while to
refer to a theory respecting Indo-European speech which
has found of late a few supporters of some note and authority, and which, if accepted, would altogether deprive it
of ethnological value. The assertion, namely, is put forth,
that the apparent unity of the languages of this family is not
due to a prevailing identity of descent in the nations to
which they belong, but to the influence of some single tribe,
whose superior character, capacity, and prowess enabled it
to impose its linguistic usages on distant and diverse races.

By some it is even, assumed that the correspondences of
words and forms exhibited by the so-called Indo-European
tongues are not fundamental and pervading, but superficial,
consisting in scattered particulars only, in such designations
of objects and conceptions as one race might naturally make
over into the keeping of another, along with a knowledge of
the things designated. This assumption, however, the expositions and reasonings of our fifth and seventh lectures
will have shown to be wholly erroneous : the correspondences
in question *are* fundamental and pervading ; they constitute
an identity which can only be explained by supposing those
who founded these tongues to have been members together
of the same community. Others, who know the European
languages too well to maintain respecting their relations any
so shallow and untenable theory, yet try to persuade themselves that the analogy of the Latin will sufficiently account
for their extension over so wide a region ; that, as Etruscans,
Celts, Iberians, Germans, learned to speak a tongue of
Roman origin, so the populations of Europe and Asia, of diverse lineage, learned to speak a common Indo-European
dialect ; and that, accordingly, the differences of Greek,
Sanskrit, Celtic, and Slavonic are parallel to those of Italian,
French, and Spanish. But this theory, though more plausible
and defensible than the other, is hardly less untenable. It
exhibits a like neglect of another class of linguistic principles : of those, namely, which underlie and explain the
abnormal extension of tongues like the Latin and the Arabic :
we have more than once had occasion to set them forth
above. In order to establish an analogy between the history
of Latin and that of Indo-European speech, and to make the
former account satisfactorily for the latter, it would be necessary to prove, or at least to render probable, the existence
in a very remote antiquity of those conditions which in
modern times have been able to give such a career to the
language of Rome. But, so far as we can at present see,
there must have been a total lack of the required conditions.
Force of character, warlike prowess, superiority of inherent
mental capacity, undeveloped or partially developed, the
Indo-Europeans may probably have possessed, as compared

with the more aboriginal races of Europe; but these are not
the forces which enable the language of a small minority to
stifle that of the masses of a people and to take its place;
if it were so, southern Europe would now be talking Germanic instead of Romanic dialects.   The rude beginnings of
a higher civilization, as metals, instruments, seeds, domestic
animals, arts, may possibly have been theirs; yet even these
would merely engraft upon the languages of the peoples to
whom they were made known certain words and phrases.
Only the resources of an enlightened culture, supplemented
by letters, literature, and instruction, could give to any
tongue the expansive force demanded by the theory we are
considering; and of these, it is needless to say, no traces
are to be found in Indo-European antiquity.   We have no
good ground, then, for doubting that the great extension of
the languages of our family was effected by the usual causes
which act among uncultivated tongues : that is to say,
mainly by the growth, spread, and emigration of a single
race; by its occupancy of ever new territory, accompanied
with the partial destruction and partial expulsion, sometimes
also with the partial incorporation and absorption, of the
former inhabitants; the element of population which inherited the speech and institutions of the original Indo-
European tribe being ever the predominant one in each new
community that was formed.   How many fragments of other
races may have been worked in during the course of the
family's migrations—how far the purity of blood of one or
another of its branches or sub-branches may have been thus
affected by successive partial dilutions, so that some of their
present peculiarities of type are attributable to the mixture—
is, of course, a legitimate matter for inquiry, and one upon
which we may even look for information from their languages, when these shall have been more narrowly examined.
But upon the whole, in the light of our present knowledge,
we are justified in regarding the boundaries of Indo-European
speech as approximately coinciding with those of a race ; the
tie of language represents a tie of blood.

   If the limitations and imperfections of the two kinds of
evidence are thus in certain respects somewhat evenly bal-

anced, there are others in which linguistic evidence has a
decidedly superior practical value and availability. The
differences of language are upon a scale almost infinitely
greater than those of physical structure. They are equal in
their range and variety to those found in the whole animal
kingdom, from the lowest organisms to the highest, instead
of being confined within the limits of the possible variation
of a single species. Hence they can be much more easily
and accurately apprehended, judged, and described. Linguistic facts admit of being readily collected, laid down with
authentic fidelity, and compared coolly, with little risk of
error from subjective misapprehension. They are accessible
to a much greater number of observers and investigators.
Exceptional capacity, special opportunity, and a very long
period of training, are needed to make a reliable and authoritative describer of race-characteristics. It is true that to
distinguish from one another very diverse types, like the
European and African, is a task which presents no difficulty.
But, though we should all, in nine cases out of ten, recognize a native of Ireland at sight, who among us could trust
himself to make a faithful and telling description of the ideal
Irishman, such that, by its aid, a person not already by long
experience made familiar with the type would recognize it
when met with? The peculiarities of the native Irish
dialect, however, are capable of being made unmistakably
plain to even the dullest apprehension. A few pages or
phrases, often even a few words, brought back by a traveller
or sojourner in distant lands from some people with which
he has made acquaintance, are likely to be worth vastly more
for fixing their place in the human family than the most
elaborate account he can give of their physical characteristics. Photography, with its utter truth to nature, can
now be brought in as a most valuable aid to physical de-
scriptions, yet cannot wholly remove the difficulty, giving
such abundant illustration as shall enable us to analyze and
separate that which is national and typical from that which
is individual and accidental. This last, indeed, is one of the
marked difficulties in physical investigations. Two persons
may readily be culled from two diverse races who shall be

less unlike than two others that may be chosen from the
same race. While, on the contrary, words and phrases
taken down from the lips of an individual, or written or en-
graved by one hand, can be no private possession ; they must
belong to a whole community.

The superior capacity of the remains of language to cast
light upon the affinities of races needs only to be illustrated
by an instance or two. What could have impregnably
established the ethnological position of the ancient Persians
like the decipherment of the inscriptions of Darius and his
successors, which show that they spoke a dialect so nearly
akin with those of Bactria and India that it can be read by
the latter's aid ? What could exhibit the intimate mixture
of races and cultures in the valley of the Euphrates and
Tigris, and the presence there of an important element which
was neither Indo-European nor Semitic, except the trilingual
inscriptions of the Mesopotamian monuments ? What a
pregnant fact in African ethnology will be, if fully and irrefragably proved, the relationship of the Hottentot dialects
with the ancient Egyptian! What but the preserved fragments of their speech could have taught us that the Etruscans had no kindred with any other of the known races
inhabiting Europe ? And when would physical science ever
have made the discovery that the same thing is true of the
Basques, whom yet it has all the opportunity which it could
desire to study ? But the most important of the advantages
belonging to linguistic science, in its relation to ethnology,
is that to which allusion was made at the very outset of our
discussions : namely, that language tells so much more respecting races than lies within the reach or scope of the
physicist. In every part and particle, it is instinct with
history. It is a picture of the internal life of the community
to which it belongs ; in it their capacities are exhibited, their
characters expressed; it reflects their outward circumstances, records their experiences, indicates the grade of
knowledge they have attained, exhibits their manners and
institutions. Being itself an institution, shaped by their
consenting though only half-conscious action, it is an important test of national endowment and disposition, like

political constitution, like jural usage, like national art. Even where it fails to show strict ethnic descent, it shows race-history of another sort—the history of the influence which, by dint of superior character and culture, certain races have exercised over others. The spread of the Latin has swept away and obliterated some of the ancient land-marks of race, but it has done so by substituting another unity for that of descent ; its present ubiquity illustrates the unparalleled importance of Rome in the history of humanity.

For these reasons, and such as these, the part which language has to perform in constructing the unwritten history of the human race must be the larger and more important. There are points which physical science alone can reach, or upon which her authority is superior : but in laying out and filling up the general scheme, and especially in converting what would else be a barren classification into something like a true history, the work must chiefly be done by linguistic science.

The considerations we have been reviewing will, it is hoped, guide us to a correct apprehension of the relations of these two branches of ethnological study. Discord between them, question as to respective rank, there is or should be none. Both are legitimate and necessary methods of ap-proaching the solution of the same intricate and difficult question, the origin and history of man on the earth—a question of which we are only now beginning to understand the intricacy and difficulty, and which we are likely always to fall short of answering to our satisfaction. There was a time, not many years since, when the structure and history of the earth-crust were universally regarded as a simple matter, the direct result of a few *fiats*, succeeding one an-other within the space of six days and nights: now, even the school-boy knows that in the brief story of the Genesis are epitomized the changes and developments of countless ages, and that geology may spend centuries in tracing them out and describing them in detail, without arriving at the end of her task. In like manner has it been supposed that the first introduction of man into the midst of the prepared

creation was distant but six or seven thousand years from
our day, and we have hoped to be able to read the record
of so brief a career, even back to its beginning; but science
is accumulating at present so rapidly, and from so many
quarters, proofs that the time must be greatly lengthened
out, and even perhaps many times multiplied, that this new
modification of a prevailing view seems likely soon to win
as general an acceptance as the other has already done. And
the different historical sciences are seeing more and more
clearly their weakness in the presence of so obscure a problem, and confessing their inability to give categorical answers to many of the questions it involves.

Such a confession on the part of linguistic science,
with reference to one point of the most fundamental interest
and importance in human history, it next devolves upon us
to make.

A second question, namely, which cannot but press itself
upon our attention, in connection with the survey we have
taken of the grand divisions of human speech, is this: What is
the scope and bearing of the division into families? Does
it separate the human race into so many different branches,
which must have been independent from the very beginning?
Does linguistic science both fail to find any bond of connection between the families and see that no such bond exists?
Or, in short, what has the study of language to say respecting the unity of the human race?

This is an inquiry to which, as I believe, the truths we
have established respecting the character and history of language will enable us readily to find a reply. But that reply
will be only a negative one. Linguistic science is not now,
and cannot hope ever to be, in condition to give an authoritative opinion respecting the unity or variety of our species.
This is not an acknowledgment which any student of language likes to make; it may seem to savour, too, of pre-
cipitation on the part of him who makes it; of a lack of
faith in the future of his science—a science which, although
it has already accomplished so much, has yet confessedly
only begun its career. That those linguistic scholars—for
such there are—are over-hasty and over-credulous who sup-

pose themselves to have proved already, by the evidence of language, that all mankind are akin by blood as well as by nature, will be conceded by many who are yet unwilling to give up all hope of seeing the proof one day satisfactorily made out. Let us, then, enter into a brief examination of the point, and a consideration of the grounds upon which is founded the view we have taken.

To show, in the first place, that linguistic science can never claim to prove the ultimate variety of human races will be no long or difficult task. That science, as we have seen, regards language as something which has grown up, in the manner of an institution, from weak and scanty beginnings; it is a development out of germs; it started with simple roots, brief in form and of indeterminate meaning, by the combination of which words came later into being. And the existing differences of speech among men are, at least to a very considerable extent, the result, not of original diversity, but of discordant growth. Now we cannot presume to set any limits to the extent to which languages once the same may have grown apart from one another. It matters not what opinion we may hold respecting the origin of the first germs of speech: if we suppose them to have been miraculously created and placed in the mouths of the first ancestors of men, their present differences would not justify us in believing that different sets must have been imparted to different pairs, or groups, of ancestors; for the same influences which have so obscured the common descent of English, Welsh, and Hindustani, for example, may, by an action more prolonged or more intense, have transformed germs originally common beyond even the faintest possibility of recognition. And if, on the other hand, we regard them as originated by the same agency which has brought about their later combinations and mutations, by men, namely, using legitimately and naturally the faculties with which they have been endowed, under the guidance of the instincts and impulses implanted in them—and no linguist, certainly, as such, has any right to deny at least the possibility of this origin of language—then the case is yet clearer. For we cannot venture to say how long a time the formation of roots may have demanded, or during what period universal language may have remained nearly stationary in this its inceptive stage. It is entirely conceivable that the earliest human race, being one, should have parted into disjoined and thenceforth disconnected tribes before the formation of any language so far developed and of so fixed forms as to be able to leave traceable fragments in the later dialects of the sundered portions. These possibilities preclude all dogmatic assertion of the variety of human species on the part of the linguist. Among all the known forms of speech, present and past, there are no discordances which are not, to his apprehension, fully reconcilable with the hypothesis of unity of race, allowing the truth of that view of the nature and history of speech which is forced upon him by his researches into its structure. It is certain that no one, upon the ground of linguistic investigations alone, will ever be able to bear witness against the descent of all mankind from a single pair.

That no one, upon the same grounds, can ever bear witness in favour of such descent is, as it appears to me, equally demonstrable, although not by so simple and direct an argument, and although the opinions of eminent authorities are at variance upon the point, and may fairly continue to be so for some time to come, until more of the fundamental facts and principles in linguistic science shall have been firmly established and universally accepted than is the case at present. We have here no theoretical impossibility to rely upon ; no direct argument from necessary conditions, cutting off all controversy. As the linguist is compelled to allow that a unique race may have parted into branches before the development of abiding germs of speech, so he must also admit the possibility that the race may have clung together so long, or the development of its speech have been so rapid, that, even prior to its separation, a common dialect had been elaborated, the traces of which no lapse of time, with all its accompanying changes, could entirely obliterate. Nay, he was bound to keep that possibility distinctly before his mind in all his researches, to cherish a hope of making language prove community of blood in all members of the human family, until conscientious study should show the hope to be groundless. The question was one of fact, of what existing and accessible testimony was competent to prove; it was to be settled only by investigation. But I claim that investigation, limited as its range and penetration have hitherto confessedly been, has already put us in condition to declare the evidence incompetent, and the thesis incapable of satisfactory proof.

In order to make clear the justice of this claim, it will be necessary to recapitulate some of the results we have won in our previous discussions.

The processes of change which are constantly at work in language, altering both the form and the meaning of its constituent words, were set forth and illustrated with sufficient fulness in our early lectures. The degree of alteration which they may effect, and the variety of their results, are practically unlimited. As they can bring utter apparent diversity out of original identity, so they can impress an apparent similarity upon original diversity. Hence the difficulties which beset etymological science, its abuse by the unlearned and incautious, the occasional seeming arbitrariness and violence of its procedures, even in skilled and scientific hands. Voltaire's witty saying, that in etymologizing the vowels are of no account at all, and the consonants of very little—to which he might have added, that the meaning is equally a matter of indifference—was true enough as regarded the science of his day; but we must also confess that in a certain way it possesses an applicability to that of our own times. Even modern etymology acknowledges that two words can hardly be so different, in form or in meaning, or in both form and meaning, that there is not a possibility of their being proved descendants of the same word : any sound, any shade of idea, may pass by successive changes into any other. The difference between the old hap-hazard style of etymologizing and the modern scientific method lies in this : that the latter, while allowing everything to be theoretically possible, accepts nothing as actual which is not proved such by sufficient evidence ; it brings to bear upon each individual case a wide circle of related facts ; it imposes upon the student the necessity of extended comparison and cautious deduction; it makes him careful to inform himself as thoroughly as circumstances allow respecting the history of every word he deals with.

Two opposing possibilities, therefore, interfere with the directness of the etymologist's researches, and cast doubt on his conclusions. On the one hand, forms apparently unconnected may turn out to be transformations of the same original: since, for example, the French *évêque* and the English *bishop*, words which have no common phonetic constituent, are yet both descended, within no very long time, from the Greek *episkopos;* since our *alms* comes from the Greek *eleêmosunē;* since our *sister* and the Persian χāhar are the same word; since the Latin *filius* has become in Spanish *hijo;* and so on. On the other hand, what is of not less importance in its bearing upon the point we are considering, he must be equally mindful that an apparent coincidence between two words which he is comparing may be accidental and superficial only, covering radical diversity. How easy it is for words of different origin to arrive at a final identity of form, as the result of their phonetic changes, is evident enough from the numerous homonyms in our own language, to which we have more than once had occasion to refer. Thus, *sound* in "safe and sound" comes from one Germanic word, and *sound* in "Long Island Sound" from another; while *sound*, 'noise,' is from the Latin *sonus.* So we have a *page* of a book from the Latin *pagina,* and a *page* in waiting from the Greek *paidion,* 'a little boy;' we have *cleave*, 'to stick together,' from the Anglo-Saxon *clifian,* and *cleave*, 'to part asunder,' from the Anglo-Saxon *clufan;* and numberless other instances of the same kind. Fortuitous coincidences of sound like these, in words of wholly independent derivation, are not less liable to occur between the vocables of different languages than between those of the same language; and they do so occur. It is, further, by no means infrequently the case that, along with a coincidence, or a near correspondence, or a remoter analogy, of sound, there is also an analogy, or correspondence, or coincidence, of meaning—one so nearly resembling that which would be

the effect of a genetic relationship between the two words
compared as to give us an impression that they must be related, when in fact they are not. Resemblances of this sort,
of every degree of closeness, do actually appear in abundance
among languages related and unrelated, demonstrably as the
result of accident alone, being mistaken for signs of genetic
connection only by incompetent or heedless inquirers.
Thus, an enterprising etymologist, turning over the pages of
his Hebrew lexicon, discovers that the Hebrew root *kophar*
means 'cover;' and he is at once struck with this plain
proof of the original identity of Hebrew and English:
whereas, if he only looks a little into the history of the
English word, he finds that it comes, through the Old French
covrir, from the Latin *coöperire*, made up of *con* and *operire ;*
which latter is gotten, by two or three steps of derivation
and composition, from a root *par*, 'pass:' and this puts
upon him the necessity, either of giving up his fancied
identification, or of making out some degree of probability
that the Hebrew word descended, through a like succession
of steps, from a like original.   Another word-genealogist
finds that *lars* in ancient Etruscan meant 'a chief, a head
man,' and he parades it as an evidence that the Etruscan
was, after all, an Indo-European language : for is not *lars*
clearly the same with the Scottish word *laird*, our *lord?*
He is simply regardless of the fact that *laird* and *lord* are the
altered modern representatives of the Anglo-Saxon *hlaford*,
with which *lars* palpably has about as little to do as with
brigadier-general or *deputy-sheriff*.   A Polynesian scholar,
intent on proving that South-Sea islanders and Europeans
are tribes of the same lineage, points out the almost exact
coincidence of the Polynesian *mata* and the modern Greek
mati, both signifying 'eye:' which is just as sensible as if
he were to compare a (hypothetical) Polynesian *busa*, 'a
four-wheeled vehicle,' with our *'bus* (from *omnibus*) : for
mati in Greek is abbreviated from *ommation*, diminutive of
omma, 'eye,' and has lost its originally significant part, the
syllable *om*, representing the root *op*, 'see.'

These are only a few samples of false etymologies, selected
from among the thousands and tens of thousands with which

all linguistic literature, ancient and modern, teems ; which
have been drawn out, with infinite expenditure of ill-directed
ingenuity and misapplied labour, from the vocabularies of
tongues of every age and every clime. There is not one
among them which has not a much higher *primá facie* plausibility than the identity of *évêque* and *bishop*, or of *filius* and
hijo, or than numberless others of the true etymologies
established upon sufficient evidence, by the scientific student
of languages : but their value is in seeming only ; they are
baseless and worthless, mere exemplifications of the effects
wrought by the process we are considering—the process
which brings out accidental analogies, phonetic and significant, between words historically unrelated. The greater
portion of false etymologies are to be ascribed directly to its
influence ; and their number is a sufficient and striking proof
of the wide extent of its action, the frequency and variety of
the results it produces.

The fact is well established, that there are no two languages upon the face of the earth, of however discordant
origin, between which may not be brought to light by dili-
gent search a goodly number of these false analogies of both
form and meaning, seeming indications of relationship, which
a little historical knowledge, when it is to be had, at once
shows to be delusive, and which have no title to be regarded
as otherwise, even if we have not the means of proving their
falsity.   It is only necessary to cast out of sight the general
probabilities against a genetic connection of the languages
we are comparing (such as their place and period, their
nearer connections, and the pervading discordance of their
structure and material), and then to assume between them
phonetic transitions not more violent than are actually
proved to be exhibited by other tongues—and we may find
a goodly portion of the vocabulary of each hidden in that of
the other.   Dean Swift has ridiculed the folly which amuses
itself with such comparisons and etymologies, ,in a well-
known caricature, wherein he derives the names of ancient
Greek worthies from honest modern English elements, explaining *Achilles* as ' a kill-ease,' *Hector* as ' hacked-tore,'
Alexander the Great as ' all eggs under the grate ! ' and so

on. This is very absurd; and yet, save that the absurdity of
it is made more palpable to us by being put in terms of our
own language and another with which we are somewhat
familiar, it is hardly worse than what has been done, and is
done, in all soberness, by men claiming the name of linguistic
scholars. It is even now possible for such a man to take an
African vocabulary, and sit deliberately down to see what
words of the various other languages known to him he can
explain out of it, producing a batch of correspondences like
these: *abetele,* ' a begging beforehand ' (which he himself de-
fines as composed of *a,* formative prefix, *be,* ' beg,' and *tele,*
' previously '), and German *betteln,* ' beg ' (from the simpler
root *bit, bet,* our *bid*) ; *idaro,* ' that which becomes collected
into a mass,' and English *dross ; basile,* ' landlord ' (*ba* for
oba, ' master,' *si,* ' of,' and *ile,* ' land '), and Greek *basileus,*
' king : ' and the comparer, who is specially versed in the
mathematical doctrine of chances, gravely informs us that
the chances against the merely accidental character of the
last coincidence are " at least a hundred million to one."
More than one unsound linguist has misled himself and
others by calculating, in the strictest accordance with mathematical rules, how many thousand or million of chances to
one there are against the same word meaning the same
thing in two different and unconnected languages. The
calculation is futile, and its result a fallacy. The relations
of language are not to be so simply reduced to precise
mathematical expression. If words were wholly independent entities, instead of belonging to families of connected
derivatives; if they were of such precise constitution and
application as so many chemical formulas ; if the things they
designated were as distinct and separate individualities as
are fixed stars, or mineral species, or geographical localities—
then the calculations of chances would be in place respecting
them. But none of these things are true. The evidences
on which linguistic science relies to prove genetical connection are not identities of form combined with identities of
meaning : forms may differ as much as *hijo* and *filius ;*
meanings may differ as much as German *bekommen,* ' get,'
and English *become,* ' come to be,' and *become,* ' suit ; ' form

and meaning may differ together to any extent, and yet the words may be one and the same, and good evidences of relationship between the languages to which they respectively belong. Not literal agreement, but such resemblances, nearer or more distant, clearer or more obscure, as are proved by supporting facts to have their ground in original identity, make satisfactory evidence of common descent in language.

Here, then, is the practical difficulty in the way of him who would prove all human speech a unit. On the one hand, those fortuitous coincidences and analogies which any given language may present with any other with which it is compared form a not inconsiderable body, an appreciable percentage of its general stock of words. On the other hand, the historical coincidences and analogies traceable between two languages of common descent are capable of sinking to as low, or even to a lower, percentage of its vocabulary. That is to say, there may be two related tongues, the genuine signs of whose relationship shall be less numerous and conspicuous than the apparent but delusive signs of relationship of two others which derive themselves from independent origins. The former have been so long separated from one another, their changes in the mean time have been so pervading, that their inherited points of resemblance are reduced in number and obscured in character, until they are no longer sufficient to create a reasonable presumption in favour of their own historical reality; they are undistinguishable from the possible results of chance. As we saw in the sixth lecture (p. 243), evidences of genetic connection are cumulative in their character; no single item of correspondence is worth anything until there are found kindred facts to support it; and its force is strengthened with every new accession. And, in the comparison of languages, the point is actually reached where it becomes impossible to tell whether the few coincidences which we discover are the genuine traces of a community of linguistic tradition, or only accidental, and evidence of nothing. When we come to holding together the forms of speech belonging to the diverse families, linguistic testimony fails us : it no longer has force to prove anything to our satisfaction.

To demonstrate that this is so, we do not need to enter into a detailed examination of two tongues claimed to be unrelated, and show that their correspondences fall incontestably short of the amount required to prove relationship: we may take a briefer and directer argument. We have seen that the established linguistic families are made up of those dialects which exhibit traceable signs of a common historic development; which have evidently grown together out of the radical stage (unless, as in the case of the monosyllabic tongues, they have together remained stationary in that stage); which possess, at least in part, the same grammatical structure. There are some linguistic scholars who cherish the sanguine hope that trustworthy indications of this kind of correspondence may yet be pointed out between some two or three of the great families; but no one whose opinion is of one straw's weight thinks of such a thing with reference to them all. So discordant is the whole growth of many of the types of speech that we can find no affinities among them short of their ultimate beginnings: if all human speech is to be proved of one origin, it can only be by means of an identification of roots. To give the investigation this form, however, is virtually to abandon it as hopeless. The difficulties in the way of a fruitful comparison of roots are altogether overwhelming. To trace out the roots of any given family, in their ultimate form and primitive signification, is a task whose gravity the profoundest investigators of language are best able to appreciate. Notwithstanding the variety of the present living dialects of the Indo-European family, and the noteworthy preservation of original forms on the part of some among them, their comparison would be far enough from furnishing us the radical elements of Indo-European speech. Even the aid of the ancient tongues but partially removes the difficulty; and, but for the remarkable and exceptional character of the Sanskrit, our knowledge of that stage in the history of our language out of which its present grammatical structure was a development would be but scanty and doubtful; while we have been compelled to confess (in the seventh lecture) that we know not how far even so primitive a stage may lie from the absolute beginning.

The corresponding condition of Semitic speech, its foundation
of triliteral roots, is to no small extent restorable; but we
have seen that these roots are themselves the products of a
strange and highly perplexing development, beneath which
their actual origin is not yet discernible. Among the different great branches of the Scythian family, the recognizable
radical coincidences are hardly sufficient, if they are sufficient,
to establish their unity as proceeding from the same stock :
a reliable basis for comparison with other families is certainly
not furnished us here. Nor was the Scythian the only
family in establishing whose unity we were obliged to add
the evidence of morphological structure to that of material
correspondences : there were at least two, the monosyllabic
in south-eastern Asia and the American, which were founded
almost solely on accordance of type. And the former of
them is a striking illustration of the power of phonetic
corruption to alter and disguise the bare roots of language,
without help from composition and fusion of elements. If
we cannot find material correspondences enough between the
pure radicals of Chinese, Siamese, and Burmese to prove these
three tongues akin, but must call in, to aid the conclusion,
their common characteristic of monosyllabism, what hope can
we possibly entertain of proving either of them akin with
Mongolian or Polynesian, for example, with which they have
no morphological affinity ? Who will be so sanguine as to
expect to discover, amid the blind confusion of the American
languages, where there are scores of groups which seem to be
totally diverse in constituent material, the radical elements
which have lain at the basis of their common development ?
Apparent resemblances among apparent roots of the different
families are, indeed, to be found : but they are wholly worthless as evidences of historical connection. To the general
presumption of their accidental nature is to be farther added
the virtual certainty that the elements in which they appear
are not ultimate roots at all, but the products of recent
growth. There is nothing, it may be remarked, in the
character of ultimate roots which should exempt them from
the common liability to exhibit fortuitous coincidences, but
rather the contrary. The system of sounds employed in the

rudimentary stage of linguistic growth was comparatively scanty, the circle of ideas represented by the roots was narrow and limited, the application of each root more vague and indeterminate; hence accidental analogies of form and meaning might even more reasonably be looked for between the radical elements of unconnected families than between their later developed words.

For these reasons it is that the comparison of roots is not likely to lead to any satisfactory results even in the most favourable cases, and cannot possibly be made fruitful of valuable and trustworthy conclusions through the whole body of human language. There are, it is true, not a few philologists—and among them some authorities deserving of the highest respect—who hold that correspondences enough have been found between Indo-European and Semitic roots to prove the ultimate connection of those two families of language: but the number is yet greater of those who regard the asserted proof as altogether nugatory. The attempt has been made above (in the eighth lecture) to show that the governing presumption in the case is not a purely linguistic one, but rather a historical; and it is one which is quite as likely to be weakened as to be strengthened by the results of future researches. But, as regards the point now under discussion, the admission or rejection of a genetic tie between these two particular families, or even between these and the Scythian and Chinese, would make no manner of difference: there would still remain the impossibility of extending a like tie, by linguistic means, to the other great families.

Our general conclusion, then, which may be looked upon as incontrovertibly established, is this : if the tribes of men are of different parentage, their languages could not be expected to be more unlike than they in fact are ; while, on the other hand, if all mankind are of one blood, their tongues need not be more alike than we actually find them to be. The evidence of language can never guide us to any positive conclusion respecting the specific unity or diversity of human races.

LECTURE XI.

Origin of language. Conditions of the problem. In what sense language is of divine origin. Desire of communication the immediate impulse to its production. Language and thought not identical. Thought possible without language. Difference of mental action in man and lower animals. Language the result and means of analytic thought, the aid of higher thought. The voice as instrument of expression. Acts and qualities the first things named. The "bow-wow," "pooh-pooh," and "ding-dong" theories. Onomatopœia the true source of first utterances. Its various modes and limitations. Its traces mainly obliterated. Remaining obscurities of the problem.

In the last lecture, we took up and considered certain matters which seemed naturally to present themselves to our attention in connection with our survey of the divisions and characteristics of human speech. We first examined the various systems of classification of languages, according to morphological form or to general rank, weighing briefly the value of the distinctions upon which they are founded; and we arrived at the conclusion that no other mode of classification has anything like the same worth with the genetical, or that which groups dialects together by their historical relationship. We then passed on to the subject of the general relations between linguistic science and ethnology, the history of human races. We saw that between the study of language and that of physical characteristics, as tests of race, there can be no discordance and jealousy, but only an honourable emulation and mutual helpfulness; that each, feeling its own limitations and imperfections, needs and seeks the assistance of the other; claiming, also, all the aid which recorded

history can furnish, and all that can be derived from archæology, to correct and confirm its conclusions. So intricate
and difficult of solution is the problem set before us in the
beginnings of history, the origin and ultimate connections of
races, that, as we have good reason to fear, our utmost efforts,
our most cunning combinations of all attainable evidence,
from whatever sources derived, will never bring us to a distinct and confident answer. For a little way, history and
tradition are our chief guides; then, the study of language
conducts us somewhat farther, although with feebler and
more uncertain steps; while physical science claims to give
us a few glimpses, we know not yet of what reach or sweep,
into a still remoter past. And as, in investigations of this
trying character, it is of no small consequence to know what
are the limits and defects of the evidence with which we are
dealing, that we may not waste our strength, and prepare
for ourselves bitter disappointment, by searching for conclusions where none can possibly be found, we entered upon an
inquiry as to whether it was within the province of linguistic
science to determine the vexed question of the unity or
multiplicity of the human race; and we found that this was
not the case. The beginnings of language, in at least a part
of the recognized families of languages, are too much covered
up and hidden under the products of later growth for our eyes
ever to distinguish them with any even tolerable approach to
certainty ; and the correspondences which have been already,
or may be hereafter, pointed out between the linguistic
material of different languages, now reckoned as belonging to
diverse families, may be so plausibly explained as the effects
of chance that they can never be accepted as the sure result
and sign of a common linguistic tradition. Our conclusion
here was, that human languages might well have become as
different as we now find them to be, even though all of them
descended from the rudimentary and undeveloped dialect of
some single original family or tribe ; while, on the other hand,
considering the acknowledged unity in diversity of human
nature, we should not expect to find languages any more unlike than they actually are, if there had been a separate Adam
and Eve for each one of a dozen or more human races.

Whether physical science will ever reach a more definite decision of the same question is at present, at least, very doubtful : its tendency seems now to be toward establishing such a capacity of mutation in species as would explain all the tribes of mèn as possible varieties of one type ; without, of course, at the same time disproving the possibility of their independent origin. It is likely enough that we may, at some time, reach a point where we shall be able to say that, upon the whole, the weight of probability is upon this side, or upon that : anything more certain and categorical we can hardly venture to look for. Happily, the question is one of little practical consequence : the brotherhood of men, the obligation of mutual justice and mutual kindness, rests upon the possession of a common nature and a common destiny, not upon the tie of fleshly relationship. Those who would justify their oppression of a whole race of their fellow-beings by an alleged proof of its descent from other ancestors than their own are not less perverse—more perverse they could not well be—than those who would sanctify it as the execution of a curse pronounced by a drunken patriarch upon a portion of his own offspring. It is as shameful to attempt to press science as religion into the service of organized injustice.

But if linguistic science must thus observe a modest silence with regard to the origin of the human race, what has it to say respecting the origin of language itself ? This is an inquiry to which we have made a near approach at one and another point in our discussions hitherto, but which we have carefully refrained from grappling with seriously. It has not lain in the direct line of our investigations. We have been engaged in analyzing and examining the recorded facts of language, in order to find what answer we could to our leading question, " why we speak as we do ? " and we have been brought at last to the recognition of certain elements called roots, which we clearly see to have been the germs whence the whole development of speech has proceeded, but which we do not dare affirm to have been absolutely the first utterances of speaking men. These, then, are the historical beginnings of speech ; and historical research will

take us no farther. The question as to what were the actual
first utterances, and how they were produced, must be decided,
if at all, in another way—by general considerations and analogies, by inferences from the facts of human nature and the
facts of language, taken together, and from their relations to
one another. It falls within the province rather of linguistic philosophy, as a branch of anthropology, than of the
historical science of language. But the subject is one of
such interest, and for the proper discussion of which our
historical investigations so directly prepare the way, that we
cannot refrain from taking it up. It may be that we shall
find no sharp-cut and dogmatic answer to our inquiries respecting it, but we may hope at least so to narrow down the
field of uncertainty and conjecture as to leave the problem
virtually solved.

We may fairly claim, in the first place, that the subject has
been very greatly simplified, stripped of no small part of its
difficulty and mystery, by what has already been proved as
to the history of speech. Did we find no traces of a primitive condition of language different from its later manifestations, did it appear to us as from the very beginning a completely developed apparatus, of complicated structure, with
distinct signs for objects, qualities, activities, and abstract
conceptions, with its mechanism for the due expression of
relations, and with a rich vocabulary—then might we well
shrink back in despair from the attempt to explain its origin,
and confess that only a miracle could have produced it, that
only a superhuman agency could have placed it in human
possession. But we have seen that the final perfection of
the noblest languages has been the result of a slow and
gradual development, under the impulse of tendencies, and
through the instrumentality of processes, which are even yet
active in every living tongue; that all this wealth has grown
by long accumulation out of an original poverty; and that
the actual germs of language were a scanty list of formless
roots, representing a few of the most obvious sensible acts
and phenomena appearing in ourselves, our fellow-creatures,
and the nature by which we are surrounded. We have now
left us only the comparatively easy task of satisfying our-

selves how men should have come into possession of these
humble rudiments of speech.

And our attention must evidently first be directed to the
inquiry whether those same inventive and shaping powers of
man which have proved themselves capable of creating out of
monosyllabic barrenness the rich abundance of inflective
speech were not also equal to the task of producing the first
poor hoard of vocables. There are those who insist much on
what they are pleased to term the divine origin of language ;
who think it in some way derogatory to the honour of the
Creator to deny that he devised roots and words, and, by
some miraculous and exceptional agency, put them ready-
made into the mouths of the first human beings. Of such we
would ask whether, after all, language can be in this sense
only a divine gift to man ; whether the hand of the Creator
is any the less clearly to be seen, and need be any the less
devoutly acknowledged, in its production, if we regard man
himself as having been created with the necessary impulses
and the necessary capacities for forming language, and then
as having possessed himself of it through their natural and
conscious workings. Language, articulate speech, is a
universal and exclusive characteristic of man: no tribe of
human kind, however low, ignorant, and brutish, fails to
speak ; no race of the lower animals, however highly endowed,
is able to speak: clearly, it was just as much a part of the
Creator's plan that we should talk as that we should breathe,
should walk, should eat and drink. The only question is,
whether we began to talk in the same manner as we began to
breathe, as our blood began to circulate, by a process in
which our own will had no part ; or, as we move, eat, clothe
and shelter ourselves, by the conscious exertion of our
natural powers, by using our divinely-given faculties for the
satisfaction of our divinely-implanted necessities.

That the latter supposition is fully sufficient to account
for our possession of speech cannot with any show of reason
be denied. Throughout its whole traceable history, language
has been in the hands of those who have spoken it, for manifold modification, for enrichment, for adaptation to the varying ends of a varying knowledge and experience ; nineteen

twentieths, at the least, of the speech we speak is demonstrably in this sense our own work: why should the remaining twentieth be thought otherwise ?   It is but a childish philosophy which can see no other way to make out a divine agency in human language than by regarding that agency as specially and miraculously efficient in the first stage of formation of language.   We may fairly compare it with the wisdom of the little girl who, on being asked who made her, replied : " God made me a little baby so high " (dropping her hand to within a foot of the floor) " and *I grew* the rest." The power which originates is not to be separated from that which maintains and develops : both are one, one in their essential nature, one in their general mode of action.   We might as well claim that the letters of the alphabet, that the simple digits, must have been miraculously revealed, for elements out of which men should proceed to develop systems of writing and of mathematical notation, as that the rudiments of spoken speech, the primitive signs of mental conceptions, must have had such an origin.

In short, our recognition of language as an institution, as an instrumentality, as no integral system of natural and necessary representatives of thought, inseparable from thought or spontaneously generated by the mind, but, on the contrary, a body of conventional signs, deriving their value from the mutual understanding of one man with another; and, farther, our recognition of the history of this institution as being not a mere succession of changes wrought upon something which still remains the same in essential character, but a real development, effected by human forces, whose operations we can trace and understand —these take away the whole ground on which the doctrine of the divine origin of language, as formerly held, reposed. The origin of language is divine, in the same sense in which man's nature, with all its capacities and acquirements, physical and moral, is a divine creation; it is human, in that it is brought about through that nature, by human instrumentality.

It is hardly necessary to make any farther reference to an objection, already once alluded to, which some minds may

be tempted to raise against our whole construction of the
course of linguistic history out of the evidences of composition, phonetic corruption, transfer of meaning, and the other
processes of linguistic growth, which we find in all the
material of human speech. The inquiry, namely, has sometimes been raised, whether it was not perfectly possible for
the Creator to frame and communicate to mortals a primitive
language filled with such apparent signs of previous development, as well as one which should have the aspect of a new
creation. Of course, must be our reply; nothing is theoretically impossible to Omnipotence : but to suppose that it has
pleased God to work thus is to make the most violent and
inadmissible of assumptions, one which imputes to him a
wholly degrading readiness to trifle with, even to deliberately
mislead and deceive, the reason which he has implanted in
his creatures. It is precisely of a piece with the suggestion
once currently thrown out, when the revelations of geology
were first beginning to be brought to light, that fossils and
stratifications and such like facts proved nothing ; since God,
when he made the rocks, could just as well have made them
in this form and with these contents as otherwise. With
men who can seriously argue upon such assumptions it is
simply impossible to discuss a historical question : all the
influences of historical science are thrown away upon them;
they are capable of believing that a tree which they have
not themselves seen spring up from the seed was created
whole in the state in which they find it, without gradual
growth ; or even that a house, a watch, a picture, were produced just as they are, by the immediate action of almighty
power.

We may here fittingly follow out a little farther an
analogy more than once suggested in our preceding discussions, and one which, though some may deem it homely and
undignified, is genuine and truly illustrative, and therefore
not wanting in instruction : it is the analogy between language and clothing and shelter, as alike results of men's
needs and men's capacities. Man was not created, like the
inferior races, with a frame able to bear all the vicissitudes of
climate to which he should be subjected ; nor yet with a

natural protective covering of hair or wool, capable of adapting itself to the variety of the seasons : every human being
is born into the world naked and cringing, needing protection
against exposure and defence from shame. Gifted is man,
accordingly, with all the ingenuity which he requires in order
to provide for this need, and placed in the midst of objects
calculated to answer to his requirements, suitable materials
for his ingenuity to work upon ready to his hand. And
hence, it is hardly less distinctively characteristic of man to
be clad than to speak ; nor is any other animal so universally
housed as he. Clothing began with the simplest natural
productions, with leaves and bark, with skins of wild animals,
and the like ; as shelter with a cave, a hole in the ground,
the hollow of a tree, a nest of interwoven branches. But
ingenuity and taste, with methods perfected and handed
down from generation to generation, made themselves, more
and more, ministers to higher and less simple needs : the
craving after comfort, ease, variety, grace, beauty, sought
satisfaction ; and architecture by degrees became an art, and
dress-making a handicraft, each surrounded by a crowd of
auxiliary arts and handicrafts, giving occupation to no insignificant part of the human race, calling into action some of
its noblest endowments, and bringing forth forms of elegance
and beauty—embodiments of conceptions, realizations of
ideals, produced by long ages of cultivation, and capable
neither of being conceived nor realized until after a protracted course of training. So was it also with language.
Man was not created with a mere gamut of instinctive cries,
nor yet with a song like the bird's, as the highest expression
of his love and enjoyment of life : he had wants, and capacities of indefinite improvement, which could be satisfied and
developed only through means of speech ; nor was he treated
by nature with a disappointing and baffling niggardliness in
respect to them ; he was furnished also with organs of
speech, and the power to apply their products to use in the
formation of language. His first beginnings were rude and
insufficient, but the consenting labour of generations has
perfected them, till human thought has been clothed in gar-
ments measurably worthy of it, and an edifice of speech has

been erected, grander, more beautiful, and more important
to our race than any other work whatever of its producing.
There are races yet living whose scanty needs and inferior
capacities have given them inferior forms of speech, as there
are races which have not striven after, or been able to con-
trive, any but the rudest raiment, the meanest shelter. But
the child now born among us is dressed in the products of
every continent and every clime, and housed, it may be, in
an edifice whose rules of construction have come down from
Egypt and Greece, through generations of architects and
craftsmen; as he is also taught to express himself in words
and forms far older than the pyramids, and elaborated by a
countless succession of thinkers and speakers.

This comparison might profitably be drawn out in yet
fuller detail, but I forbear to urge it farther, or to call attention to any other of the aspects in which it may be made
to cast light upon the development of speech. Enough has
been said, as I hope, to make plain that the assumption of
miraculous intervention, of superhuman agency, in the first
production of speech, is, so far as linguistic science is concerned, wholly gratuitous, called for by nothing which is
brought to light by our study of language and of its relations
to the nature and history of man.

It is next of primary and fundamental importance that
we make clear to ourselves what is the force directly and
immediately impelling to the production of speech. Speech,
we know, is composed of external audible signs for internal
acts, for conceptions—for ideas, taking that word in its most
general sense. But why create such signs? The doctrine,
now, is by no means uncommon, that thought seeks expression by an internal impulse; that it is even driven to expression by an inward necessity; that it cannot be thought
at all without incorporation in speech; that it tends to utterance as the fully matured embryo tends to burst its
envelop, and to come forth into independent life. This doctrine is, in my view, altogether erroneous: I am unable to
see upon what it is founded, if not upon arbitrary assumption,
combined with a thorough misapprehension of the relation
between thought and its expression. It is manifestly op-

posed to all the conclusions to which we have been thus far led by our inquiries into the nature and office of speech. Speech is not a personal possession, but a social; it belongs, not to the individual, but to the member of society. No item of existing language is the work of an individual; for what we may severally choose to say is not language until it be accepted and employed by our fellows. The whole development of speech, though initiated by the acts of individuals, is wrought out by the community. That is a word, no matter what may be its origin, its length, its phonetic form, which is understood in any community, however limited, as the sign of an idea; and their mutual understanding is the only tie which connects it with that idea. It is a sign which each one has acquired from without, from the usage of others; and each has learned the art of intimating by such signs the internal acts of his mind. Mutual intelligibility, we have seen, is the only quality which makes the unity of a spoken tongue; the necessity of mutual intelligibility is the only force which keeps it one; and the desire of mutual intelligibility is the impulse which called out speech. Man speaks, then, primarily, not in order to think, but in order to impart his thought. His social needs, his social instincts, force him to expression. A solitary man would never frame a language. Let a child grow up in utter seclusion, and, however rich and suggestive might be the nature around him, however full and appreciative his sense of that which lay without, and his consciousness of that which went on within him, he would all his life remain a mute. On the other hand, let two children grow up together, wholly untaught to speak, and they would inevitably devise, step by step, some means of expression for the purpose of communication; how rudimentary, of what slow growth, we cannot tell—and, however interesting and instructive it would be to test the matter by experiment, humanity forbids us ever to hope or desire to do so; doubtless the character of the speech produced would vary with difference of capacity, with natural or accidental difference of circumstances: but it is inconceivable that human beings should abide long in each other's society without efforts, and successful efforts, at intelligent interchange of thought. Again, let one who had grown up even to manhood among his fellows, in full and free communication with them, be long separated from them and forced to live in solitude, and he would unlearn his native speech by degrees through mere disuse, and be found at last unable to converse at all, or otherwise than lamely, until he had recovered by new practice his former facility of expression. While a Swiss Family Robinson keep up their language, and enrich it with names for all the new and strange places and products with which their novel circumstances bring them in contact, a Robinson Crusoe almost loses his for lack of a companion with whom to employ it. We need not, however, rely for this conclusion upon imaginary cases alone. It is a well-known fact that children who are deprived of hearing even at the age of four or five years, after they have learned to speak readily and well, and who are thus cut off from vocal communication with those about them, usually forget all they had learned, and become as mute as if they had never acquired the power of clothing their thoughts in words. The internal impulse to expression is there, but it is impotent to develop itself and produce speech : exclusion from the ordinary intercourse of man with man not only thwarts its progress, but renders it unable to maintain itself upon the stage at which it had already arrived.

Language, then, is the spoken means whereby thought is communicated, and it is only that. Language is not thought, nor is thought language ; nor is there a mysterious and indissoluble connection between the two, as there is between soul and body, so that the one cannot exist and manifest itself without the other. There can hardly be a greater and more pernicious error, in linguistics or in metaphysics, than the doctrine that language and thought are identical. It is, unfortunately, an error often committed, both by linguists and by metaphysicians. " Man speaks because he thinks " is the *dictum* out of which more than one scholar has proceeded to develop his system of linguistic philosophy. The assertion, indeed, is not only true, but a truism ; no one can presume to claim that man would speak if he did not think : but no fair logical process can derive any momentous con-

clusions from so loose a premise. So man would not wear
clothes if he had not a body; he would not build spinning
mules and jennies if cotton did not grow on bushes, or wool
on sheep's backs: yet the body is more than raiment, nor do
cotton-bushes and sheep necessitate wheels and water-power.
The body would be neither comfortable nor comely, if not
clad; cotton and wool would be of little use, but for machinery making quick and cheap their conversion into cloth;
and, in a truly analogous way, thought would be awkward,
feeble, and indistinct, without the dress, the apparatus,
which is afforded it in language. Our denial of the identity
of thought with its expression does not compel us to abate
one jot or tittle of the exceeding value of speech to thought;
it only puts that value upon its proper basis.

That thought and speech are not the same is a direct and
necessary inference, I believe, from more than one of the
truths respecting language which our discussions have already
established; but the high importance attaching to a right
understanding of the point will justify us in a brief review
of those truths in their application to it. In the first place,
we have often had our attention directed to the imperfection
of language as a full representation of thought. Words and
phrases are but the skeleton of expression, hints of meaning,
light touches of a skilful sketcher's pencil, to which the appreciative sense and sympathetic mind must supply the
filling up and colouring. Our own mental acts and states
we can review in our consciousness in minute detail, but we
can never perfectly disclose them to another by speech; nor
will words alone, with whatever sincerity and candour they
may be uttered, put us in possession of another's consciousness. In anything but the most objective scientific description, or the driest reasoning on subjects the most plain and
obvious, we want more or less knowledge of the individuality
of the speaker or writer, ere we can understand him intimately; his style of thought and sentiment must be gathered
from the totality of our intercourse with him, to make us
sure that we penetrate to the central meaning of any word
he utters; and such study may enable us to find deeper and
deeper significance in expressions that once seemed trivial or

commonplace. A look or tone often sheds more light upon character or intent than a flood of words could do. Humour, banter, irony, are illustrations of what tone, or style, or perceived incongruity can accomplish in the way of impressing upon words a different meaning from that which they of themselves would wear. That language is impotent to express our feelings, though often, perhaps, pleaded as a form merely, is also a frequent genuine experience; nor is it for our feelings alone that the ordinary conventional phrases, weakened in their force by insincere and hyperbolical use, are found insufficient: apprehensions, distinctions, opinions, of every kind, elude our efforts at description, definition, intimation. How often must we labour, by painful circumlocution, by gradual approach and limitation, to place before the minds of others a conception which is clearly present to our own consciousness! How often, when we have the expression nearly complete, we miss a single word that we need, and must search for it, in our memories or our dictionaries, perhaps not finding it in either! How different is the capacity of ready and distinct expression in men whose power of thought is not unlike! he whose grasp of mind is the greatest, whose review of the circumstances that should lead to a judgment is most comprehensive and thorough, whose skill of inference is most unerring, may be, much more than another of far weaker gifts, awkward and clumsy of speech. How often we understand what one says better than he himself says it, and correct his expression, to his own gratification and acceptance. And if all the resources of expression are not equally at the command of all men of equal mental force and training, so neither are they, at their best, adequate to the wealth of conception of him who wields them; that would be but a poorly stored and infertile mind which did not sometimes feel the limited capacity of language, and long for fuller means of expression.

But again, the variety of expression of which the same thought admits is an insuperable difficulty in the way of the identification we are opposing. To recur once more to an illustration of which we have already made use—I form and utter, for instance, the thought, *fish like water*. How

nearly bare this phrase is of all indication of relations
between the principal ideas; how ambiguous it is, but for the
tone, the connection, the circumstances in which it is used,
was pointed out before. If I say "fish, like water-rats,
swim in rivers," or "fish-like water-snakes abound here," I
have variously changed the elements of thought which these
words indicate, without any corresponding change of their
form. Were I, now, an ancient Roman, the words in which
I should have put my first thought would be *pisces amant
aquam.* Here, not only are the signs totally different, but a
host of things are distinctly expressed which before were left
to be inferred from the sum and surroundings of the statement. *Pisces* is marked not only as being a noun and
nothing else, but a noun in a certain case of the plural
number; *amant* is not less clearly a verb, and to be made
nowhere but in the third person plural of the present indicative active; while *aquam* shows by its form that it is used as
the direct object of the preceding verb, and that in all connections it is to be treated as a feminine word. If, again, I
were a Frenchman, I should have said, *les poissons aiment
l'eau,* literally, 'the fishes love the water.' Here nearly all
the expressions of relation which the Latin words conveyed
are lost again; in part, they are left to inference, as
in English; in part, they are intimated by the two
independent relational words, articles; which, moreover,
point out a new relation, that of class (fish in general, not
some fish only), not hinted at in either of the other phrases.
The Chinese would embody the same sense in still other
words, which would be even more barren than our English of
any indication of relations except such as is signified by the
respective position of the words and the requirements of the
situation. Other languages, in expressing the same idea,
would indicate yet other distinctions and relations: one,
perhaps, has a different word for fish when living from that
which denotes them when dead, or prepared for eating;
another signifies the fondness which fish have for their native
element by one term, and the higher affections of more
rational beings by another; and so on. There is thus a very
considerable discordance between the various equivalent

phrases, as to how much and what is expressed in the words signifying the three radical ideas, of *fish*, *liking*, and *water*, as to how much is expressed besides those ideas, and as to how it is expressed; and, at the same time, a total discordance between the sounds used to indicate the various elements. And yet, so far as we can judge, the thought expressed is in every instance the very same: certainly, there is no difference of thought corresponding to or measured by the difference of expression. Each speaker's intent, were he called upon to explain it fully, would be found to agree with that of the rest; only his uttered words directly signify a part, and leave the rest to be filled in by the mind of the hearer. How, now, can any one possibly maintain that thought and speech are one and the same, when identity of thought can consist with so much diversity of speech?

Look, once more, at the nature of the tie which, as repeatedly pointed out, connects any one of the spoken signs we use with the conception it represents. I learned the word *fish* at an early period of my life from my instructors, and associated it so intimately with a certain idea that the two are in my mind well-nigh inseparable: I cannot hear *fish* without having the corresponding thing called up in my imagination, nor utter it without calling up the same in the imagination of every person who has been taught as I was; nor, again, does any one of us ordinarily form the conception of a fish without at the same time having the audible complex of sounds, *fish*, uttered to the mind's ear. In later life, I have learned and associated with the same conception other words, as *piscis*, *poisson*, *ichthüs* (Greek), and so forth; any one of these I can call up at will, and employ in place of *fish*, when circumstances make it desirable. That I here use *fish* is simply for the reason that I am addressing myself to those who have mastered this sign, understand it readily, and are accustomed to employ it; the conventional usage of the community to which I belong, not anything in the character of my thought, imposes the necessity upon me: if I went to France, I should substitute the sign *poisson* for precisely the same reason. And I might stay so long in France, and say

and hear *poisson* so often, that it should become more intimately associated with its conception than *fish*, and should
come more readily and naturally than the latter into my
mind on presentation of the conception : I should then have
learned, as we phrase it, to *think* in French instead of
English.   How futile, I say again, to talk of such a thing as
identity between thought and the expression which sits so
loosely upon it, and can be so easily shifted !   As well compare the house of the hermit-crab—which, born soft and
coverless, takes refuge in the first suitable shell which chance
throws in its way, and thenceforth makes that its home,
unless convenience and opportunity lead it to move to
another—with that of the turtle, whose horny covering is a
part of its own structure, and cannot be torn off without
destruction of its life.

Is there not, in fact, something approaching to palpable
absurdity in the doctrine that words and thoughts are
identical, that the mind thinks words ?   Words are not
mental acts ; they are combinations of sounds, effects produced upon the auditory nerve by atmospheric vibrations,
which are brought about by physical agencies—agencies set in
operation, it is true, by acts of volition, but whose products are
no more mental than are pantomimic motions voluntarily
made with the fingers.   We know well, indeed, that there is
a language composed of such motions instead of uttered
words : namely, the language taught as means of communication and expression to those whose ear is numb to the
ordinary signs of thought.   Nothing brings more distinctly
to light the true nature of language, as a system of arbitrary
signs for thought, learned and made auxiliary to the processes
of thought, than a consideration of the modes of speech
practised by the deaf and dumb : whether their general language, which intimates ideas by significant gestures, possessing in the main a certain degree of evident relevancy, but
conventional in their special application ; or their finger-
speech, that most strange and anomalous mode of representation of ideas at second hand, by wholly arbitrary contortions
of certain appendages of the body, standing for another kind
of signs, namely articulate sounds, of the true nature of

which these unfortunate beings cannot form the slightest conception. But either of these kinds of language, or their combination, answers for the deaf-mute the same purpose that our speech answers for us, and in the same way, only in an inferior degree, owing to the comparative imperfection of the instrumentality—although the question may be seriously raised, whether it be not nearly or quite as effective a means of expression and aid of thought as is a rude and rudimentary spoken language like the Chinese. If, then, thought and language are identical, thought and pantomime are not less so; if we think words, the mute must think finger-twists: and who will venture seriously to maintain a proposition so manifestly preposterous?

But if we must thus deny that, in any admissible sense of the expression, language *is* thought, it still remains for us to inquire whether thought is not co-extensive with and dependent upon language; whether we can think otherwise than in and by words. The claim is sometimes roundly made, that "general ideas and words are inseparable; that the one cannot exist without the other;" that, "without words, not even such simple ideas as white or black can for a moment be realized." Let us examine for a moment this last assertion, and see whether it be well founded. Suppose, for instance, that there occurred but a single white substance, namely snow, in the nature by which we are surrounded: it is both possible and altogether likely that, while we had a name for the substance, we should have none for the colour: and yet, we should not therefore any the less apprehend that colour, as distinct from those of other objects; even as we now apprehend a host of shades of blue, green, red, purple, for which we possess no specific appellations. We conceive of them, we are able to recognize them at sight, but their practical value is not sufficient to lead us to name them separately. If, then, on going southward, we made acquaintance with cotton, we should not fail to notice and fully to realize its accordance with snow in the quality of whiteness, even though we had no name for the quality. On the contrary, we should certainly proceed to call cotton "snowy," for the precise reason that we did notice the correspondence

of the two in colour; and, as we went on to meet with other
substances of like hue, we should call them " snowy " also;
and at length—particularly, if we had left the zone of snow
behind us—*snowy* would come to mean in our use what
white does now, and *snowiness* would signify 'whiteness.'
We should have supplied the deficiency of our vocabulary in
this regard, not because we could not form a conception of
the colour without the name, but because we had found it
practically convenient to give a name to the conception we
had formed. The example is a typical one; it illustrates
the universal process of names-giving, in all its forms and in
all ages.   Our primitive ancestors were not unable to apprehend the existence and office of the earth's satellite until
they had devised for her the appellation of 'measurer;' and,
if she had a yet earlier title, it was given her in like manner,
for some quality distinctly perceived in her. We always
make a new word, or bestow upon an old word a new meaning, because we have an idea that wants a sign.   To maintain that the idea waits for its generation until the sign is
ready, or that the generation of the idea and of the sign is a
simple and indivisible process, is much the same thing as to
hold, since infants cannot thrive in this climate without
clothing and shelter, that no child is or can be born until a
layette and a nursery are ready for its use, or that along with
each child are born its swaddling-clothes and a cradle!
    It must be farther conceded, then, that the operations of
mind are at least so far independent of language that thought
is able to reach out in every direction a step beyond the border of speech; to conquer, bit by bit, new territory for
speech to occupy and hold in possession.   But our earlier
reasonings and examples have shown that there is no small
degree of incommensurability between the two in other respects also, that we do not and cannot always precisely communicate what we are conscious of having in our minds, and
that, of what we call our expression, a part consists merely
in so disposing a framework of words that those who hear us
are enabled to infer much more than we really express, and
much more definitely than we express it.   That we ordinarily
think with words may be true: but I imagine that the ex-

tent to which we do so, and the necessity of the accompaniment, are both apt to be considerably exaggerated. When we think most elaborately and most reflectively, then we formulate our thoughts as if we were speaking or writing them; but we need not always think in that style. If I hold up two sticks together, to see which is the longer, my comparison and conclusion are assuredly, both of them, independent of any use of language, spoken or conceived of. When I taste a bit of strong sea-duck, which has been put upon my plate for mallard, my perception of its flavour and my judgment that "the bird is fishy" are wholly instantaneous, and simple mental acts: I may then proceed to state my judgment, either to myself or to others, in whatever style of elaboration I may choose. This, if I mistake not, is the normal order of procedure: the mental act is momentary, its formulation in words occupies time; we have our thought to start with, and then go on to give it deliberate expression. The operation of thinking in words is a double one; it consists of thinking and of putting the thought into words; we conceive the thought and conceive also its expression. That, when we turn our attention full upon our own minds, we read there the act and its expression together, does not necessarily prove more than the intimacy of the association we have established between our conceptions and their signs, and the power over us of the habit of expression. Every deliberate thought, doubtless, goes through the mind of the deaf-mute accompanied by an image of the dactylic writhings which would be his natural mode of expressing it; * but his mental action is not slavishly dependent upon such an external auxiliary.

The only way, in fact, to prove the necessary connection and mutual limitation of thought and speech is to lay down such a definition of the former as excludes everything which

---

* Indeed, I know that the children of a late principal of the Hartford deaf-and-dumb asylum, who had grown up in the asylum, and knew the peculiar language of the inmates as familiarly as their English, could always tell what their father was thinking of, as he walked up and down in meditation, by watching his hands: his fingers involuntarily formed the signs which were associated in his mind with his subjects of thought; while at the same time, doubtless, he imagined also their spoken signs.

is not done by means of the latter. If thought is only that kind of mental action which is performed in and through words, all other being mere—what shall we call it?—preliminary and preparatory to thought, the question becomes simply a verbal one, and is settled. But it were futile to attempt thus to narrow the application of the term. Apprehension of generals and particulars, comparison, distinction, inference, performed under the review of consciousness, capable of being remembered and applied to direct the conduct of life—these are the characteristics of the action of mind, in every grade; where they are present, there is thought. And who will dare to deny even to the uninstructed deaf-mute the possession of ideas, of cognitions multitudinous and various, of power to combine observations and draw conclusions from them, of reasonings, of imaginings, of hopes? Who will say, then, that he does not think, though his thinking faculty has not yet been trained and developed by the aid of a system of signs? But neither can we refuse to believe that some of the lower animals have a capacity of thinking, although they are incapable of the production of any signs of their ideas which we may venture to dignify by the name of language. A dog, for instance, as surely apprehends the general ideas of a tree, a man, a piece of meat, cold and heat, light and darkness, pleasure and pain, kindness, threatening, barking, running, and so on, through the whole range, limited as compared with ours, of matters within his ken, as if he had a word for each. He can as clearly form the intention "I mean to steal that bone, if its owner turns his back and gives me a fair chance," as if he said it to himself in good English. He can draw a complex of syllogisms, when applying to present exigencies the results of past experience, and can determine "that smoking water must be hot, and I shall take good care not to put my foot into it"—that is to say, "water that smokes is hot; this water smokes; therefore, this water is hot: hot water hurts; this water is hot; *ergo*, it will hurt my foot." He is, to be sure, far enough from being able to put his process of thought into that shape; but so is many a human being who can not only draw the conclusion with unerring judgment, but also state it with perfect intelligibility. That the dog and many other animals make no very distant approach to a capacity for language is shown farther by their ability to understand and obey what is said to them. They are able so distinctly to associate certain ideas with the words we utter as to govern their actions accordingly. Even the dull ox knows which way to turn when his driver cries *gee* or *haw* to him ; and the exceeding intelligence with which some dogs will listen to directions, and even overhear conversation, has been the subject of many striking and authentic anecdotes. It is vain and needless to deny a correspondence up to a certain point between men and other animals in regard to the phenomena of mental activity, as well as the other phenomena connected with animal life, like digestion, motion, enjoyment and suffering. But their power of thinking is not, like ours, capable of free and indefinite development by education, whereof language is the chief means, as it is the sign also of a capacity for it. There is, it need not be doubted, no small difference between the thought of the most intelligent of the lower races, and that of the least cultivated speechless human being. Yet what a chaos of unanalyzed conceptions, undefined impressions, and unreasoned conclusions the mind of every one of us would be without speech, it is well-nigh impossible for us to have even a faint idea—for us who have so long enjoyed the advantage of expression, and so accustomed ourselves to lean upon it, that we can now even differ and dispute as to whether thought and its instrument are not one and the same thing. The mental action of the wholly wild and untrained man is certainly less unlike to that of the beast than to that of the man who has been educated by the acquisition and use of language. The distinction of the two former is mainly that of potentiality ; they are like the fecundated and the unfecundated egg : the one can develop into organized life ; the other cannot. Let us look at an illustration which shall set forth both their correspondence and their difference.

It has been often remarked that the crow has a capacity to count, up to a certain number. If two hunters enter a hut and only one comes out, he will not be allured near the place by any bait, however tempting; the same will be the case, if three enter and two come out, or if four enter and three come out—and so on, till a number is reached which is beyond his arithmetic; till he cannot perceive that one has been left behind, and so. is led to venture within reach of the hidden gun, to his destruction. Something very like this would be true of men, without language. Open for the briefest instant a hand with one corn in it, and then again with two, and any one who has an eye can tell the difference; so with two and three, with three and four—and so on, up to a limit which may vary with the quickness of eye and readiness of thought of the counter, results of his natural capacity or of his training, but which is surely reached, and soon. Open the hand, for instance, with twenty corns, then drop one secretly and open it again, and the surest eye that ever looked could not detect the loss. Or put near one another two piles or rows, one of nineteen, the other of twenty, and it would be not less impracticable to distinguish them by immediate apprehension. But here appears the discordance between the human mind and that of the brute. The crow would never find out that the heap of twenty is greater than that of nineteen; the man does it without difficulty: he analyzes or breaks up both into parts, say of four corns each, the numerical value of which he can immediately apprehend, as well as their number; and he at last finds a couple of parts, whereof both he and the crow could see that the one exceeds the other.

In this power of detailed review, analysis, and comparison, now, lies, as I conceive, the first fundamental trait of superiority of man's endowment. But this is not all. This would merely amount to a great and valuable extension of the limits of immediate apprehension; whereas the crow knows well that three corns are more than two corns, man would be able also to satisfy himself, in every actual case which should arise, that twenty corns are more than nineteen corns, or a hundred corns than ninety-nine corns; and he would be able to make an intelligent choice of the larger heap where a crow might cheat himself through ignorance. So much is possible without language, nor would it alone ever lead to the possession of language. In order to this, another kind of analysis is necessary, an analysis which separates the qualities of a thing from the thing itself, and contemplates them apart. The man, in short, is able to perceive, not only that three corns are more than two corns, but that three are more than two—a thing that the bird neither does nor can do. Such a perception makes language possible—for language-making is a naming of the properties of things, and of things themselves through those properties—and, combined with the other power which we have just noticed, it creates the possibility also of an indefinite progression in thinking and reasoning by means of language. Signs being found for the conceptions 'one,' 'two,' 'three,' and so on, we can proceed to build them up into any higher aggregate that we choose, following each step of combination by a sign, and with that sign associating the result of the process that made it, so as to be effectually relieved of the necessity of performing the process over again in each new case. Thus, from the recognition that three is more than two, that two and one are three, that twice two is four—all which truths are virtually within reach of the crow, since he would determine aright any practical question that involved them—we rise to the recognition that twenty is more than nineteen, that fifteen and five are twenty, that seven times seven are forty-nine, or ten times ten are a hundred : and these are truths which we could only reach by means of language ; they are inferences, circuitously arrived at, and made by means of language not less manageable than the simpler truths which are matters of direct synthetic apprehension. He who, having learned only to count, constructs for his own use a multiplication-table, has to work onward from step to step in somewhat the same way as he who has no speech ; but every product that he attains and fixes in memory with its factors, is an acquisition made once for all. Indefinite progress is thus ushered in ; every new result of mathematical reasoning is rendered capable of being handled, and the whole career of mathematical science is initiated. Yet not to be carried on by words alone. The most skilful mathematician cannot perform any of the more complicated processes

27

of calculation with signs merely uttered or conceived of as
uttered; he must write down his equations and series, and
work out painfully, in long rows of figures, his numerical results: for, though all was implied in his first assumption, as
evolved according to the unvarying relations of numbers,
and the principles of mathematical reasoning, he is unable to
grasp the various quantities with his mind, and to follow out
unerringly the successive steps of the processes, without recording each as he takes it. It is none the less true, however, that the whole work is a mental one: mathematical
quantities are identical neither with the written figures and
symbols, nor with the spoken signs; nor is mathematical
reasoning dependent for its existence upon the one or the
other: both are kindred instrumentalities, whereby the mind
is enabled to accomplish what would otherwise be wholly
beyond its power.

The main truths which we have to accept as touching the
relation of language to thought are, I think, brought out by
this illustration. It is, indeed, an extreme illustration on
the side of the indispensability of language. For no other
class of conceptions are so eminently abstract as are the
mathematical, none so wholly dependent upon spoken and
written signs and symbols. They are so essentially ideal in
their character, so divorcible from concrete objects, that they
can be worked with mechanically, can be put together and
taken apart without constant reference to real conditions—
though only according to rules and methods ultimately
founded on concrete exemplification, on immediate synthetic
apprehensions which are capable of being grasped by minds
lower than human. Yet, even here, the signs are merely
the instruments of thought, and created by it. The symbols
of the calculus are not more truly the device of the master-
minds which, exalted upon the vantage-ground of their own
and others' previous studies, apprehended the higher and
more recondite relations involved in this new mode of
mathematical reasoning, than the whole nomenclature of
numbers is the gradually elaborated work of men who saw
and felt impelled to signify the simpler and more fundamental
relations, those which seem to lie within the reach of every

intellect. That, however, they are not so easily attained,
that not a little time and reflection, and some special insight,
were required for generating even an ordinary system of
numeration, is clearly shown by the facts of language. There
are dialects that name no higher numbers than 'three' or
'four:' all beyond is an undistinguished "many," the definite
relations of which are as unmanageable by the speakers of
those dialects as if they were speechless. Many others have
not risen to the apprehension of a hundred; the Indo-
European race, before its dispersion, had apparently formed
no word for 'thousand;' the Greek popular mind had distinctly conceived no higher group than 'ten thousand'
(*myriad*). We have ourselves given names only to a few of
the first numbers in that infinite series which, having once
hit upon the method of decimal multiplication and notation,
we are capable of apprehending and of managing. And
what more significant mark of the externality of the whole
system of numerical names and signs could we ask to find
than its decimal character, which, as every one knows, is
altogether based upon the wholly irrelevant circumstance of
the number of our fingers, those ready aids to an unready
reckoner? Had we chanced to possess six digits on each
hand, our series of arithmetical "digits" would also be
twelve, and we should now be rejoicing in the use of a
duodecimal system—the superior advantages of which in
many respects are generally acknowledged.

In every department of thought, the mind derives from
the possession of speech something of the same advantage,
and in the same way, as in mathematical reasoning. The
idea which has found its incarnation in a word becomes
thereby a subject of clearer apprehension and more manageable use: it can be turned over, compared, limited, placed in
distinct connection with other ideas; more than one mind,
more than one generation of minds, can work at it, giving it
shape, and relation, and significance. In every word is
recorded the result of a mental process, of abstraction or of
combination; which process, being thus recorded, can be
taught along with its sign, or its result can be used as a step
to something higher or deeper. There are grades of thought,

spheres of ratiocination, where our minds could hardly work
at all without the direct aid of language; as there are also
those where they could not surely hold and follow the chain
of reason and deduction without the still further assistance
afforded by writing down the argument. It may be freely
conceded that such mental processes as we are in the constant
habit of performing would be too difficult for us to compass
without words—as they certainly also lie far beyond what
would have been our mental reach had we not been trained
through the use of language to orderly thought, and enriched
with the wealth of mental acquisitions accumulated by our
predecessors and stored up in words. But this is a very
different thing from acknowledging that thought is impossible
without language. So, also, to build steam-engines and
tubular-bridges, to weave satins and Brussels carpets, to
tunnel mountains, to fill up valleys, is impossible without the
aid of complicated and powerful machinery; yet we do not
on that account deny all power and efficiency to the bare
human hands. On the contrary, we see clearly that machinery is, in every part and parcel, ultimately the work of
human hands, which can do wondrous things without it, if
still more wondrous with it. Language, in like manner is
the instrument of thought, the machinery with which the
mind works; an instrument by which its capacity to achieve
valuable results is indefinitely increased, but which, far from
being identical with it, is one of its own products; with and
by which it works with freedom, depending upon it now
more, now less, according to circumstances—as the matter in
hand, the style of elaboration, the deliberation required or
permitted; and fully able to carry on the same operations
with instrumentalities greatly differing in completeness and
inherent adaptation to their purpose.

Our conclusion stands fast, then, that thought is anterior
to language, and independent of it; it is not compelled to
find expression in order to be thought. The immense and
incalculable advantage which it gains from its command of
speech is something incidental : something intended, indeed,
and a necessary implication in the gift of speech to the
human race; yet coming as a consequence of something else,

growing out of that communication which men must and will
have with their fellows.   True it is that the individual mind,
without language, would be a dwarfed and comparatively
powerless organ: but this means simply that man could
develop his powers, and become what he was meant to be,
only in society, by converse with his fellows. He is by his
essential nature a social being, and his most precious individual possession, his speech, he gets only as a social being.
The historical beginnings of speech, therefore, were no spontaneous outbursts, realizing to the mind of the utterer the
conceptions with which he was swelling; they were successful results of the endeavour to arrive at signs by which
those conceptions should be called up also in the minds of
others.

These considerations, if I am not mistaken, will be found
to relieve the remaining part of the problem we are considering of not a little of its perplexity. Recognizing the
external and non-essential nature of the bond which unites
every constituent of language to the idea represented by it,
and also the external nature of the force which brings about
the genesis of the sign, we are enabled to reduce the inquiry
to this form: how should the first language-makers, human
beings gifted like ourselves, with no exceptional endowments,
but with no disabilities other than that of the non-develop-
ment of their inherent capacities, have naturally succeeded
in arriving at the possession of signs by which they could
understand one another? Before we take up and examine
the theories which have been proposed to explain the first
processes of sign-making, however, we must look for a
moment at one or two preliminary points, of a more general
character.

Our first point concerns the office of the voice as instrument of expression. If the tie between idea and sign be so
loose, it may be asked, why is the sign always a spoken one,
and language, as we use the term, a body solely of articulated
utterances? In answering this, it is sufficient to point out
the superior convenience and availability of spoken signs, as
compared with those of any other kind. These qualities,
and these alone, designate the voice to its office. There is

no necessary connection between mental acts and vocal utterances. The one thing necessary is, that thought, tending irresistibly toward expression under the impulse to communication, should find the means of intelligibly expressing itself. With the mental powers and social tendencies which men have, they would, even if unendowed with voice, have nevertheless put themselves in possession of language—language less perfect and manageable, to be sure, than is our present speech; but still, real language. Resort, doubtless, would first have been had to gesture: it is hardly less natural to men to use their hands than their tongues to help the communication of their ideas; the postures of the body, the movements of the face, can be made full of significance; the resources of pantomime are various and abundant, and constitute a means of expression often successfully employed, between those who are unacquainted with the conventional signs of one another's spoken language. Those human beings whose vocal powers are rendered useless by the deadness of their ears learn a pantomimic language which answers their needs, both of communication and of mental training, in no stinted measure. It has, indeed, its limitations and defects; but what it might be made, if it were the only means of communication attainable by men, and were elaborated by the consenting labour of generations, as spoken speech has been, we perhaps are slow to realize. I do not doubt that it might far exceed, both in wealth of resources and in distinct apprehensibility, many an existing spoken language, might ally itself with a mode of writing, and become an efficient means and aid of human progress. How easy a language of gestures is to acquire, and how natural to use, is clearly shown by the fact that the fully endowed children of the instructors in deaf-and-dumb asylums, brought up among those who employ both it and the spoken tongue, are accustomed to learn the former first, and to avail themselves of it in preference to the other, till long after the time when other children usually talk freely. It is past all reasonable question that, in the earliest communication between human beings, gesture long played a considerable, if not the principal, part, and that our race learned only by

degrees the superior capacities of spoken signs, and by
degrees worked them out to a sufficiency for all the ordinary
needs of expression; when gesture was relegated to the department of rhetoric, to the office of giving individual colouring
and intensity to intellectual expression—as, in all well-
developed languages, has been the case with tone also. We
do not need to enter here into any detailed inquiry as to the
modes and reasons of the special adaptedness of vocal utterance to the uses of expression. The fact is palpable, recognized by every mind, and illustrated by the whole history of
human communication. We feel that those who learn to
talk well without speaking are to be compared with the
mutilated beings who, deprived of hands, learn to make their
feet do the ordinary and natural work of hands. Many of
us have seen toys constructed, figures cut out, pictures
painted by such beings, with the help of instruments grasped
by the toes, which we who possess the most supple of fingers
might try in vain to imitate : and in the possibility of such
things we note the controlling power of the true actor, the
human mind and soul, which, in the direction of its special
gifts, can work out beautiful and wonderful results with
instrumentalities that appear to us awkward, feeble, and
inefficient. The voice, the articulating power, was the
appointed and provided means of supplying the chief want
of man's social nature, language ; and no race of men fails
to show, by its possession of articulate speech, that the provision was one natural, recognizable, and sufficient.

Our second point concerns the general class of ideas
which should have first found incorporation in speech.
What we are brought by our historical analysis of language
to recognize as the beginnings of speech was set forth in the
seventh lecture. Roots, directly significant of quality or
action, were there shown to be the starting-points, the germs,
of our whole vast system of nomenclature, for qualities,
beings, and relations. Many minds, however, find a difficulty
in accepting such a result. They are unwilling to believe
that language can have begun with the expression of anything so abstract as a quality ; they feel as if the first words
must have been designations for concrete things, for the

familiar objects of primitive life. The source of their difficulty lies in the fact that they would confound the *prima
denominata*, the things first named, with the *prima cognita*,
the things first cognized, apprehended by the mind, either
as individuals or as classes. In truth, however, the two are
quite distinct. It is not to be doubted that concrete things
are first recognized, distinguished, and classified, in the
earliest synthetic operations of the intelligence ; so are they
also in the inferior intelligences of the lower animals ; but
these synthetic cognitions do not and cannot lead to language. Language begins with analysis, and the apprehension of characteristic qualities. Not what the mind first
consciously contemplated, but what was most readily capable of being intelligibly signified, determined the earliest
words. Now a concrete object, a complex existence, is just
as much out of the immediate reach of the sign-making
faculty as is a moral act or an intellectual relation. As,
during the whole history of language, designations of the
latter classes of ideas have been arrived at through the medium of names for physical acts and relations, so have appellations for the former been won by means of their perceived
characteristics. No etymologist feels that he has traced out
the history of any concrete appellation till he has carried it
back to a word expressive of quality. We saw in the third
lecture that, when we would make a name for a thing, we
have recourse always to its qualities ; we take some general
word designating one of its distinguishing properties, and
limit it to signifying the thing itself (as when we derived
board from *broad, moon* from *measuring, smith* from *smooth-
ing*) ; or else we identify by some common property or properties, or connect by some other equivalent tie of association,
the thing to be named with another thing already named,
and call it by the latter's title (as in deriving Jupiter's *moons*
from *moon, Board* of Trade from *board, Smiths* from *smith*).
Let any one of us, even now, after all our long training in
the expression of our conceptions, attempt to convey to another person his idea of some sensible thing, and he will
inevitably find himself reviewing its distinctive qualities, and

selecting those which he shall intimate, by such signs as he
can make intelligible : there is no other way in which we
can make a definition or description, whether for our own
use or for that of anybody else.   If, for example, a dog is
the subject of our effort, we compare our conception of him
with those of other sensible objects, and note its specific differences—as his animality, shape, size, disposition, voice.
This is so essentially a human procedure that we cannot conceive of the first makers of language as following any other.
Then, in finding a designation, it would be impossible to include and body forth together the sum of observed qualities :
in the first instance, not less than in all after time, some one
among them would necessarily be made the ground of appellation.   The sign produced would naturally vary with the
instrumentality used to produce it, and the sense to which it
was addressed : in the instance which we have supposed, if
the means of communication were writing, it would probably
be the outline figure of a dog ; if gesture, an imitation of
some characteristic visible act, like biting, or wagging the
tail ; if the voice, not less evidently an imitation of the
audible act of barking : the dog's primal designation would
be *bow-wow*, or something equivalent to it.   But in this
designation would be directly intimated the act ; the actor
would be suggested by implication merely : *bow-wow*, as name
for ' dog,' would literally mean ' the animal that *bow-wows*.'
So in the case of a word like *splash*, used to imitate and call
up before the mind the fall of a stone into water—the collision of the stone and the water would be the immediate
suggestion ; but a natural act of association might make the
sign mean the stone, or the water, or the act of throwing, or
the fall.   One sign would turn more readily to the designation of a property or action, another to that of a concrete
thing, an actor, according to the nature of each, and the
exigencies of practical use as regarded it ; but both would
be inherently a kind of indifferent middle, capable of conversion to either purpose : and, in the poverty of expression
and indistinctness of analysis belonging to the primitive stage
of linguistic growth, would doubtless bear various offices at

once. In short, they would be such rudiments of speech, rather than parts of speech, as we have already found the radical elements of language to be.

Thus we see that the necessary conditions of the act of production of our language, as being the creation of a spoken sign for mutual intelligence between speaker and hearer, determine the kind of significance belonging to the first produced words. An acted sign, and a language of such, would have been of the same quality. While, on the other hand, a language of written characters, beginning with pictorial signs, would be of a very different structure : its first words would be designations of concrete sensible objects—since drawings are fitted to suggest concrete objects rather than their individual qualities—and, from these, designations of qualities would have to be arrived at by secondary processes.

Our reasonings have now at length brought us very near to a positive conclusion respecting the mode of genesis of even the first beginnings of spoken speech. But, rather than follow them farther, to a yet more definite result, we will proceed to examine the various theories that have been framed to explain how men should have found out what their voice was given them for, and should have begun to apply it to its proper uses, producing with it significant words.

Of such theories there are three which are especially worthy of note. The first holds that the earliest names of objects and actions were produced by imitation of natural sounds : animals, for instance, were denominated from their characteristic utterances, as, with us, the cuckoo is so named : the dog was called a *bow-wow*, the sheep a *baa*, the cow a *moo*, and so on ; while the many noises of inanimate nature, as the whistling of the wind, the rustling of leaves, the gurgling and splashing of water, the cracking and crashing of heavy falling objects, suggested in like manner imitative utterances which were applied to designate them ; and that by such means a sufficient store of radical words was originated to serve as the germs of language. This is called the onomatopoetic theory. The second is to this effect : that the natural sounds which we utter when in a state of excited feeling, the *oh's* and *ah's*, the *pooh's* and *pshaw's*, are the ultimate beginnings of speech. This is styled the interjectional theory. A recent writer of great popularity, Professor Max Müller,* entirely rejects both these, stigmatizing them as "the *bow-wow* theory " and " the *pooh-pooh* theory" respectively, and adopts from a German authority (Professor Heyse, of Berlin) a third, which is, abridged from his own statement, as follows : " There is a law which runs through nearly the whole of nature, that everything which is struck rings. Each substance has its peculiar ring. . . . It was the same with man, the most highly organized of nature's works "— and so on. Man possessed an instinctive "faculty for giving articulate expression to the rational conceptions of his mind." But " this creative faculty, which gave to each conception, as it thrilled for the first time through the brain, a phonetic expression, became extinct when its object was fulfilled," etc. This, in its turn, has been very appositely termed " the *ding-dong* theory."

What value we have to attribute to these various theories is readily to be inferred from the principles already laid down and established. The third may be very summarily dismissed, as wholly unfounded and worthless. It is, indeed, not a little surprising to see a man of the acknowledged ability and great learning of Professor Müller, after depreciating and casting ridicule upon the views of others respecting so important a point, put forward one of his own as a mere authoritative *dictum*, resting it upon nothing better than a fanciful comparison which lacks every element of a true analogy, not venturing to attempt its support by a single argument, instance, or illustration, drawn from either the nature or the history of language. He tells us, virtually, that man was at the outset a kind of bell; and that, when an idea struck him, he naturally rang. We wonder it was not added that, like other bells, he naturally rang by the tongue: this would have been quite in keeping with the rest, and would merely have set more plainly before our minds the real character of the whole theory. It fully implies the doctrine, which we have shown above to be erroneous, that

---

* In his Lectures on the Science of Language, first series, last lecture.

thought tends to burst into expression by an internal
impulse, instead of under an external inducement; and with
this it couples the gratuitous assumption that the impulse
ceased to act when a first start had thus been given to the
development of human speech. In effect, it explains. the
origin of language by a miracle, a special and exceptional
capacity having been conferred for the purpose upon the
first men, and withdrawn again from their descendants.
The formation of language is never over in any such manner
as should release an instinct like this from farther service, if
it really existed in human nature. New cognitions and
deductions still thrill through the brains of men, yet without
setting their tongues swinging, any more than their fingers
working. In all our investigations of language, we find
nothing which should lead us to surmise that an intellectual
apprehension could ever, by an internal process, become
transmuted into an articulated sound or complex of sounds.
We do, indeed, see that what strongly affects the emotional
nature prompts utterance, as it also prompts gesture: fear,
surprise, joy, lead to exclamations; and delight at a new
cognition might find vent in an interjection; but this interjection would express the delight, not the cognition; if language commenced in such a way, the historical beginnings
of speech would be names of emotions, not of the qualities of
objects.

The fatal weakness of such attempts as this to explain the
earliest steps in the formation of language lies in the fact
that they would fain discover there some force at work
differing entirely from that which directs the whole after-
course of linguistic development. We, on the contrary,
having fully recognized the truth that all language-making,
through the long recorded periods of linguistic history, consists in a succession of attempts to find an intelligible sign for
a conception which the mind has formed and desires to communicate, must look to find the same principle operative also
at the very outset of that history.

Regarding the matter in this light, we shall not fail to see
clearly what and how much value we are to ascribe to the
other two theories, the onomatopoetic and the interjectional.

Each of them furnishes a good and sufficient explanation of
a part of the facts for which we are seeking to account,
since each suggests available means by which the first
speakers should have arrived at mutually intelligible signs.
Especially great and undeniable are the capabilities of the onomatopoetic principle. We saw in one of our recent illustrations that, since qualities or acts are the immediate objects
of the first designations, and since the voice is the appointed
means of designating, audible acts, utterances or accompanying noises, would be most naturally chosen to be designated.
That words have been and may be formed through the
medium of imitation of natural sounds is palpably true ;
every language has such to show in its vocabulary. That,
for example, an animal can be named from its cry, and the
name thus given generalized and made fertile of derivatives,
is shown by such a word as *cock*, which is regarded by ety-
mologists as an abbreviated imitation of chanticleer's *cock-a-
doodle-doo!* and from which come, by allusion to the bird's
pride and strut, the words *coquette, cockade,* the *cock* of
a gun, to *cock* one's eye, to *cock* the head on one side, a
cocked hat, and so on. Through all the stages of growth of
language, absolutely new words are produced by this method
more than by any other, or even almost exclusively ; there is
also to be seen an evident disposition to give an imitative
complexion to words which denote matters cognizable by
the ear; the mind pleases itself with bringing about a sort
of agreement between the sign and the thing signified.
Both theory and observed fact, therefore, unite to prove the
imitative principle more actively productive than any other
in the earliest processes of language-making. But neither
is a noteworthy degree of importance to be denied to the
exclamatory or interjectional principle. It is, beyond all
question, as natural for the untaught and undeveloped man
to utter exclamations, as to make gestures, expressive of his
feelings ; and as, in the absence of a voice, the tendency to
gesture might have been fruitful in suggesting a language of
significant motions, so we may most plausibly suppose that
the tendency to exclaim was not without value in aiding men
to realize that they had in their voices that which was capable

of being applied to express the movements of their spirits.
Perhaps the principal contribution of exclamations to the
origin of language was made in this way, rather than by the
furnishing of actual radical elements: for the latter work,
their restricted scope, their subjective character, their in-
fertility of relations, would render them less fitted.

There is no real discordance between the onomatopoetic
and interjectional theories, nor do the advocates of either, it
is believed, deny or disparage the value of the other, or refuse
its aid in the solution of their common problem. The definition of the onomatopoetic principle might be without difficulty
or violence so widened that it should include the interjectional. We must, indeed, beware of restricting its action
too narrowly. It is by no means limited to a reproduction
of the sounds of animate and inanimate nature: it admits
also a kind of symbolical representation—as an intimation of
abrupt, or rapid, or laborious, or smooth action by utterances
making an analogous impression upon the ear. A yet more
subjective symbolism has been sought for among some of the
earlier constituents of speech; it has been suggested, for example, not without a certain degree of plausibility, that the
pronominal root of the first person in the Indo-European (and
in many other) languages, *ma* (our *me*), has in its internality
of formation, its utterance with closed lips, as if shutting out
the external world, a peculiar adaptedness to express one's
own personality; and that the demonstrative *ta* (which has
become our *that*) was prompted by the position it calls for
in the tongue, which is thrust forward in the mouth, as it
were to point out the object indicated. Very little of this
kind, if anything at all, can be satisfactorily made out in the
material of language; that, however, some degree of such
subjective correspondence, felt more distinctly in certain
cases, less so in others, may have sometimes suggested to a
root-proposer, by a subtile and hardly definable analogy, one
particular complex of sounds rather than another, as the
representative of an idea for which he was seeking expression,
need not be absolutely denied. Only, in admitting it, and
seeking for traces of its influence, we must beware of
approximating in any degree to that wildest and most

absurd of the many vagaries respecting language, the doctrine of the natural and inherent significance of articulate sounds.

It is quite unnecessary that we should attempt to determine the precise part played by these principles, or these different forms of the onomatopoetic principle, in generating the germs of speech. We cannot go far astray, either in overestimating or in underestimating the value of each one of them, if we bear always distinctly in mind the higher principle under which they all alike exercised their influence : namely, that the language-makers were not attempting to make a faithful depiction of their thought, but only to find for it a mutually intelligible sign ; and that everything which conduced to such intelligibility would have been, and was, resorted to, and to an extent dependent on its degree of adaptedness to the purpose—the extent being a fair matter for difference of opinion, and for ascertainment by further detailed investigation, both theoretical and historical. There are many ideas which would be much more clearly intimated by a gesture, a grimace, or a tone, than by a word ; and, as has been already remarked, we cannot doubt that tones, grimaces, and gestures constituted no small portion of the first sign-language, both as independently conveying meaning, and as helping to establish the desired association between articulate signs and the ideas which they were intended to signify. Language, indeed, never fully outgrows the need of their assistance : it is only the most highly developed and cultivated tongues, wielded by the most skilful writers, that can make a written passage, even when addressed to the intellect alone, as clear and effective as the same would be when well uttered, with the addition of due emphasis and inflection : and where the emotions and passions are appealed to, we have the opinion of one of the greatest word-artists of antiquity (Demosthenes) that " action " is far more than words.

We are not, of course, to look upon the imitative signs of which we have been treating as servile copies of natural sounds, or their exact reproductions. Nothing of that kind is either called for or possible. Inarticulate noises are not

faithfully representable by articulate, nor is more than a distant likeness needed in the sign that shall suggest and recall
them. The circumstances in which a new word is generated
and used contribute no small part toward its correct apprehension, in the first, as in all the after-stages of linguistic
growth. The most violent mutilations of form, the most absurd confusions of meaning, committed upon words by very
young children, when just learning to talk, do not prevent
those who are familiar with them from understanding which
of their contracted circle of ideas they are intending to signify: and many a change almost as violent, or a transfer
almost as distant, has made part of the regular history of
speech, being justified by the exigency that called it forth,
and explained by the suggestive conditions of the case. The
process of language-making was always in a peculiar sense
a tentative one; a searching after and experimental proposal
of signs thenceforth to be associated with conceptions.
There was not less eagerness and intelligence on the part of
the hearer to catch and apprehend than on that of the
speaker to communicate; the impulse to a mutual understanding was so strong as to make even a modicum of connection between sign and sense sufficient for its purpose.
A wide range of possibilities was thus opened for the designation of any given idea, even though resting upon the same
onomatopoetic ground: as, indeed, the present facts of language show us no little variety and dissimilarity in the confessedly imitative names of the same objects.

That distinct and unequivocal signs of onomatopoetic
action are not abundantly to be recognized among the earliest
traceable constituents of our language is no valid argument
against the truth of that view of the origin of speech which
we have been defending. It has been a common weakness
with the upholders of the onomatopoetic theory, and one
which more than anything else, perhaps, has tended to dis-
credit them and it with linguistic scholars, that they claim to
point out too much in detail, endeavouring to find imitative
etymologies where a more thorough comprehension of the
facts and a sounder and less prepossessed judgment see an
origin of another and less immediate character. But their

doctrine is so impregnably founded in the properly under-stood facts of linguistic history, and in the necessary con-ditions and forces of its earliest period, that they can well afford to be modest, and even reserved, in their attempts to explain particulars. Always and everywhere in language, as we have abundantly seen in our earlier inquiries into the processes of linguistic growth, when once the mutually intel-ligible sign is found, its origin is liable to be forgotten and obscured. There was doubtless a period in the progress of speech when its whole structure was palpably onomatopoetic ; but not a long one: the onomatopoetic stage was only a stepping-stone to something higher and better. Especially, perhaps, was this the case in the language of our own branch of the human race, whose nobler endowments must have begun very early their career of superior development. If we could trace the roots of the other families of language back to the same remote stage, we might find in some of them more evident traces of the primal imitative condition ; we may even yet find the same principle dominant to a much higher degree through the whole history of one or other of those families than in our own.

How many may have been the individual proposals of signs which were made ineffectively, to be disregarded or soon forgotten again, or how many the special signs which gained a certain currency in the minor groups of the language-making community, but failed to win that general acceptance which should make them the germs of a transmitted and perpetuated language, we do not and cannot know. Nor can we know how numerous, or of what social constitution, or in what condition of life, was the community which thus formed the speech of a linguistic family or of the whole hu-man race; nor how rapid was the accumulation of uttered words of general intelligibility, nor how great the store gathered by direct imitative process, nor how long the period during which they and their like were made to answer the purposes of communication, anterior to the beginning of structural development. On all such topics as these—as we have found occasion to remark before (in the seventh lec-ture), when treating of similar subjects—even our guesses are now worth nothing, or so nearly nothing as not to deserve recording. But we have no reason to suppose that any language of roots alone was ever otherwise than scanty and feeble ; those are greatly mistaken who imagine that the beginnings of speech were produced in a profusion, a superfluity, which later times have rather tempered down and economized than increased. We can see clearly also that the imitative principle, on the one hand, has its natural limits, and, on the other hand, would soon begin to admit the concurrence of a new principle of word-making: namely, the differentiation and various adaptation of the signs already established in use. There would come a time, before very long, when a designation of certain ideas would be more easily won out of existing material than by the creation of new ; and this facility would rapidly increase as the body of accepted expression was augmented; until finally the condition of things was reached which we find prevailing during the historical periods of language, when additions to our store of expression are almost exclusively elaborated out of modes of expression in previous use, and onomatopœia is resorted to only in rare and exceptional cases.

The imitative principle is limited in kind as well as in extent of action, and it may sometime become a practical inquiry what were the individual conceptions to which the first signs were fitted. In the present state of advancement of linguistic science, as also of our knowledge of the earliest human conditions, such an investigation, though an interesting one, would doubtless lead to no valuable result.

The view of language and of its origin which has been here set forth will, as I well know, be denounced by many as a low view : but the condemnation need not give us much concern. It is desirable to aim low, if thereby one hits the mark ; better humble and true than high-flown, pretentious, and false. A considerable class of linguistic scholars, fearful lest they should not otherwise make out language to be a sufficiently exalted and sacred thing, confound it with thought, and arrogate to the instrumentality a part of the attributes which belong only to the agent; thus becoming involved in inconsistencies and absurdities, or blinding them-

selves and those who depend upon them with mystical dog-
mas, irreducible to the language of fact and common sense.
Mind and its operations are full of real mystery ; in language,
there are no mysteries, but only the obscurities and difficulties inseparable from the rise and development of the
oldest and most important of all human institutions.

LECTURE XII.

Why men alone can speak. Value of speech to man. Training involved
in the acquisition of language. Reflex influence of language on mind
and history. Writing the natural aid and complement of speech.
Fundamental idea of written speech. Its development. Symbolic
and mnemonic objects. Picture writing. Egyptian hieroglyphs.
Chinese writing. Cuneiform characters. Syllabic modes of writing.
The Phenician alphabet and its descendants. Greek and Latin
alphabets. English alphabet. English orthography. Rank of the
English among languages.

OUR last inquiries, into the origin of language and the
nature of its connection with thought, brought us to conclusions accordant with those we had reached in the course of
our earlier discussions, and foreshadowed by them. As we
had found before that the only forces immediately concerned
in the growth and changes of language were human, so now
we saw that there was no reason to regard any others as
having borne a share in its origination: in its incipient
stage, no less than in its succeeding phases, speech has been
the work of those whose needs it supplies; it is in no
other sense of divine origin than as everything which man
possesses is a divine gift, the product of endowments and
conditions which are not of his own determining. As,
further, we had recognized the arbitrariness and conventionality of the means whereby each individual among us signifies
his conceptions to his fellows—namely, utterances learned by
each from those among whom his lot chanced to be cast, he
being forced to speak as they were in the habit of speaking

—so now we perceived that the same qualities had attached from the very outset to the signs chosen for expression; that, as there is at present no internal and necessary reason why we employ one particular complex of sounds rather than another as the representative of a particular idea, so there had never been any such reason; that words never meant thoughts, but always simply designated them. It had formerly appeared to us that, although there has been in every case an etymological reason for a word, this reason is one of convenience only, founded in the prior acquisitions and habitudes of the word-makers; efficient, indeed, at the moment of origination of the word, whose association with the intended meaning it is instrumental in initiating, but idle when the association has once been formed, and therefore soon neglected by the language-users, and often forgotten beyond power of recovery—and now we were brought to acknowledge that the very first words had only a similar reason, being such utterances as the natural endowments and habits of man, his imitative faculty and his tendency to exclaim, made the feasible means of arriving at a mutual comprehension between utterer and listener. Onomatopœia, in all its varieties of application, thus came in at the outset, aided and supplemented by tone and gesture, to help the language-makers to find intelligible signs, but ceased to control the history of each sign when once this had become understood and conventionally accepted; while the productive efficiency of the principle gradually diminished and died out as a stock of signs was accumulated sufficient to serve as the germs of speech, and to increase by combination and differentiation. Thus, as mutual intelligibility had been before proved to be the only test of the unity of language, and its necessity the force that conserved linguistic unity, it was further demonstrated that the desire to understand and be understood by one another was the impulse which acted directly to call forth language. In all its stages of growth alike, then, speech is strictly a social institution; as the speaking man, when reduced to solitude, unlearns its use, so the solitary man would never have formed it. We may extol as much as we please, without risk of exaggeration, the

advantage which each one of us derives from it within his
inmost self, in the training and equipment of his own powers
of thought : but the advantage is one we should never have
enjoyed, save as we were born members of a community :
the ideas of speech and of community are inseparable.

By thus tracing back, as well as our knowledge and our
limited time have allowed, the course of the history of human
speech even to its very beginning, we have made such answer
as was within our power to our introductory question, " Why
we speak as we do, and not otherwise ? "   But, before bringing our discussions to a close, it will be well for us, varying a
little the emphasis of our inquiry, to present and consider it
in one or two new aspects.

And, in the first place, why do *we* speak—we human
beings and we alone, and not also the other races of animals
which have been endowed with faculties in many respects so
like our own ?   The fact is a patent one : although some of
the lower animals are not entirely destitute of the power of
communicating together, their means of communication is
altogether different from what we call language.   The
essential characteristic of our speech is that it is arbitrary
and conventional; that of the animals, on the other hand, is
natural and instinctive : the former is, therefore, capable of
indefinite change, growth, and development; the latter is
unvarying, and cannot transcend its original narrow limits :
the one is handed down by tradition, and acquired by instruction; the other appears independently, in its integrity,
in every individual of the race.   Now, for the superiority of
man in this particular, the general reason, that his endowments are vastly higher than those of the inferior races,
though by no means so definite as could be desired, is perhaps the truest and most satisfactory of which the case at
present admits.   When philosophers shall have determined
precisely wherein lies the superiority of man's mind, they will
at the same time have explained in detail his exclusive possession of speech.   We are accustomed to agree that man is
distinguished from the brute by the gift of reason ; but then
we can only define reason as that whereby man is distinguished from the brute ; for as to what reason is, how far it

is a difference of kind, and how far one of degree only, we are quite at a loss to tell. To say that the animal is governed by instinct instead of reason does not help the difficulty; it is but giving a name to a distinction of which we do not comprehend the nature. Wherever the line may require to be drawn between the "blind instinct," as we sometimes style it, of the bee and ant, and the "free intelligence" of man, that line is certainly long passed when we come to some of the higher animals—as, for example, the dog. No one can successfully deny to the dog the possession of an intelligence which is real, even though limited by boundaries much narrower than those that shut in our own; nor of something so akin with many of the nobler qualities on which we pride ourselves that their difference is evanescent and indefinable. And anything wearing even the semblance of intelligence necessarily implies the power to form general ideas. It is little short of absurdity to maintain, for instance, that the dog, and many another animal, does not fully apprehend the idea of a human being; does not, whenever it sees a new individual of the class, recognize it as such, as having like qualities, and able to do like things, with other individuals of the same class whom it has seen before. If the crow did not comprehend what a man is, why should it be afraid of a scarecrow? And how is any application of the results of past experience to the government of present action—such as the brutes are abundantly capable of—possible without the aid of general conceptions? To identify reason, then, with the single mental capacity of forming general ideas, and to trace the possession of speech directly to this faculty, is, in my view, wholly erroneous: it is part of that superficial and unsound philosophy which confounds and identifies speech, thought, and reason. Speech is one of the most conspicuous and valuable of the manifestations of reason; but, even without it, reason would be reason, and man would be man, though far below what he was meant to become, and is capable of becoming through the aid of speech: and there are many other things besides talking which man can do in virtue of his reason, and which are out of the power of any other creature. If we are pressed to say in what mode of action, more than in any other, lies that deficiency in the powers of the lower animals which puts language beyond their reach, we need have little hesitation in answering that it is the inferiority of the command which consciousness in them exercises over the mental operations : in their inability to hold up their conceptions before their own gaze, to trace out the steps of reasoning, to analyze and compare in a leisurely and reflective manner, separating qualities and relations from one another, so as to perceive that each is capable of distinct designation.   That many animals come so near to a capacity for language as to be able to understand and be directed by it when it is addressed to them by man, was pointed out in the last lecture ; nor can I see that their condition is destitute of analogy with that of very young children, whose power of understanding language is developed sooner and more rapidly than their power of employing it ; who learn to apprehend a host of things before they learn to express them.   In respect to speech, it is very evident that the distance from the oyster, for instance, which no amount of training can bring to the slightest apprehension of anything you may wish to signify to it, to the intelligent and docile dog, is vastly greater than that which separates the dog from the undeveloped man, or from a man of one of the lower and more brutish races.

But once more, *why* do we speak ? what is the final cause of the gift of language to man ? in what way is the possession of such a power of advantage to us ?   These inquiries open a great and wide-reaching subject ; one far too great, indeed, for us to attempt dealing with it, in the contracted space at our command, otherwise than in the briefest and most superficial manner.   A detailed reply can be the more easily dispensed with, inasmuch as, on the one hand, the worth of speech is too present to the mind of every one to need to be called up otherwise than by a simple allusion ; and as, on the other hand, our previous discussions have brought more or less distinctly to view the chief points requiring notice.

The general answer, in which is summed up nearly the whole array of advantages derived from language, is this : that it enables men to be, as they are intended to be, social, and not merely gregarious beings. As it is the product, so it is also the means and instrument, of community. It converts the human race from a bare aggregate of individuals into a unity, having a joint life, a common development, to which each individual contributes his mite, receiving an untold treasure in return. It alone makes history possible. All that man possesses more than the brute is so intimately bound up with language that the two are hardly separable from one another; and, as we have already seen, are regarded by some erroneously, but naturally and excusably, as actually identical. Our endowments, so infinitely higher than the brute's, need also, as being so much freer and less instinctive, to be brought to our knowledge, to be drawn out and educated. The speechless man is a being of undeveloped capacities, having within him the seeds of everything great and good, but seeds which only language can fertilize and bring to fruit; he is potentially the lord of nature, the image of his Creator; but in present reality he is only a more cunning brute among brutes. There is hardly to be found in the whole animal creation any being more ignoble and shocking than those wild and savage solitary men, of whom history affords us now and then a specimen; but what we are above them has been gained through the instrumentality of language, and is the product of a slow progressive accumulation and transmission. If each human being had to begin for himself the career of education and improvement, all the energies of the race would be absorbed in taking, over and over again, the first simple steps. Language enables each generation to lay up securely, and to hand over to its successors, its own collected wisdom, its stores of experience, deduction, and invention, so that each starts from the point which its predecessor had reached, and every individual commences his career, heir to the gathered wealth of an immeasurable past.

So far, now, as this advantage comes to us from the handing down, through means of speech, of knowledge hoarded up by those who have lived before us, or from its communication by our contemporaries, we appreciate with a tolerable degree of justness its nature and value. We know full well that we

were born ignorant, and have by hearing and reading possessed ourselves in a few short years of more enlightenment
than we could have worked out for our own use in many
long centuries; we can trace, too, the history of various
branches of knowledge, and see how they have grown up
from scanty beginnings, by the consenting labour of innumerable minds, through a succession of generations. We are
aware that our culture, in the possession of which we are
more fortunate than all who have gone before us, is the
product of historical conditions working through hundreds,
even thousands, of years; that its germs began to be
developed in the far distant East, in ages so remote that
history and tradition alike fail to give us so much as glimpses
of their birth; that they were engendered among exceptionally endowed races, in especially favouring situations, and
were passed on from one people to another, elaborated and
increased by each, until, but a thousand years ago, our own
immediate ancestors, a horde of uncouth barbarians, were
ready to receive them in their turn—and that this whole
process of accumulation and transfer has been made possible
only by means of speech and its kindred and dependent art
of record. What we are far less mindful of is the extent to
which we derive a similar gain in the inheritance of language
itself, and that this very instrumentality is in like manner
the gradually gathered and perfected work of many generations—in part, of many races. We do not realize how much
of the observation and study of past ages is stored up in the
mere words which we learn so easily and use so lightly, and
what degree of training our minds receive, almost without
knowing it, by entering in this way also into the fruits of
the prolonged labour of others. To this point, then, we owe
a more special consideration.

Learning to speak is the first step in each child's education,
the necessary preparation for receiving higher instruction of
every kind. So was it also with the human race; the acquisition of speech constituted the first stage in the progressive
development of its capacities. We, as individuals, have forgotten both the labour that the task cost us and the enlightenment its successful accomplishment brought us: the whole

lies too far back in our lives to be reached by our memories ;
we feel as if we had always spoken, as directly and naturally
as we have thought.   As a race, too, we have done the same
thing : neither history nor tradition can penetrate to a period
at all approaching that of the formation of language ; it was
in the very childhood of our species, and men learned thinking and talking together, even as they learn them now-a-
days : not till they had acquired through language the art of
wielding the forces of thought, were they qualified to go on
to the storing up of various knowledge.   Into a few years of
instruction are now crowded, for the young student, the net
results of as many tens of centuries of toiling after wisdom
on the part of no small portion of mankind ; and, in like
manner, into the language-learning of the first few months
and years is crowded the fruit of as many ages of language-
making.   We saw in the last lecture that, if two human
beings were suffered to grow up together untaught, they
would inevitably frame some means of communication, to
which we could not deny the name of language : but we know
not how many generations would succeed one another before
it could reach a fulness comparable with that of even the
rudest existing human dialects.   Men invent language, their
mental instrument, as truly as they invent the mechanical
appliances whereby they extend and multiply the power of
their hands ; but it would be as impossible for a man, or a
generation, to invent a language like one of those which we
know and use, as, for example, to invent a locomotive engine.
The invention of the engine may be said to have begun when
the first men learned how to make a fire and keep it alive
with fuel ; another early step (and one to which many a
living race has not even yet ascended) was the contriving of a
wheel ; command was won, by degrees, of the other mechanical powers, at first in their simplest, then in their more complicated, forms and applications ; the metals were discovered,
and the means of reducing and working them one after
another devised, and improved and perfected by long accumulated experience ; various motive powers were noted and
reduced to the service of men ; to the list of such, it was at
length seen that steam might be added, and, after many vain

trials, this too was brought to subjection—and thus the work
was at length carried so far forward that the single step, or
the few steps, which remained to be taken, were within the
power of an individual mind. When one of us now undertakes to invent a language (as in fact happens from time to
time), it is as if one who had been all his life an engineer
should sit down to invent a steam-engine : he does nothing
but copy with trifling modifications a thing which he is
already familiar with ; he reärranges the parts a little, varies
their relative dimensions, uses new material for one and
another of them, and so on—perhaps making some improvements in matters of minor detail, but quite as probably turning out a machine that will not work. To call upon a man
who has never spoken to produce a complete language is like
setting a wild Fijian or Fuegian at constructing a power-loom
or a power-press : he neither knows what it is nor what it
will be good for. The conditions of the problem which is
set before the language-makers are manifest : man is placed
in the midst of creation, with powers which are capable of
unlocking half its secrets, but with no positive knowledge
either of them or of himself ; with apprehensions as confused,
with cognitions as synthetic, as are those of the lower
animals ; and he has to make his way as well as he can to a
distinct understanding of the world without and the world
within him. He accomplishes his task by means of a continuous process of analysis and combination, whereof every
result, as soon as it is found, is fixed by a term, and thus
made a permanent possession, capable of being farther
elaborated, and communicated by direct instruction. It is
necessary to study out what needs to be expressed, as well
as the means of its expression. Even the naming of concrete
objects, as we saw, demands an analysis and recognition of
their distinctive qualities ; and to find fitting designations
for the acts and relations of the external sensible world, and
then, by an acute perception of analogies and a cunning
transfer, to adapt those designations to the acts, states, and
relations of the intellectual and moral world within the soul,
was not an easy or rapid process ; yet, till this was measurably advanced, the mind had no instrument with which it

could perform any of the higher work of which it was capable. But as each generation transmitted to its successor what it had itself inherited from its predecessor, perfected and increased by the results of its own mental labour, the accumulation of language, accompanying the development of analytic thought and the acquisition of knowledge, went steadily and successfully forward ; until at last, when one has but acquired his own mother-tongue, a vocabulary of terms and an understanding of what they mean, he already comprehends himself and his surroundings ; he possesses the fitting instrument of mental action, and can go on intelligently to observe and deduce for himself.   Few of us have any adequate conception of the debt of gratitude we owe to our ancestors for shaping in our behalf the ideas which we now acquire along with the means of their expression, or of how great a part of our intellectual training consists in our simply learning how to speak.

One thing more we have to note in connection herewith. The style in which we shall do our thinking, the framework of our reasonings, the matters of our subjective apprehension, the distinctions and relations to which we shall direct our chief attention, are thus determined in the main for us, not by us.   In learning to speak with those about us, we learn also to think with them : their traditional habits of mind become ours.   In this guidance there is therefore something of constraint, although we are little apt to realize it.   Study of a foreign language brings it in some measure to our sense. He who begins to learn a tongue not his own is at first hardly aware of any incommensurability between its signs for ideas and those to which he has been accustomed.   But the more intimately he comes to know it, and the more natural and familiar its use becomes to him, so much the more clearly does he see that the dress it puts upon his thoughts modifies their aspect, the more impossible does it grow to him to translate its phrases with satisfactory accuracy into his native speech.   The individual is thus unable to enter into a community of language-users without some abridgment of his personal freedom—even though the penalty be wholly insignificant as compared with the accruing benefit.   Thus, too,

each generation feels always the leading hand, not only of
the generation that immediately instructed it, but of all who
have gone before, and taken a part in moulding the common
speech ; and, not least, of those distant communities, hidden
from our view in the darkness of the earliest ages, whose
action determined the grand structural features of each tongue
now spoken. Every race is, indeed, as a whole, the artificer
of its own speech, and herein is manifested the sum and general effect of its capacities in this special direction of action ;
but many a one has felt through all the later periods of its
history the constraining and laming force of a language un-
happily developed in the first stages of formation ; which it
might have made better, had the work been to do over again,
but which now weighs upon its powers with all the force of
disabling inbred habit. Both the intellectual and the historical career of a race is thus in no small degree affected by
its speech. Upon this great subject, however, of the influence reflected back from language upon the thought and
mind of those who learn and use it, we can here only touch ;
to treat it with any fulness would require deep and detailed
investigations, both linguistic and psychological, for which
our inquiries hitherto have only laid the necessary foundation.

The extent to which the different races of men have availed
themselves of language, to secure the advantages placed
within their reach by it, is, naturally and necessarily, as
various as are the endowments of the races. With some, it
has served only the low purposes of an existence raised by
its aid to a certain height above that of the brutes, and remaining stationary there. Their whole native capacity of
mental development seems to have exhausted itself in the
acquisition of an amount of language even less than is
learned by the young child of many another race, as the first
stage upon which his after-education shall be built up. Their
life is absorbed in satisfying the demands of the hour ; past and
future are nothing to them ; the world is merely a hunting-
ground, where means of gratifying physical desires, and of
lengthening out a miserable existence, may be sought and
found ; its wonders do not even awaken in their minds a
sense of a higher power ; the barest social intercourse, per-

petuation by instruction of the petty arts of living, and the scantiest adaptation to the changes of external circumstances, are all they ask of the divine gift of speech. Through such a condition as this we may suppose that all human language has passed; but while in parts of the world it still stays there, and gives no prospect of a higher development except through the influence and aid of races of better gifts and richer acquisitions, it shows elsewhere every degree of progression, up even to the satisfaction of the wants of an advanced and advancing culture like our own, where the knowledge of the past, aiding the understanding of the present and preparing for the future, is laid up in such abundant store, that he who studies longest and deepest, and with most appreciative and inquisitive industry, hardly does more than realize better than his fellows how little he can know of that which is known; how short is life, compared with the almost infinite extent of that series of truths, the infinite variety of that complication of cognitions, which life puts within our reach, and whose apprehension constitutes one of the highest and noblest pleasures of life.

Such full development as this, however, of the uses and advantages of speech would be impossible by the instrumentality of spoken speech alone; it demands a farther auxiliary, in the possession of written speech. The art of writing is so natural a counterpart and complement of the art of speaking, it so notably takes up and carries farther the work which language has undertaken on behalf of mankind, that some consideration of it is well-nigh forced upon us here : our view of the history and office of language would otherwise lack a part essential to its completeness. Speech and writing are equally necessary elements in human history, equally growing out of man's capacity and wants as a social and an indefinitely perfectible being. He would be, without language, hardly man at all, a creature little raised above the brutes ; without the art of record, his elevation would soon find its limits; he could never become the being he was meant to be, the possessor of enlightenment, the true lord of nature and discoverer of her secrets. Language makes each community, each race, a unit; writing tends to bind to-

gether all races and all ages, forcing the whole of mankind
to contribute to the education and endowment of every
individual. Moreover, there is in many respects so close a
parallelism and analogy between the histories of these two
sister arts, that, were it only for the value of the illustration,
we should be justified in turning aside for a time to follow
out the growth of letters.

As in the case of language, it may be remarked, so also in
that of writing, we hardly realize, until we begin to investigate the subject, that the art has had a history at all. It
seems to us hardly less " natural " to write our thoughts than
to speak them : such is the power of educated habit, that we
take both alike as things of course. But what we have above
shown to be true of spoken language is still more palpably
and demonstrably true of written; it was a slow and laborious
task for men to arrive at the idea and its realization : more
than one race has been engaged in the work of elaborating
for our use the simple and convenient means of record of
which we are the fortunate possessors ; many have been the
failures or only partial successes which have attended the
efforts of portions of mankind to provide themselves with such
means. As it is impossible to trace the history of our own
alphabet back to its very beginning, some review of those
efforts will be our best means of inferring what its earliest
stages of growth must have been, and will prepare us to
understand what it is, and what are its advantages. *

We have first to notice that the force which impels to the
invention of writing, which leads men to represent thought
by visible instead of audible signs, is the desire to communicate to a distance, to cut expression loose from its natural
limitation to the personal presence of him whose thought is
expressed, and make it apprehensible by persons far away.
Even the intention of record, of conveying the thought to a
distance in time also, making it apprehensible by generations
to come, shows itself only secondarily, as experience suggests

* In drawing up this sketch of the history of writing, I have to acknowledge my special obligations to Professor Steinthal's admirable essay on the
Development of Writing (*Die Entwickelung der Schrift*), published at Berlin,
in 1852 (8vo, pp. 113).

such use; and as for the advantage which the individual himself derives from recording his thought, so as to be able to
con it over, to apprehend it and its relations more distinctly,
as well as that other incalculable advantage which the
individual and the race derive from the transmission and accumulation of knowledge by this means—these are matters
which are still farther from the minds of the earliest inventors. Here is a first most notable analogy between the
histories of spoken and written speech: the satisfaction of a
simple social impulse, arising out of the ordinary needs
of intercourse between man and man, brings forth by degrees
an instrumentality of supreme importance to the progress of
the whole human race. The earliest writers, like the earliest
speakers, wrought far more wisely than they knew.

Again, the conveyance of thought by means of writing was
not primarily conceived of as a conveyance of the spoken language in which the thought would be expressed: it dealt
immediately with the conception itself, striving to place this
by direct means before the apprehension of the person addressed. Speech and writing were two independent ways of
arriving at the same end. We may add that, so long as it
remains in this stage, writing is a tedious and bungling
instrumentality; the great step towards its perfection is
taken when it accepts a subordinate part, as consort and
helpmate of speech.

A first feeble effort toward the realization of the fundamental object of writing is to be seen in the custom—not
infrequent at a certain period of culture, and even retained
in occasional use among peoples of every grade of civilization
—of sending along with a messenger some visible object,
symbolical of his errand, and helping both to authenticate
and to render it impressive. Thus, the prophet Jeremiah
(Jeremiah, ch. xix.) is directed to take an earthen bottle and
break it before the ancients of his people, to signify the sudden and irremediable destruction with which he is to threaten
them. Thus ambassadors and heralds in ancient times were
charged with the delivery of something typical of the peace
or war they were sent to proclaim. And the knight's glove,
thrown down in defiance and taken up by him who accepts

the challenge, and the staff still broken in Germany over the head of the condemned criminal, are instances of the same general style of instrumentality for expressing meaning. Objects, too, are used in a more arbitrary and conventional way, as reminders, helps to the recollection of that which is communicated orally. So the North American Indians, on solemn occasions, had his strips of wampum, corresponding to the heads of the discourse he had prepared; and handed them over, one after another, as each announcement was made or each argument finished, to the person addressed. We should hardly need to take any notice of a method of intimation so rude and indefinite as this, but for the development which we know it to have attained, as a practical means of communication and record, in the usage of one or two nations. It received its greatest elaboration in the system of the *quippos*, or knotted cords, employed in Peru at the time of its discovery and conquest. With these cords the state messengers were provided, and by their numbers, their colours, their groupings, their style of knotting, they were made conventionally significant of each one's message, even to partial independence of his own oral explanation. The accounts, and, to a certain extent, the annals also, of the empire of the Incas are claimed to have been intelligibly kept by means of the *quippos*. The Peruvians doubtless made out of this coarse instrumentality all that it was capable of becoming; but the essentially low grade of their capacity and culture is indicated by the fact that they had risen to the invention of nothing better. The Chinese, too, curiously enough, have preserved the tradition that their earliest ancestors wrote by means of knotted cords, until the mythical emperor Fo-hi devised the beginnings of the better system of which we shall have presently to speak.

A higher degree of ingenuity, and a greatly superior capacity of progression and development, are to be seen in the contrivance of a picture-writing. This, in its simplest form, is found all over the world, among peoples of a certain degree of civilization. Let us look at an example furnished by the aborigines of our own country.*

---

* It is one of those given by Steinthal, who extracts it from Schoolcraft's work on the Indian Tribes, vol. i. p. 352.

Two hunters have gone up the river on an expedition, and have killed a bear and taken many fish. They endeavour to commemorate their success, and make it known to whosoever shall pass that way after them, by a monument raised upon the spot. On a piece of wood they draw two boats, and over each the *totem*, or symbolic animal, indicating the family to which each hunter respectively belongs—his sur-name, as it were. The figures of a bear and of half-a-dozen fish tell the rest of the simple story. There is here no idea of a narrative, of an orderly setting forth of the successive incidents making up an act or occurrence : the whole com-plex is put before the eye at once, unanalyzed, in the form in which we might suppose it to lie in the mind of a brute— or, more properly, as it would lie in the mind of a man desti-tute of language, and lacking that education in progressive thought which the possession and use of language give ; it abnegates, in short, the advantages conferred by language, and is confusedly synthetic, like the conceptions of an un-taught human being. It offers but one element implying a possibility of something higher—namely, the *totems*, which are signs, not for things, but for the conventional and com-municable names of things : here is contained in embryo the idea of a written language representing speech, and such might be made to grow out of it, if the picture-writers had but the acuteness to perceive it, and the ingenuity to make the conversion.

The pictorial mode of writing is analogous with that primi-tive stage of language in which all signs are still onomato-poetic, immediately suggestive of the conceptions they desig-nate, and therefore, with due allowance for the habits and knowledge of those who use them, intelligible without in-struction. To the most prominent and important difference between the two allusion was made in the last lecture : in virtue of the character of the medium through which com-munication is made, the earliest written signs denote concrete objects, while the earliest spoken signs denote the acts and qualities of objects.

One of the American nations, the Mexican, had brought the art of picture-writing to a high state of perfection,

29 *

making it serve the needs of a far from despicable civilization.
The germ of a superior development which we saw in the
totem-figures of the Indian depiction was in their use made
to a certain extent fruitful.   Every Mexican name, whether
of place or person, was composed of significant words,
and could in most cases be signified hieroglyphically—
just as we, for instance, might signify ' Mr. *Arrowsmith*, of
Hull,' by an arrow and a human figure holding a hammer,
placed within or above the hull of a vessel.   So also, the
periods, of greater or less length, which made up their intricate and skilfully constructed calendar, all derived their appellations from natural objects, and were intimated in writing
by the figures of those objects.   Thus the Mexican annals
were full of names and dates composed of figures designating
the spoken signs of things ; and the idea of a hieroglyphic
method of writing, which should found itself on spoken language, following the progress of oral narration and attempting to signify this alone, lay apparently within their easy
reach ; and would, possibly, have been reached in due time,
had the Mexican culture been allowed to continue its career
of progress uninterfered with.   Authorities are somewhat at
variance, indeed, as to what was the real condition and character of the Mexican picture-writing at the 'time of the
Conquest, some holding that it had already become a representation of continuous spoken texts.   That there was a
quite extensive Mexican literature is certain ; but the ignorant fanaticism and superstition of the Spanish conquerors
almost swept it out of existence, destroying at the same
time the key to its comprehension, which has not yet been
fully recovered.

In Egypt, the same beginnings have grown into an institution of quite a different character.   The Egyptian hieroglyphs, in even the very earliest monuments preserved to us,
form a completely elaborated system, of intricate constitution and high development ; it undergoes hardly a perceptible
change during all the long period covered by the monumental
records : yet its transparency of structure is such that it
exhibits in no small degree, like the grammatical structure
of the Sanskrit language, its own history.   In its origin and

application, it is peculiarly a commemorative and monumental mode of writing, and it retains to the last strictly its pictorial form; every one of its separate signs is the representation of some visible object, however far it may be removed in use from being a designation of that object. It is in this respect like a language which has never forgotten the derivation of its words, or corrupted their etymological form, however much it may have altered their meaning. On the Egyptian monuments are found, accompanied and described by the hieroglyphics, many and various pictorial scenes—such as kings besieging cities or leading trains of captives, individuals making offerings to divinities, souls undergoing judgment and retribution, and other the like—all of which are cast in conventional form, and often contain symbolic elements : their intent is much more didactic than artistic ; they are meant to inform rather than to illustrate : these, then, are with evident plausibility assumed still to represent the earliest, purely pictorial, stage of Egyptian writing, corresponding with that illustrated above by an example furnished by our own aborigines ; while the hieroglyphs grew out of the attempt—also finding its analogue in the *totem*-figures of that example, and still more fully in the Mexican delineations—to designate and explain the persons and actions depicted. The ways in which this end was attained, and figured signs made indicative of names and abstract ideas, were various : homonymy and symbolism were both fertile of characters : thus, the name of the god Osiris, *Hesiri*, was written by the two figures of a kind of seat (?), *hes*, and an eye, *iri;* the figure of a basket, *neb*, signified also *neb*, 'a lord:' a hand pouring libations from a vase meant 'offer in sacrifice;' an extended hand bearing some object meant *ti*, 'give;' the wallowing hippopotamus denoted 'filth, indecency;' and so on.   But the Egyptians showed in this part of the development of their system a much higher aptitude than the Mexicans for analytic representation, for paralleling, and then identifying, the process of writing with that of speaking.   In the first place, they came to be able to write symbolically such a sentence as "Young! old! God hates indecency," by the five figures of a child, an old man, a hawk,

a fish, a hippopotamus, placed one after the other, while the
Mexican would have given a synthetic symbolic representation of the action by a picture of the Great Spirit chastising
an evil-doer, or in some other like way. But, in the second
place, the Egyptian system had taken the yet more important
step—one which, if followed up, would have brought it to
the condition of a real alphabet—of indicating simple sounds,
phonetic elements, by a part of its figures. That such a step
lies not far off from the homonymic designation of a thing by
something which called to the mind the sounds of which its
name was composed, is evident enough ; still, no little insight
and tact was needed in order to bridge over and cross the
interval, and we do not apprehend so fully as we could desire
the details of the movement. It appears, however, that the
figure of an object was first made to designate some other
conception whose name agreed with its own in the consonantal elements, to the exclusion of the more variable vowels ;
and then, by a farther abstraction, instead of designating
thus a part of the phonetic elements of its own name, it
came to signify the initial element only, whether consonant
or vowel. For example, the figure of a lion, *labo*, is used to
represent *l*; that of an eagle, *ahom*, to represent *a*. Proper
names are written almost exclusively in this style of characters, and the decipherment of the names *Ptolemy* and
Cleopatra on the inscription of the famous Rosetta stone, as
set down distinctly in pure phonetic signs, was the first step
in our recovery of the key to the hieroglyphs. In ordinary
texts, the phonetic, homonymic, and symbolical characters
are intricately mingled, variously aiding, explaining, and sup-
plementing one another's meaning. Thus, the signs for
Osiris (*Hesiri*), already given, are always accompanied by
the figure of a peculiar hammer or hatchet, which some unknown reason has made one of the standard symbols of
divinity ; the verb *ti*, 'give,' having been once written phonetically, has the symbolic outstretched arm with gift added
by way of farther explanation ; and so on.

In monumental, and to some extent also in literary use,
the hieroglyphs maintained, as already remarked, their pictorial form unaltered, as long as the kingdom and civilization

of Egypt had an existence: reverence for ancient custom, as well as their peculiar adaptedness to the purposes of architectural decoration, to which they were so largely applied, preserved them from corrupting change. But how easily, under the exigencies of familiar practical use, a true alphabet might have grown out of this cumbrous, long-winded, and intricate mode of writing, is shown in the history of its two derivative forms, the hieratic, and the demotic or enchorial. The former, the hieratic, is simply an abbreviated and cursive style of hieroglyphic, in which each figure is represented by a part of its outline, or otherwise so altered as to be hardly recognizable. It was the common written character of the priests and sacred scribes, from a very early period. The demotic was a still later adaptation of the same, and has lost all relics of a pictorial character, being composed of a limited, though large and unwieldy, number of arbitrary signs, chiefly phonetic. What farther improvement and reduction toward a true alphabetic form the demotic might in time have undergone, we cannot tell. For Greek influence and Christianity came in to interrupt the regular course of development; the Christian Coptic literature, casting aside the native modes of writing, adopted a new alphabet, founded upon the Greek.

The history of writing in China, although its final products are in appearance so different from the Egyptian hieroglyphs, goes back to a very similar origin. The Chinese themselves, with that love for historical research and record and the explanation of subsisting ihstitutions which has always distinguished them, have set down for our benefit all the steps of the process by which their immense and unique system of signs has been elaborated out of its scanty beginnings; and both product and process present more numerous and striking analogies with spoken language and its growth than are to be found anywhere else in the whole history of written characters. We have already noticed the Chinese tradition that their earliest ancestors used knotted cords as a means of communication and record. Their first written signs were no development out of these, but a substitution for them. They were, like the Egyptian hieroglyphs, simple pictures of

the objects represented : such are, in fact, the beginnings of
every system of written signs for thought, not less necessarily
than onomatopoetic utterances, designating acts and qualities,
are the beginnings of every system of spoken signs. Thus,
the sun was denoted by a circle with a point within, the
moon by a crescent, a mountain by a triple peak, a tree and
a man by rude figures representing their forms, and so on.
Signs were provided thus for a considerable number of
natural objects ; those, namely, which are most familiarly
noted and most easily depicted. But such cannot supply
otherwise than in small part the needs of a written language,
any more than onomatopoetic signs those of a spoken language. Their store was notably increased by the compounding of two or more simple signs ; as the vocabulary of
a language by the composition of spoken elements. For
example, the signs for 'mountain' and 'man,' put together,
signified 'hermit;' those for 'eye' and 'water' signified
'tear;' those for 'woman,' 'hand,' and 'broom,' meant
'housekeeper.' A simple symbolism often came in to aid,
both in the case of single and of compound signs. A banner
pointing one way signified 'left;' the other way, 'right;'
an ear between two doors gave the meaning of 'listen;'
'sun' and 'moon,' taken together, indicated 'light;' 'mouth'
and 'bird' made up 'song,' and so on. This is equivalent
to the transfer of meaning of a word, effected through a
simple association. But the most abundant means of multiplication of the resources of Chinese expression was found in
the introduction of a phonetic principle, and the combination
of phonetic and ideographic elements into a compound sign.
The language, as we saw in the ninth lecture, is full of
homonyms, words identical in phonetic form but of different
meaning : a sign being found for a word in one of its many
senses, either by direct representation or by symbolism, the
device was very naturally suggested of making the same sign
answer for some of its other meanings also, by the aid of an
appended diacritical sign. It was quite as if we, for instance,
had learned to signify *sound* in " safe and *sound* " symbolically by a circle (as being peculiarly the complete, unbroken
figure), and had then suffered it to represent the same

phonetic compound in its other senses, distinguishing each
by some suggestive mark: thus, adding an ear on either side
might make it signify '*sound*, audible noise;' a sign for
'water' written within it would intimate the meaning of
'*sound*, an arm of the sea;' a depending line and plummet,
that of '*sound*, to try the depth of anything.' For example,
there is in China a certain simple sign having the pronunciation *pe*, and meaning 'white' (what the object represented
is, and in virtue of what property it was chosen to signify
this conception, is now no longer known); then, with the
sign for 'tree' prefixed, it means '*pe*, a kind of cypress;'
with the sign for 'man,' it means '*pe*, elder brother;' with
the sign for 'manes,' it means '*pe*, the vital principle in its
existence after death;' and so forth. Some signs are thus
very extensively used to form compound characters, in connection with various others that bear a phonetic value in the
compound; two of those already instanced are among the
most common of them: the sign for 'man' enters into nearly
six hundred combinations, all denoting something that has a
special relation to man; that for 'tree' enters into more
than nine hundred, which denote kinds of trees, wood and
things made of wood, and such like matters. Their analogy
with the formative elements of spoken language is very
evident; they are signs which limit the general value of the
phonetic radical, putting it in a certain class or category of
meanings.

The Chinese mode of writing, unlike the Egyptian, has
been ready to forget and lose sight of its hieroglyphic origin,
to convert its characters, when once the needed association
was formed between them and their significance, into signs
wholly conventional, bearing no traceable resemblance to the
objects they originally depicted, and made liable to any
modifications which practical convenience, or a sense for
symmetry, or mere fancy, should suggest and recommend.
In this, again, it offers a manifest analogy with what we have
repeatedly shown to be the legitimate and laudable tendency
of spoken language. The characters have passed through a
variety of transitional forms on their way to that in which
they are at present ordinarily written, and which was itself

established more than a thousand years since : some of these
intermediate forms are still preserved in monuments and
ancient documents, and to a certain extent even now employed for special uses—as the older phases of many a spoken
tongue are kept to the knowledge of posterity by like
means ; and as a Frenchman, for example, of the present day
may clothe his thoughts, upon occasion, in an Old French or
a Latin dress. Their current shape has been determined
mainly by the customary instruments of writing and the
manner of their use—these have exercised all the modifying
and adapting force which in a spoken tongue belongs to a
powerful euphonic tendency, like that which has made all
Italian words end in vowels, and has worn off from French
vocables the syllables which followed after the accented one
in their Latin originals. And so thoroughly has their hieroglyphic origin been covered up and concealed by these transformations that no one, from their present aspect, would
venture even to conjecture that they had started from outlines of natural objects ; nor would the older preserved
documents suffice to prove this ; the truth lay only within
reach of the Chinese themselves, as having access to traditional information from yet more ancient times. We have
no right to be surprised, then, if the onomatopoetic beginnings of speech, dating from a period compared with which
the origin of Chinese writing is but as yesterday, are no
longer to be distinctly traced in the worn and altered facts
of such language as is now accessible to our researches.

Another set of causes has powerfully influenced the development of the Chinese written expression : namely, the
poverty of the spoken tongue, and the felt need of giving it
an aid and support from without. The system of signs combines a phonetic and ideographic nature in a manner
peculiarly its own. It is rather an auxiliary language, than
a reduction of speech to writing. It supplies the defects
and removes the ambiguities of the language it represents ;
it might be learned and used without any regard paid to its
phonetic equivalents ; and if the Chinese were but willing to
forego converse by the tongue and ear, substituting for them
the hand and eye, it would answer the purposes of their

communication vastly better, with its forty thousand signs for ideas, than the spoken means now chiefly employed, with its scant thousand or two. While the uttered vocabulary of the Chinese is one of the poorest in the world, their written one is eminently rich and abundant. This farther analogy with spoken languages it has, that, as was in the first lecture (p. 18) shown to be true of the latter, only a part of its resources are required for the ordinary uses of life: not more than eight or ten thousand of its characters are otherwise than very rare, and all common needs are supplied by from three to five thousand.

One more important mode of writing is said to be distinctly traceable to a hieroglyphic origin: namely, the cuneiform, the character of the monuments of Mesopotamia and the neighbouring countries. Its signs are made up of various combinations of wedge-shaped elements: hence the name "cuneiform" (from Latin *cuneiformis*, 'wedge-shaped'); they are also sometimes called "arrow-headed characters," from the same peculiarity. There are several different cuneiform alphabets, the older of them being exceedingly intricate and difficult, made up of phonetic, ideographic, and symbolic signs, variously intermingled; and sometimes farther complicated, it is said, with combinations which were phonetic in the language for which they were originated, and have been transferred to the use of another with their old meaning, but a different spoken value (somewhat, as has been pointed out, as we write *viz.*, an abbreviation of Latin *videlicet*, and read it "namely"). Much that regards the history and relations of the different systems of cuneiform characters is, and may always remain, obscure: but it is confidently claimed that evidences are found which prove their beginnings to have been pictorial; and the peculiar form of their component elements is fully recognized as a consequence of the way in which they were originally written—namely, by pressure of the corner of a square-ended instrument upon tablets of soft clay; these being afterwards dried or burned, to make the record permanent. That, through such intermediate steps even as these, a hieroglyphic system may finally pass over into one truly alphabetic, is shown by the derivation from the Mesopotamian cuneiform of the Persian, which is by far the simplest and the best understood of all the systems of its class, being purely phonetic and almost purely alphabetic. It contains about thirty-five signs of simple sounds, some of those for the consonants being partially of a syllabic character—that is to say, being different according as the consonant was to be followed by one or another vowel. In this simpler cuneiform are written the Achæmenidan inscriptions, of which we have already more than once had occasion to take notice, as preserving to us an Indo-European dialect. The history of its formation is unknown.

I have called the Achæmenidan cuneiform a partially syllabic mode of writing; and syllabic systems have played so important and prominent a part in the general history of writing—in the main, traceable as derivatives from methods of a different character—that it is necessary for us to pay them here a little special attention. A pure syllabic alphabet is one whose letters represent syllables, instead of articulations; which makes an imperfect phonetic analysis of words, not into the simple sounds that compose them, but into their syllabic elements; which does not separate the vowel from its attendant consonant or consonants, but denotes both together by an indivisible sign. Such an analysis is more natural and easy to make than one which distinguishes all the phonetic elements—especially in the case of languages of a simple structure, which do not favour difficult consonantal combinations, and therefore make up but a limited number of syllables. Many times, accordingly, when some race has made acquaintance with the art of writing as practised by another, and, instructed and incited by the latter's example, has set about representing its own spoken tongue by written signs, it has fallen first upon the syllabic method. One of the most noted alphabets of this kind is the Japanese *kata-kana*, or *irofa* (so called from the names of its first signs, like *alphabet*, from *alpha, beta*), to which we have already once had occasion to allude (in the ninth lecture): it was made out of fragments of Chinese characters, and contained forty-seven different signs, one for each of the syl-

lables of which the Japanese words were made up : for the
spoken alphabet of the language then included only ten
consonants and five vowels, and no syllable contained more
than one vowel, with a single preceding consonant. A
similar alphabet was devised for the Cherokee language, not
many years ago, by an ingenious member of the tribe, George
Guess, who, though he had never learned to read English, had
seen and possessed English books, and knew in general what
was their use : it contained eighty-five signs, mostly fashioned
out of English letters, though with total disregard of their
original value.

Another and a less pure form of syllabic alphabet is that
which treats the consonant alone as the substantial part of
the syllable, and looks upon the vowel as something of subordinate consequence—as it were, a colouring or affection of
the consonant. In its view, then, only the consonant has a
right to be written, or to be written in full ; the accompanying vowel, if taken note of at all, must be indicated by some
less conspicuous sign, attached to the consonant. Peculiar
and arbitrary as this mode of conceiving of the syllable may
seem to us, it is historically of the highest importance ; for
upon it was founded the construction of the ancient Semitic
alphabet, which has been the parent of the methods of writing
used by the great majority of enlightened nations, since the
beginning of history. It is not difficult to see how the character of Semitic language should have prompted, or at least
favoured, such an estimate of the comparative value of vowel
and consonant. In Semitic roots and words (as was explained
in the eighth lecture), the consonants are the principally significant, the substantial, element ; the vowels bear a subordinate office, that of indicating, as formative elements, the
modifications and relations of the radical idea ; the former are
stable and invariable, the latter liable to constant change.
Perhaps we should not be going too far, if we were to say that
only a language so constructed could have originally suggested
such an alphabet. Be this as it may, the ancient Semitic
alphabet—of which the Phenician is the generally accepted
type, being, whether original or not, its oldest traceable form
—was a system of twenty-two signs, all of them possessing

consonantal value : three, however—namely, the signs for the
semi-vowels *y* and *w*, and for what we may call the "smooth
breathing"—partaking somewhat of a vowel character, and
being under certain circumstances convertible into representatives of the vowels, *i*, *u*, and *a*.

The Phenician alphabet was thus strictly and exclusively
a phonetic system, though one of a peculiar and defective
type. We cannot possibly regard it, therefore, as an immediate and original invention; it must have passed, in the
hands either of the Semites themselves or of some other people,
through the usual preliminary stages of a pictorial or hieroglyphic mode of writing. More probably, its elements were
borrowed from one or another of the nations, of yet earlier civilization, by whom we know the Semitic races to have been surrounded, before they entered on their own historic career. The
traditional names of its characters are the recognizable appellations of natural objects, and each name has for its initial letter
that sound which is designated by the character: thus, the sign
for *b* is called *beth*, 'house;' that for *g*, *gimel*, 'camel;' that
for *d*, *daleth*, 'door;' in some cases, moreover, a degree of resemblance is traceable between the form of the letter and the
figure of the object whose name it bears. This, so far as it
goes, would evidently point toward that application of the
hieroglyphic principle which, as we saw above (p. 454), made
the figures of the lion and eagle represent in Egyptian use
the letters *l* and *a*. The subject of the ultimate history of
the Phenician alphabet, however, is too obscure and too much
controverted for us to enter here into its discussion; investigations of it have reached hitherto no satisfactory results.

The diffusion which this alphabet and its derivatives have
attained is truly wonderful. From it come, directly or in-
directly, the three principal Semitic alphabets, the Hebrew,
the Syriac, and the Arabic, the last of which has gained
currency over no inconsiderable part of the Old World, being
employed by nations of diverse race, Indo-European (Persian,
Afghan, and Hindustani), Scythian (Turkish), and Polynesian
(Malay) ; while the Syriac has spread, through the Uigur
Turkish, Mongol, and Manchu, to the farthest north-eastern
Asia. The eastern Iranian and the Indian alphabets have

been traced, though more doubtfully, to the same source; and
India, especially, has been a home where it has developed into
new and richer forms, and whence it has been extended over
a vast region, in Asia and the islands lying southward from
Asia—reaching at last, in its remote derivatives, conditions as
unlike to the original and to one another as are the late
dialects of a widely disseminated family of languages. In
nearly all these countries, through all its various metamorphoses, it has held fast, in the main, to its primitive character
of a consonantal alphabet, with omission, or with partial or
subordinated designation, of the vowels. But in its progress
in the other direction, toward Europe, it fell first into the
hands of the Greeks; and from them it received its final perfection, by the provision of signs enabling it to represent the
vowels not less distinctly than the consonants. In the Greek
alphabet, for the first time in all our review of the history of
written speech, we find realized what we cannot but regard as
the true ideal of a mode of writing—namely, that it be simply
a faithful representation of spoken speech, furnishing a visible
sign for every audible sound that the voice utters, not attempting to distinguish any class of sounds as of more importance
than another, nor to set itself up as an independent instrumentality for the conveyance of thought by overpassing the
limits of utterance, and assuming to give more or other than
the voice gives in speaking.

From the Greek alphabet have been derived, by modifications and adaptations of greater or less consequence, several
others, used by peoples of each of the grand divisions of the
eastern continent—as the Coptic of later Egypt, already
referred to, and the Armenian; the runes of some of the
Germanic tribes also, and the early Celtic modes of writing,
trace their origin back to it, mainly through the Latin; as
does the modern Russian, the most ungainly and unsymmetri-
cal, perhaps, of all its descendants. But the Latin alphabet
itself is beyond all comparison the most important of its
derivative forms. The Greek colonies of southern Italy were
the means of bringing Greek letters to the knowledge of the
inhabitants of the peninsula, and several of the Italian nations
—the Etruscans, Umbrians, and Oscans, as well as the Latins

—provided themselves with alphabets derived from the Greek. All these excepting the last have passed away, along with the nationalities and languages to which they belonged; but the Latin alphabet has become the common property of nearly all the enlightened nations of modern times whose civilization is derived from that of Greece and Rome; while, under European influence, its use has also extended and is extending among the races of inferior endowments and culture, even crowding out, to some extent, their indigenous and less convenient modes of writing.

Our examination of the history of writing might here properly enough be closed; yet the particular interest which we take in our own alphabet will justify us in delaying a little, to note the principal steps of the process by which it has been derived from the Phenician—so far, at least, as it is possible to do this without graphic illustration. We shall also thus see more clearly how a borrowed system is wont to be modified and expanded, in passing from the service of one language into that of another. There is never a precise accordance between the phonetic systems, the spoken alphabets, of any two languages, so that a written alphabet which suits the one can be immediately applied to the other's uses; and hence the history of every scheme of characters which has won a wide currency, among various nations, presents a succession of adaptations, more or less wisely and skilfully made.

The chief change wrought upon the Phenician alphabet by the Greeks consisted, as has been already pointed out, in the provision of signs for the vowels. The Semitic tongues, as compared with the Greek, were characterized by an excess of guttural and sibilant sounds : the superfluous signs representing these, then, were put to divers new uses in Greece; our **A, E,** and **O** were to the Phenicians designations of certain guttural breathings, having the value of consonants; the semivowel *y* being wanting in Greek, its sign was greatly altered and simplified to form our **I**; the sign for *w* was retained by the early Greeks as the *digamma* (though abandoned later); for *u*, they invented a wholly new character, **V** or **Y** (which are by origin only varying graphic forms of the same letter).

The other Greek alterations and additions may be passed over, as of less account.

The Latin alphabet was taken from one of the older forms of the Greek, before the characters of the latter had assumed in all points the form and value with which we are most familiar—when the H, for example, had still its value as a breathing, and had not been converted into a long *ē*. The system of spoken sounds for which the Latin required written representatives was but a simple one : to the fifteen articulations which, as we saw in the seventh lecture (p. 265), had been the primitive possession of the Indo-European family, it had added but three, the medial vowels *e* and *o*, and the labial spirant *f* (it had, indeed, the semivowels *y* and *w* also, but did not distinguish them in writing from the vowels *i* and *u*, with which they are so nearly identical : I and J, U and V, are but graphic variations of the same sign). Nearly all the Latin letters are the same with the Greek, or differ from them only by slight diversities of form : but one or two points of discordance need a word of explanation. The Latin system is most peculiar in rejecting the K, which was found in every Greek alphabet, of whatever period or locality, and in writing both its *k* and *g* sounds at first by a single letter, C, the ancient sign for the *g*-sound only : then, when it came to itself, and felt again the need of a separate designation for each, it knew no better than to retain the C for the *k*-sound, and to add a diacritical mark at its lower end, making a G, for the purpose of denoting the corresponding sonant, *g*. By a somewhat similar process of transfer, we have come to write the *p*-sound by the sign, P, which formerly belonged to the *r* : when the older sign for *p*, Γ, had assumed a shape so nearly agreeing with the P that the two were not readily distinguished from one another, a tag was hung upon the crook of the latter as a further diacritical mark, and it was thus made into R. For the *f*-sound, the ancient sign for *w*, the Greek *digamma*, F, was somewhat arbitrarily adopted, its only special recommendation being that both *w* and *f* were labials. The Q represents an old Phenician letter, a deeper guttural than *k*, rejected by the later Greek alphabets as superfluous—and really no better than superfluous in the Latin, where the pronunciation of the *k*-sound before *u* did not differ enough from its pronunciation before *a* and *o* to call for an independent notation. Of the remaining three Latin letters, the **X** is a Greek invention (used in some Greek alphabets also with its Latin value, or representing *xi*, instead of *chi*), and, as standing for the double sound *ks*, not less needless than **Q**; **Y** and **Z** are later importations out of the Greek alphabet, and used only in Greek words, to signify peculiar Greek sounds (the Greek *upsilon* having by this time changed its value of *u* for that of the French *u*, German *ü*).

The changes which we, in our turn, have introduced into the Latin alphabet, in adapting it to our purposes, are not insignificant, although far from being enough to make it represent our spoken language as fully and consistently as it formerly did that of the Romans. Besides the eighteen articulations of the early Romans, we have (as was shown above, in the third lecture) at least fourteen others which call more or less imperatively for separate designation. There are the *a* of *cat* and *care*, the *a* of *what* and *all*, and the *u* of *cut* and *curl;* there are the two semi-vowel sounds, *y* and *w*, the palatal nasal (which we commonly write with *ng*, as in *singing*), the three sibilants, *z*, *sh*, and *zh* (the *z* of *azure*), the two sounds of *th*, in *thin* and *thine*, and the *v* of *valve;* and, finally, the compound consonants *ch* (in *church*) and *j* (in *judge*). Some of these needs we have managed to provide for: we have turned the two forms of the Latin *i*, **I** and **J**, into two separate letters, with very different values; we have done the same thing with the two forms of *u*, **V** and **U**, converting the former into a sign for the sonant labial spirant; by doubling the same character, we have made one wholly new letter, *w*, for the labial semi-vowel; and we have utilized *y* and *z*, as semi-vowel and sonant sibilant. We have also brought *k* back into its old place—yet without perceptible gain, since its introduction makes *c* superfluous; *k*, *c*, and *s* having but two sounds to designate among them. The new characters which the Anglo-Saxons had devised for expressing the two *th*-sounds we have unfortunately suffered to go out of use again. And *q* and *x* are still as useless to us as they were of old to the Romans. Hence, we have virtually only twenty-three letters wherewith to write at least thirty-two sounds. In the process of phonetic change, whose tendency is always toward the increase of the spoken alphabet, the filling up of the system of articulated sounds by the distinction of slighter and more nicely differentiated shades of articulation, our spoken alphabet has very notably outgrown the limits of our written alphabet.

To this cause are to be attributed, in part, the anomalies of our orthography. But only in the lesser part. If an alphabet is hardly able to enlarge itself to the dimensions of a growing body of sounds, it is because men do not easily learn to write their words otherwise than as they have been accustomed to do, even when they have learned to pronounce them otherwise —and the same cause operates in other ways yet more effectually to bring about a discordance between the spoken and the written language. It has been the misfortune of the English to pass, during its written period, through the most important crisis in its history, its mixture with the Norman French, also a written tongue: not only were the discordant orthographic usages of the two thus forced together within the limits of the same language, but a period of both orthoëpic and orthographic confusion was introduced—and the orthographic confusion has been, in great measure, only stereotyped, not remedied, by the usage of later times.

We of the present age have thus been in a measure deprived, not by our own fault, of the advantages belonging to a phonetic mode of writing—advantages which seemed to have been secured to us by the joint labours of so many races and so many generations. And yet, we are not altogether without fault in the matter, for we are consenting unto the deeds of our fathers and predecessors. As a community, we are not content with accepting as inevitable our orthographical inheritance, and resolving to make the best of it, despite its defects; we even defend it as being better than any other; we strive to persuade ourselves that an etymological or a historical mode of spelling, as we phrase it, is inherently preferable to a phonetic. Now it is altogether natural and praiseworthy that we should be strongly attached to a time-honoured institution, in the possession of which we have grown up,

and which we have learned to look upon as a part of the subsisting fabric of our speech; it is natural that we should love
even its abuses, and should feel the present inconvenience to
ourselves of abandoning it much more keenly than any pro-
spective advantage which may result to us or our successors
from such action; that we should therefore look with jealousy
upon any one who attempts to change it, questioning narrowly his right to set himself up as its reformer, and the
merits of the reforms he proposes. But this natural and
laudable feeling becomes a mere blind prejudice, and justly
open to ridicule, when it puts on airs, proclaims itself the de-
fender of a great principle, regards inherited modes of spelling
as sacred, and frowns upon the phonetist as one who would
fain mar the essential beauty and value of the language. Of
all the forms of linguistic conservatism, or purism, orthographic
purism is the lowest and the easiest; for it deals with the
mere external shell or dress of language, and many a one can
make stout fight in behalf of the right spelling of a word
whose opinion as to its pronunciation even, and yet more its
meaning and nice application, would possess no authority or
value whatever: hence it is also the commonest, the least
reasonable, and the most bigoted. When it claims to be as-
serting a principle, it is only defending by casuistry a prejudice; it determines beforehand to spell in the prevailing mode,
and then casts about to see what reasons besides the mode it
can find for doing so, in each particular case. It overwhelms
with misapplied etymologic learning him who presumes to
write *honor* and *favor* for *honour* and *favour* (as if it were
highly desirable to retain some reminiscence of the French
forms, *honneur* and *faveur*, through which we have derived
them from the Latin *honor* and *favor*), and then insists just as
strongly upon *neighbour* (which is neither French nor Latin);
it is not more concerned to preserve the *l* of *calm* (Latin
calmus) than that of *could* (Anglo-Saxon *cudhe*: the *l* has
blundered in, from fancied analogy with *would* and *should*),
the *g* of *sovereign* (Old-English *soveraine*, French *souverain*,
Italian *sovrano*) than that of *reign* (Latin *regnum*), the *s* of
island (Anglo-Saxon *ealand*) than that of *isle* (Old-French
isle, Latin *insula*); it upholds such anomalies as *women*, which

offends equally against the phonetic and the etymological principle (it comes from Anglo-Saxon *wif-men*). How much better were it to confess candidly that we cling to our modes of spelling, and are determined to perpetuate them, simply because they are ours, and we are used to and love them, with all their absurdities, rather than try to make them out inherently desirable! Even if the irregularities of English orthography were of historical origin throughout—as, in fact, they are so only in part—it is not the business of writing to teach or suggest etymologies. We have already noted it as one of the distinguishing excellencies of the Indo-European languages, that they are so ready to forget the derivation of a term in favour of the convenience of its practical use: he, then, is ready to abnegate a hereditary advantage of his mode of speech, who, for the sake of occasional gratification to a few curious heads, would rivet for ever upon the millions of writers and readers of English the burden of such an orthography. The real etymologist, the historic student of language, is wholly independent of any such paltry assistance, and would rejoice above measure to barter every " historical " item in our spelling during the last three hundred years for a strict phonetic picture of the language as spoken at that distance in the past. Nor do we gain a straw's weight of advantage in the occasional distinction to the eye of words which are of different signification, though pronounced alike: our language is not so Chinese in its character as to require aid of this sort; our writing needs not to guard against ambiguities which are never felt in our spoken speech; we should no more miss the graphic distinction of *meet*, *meat*, and *mete*, of *right*, *write*, and *rite*, than we do now that of the two *cleave's* and *page's*, the three or four *found's* and *sound's*, or the other groups of homonyms of the same class.

It may well be the case that a thorough reform of English orthography will be found for ever impracticable; it certainly will be so, while the public temper remains what it now is. But let us at any rate acknowledge the truth, that a reformation is greatly to be desired, and perhaps, at some time in the future, a way will be found to bring it about. If we expect and wish that our tongue become one day a world-language, understood and employed on every continent and in every clime, then it is our bounden duty to help prepare the way for taking off its neck this heavy millstone. How heavy, we are hardly able to realize, having ourselves well-nigh or quite forgotten the toil it once cost us to learn to read and speak correctly; yet we cannot help seeing how serious an obstacle to the wide extension of a language is a mode of writing which converts it, from one of the easiest in the world, into one of the hardest, for a foreigner to acquire and use.

The English is already, perhaps, spoken and written as mother-tongue by a greater number of persons than any other existing dialect of high cultivation; and its sphere seems to be widening, at home and abroad, more rapidly than that of any other. If it ever becomes a world-language, it will do so, of course, not on account of its superiority as a form of human speech—since no one ever yet abandoned his own vernacular and adopted another because the latter was a better language—but by the effect of social and political conditions, which shall widen the boundaries of the English-speaking community. Yet we cannot but be desirous to convince ourselves that it is worthy of so high a destiny. To trust our own prepossessions upon this point may be very easy and comfortable, but is not quite safe. The universal tendency among men to exaggerate the advantages of their own mode of speech and depreciate those of others would make us, in spite of our sincere attempts at impartiality, more than just to our beloved mother-tongue—even though we might be willing to allow that, as all advantages cannot be found united in one individual, each of its rivals among the cultivated dialects of the present or of the past may surpass it in one or another respect. It does not lie in our way to take up the matter seriously, inquiring and determining what is the absolute rank of the English among languages; yet it may be worth while to give a few moments' consideration to one or two points that bear upon the question.

We have, in the first place, already had occasion to notice that a language *is* just what the people to whom it belongs have made it by their use; it is the reflection of their minds, and of their minds' contents; its words and phrases are instinct with all the depth, the nobility, the subtilty, and the beauty that belongs to their thought; it can be made to express at least as much, and as well, as it has been made to express. A literature, then, is one grand test of the worth of a language—and it is one by which we need not fear to see tried that of our own. It is not national prejudice that makes us claim for English literature, in respect to variety and excellence, a rank second to none. We can show, in every or nearly every department, men who have made our English tongue say what no other tongue has exceeded.

This is not, however, the only test. We cannot but ask also how our language is fitted to admit and facilitate that indefinite progress and extension of thought and knowledge to which we look forward as the promise of the future. Has it all the capacity of development which could be desired for it? In their bearing upon this inquiry, two of its striking peculiarities—the two most conspicuous, in the view of the historical student of language—call for special notice: namely, its uninflective or formless character, and its composition out of two somewhat heterogeneous elements, Germanic and Romanic.

Both these peculiarities have been made the subject of repeated reference in our discussions hitherto. For its poverty in formative elements, for its tendency to monosyllabism, for its inclusion of many parts of speech in the same unvaried word, we have compared English more than once with Chinese. But we must beware of misapprehending the scope and reach of the comparison. There is a curious and suggestive analogy between the present geographical position of the English and Chinese races and the present character of their languages. Since our occupation of the whole breadth of the American continent, the speakers of these two tongues look over to one another as nearest neighbours across the intervening Pacific. But the situation of the Chinese people is the result of simple quiescence in their primeval abode; while the English, setting forth probably from the depths of the same Orient, have reached the seats

they now occupy, in the sequel of an adventurous and conquering career which has led them around nearly the whole
earth, and leaves them masters of many of its fairest portions,
under the most varied skies. The virtual distance between
the two is therefore almost world-wide; it is to be measured
by the course which the English race has traversed, rather
than by the distance which still separates its outposts from
China. So the English language, starting in that monosyllabism which the Chinese has never quitted, has made the
whole round of possible development, till its most advanced
portions have almost come back again to their original state;
but it still holds in possession much of the territory over
which it has passed, and is dowered with all the wealth
which it has gathered on its way; it has passed through all
stages and varieties of enrichment, and has kept fast hold of
their most valuable products. It is therefore in its essential
character as far removed from the Chinese as is the Greek.
Its resources for the expression of relations, for the sufficient
distinction of the categories of thought, are hardly inferior
to those of the tongues of highest inflective character: they
are of another kind, it is true, but one which, if it has its
disadvantages, has its advantages as well. Our analytic
flection has a practical value equivalent to that even of the
rich synthesis of the classical tongues; and in this respect
also we need confess to no disabling inferiority, as compared
with the speakers of other cultivated languages.

That, again, the English is a mixed tongue, may not be
denied. There has not been that assimilation of its two
elements which is the natural result of a complete fusion.
The length of our words of Latin origin, as compared with the
Saxon, is a plain external indication of this: take anywhere
a page of English, and you will find that its Saxon words
average less than half as long as those of other derivation.
What would have been the natural tendency of the language
with respect to these long forms is shown by its treatment
of words borrowed earlier from the classical tongues: thus,
it has worked down *moneta* into *mint*, *küriake* into *church*,
presbüteros into *priest*, *eleēmosünē* into *alms*, and so on. Only
the specially conservative forces of learned culture and the

habit of writing have saved many others of our sesquiped-
alian Latin elements from a like fate. We have, then, in a
certain sense, two languages combined: one of root-words,
prevailingly monosyllabic; the other of long derived forms,
whose roots and derivation are in the main unrecognizable
by the mass of speakers: and the latter must often lack something of that freshness and direct force which belong to the
former. But, on the one hand, we have seen above (toward
the end of the third lecture) that the etymological connections of a word are, after all, of very subordinate consequence
in determining its degree of significant force and suggestiveness; and, on the other hand, there has been, to no small extent, a real amalgamation of our two vocabularies, the Germanic and Romanic: among the words, mainly Saxon, which
answer the commonest and simplest uses of communication,
there are not a few also of Latin origin; and some Latin
suffixes are familiarly added to Saxon themes, as well as the
contrary. Our Latin words thus range from the extreme of
homeliness and familiarity to the extreme of learned stateli-
ness, and furnish the means of attaining a great diversity of
styles. At the same time, the partial Romanization of our
language throughout its whole structure renders it possible
for us to naturalize more thoroughly, and use more adroitly,
the words which, in common with all other tongues of enlightened nations at the present day, we are obliged to import
in great numbers for the designation of objects and relations of learned knowledge. Richness of synonymy, variety
of style, and power of assimilation of new learned material,
are, then, our compensation for whatever of weakness may
cling to our language by reason of the discordance of its
constituent elements.

Our general conclusion must be that, if the English is not
entitled to all the exaggerated encomiums which are sometimes heaped upon it, if it has no right to be set at the
head of all languages, living or extinct, it is at least worthy
of all our love and admiration, and will not be found un-
equal to anything which the future shall require of it—even
should circumstances make it the leading tongue of civilized
humanity. For what it is to become, every individual who em-

ploys it shares in the responsibility. The character of a language is not determined by the rules of grammarians and lexicographers, but by the usage of the community, by the voice and opinion of speakers and hearers; and this works most naturally and effectively when it works most unconsciously. Clear and manly thought, and direct and unaffected expression, every writer and speaker can aim at; and, by so doing, can perform his part in the perfecting of his mother-tongue.

With these few words respecting our own language, which must be the subject of highest interest with every student of language to whom it is native, I bring to a close our consideration of the subject of these lectures, thanking you for your kind and patient attention to my exposition of it, and hoping that what I have said may not be without effect in helping you to clear apprehensions of the nature and history of one of man's noblest gifts and most valuable acquisitions.

THE END.

JOHN CHILDS AND SON, PRINTERS.

INDEX.

A, the letter, derivation of, 464.
a, flattening of, in *dance*, etc., 43.
a or *an*, article, 115.
-able, 40-41.
abstract, 112.
Abyssinia, Semitic languages of, 297, 299.
Abyssinian group of Hamitic languages, 341, 343.
Accent, makes unity of word, 56; how produced, 89; its various place in different languages, 95-6.
Accidental correspondences between words unrelated, 185, 243-4, 387-91.
Achæmenidan monuments, 222; character in which they are written, 460.
Acquisition of language, how made, 11-20; acquisition of mental training and knowledge involved in it, 442-5.
Adelung, referred to, 4.
Adjectives, in Indo-European language, 275; English nouns directly convertible into, 282.
Adverbs in Indo-European language, 275-6.
Æolic dialect of ancient Greek, 221.
Afghan or Pushto language, 192, 224.
Africa, languages of, 297, 299, 340-46.
again, 115.
Agglutinative structure of Scythian languages, 316-20; of Dravidian, 327.
Agglutinative tongues, their characteristics, classification, and relations, 360-65.
Ainos, language of, 329.
alas, 277.
Albanian language, descendant of ancient Illyrian, 191, 290-91, 355.
Alemannic dialect of Old High-German, 163, 211.
Alforas of Australia, language of, 340.
Algonquin group of American languages, 350.
ally, 29.
alms, 29, 102, 387.
alphabet, 460.

Alphabet, spoken, structure and relations of, 91; primitive alphabet of Indo-European language, 265; its development, 266; limited alphabets of Polynesian languages, 338.
Alphabet, written, germs of in Egypt, 454-5; derivation of alphabetic cuneiform, 460; syllabic alphabets, 460-61; Semitic alphabet and its derivatives, 461-3; Greek and its derivatives, 463; Latin, 464-6; English, 466-7.
also, 111, 114.
Altaic family of languages — see Scythian.
am, 62-3, 115, 135, 267.
America, the English language in, 151, 171-4.
America, aboriginal languages of, 346-53; their variety and changeableness, 346-7; probable unity, 348; polysynthetic structure, 348; principal groups in North America, 350 -51; question of their relation to Asiatic languages, 350, 351; absurd theories respecting this, 352; importance to us of their study, 352.
American aborigines, examples of picture-writing by, 450-52.
Amharic language, of Abyssinia, 297, 299.
an or *a*, article, 115.
-ana, 140.
Analogies, extension of prevailing, its influence in producing the changes of language, 27-8, 82, 85.
Analogies between linguistic and certain physical sciences, 46-7, 52.
Analysis, etymological, of words, 55 seq.; is the retracing of a previous historical synthesis, 65-7, 251-4; indispensable in comparison of languages, 246.
Analytical tendency in modern languages, 120, 279; its ground, 280-86.
and, 115.

31   (475)

Andaman islands, people and language of, 339.
Anglo-Saxon language, ancestor of English, 24; its relations to the other Germanic languages, 210.
Animals lower than man, mental action of, 414–17, 439; how near some of them approach to capacity of language, 415, 440; reason of their incapacity, 438–40.
Annamese language, 336.
Antiquity of human race, 205, 382–3.
apprehend, 112, 133.
Arabic alphabet, origin and diffusion of, 462.
Arabic language, 294, 296–7, 301 seq., 306; its literature, 299–300; its spread, 299, 300, 346, 375.
Aramaic branch of Semitic languages, 297, 298.
Arbitrariness and conventionality of words, as signs for ideas, 14, 32, 71, 102, 438.
Armenian language, 192, 224; character in which it is written, 463.
Armorican language of Brittany, 190, 218.
Arrow-headed characters — see Cuneiform.
Articles, origin of, 115, 276.
Articulate sounds, how produced, 70, 87–91; their systematic arrangement and relations, 91; transitions, 92–8; office as means of expression, 421–3; have no inherent natural significance, 430–31; cannot represent exactly inarticulate sounds, 431–2.
Artificial languages, 50–51, 444; artificial terminology, 122.
Aryan branch of Indo-European language, 192, 201.
Aryan, name for Indo-European, 192.
as, 111, 114.
Asia, languages of, 192, 222–7, 294–337, 354–5.
Aspirates, or aspirated mutes, 93, 265 note.
Assimilation of consonants, 93–4.
Assimilation of dialects, 160–61, 181.
Association, mental, the only tie between words and their meanings, 14, 71, 128, 409–10.
Assyrian people and language, 295, 297.
Athapaskan group of American languages, 350.
attend, 178.
Attenuation of the meaning of words and elements of words, 114–20.
Attic dialect of ancient Greek, 221.

Augment in Indo-European verbs, 267, 292.
Australia, language of, 339–40.
Austrian dialect of Old High-German, 211; Austrian dialectic elements in modern German, 163.
Auxiliary and relational words, their production, 117–20.
Avesta, Zoroastrian scripture, 222.
Aztecs, language of, 351.

Baber, the emperor, memoirs of, 313.
Bantu family — see South-African.
Bashkir, Turkish language, 310.
Basque language, in Spain, 191, 353–4, 363.
Bavarian dialect of Old High-German, 163, 211.
be, 115.
bear, 242.
become, 108.
befall, 113.
Beginnings, of Indo-European language, 250 seq.; of language in general, 423–6.
Bengali language, 224.
Beowulf, Anglo-Saxon poem, 210.
Berber languages, 341, 343.
better, 331.
bishop, 244, 387.
blame, 262.
blast, 262.
Bleek, Dr. W. H. J., referred to, 344 note.
board, 107.
boatswain, 72.
body, 115.
Bohemian language, 191, 214.
Bopp, Professor Franz, referred to, 5, 200, 245 note.
Bornu, language of, 346.
Borrowing of foreign words, its range and amount, 185, 197–8; into English vocabulary, 143–7.
bow-wow, 425.
Bow-wow theory of origin of language, 426 seq.
Brahui language, 327.
breakfast, 56.
Breton language, 190, 218.
brother, 196.
Brown, Rev. N., referred to, 337 note.
Bulgarian language, 191, 214.
Buriats, language of, 312.
Burmese language, 336, 359.
Burnouf, M. Eugène, referred to, 5
Bushmen, language of, 341, 345.
butterfly, 71.

C, the letter, derivation of, 465.
Cæsar, 105–6.
calculate, 130.
Caldwell, Rev. R., referred to, 327 note.
calm, 468.
Cambodian language, 336.
can, 111.
Canaanitic branch of Semitic languages, 297.
Canarese language, 326.
candid, 127, 133.
candidate, 126, 127, 131, 133.
Carthage, language of, 295, 298.
Cases, their number, origin, and office in Indo-European language, 271–5; their loss in English, 77; in other languages, 274; replacement, 280–81; cases in Semitic language, 304; in Scythian, 319.
Castrén, Professor Alexander, referred to, 310, 315.
Caucasian languages, 354–5.
Celtic languages, obliterated by Latin in southern Europe, 166, 216–17; by Germanic language in England, 169; their classification, age, literatures, etc., 190, 215–18; their position in Indo-European family, 204.
Celtomania, 216.
Central America, language and culture of, 347, 351.
Chaldee language, 297, 298.
Champollion, referred to, 341.
Chances, doctrine of, as applied to linguistic resemblances, 390.
Change, linguistic, its kinds, necessity, and universality, 24–33; forces producing it, 35–46, 48–9; considerations determining it in special cases, 41; phonetic or external change, 42–3; constructive, 55–65, 70, 73–4; destructive, 74–98; internal change, of meaning, 100–135, 141–2; relations of external and internal change, 101; varying rate and kind of change, 137–53; processes of change are what, 154; linguistic change causes the growth of dialects, 154–5, 159; generally of slow and gradual progress, 44, 123, 183, 277–8; exceptional cases of rapid change, 137, 291, 347.
charity, 102.
Cheremiss language, 309.
Cherokee language, 350; word-phrase of, 349; alphabet of native invention, 461.
Chinese language, its age, 233–4, 332; monosyllabic character, 257, 330–31, 359; history, literature, etc., 332–6;

merit, 336, 367; supplemented by its written characters, 458; compared with English, 331, 471–2.
Chinese writing, preceded by use of knotted cords, 450, 455; history of, 455–9; relation to the spoken language, 458.
Choctaw language, 350.
Chuana family — see South-African.
Chukchi language, 329.
church, 472.
Church-Slavic language, 214.
Circassian language, 354.
Civilization, degree of, of Indo-European mother-tribe, 207–8.
Classification of languages, by genetic relationship, how effected, 185–6, 290; review of families thus established, 292–357; its uncertainties, 323, 357–8; its preëminent value, 369–70; classification by structural correspondence, 358–67; by positive value, 367–9.
Classification of conceptions, learned along with language, 12.
cleave, 387.
Clicks in South African languages, 345.
Clothing, analogy between language and, 401–3.
Cochin-China, language of, 336.
cock, 429.
cockade, 429.
Comanche language, 351.
Combination of independent elements into words, 55–67; our words universally so made up, 65–7, 251–5; combination promotes, and is aided by, phonetic change, 70, 73–4; accompanied by change of meaning, 116; now of limited range in English, 143, 147–8, 282.
comfort, 133.
Communication, its possibility makes the unity of a language, 22, 157; it keeps language uniform, 155–61, 183; impulse to it, the immediate producer of spoken language, 403–5; of writing, 448–9.
Community, makes and changes language, 45, 123, 148, 404; preserves unity of a language, 155; how and within what limits it works, 156–8, 161; effects of external conditions upon, 159.
Comparative method in modern study of language, 3, 240–48; how to be applied, 241–6; not a mere comparison of words, 246–7; its universal reach, 248.

Comparative philology, 3, 241.
Composition of words — see Combination.
concrete, 112.
Confucius, representative man of China, 333.
Conjugation, forms of, in Indo-European language, 266–9 ; in its later dialects, 269–70; their loss by phonetic corruption in English, 75–7, 86–7 ; conjugational forms in Semitic language, 303 ; in Scythian, 319–20.
Conjugations, irregular and regular, in English, 79–82.
Conjugations, of Semitic verb, 304; of Scythian, 319; of South-African, 345.
Conjunctions, in Indo-European language, 276.
Consciousness, different degrees of, in the processes of language-making, 40–41, 50, 121–4.
Consciousness, different subjection of mental action to, in man and lower animals, 440.
Conservative forces in linguistic tradition, 31, 43–4, 148–51, 159.
Consonants and vowels, relation of, 89, 91.
Constraining influence of acquisition of language on mental action, 445–6.
Conventionality of words, as signs of ideas, 14, 32, 71, 128, 148, 409–10, 438.
copper, 130.
Coptic language, 340–41; writing, 455.
coquette, 429.
Corean language, 329.
Cornish language, 216, 218.
could, 468.
count, 261.
court, etc., 108.
cover, 388.
Craik, Rev. G. L., referred to, 211 note.
Creek language, 350.
Crow, its power of numeration, 415–17.
Cultivated or learned dialects, 149–51, 182–4.
Cultivation of a language, its meaning and effect, 182–4.
Culture and education, conservative influence of, on language, 17, 149–51, 158–9.
Culture, only possible by means of language, 441; won in the acquisition of language, 441–5.
Cuneiform characters, origin of, 459–60; monuments, in these characters, of Persia, 222; of Assyria, 295; Persian

language of, 222; Semitic, 306; asserted Ugrian, 314–15.
Curtius, Professor George, referred to, 200.
Cymric group of Celtic languages, 190, 217.
Cyril, Slavic Bible-version of, 214.
czar, 106.

-d, ending of English preterits, origin of, 60, 81–2, 117, 235.
daguerreotype, 39.
dahlia, 146.
Dakota language, 350.
Danish language, 212.
Darfur, language of, 346.
daughter, 196.
Dead languages, 149–50.
Deaf-mutes, language of, 410–11, 413, 422; thought of, 414.
dealt, 79.
dear me !, 277.
Decimal system of numeration, on what founded, 419.
Declension, forms of, in Indo-European language, 270–74; in its later dialects, 274–5; their loss by phonetic corruption, 77–9. — See also Cases.
Dekhan, languages of, 224, 326.
Delaware or Algonquin group of American languages, 350.
Demotic, later Egyptian, alphabet, 455.
Dialects, their prevalence, 153–4; their explanation, 154–62 ; causes which bring about dialectic diversity, 154–5; which restrain it, 155–6, 159; which reduce it, 160–61; illustrations of dialectic divergence and convergence, 162–74; dialects of English, 170–71; in America, 171–4; dialectic growth everywhere inevitable, 174, 181–2; dialect °and language convertible terms, 175; erroneous views respecting dialects, 177–84; dialectic differences always imply original unity, 178–81.
did, 268; forms ending of English preterits, 60–61, 81–2, 235; auxiliary, 117.
Ding-dong theory of origin of language, 427.
discuss, 112.
Divine origin of language, in what sense to be accepted, 399–403.
doff, 116, 262.
don, 116, 262.
Doric dialect of ancient Greek, 221.
double, 62.
Dravidian languages of southern India, 198, 326–7.

Dual number, in verbs, 267; in nouns, 273; its loss, 274.
Dutch language, 164, 211.

E, the letter, derivation of, 464.
Eddas, Old Norse collections, 212.
Education gained in the acquisition of language, 13, 15–16, 441–5.
Education, conservative influence of, upon language, 17, 149–51, 158–9.
Egypt, languages of, 150, 234, 340–43.
Egyptian modes of writing, 452–4.
Ehkili language, 299.
either or *either*, 43, 95.
electricity, 129.
English language, how acquired by its speakers, 10–22 ; its differences in individuals, 16–22; what, in general, it is, 22; how kept in existence, 23; its constant change, 24; causes and modes of this change, 25–31, 140–48; examples of the changes which have brought it into its present state, 55–65, 70–87, 92–5, 97, 102–34; its derivation and history, 24, 31, 99, 147, 169–70; its periods, 210; mixture of Germanic and other elements in it, 84, 144, 170, 185, 198, 373, 472–3; its fundamental structure chiefly Germanic, 170, 198; position and relations as a Germanic language, 187–9, 210–13 ; as an Indo-European language, 189–200; its analytical character, 279, 232, 284; prevailing monosyllabism, 264–5, 279 ; comparison with Chinese, 331, 471–2; its dialects, 170–71; transfer to America, 171–2; British and American forms of, 172–4 ; prospects as a world-language, 470; merits, 470–74.
English orthography, anomalies of, 94, 467–9; reform desirable, 469–70.
English spoken alphabet, structure and relations of, 91.
English written alphabet, derivation and character of, 466–7.
Erse, or Scotch Gaelic, language, 190.
Eskimo language, 330, 350, 351.
Esthonia, Scythian languages in, 309.
Ethiopian or Abyssinian group of Hamitic languages, 341, 343.
Ethiopic or Geëz, a Semitic, language, 297, 299.
Ethnology, bearing of linguistic science on, 8, 370–94.
Etruscan language, 354.
Etymology, the foundation of linguistic science, 54–5, 238; its uncertainties,

dangers, and ill-repute, 239, 386–94; modern improvements of, 240, 244, 386–7; is not the whole science, 247; false etymologies, 388–90.
Etymology of a word the explanation of its origin, not the ground of its use, 14, 128–9, 132–4.
Euguvine tablets, Umbrian monuments, 220.
Euphony, seat of, in the mouth, not the ear, 90.
Europe, languages of, 186–91, 209–21, 309–10, 353–5.
Expression, dependent upon an external inducement, not an internal impulse, 403–5, 420–21; always incomplete, 20, 109–11, 406–7; variety of expression for same idea in different languages, 407–9; the voice as means of, 421–3.
eye, 101.

F, the letter, derivation of, 465.
Families of languages, how established, 290–92.
Family languages, so called, 363.
Farrar, Rev. F. W., referred to, vi. note.
Farther India, languages of, 336–7.
father, 179.
Fellatah language, 346.
Finnish language, 191, 309, 320, 361; its literature, 314.
Finno-Hungarian branch of Scythian language — see Ugrian.
Firdusi, Persian poet, 223, 325.
five, 196.
Flemish language, 211.
Florida group of American languages, 350.
for, 114.
forehead, 56.
forget, 113.
forgive, 113.
Formative elements, 63–7 ; derived from words originally independent, 66, 251–5; their production gradual and unreflective, 124; aided by phonetic corruption, 73–4; accompanying change of meaning, 117; extensibility of their application, 83–4 ; their distinction as primary and secondary, 255.
fortnight, 56.
frail, 111.
Frankish dialect of Old High-German, 163, 211.
Freedom of mental action restricted by acquisition of language, 445–6.
French language, 164–5, 189, 218–19;

Germanic and Celtic elements in, 168, 169, 374.
Fricative sounds, in alphabet, 91.
Frisian language, 211.
-*ful*, suffix, 57, 73.
Fulah language, 346.
Fusion of dialects into one, 161; causes determining character of result, 168–9.
Future in Romanic languages, 118; in Anglo-Saxon and English, 119 ; in Indo-European language, 268.

G, the letter, derivation of, 465.
Gabelentz, H. C. von der, referred to, 339 note.
Gadhelic group of Celtic languages, 190, 217.
Gaelic languages, 190, 217.
Galla language, 341.
Gallatin, Albert, referred to, 349 note.
galvanism, 39, 129.
Gaulish languages of France etc., 216–17.
Geëz or Ethiopic language, 297, 299.
Gender, grammatical, in Indo-European languages, 77–8, 273–4; lost in English, 78 ; in other languages, 275; gender in Semitic languages, 303; nouns, 304; in Hamitic languages, 342; gender wanting in Scythian languages, 319; in other families, 342–3.
Genetic relationship of languages, 186, 290; their classification by it — see Classification.
Genius of individuals, its effect on language, 123.
genteel, *gentile*, *gentle*, 111.
Geology, general analogy between and linguistic science, 47 ; analogies in special points, 62, 184, 253, 265, 382.
Georgian language, 354–5.
German language, history of, 162–4.
Germanic languages, 187–9; their classification, age, literatures, etc., 210–13 ; permutation of consonants in, 97–8; verbal conjugation of, 80–82, 269–70.
Germanic race, its part in history, 231.
Gesture as means of expression, 422–3, 431.
get, 108.
Gonds, language of, 327.
Gothic language, 213.
-*graph*, 140.
Greece, founder of Indo-European pre-eminence, 230–31.
Greek language, 190, 220–22.
green, 125.
Greenland, language of, 350.

Grimm, Professor Jacob, referred to, 4, 5; his law of permutation of consonants in Germanic languages, 97–8.
Grout, Rev. L., referred to, 344 note.
grow, 115.
Guess, George, inventor of Cherokee alphabet, 461.
Gypsy language, 225.

H, the letter, derivation of, 465.
Habit, the ground of ability in language, 117, 147–8, 282.
Hadley, Professor James, referred to, 84 note, 211 note.
Hamitic family of languages, 341–3.
hand, 115.
Harmonic sequence of vowels in Scythian languages, 318, 362.
have, 117–18, 199.
head, 107, 115.
Hebrew language, 294, 296, 297, 306, 308; its alphabet, 462.
Heldensagen, Middle High-German, 212.
Heliand, Old Saxon poem, 211.
help, 30, 81, 82.
Heyse, Professor K. W. L., referred to, 427.
Hieratic, later Egyptian, writing, 455.
Hieroglyphic writing, 450–59; of Egypt, 452–5; of China, 455–6; hieroglyphic origin of cuneiform writing, 459.
High-German languages, 163–4, 188, 210, 211–12.
hill, 14.
Himalayas, languages of, 337.
Himyaritic language, 297, 299.
Hindi language, 224.
Hindustani language, 224.
Historical spelling in English, 94, 467.
Hodgson, Mr. B. H., referred to, 337 note.
home, 133.
Homer, poems of, 221.
Homonyms in English, 334–5, 387 : in Chinese, 334; how distinguished in Chinese writing, 456–7.
horse, 195.
Hottentots, language of, 341; clicks in it, 345.
Human race, its antiquity, 205, 382–3; its unity not determinable by language, 383–94.
Humboldt, Wilhelm von, referred to, 5, 367.
Hungarian language, 191, 309, 320, 361; its literature, 314; traces of polysynthesis in, 349.
Huzvaresh or Pehlevi language, 223.

I, the letter, derivation of, 464, 465.
I (pronoun), 101.
Icelandic language, 203, 212.
Ideas antecedent to their names, 125, 412.
Illyrian language, 191.
Imitation of natural signs, efficient principle in the origin of language, 426–31; not servilely precise, 431–2.
important, 112.
Inaccuracies of speech, their causes and their part in the history of language, 27–31, 36–7.
inapplicabilities, 64.
Incorporative or polysynthetic structure, 348–9, 354, 363.
India, languages of, 224–9, 326–7; occupation of its northern part by Indo-European peoples, 201, 326.
Indian, 130.
Individuals, all changes of language ultimately their work, 35–46, 123–4, 125, 148, 154–5, 404; their diversity causes divergence of dialects, 154–5; differences of their speech within the same community, 16–22, 156–8, 181.
Indo-European family of languages, other names for, 192; how composed, 186–92, 210–29; genetic relationship of its constituents, 193, 197, 378; evidences of their common descent, 193–200; interconnections of its branches, 203–4; place and time of its original speakers unknown, 200–205; their civilization, 205–8; importance of the family to linguistic science, 3, 229–37; age and variety of its dialects, 233–6; earliest history of development, 250–87; historical beginnings, 250–66; roots, pronominal and verbal, 258–63; primitive spoken alphabet, 265; growth of forms and parts of speech, 266–77; rate and continuousness of growth, 277–8; synthetic and analytic development, 279–86; characteristic structure of Indo-European language, 292–4, 361–3; question of its ultimate connection with Semitic language, 307, 361, 394; its limits probably mainly coincident with those of a race, 377–9.
Indo-Germanic family — see Indo-European.
Inflectional languages, 358.
Inflective character of Indo-European language, 293, 361; wherein it consists, 293–4, 366 note; Semitic language inflective, 300, 361; value of inflective principle, 362.

Instinct and reason, 439.
intellect, 112.
Intellectual terms derived from physical, 111–13.
Interjectional theory of origin of language, 426–7, 429–30.
Interjections, 276–7.
Internal change in language, 100–121.
Invention of language by men, what is meant by, 443–4.
Ionic dialect of ancient Greek, 221.
Iranian branch of Indo-European language, 192, 222–4.
Irish language, 190, 217, 218.
Iroquois group of American languages, 350.
Irregularities in English declension and conjugation, 78–81.
irrevocability, 254.
is, 63, 115, 179.
island, 468.
isle, 468.
-ism, 140.
Isolating languages — see Monosyllabic.
Italian language, 165, 168, 189, 219.
Italic group of Indo-European languages, 220.
its, 30.

J, the letter, derivation of, 465, 466.
Jagataic Turkish language, 313.
Japanese language, 328–9; modes of writing, 329, 460–61.
Japhetic family — see Indo-European.

K, the letter, derivation of, 465.
Kafir group of South-African languages, 345.
Kalevala, Finnish poem, 314.
Kalmucks, language of, 312.
Kamchatkan language, 329.
Karen language, 336.
Khalkas, language of, 312.
Khitan, Tungusic dynasty, 312.
Khonds, language of, 327.
Kin, Tungusic dynasty, 312.
kind, 108.
kine, 44.
Kirghiz language, 310.
knight, 42.
Kols, language of, 327.
Koran, Mohammedan scripture, 299.
Koriak language, 329.
Kotars, language of, 327.
Kroatian language, 214.
Kurdish language, 192, 224.
Kurilian language, 328, 329.
Kwanto, of Farther India, 336.

kye, 44.

Labial series of articulate sounds, 91.
laird, 388.
Language, in what aspect the subject
of linguistic science, 6, 10, 54; interest of inquiries into, 7–8; how acquired by those who speak, 11–22;
what a language is, 22; how kept in
existence, 23; dead languages, 149–
50; constant change or growth of
language, 24–33 ; by what instrumentality produced, 35–46, 125, 154;
processes of growth, 55–135 ; rate
and kind of growth, and causes affecting it, 137–53; dialects, 153–85;
the various forms of human language and their genetic classification, 185–229, 294–357; other modes
of classification, 357–70; relation of
language to race, 14–15, 370–83; its
evidence incapable of determining
the question of human unity, 383–94;
language an institution, the work of
its speakers, 48, 401–3, 442–5; its
conventional character, 32, 409–10;
it is a social product and possession,
404; part taken by individuals and
by the community, respectively, in its
production, 45, 148, 154–6, 171; language not identical with thought, nor
indispensable to it, but its instrument
and aid, 405–21; its imperfection as
means of expression, 20, 109–11,
406–7 ; its value to man, 440–47;
education involved in its acquisition,
13, 15–16, 441–3; its constraining influence on mental action, 445–6; its
work supplemented by writing, 447–
9; origin of language, in what sense
divine, 399–403; desire of communication its direct impulse, 403–5; its
beginnings of what kind, 421–6; how
produced, 426–34 ; example of development of a language from such
beginnings, 250–87; language a human possession only, 399, 414–17,
438–40.
Language, science or study of — see
Linguistic science.
Langue d'oc, 164, 218.
Lapps, language of, 191, 309.
Latin language, its age, literature, etc.,
219–20; its relations in Italy, 165,
220; history of its extension in southern Europe, 165–9; causes of this,
375, 378, 382; its artificially prolonged existence, 150; its modern
descendants, 167, 218–19; its spoken

alphabet, 465; its written alphabet,
463–4, 465–6.
Latin words, introduction of, into English, 143–6; Latinized style of English, 146.
learn, 262.
led, 80.
Lena, branch of Turkish language upon, 310–11.
Lepsius, Professor R., referred to, 92
note, 341 note, 344 note.
Lesghian language, 355.
-less, 58.
Lettish language, 191, 215.
Libyan languages, 341, 343.
lie, 75–6.
Life of a language, what is meant by,
32, 35; its analogy with that of an
organized being, or of a race of such,
46 ; the processes constituting —
see Change, linguistic.
like, in *such* and *which*, 57, 70; in *-ly*,
58–60, 70, 73; the verb, 108, 113.
likewise, 114.
Lingual series of articulate sounds, 19.
Linguistic change or growth — see
Change, linguistic.
Linguistic evidence of race, its nature
and limitations, 371–9.
Linguistic scholars, differences of temperament among, 324.
Linguistic science, of recent development, 1; its preparatory stages, 1–3;
its progress, 3–6; its material, 6, 50,
230; its objects and their interest,
6–8; what it seeks in language, 10, 54,
237; analogies between it and certain
physical sciences, 46–48, 52; it is a
historical science, 48–52 ; its truly
scientific character, 53; its method,
52, 54–5, 237–48; its dependence on
Indo-European comparative philology, 4, 233–7.
Literary culture, its influence on the
history of language, 23, 37, 43–5,
148–51, 159–60, 182–4.
Literary languages, 149–50, 174; their
usual origin, 164.
Lithuanian group of languages, 191,
215.
Little-Russian language, 214.
Livonia, Scythian languages of, 309.
Livonian language, 191, 215.
Local dialects, acquired in learning to
talk, 16–17.
Loo-Choo islands, language of, 329.
lord, 388.
lore, 262.

Loss of words from the vocabulary of a language, 27, 98–100.
Louis, St., of France, as language-maker, 38.
love, 260.
Low-German languages, 188, 210–11.
luna etc., 103, 104.
lunatic, 105, 130, 131.
Luther's influence on history of German language, 163.
-ly, 58–60, 63, 83, 124, 235.
Lyell, Sir Charles, referred to, 47 note.

magnet, 130.
Magyar — see Hungarian.
Mahratta language, 224.
Malayalam or Malabar language, 326.
Malay language, 338.
Malay-Polynesian family of languages, 337–9.
Man, Isle of, its language, 190.
Man, sole possessor of language, 399, 438 ; difference of his mental capacity and action from that of the lower animals, 414–16, 438–40; the artificer of his own speech, 48, 401–3, 442–5; value of speech to him, 440–47.
Manchu language, 312, 313, 320; its written character, 313, 462.
Mandingo language, 346.
manumit, 130.
manure, 111.
Marsh, Mr. G. P., referred to, 211 note.
me, 196, 430.
mean, 263.
Melanesian family of languages, 339.
men, 79.
Mental action of men and animals, comparison of, 414–17, 438–40.
Mesopotamia, Semitic languages of, 295.
Mexico, language and culture of, 347, 349, 351; writing of, 451–2.
Middle High-German period and literature, 212.
Migration, effect of, on language, 202.
Minnesingers, 212.
mint, 130.
minute, 111.
Mishna, Rabbinic Hebrew work, 297.
Mithridates, work of Adelung etc., 4.
Mitsjeghian language, 355.
Mixture of language, 197–9; of elements in English language, 84, 143–4, 170, 185, 472–3.
Mixture of races, 374; its effect upon language, 160–61, 168, 374–6.

Mnemonic objects, as forerunners of writing, 450.
Modern Greek language, 221.
Mœso-Gothic language, 60, 199, 213, 235.
Mohammed, arouser of the Arab race, 296.
money, 130, 131, 247–8.
Mongolian family — see Scythian.
Mongolian branch of Scythian languages, 311–12, 313, 320; its written character, 313, 462.
Monosyllabic family of languages, 330–37; monosyllabic class, 358–65.
Monosyllabism, primitive, of Indo-European language, 255–66, 279–86; secondary monosyllabism of English etc., 264, 279; compared with Chinese, 331, 472.
month, 104.
Moods of Indo-European verb, 268; of Semitic, 303.
moon, 103–5.
Moral terms derived from physical, 111–13.
Moravian language, 214.
Mordwinian language, 309.
Morphological correspondence as sign of genetic relationship, 291, 332, 357–8 ; systems of morphological classification, 358–67.
mother, 196.
mountain, 14.
Müller, Professor Max, quoted or referred to, vii., 4 note, 35, 51 note, 177 note, 180, 317, 360, 363, 427.
Mutes, class of articulations, 91; aspirated, 265 note.
Mutes, language of — see Deaf-mutes.

Nabatean literature, 298.
Names-giving, processes of, 25–6, 38–42, 103–31, 411–12, 424–6; different degrees of reflectiveness in, 121–4, are historical, and founded in convenience only, 127, 129; comparative ease of naming different classes of conceptions, 194–5.
Namollo language, 329.
Nasal articulations, 91.
National character as expressed in speech, 152.
Negative prefix, 292.
Negritos, language of, 339.
Nestorian people and language, 298.
Netherlands, language of, 211.
Newfoundland, 71–2.
New Guinea and neighboring islands, language of, 339.

New High-German period of German, 212.
Nibelungen-lied, old German epic, 212.
Nomadic languages, so called, 363.
Normans, adoption of French language by, 169; their introduction of it into England, 169, 189.
Norwegian language, 212.
Nouns, substantive and adjective, their development from roots, 270–75 ; question whether nouns or verbs are original, 423–6.
Numbers, in conjugation, 267; in declension, 273; in Semitic languages, 303, 304; in Polynesian languages, 339.
Numerals as proofs of Indo-European unity, 194; examples, 196.
Numeration in Indo-European and other languages, 419; reason of its usual decimal basis, 419.

O, the letter, derivation of, 464.
Obsolete and obsolescent words, 98–9.
of, 111, 114, 120.
off, 111, 114.
Old Bactrian language, 222.
Old High-German period of German, 211.
Old Norse language — see Icelandic.
Old Prussian language, 191, 215.
Old Saxon language, 211.
Old Slavonic language, 214.
-ology, 140.
Onomatopœia, the main effective principle in the origination of language, 425–6, 428–34.
Onomatopoetic theory of origin of language, 426.
or, 115.
Organism of language, what is meant by, 35, 46.
Origin of language, approximation to it by historical research, 397–8; doctrine of divine origin, in what sense alone true, 399–403 ; due to an external inducement, the desire of communication, 403–5; language not originated by thought, but by men for the uses of thought, 405–21; characteristic mental action of men, leading to it, 414–18, 438–40; beginnings of language, of what kind, 421–6; exemplified in beginnings of Indo-European language, 250–61; various theories to account for their production, 426–7; onomatopœia, or imitation of natural sounds, the main efficient principle, 427–34, 437.

Orochon, Tungusic tribes, 312.
Oscan language, 165, 220.
Osmanli Turkish, 314.
Ossetic language, 192, 224.
Ossianic poems, 217.
Ostiaks, language of, 309.
Otomi language, 348 note.
Ottoman Turkish, 314.
ought, owed, owned, 111.

P, the letter, derivation of, 465.
pagan, 131.
page, 387.
Palatal series of articulations, 91.
Pali language, 225
Papuans, language of, 339.
parchment, 130.
Parsis, and their language, 222–3.
Passives, origin of, in Indo-European language, 268.
Past time, Indo-European verbal forms indicating, 267–8.
Pazend language, 223.
Pegu, language of, 336.
Pehlevi language, 223.
Permian language, 309.
Permutation of consonants in Germanic languages, 97–8.
Persian or Iranian branch of Indo-European languages, 192, 198, 222–4.
Person, verbal endings of, their origin, 75, 266–7, 303, 319; their loss in English, 75–7; they distinguish gender in Semitic, 303; double form of first person in Polynesian languages, 339.
Peru, its culture, 347; its mode of writing, 450.
Peshito, Syriac Bible-version, 298.
Petra, inscriptions of, 299.
petroleum, 146.
Phenician language, 294–5, 297; alphabet of, 461–2; its diffusion, 462–3.
Phonetic change, 27–31, 42–3, 51, 69–98; how brought about, 28, 42, 69; most rife in compound forms, 70; aids the constructive processes of language, 73–4; its destructive action, 74–87 ; conversion of sounds into one another, 87–94; this dependent on the mode of physical production of sounds, 87–91; its causes only partially explainable, 95–7; permutation of consonants, peculiar phonetic change in Germanic languages, 97–8.
Phonetic principle in writing, its development in Egyptian writing, 454; its introduction into Chinese, 456; phonetic cuneiform, 460 ; steps of

development of a purely phonetic alphabet, 460–63.

Phonetic spelling for English, 467–70.

Phrases, formation of, 116.

Physical causes, their effect on language, 138, 152–3.

Physical evidence of race, compared with linguistic, 370–82, 397.

Physical sciences, analogies of linguistic science with, 46–7, 52.

Physical structure of men does not determine their language, 371–2.

Physical terms converted to intellectual and moral, 111–13.

Picture-writing, 450–53 ; its analogy with onomatopoetic speech, 451.

Plan of this work, 8–10.

-ple, 62.

please, 113.

Plural, irregular and regular in English, 78–9, 82–3; in Indo-European language, 272–3; in Scythian, 319; pluralizing words in Chinese, 335.

Polabian language, 214.

Polish language, 191, 214.

Polynesia, languages of, 337–40.

Polysynthetic structure* of American languages, 348–9; of Basque, 354; traces of it in Hungarian, 349; polysynthetic class, 363.

pono (Latin), derivatives of, in English, 120–21.

Pooh-pooh theory of origin of language, 426.

Portuguese language, 189, 219.

possess, 112.

Possessive case in English, 77, 82, 274.

post, 107.

Pott, Professor A. F., referred to, 5.

Prakrit languages, 225.

preach, 262.

Prefixes, their rarity in Indo-European language, 292; their prevalence in Polynesian, 339 ; in African, 344–5.

Prepositions, in Indo-European language, 274, 276, 292.

Present tense in Indo-European language, special theme of, 269.

priest, 102.

Process of linguistic growth, what it is, 154.

Processes of linguistic growth — see Change, linguistic.

Pronominal roots, Indo-European, 258–9; whether primitive, 261.

Pronouns, their nature, 258; derivation, in Indo-European language, 258–9; declension, 275; part played by pronouns in form-making, 266, 271, 290,
303, 319; pronouns as evidences of Indo-European unity, 194; examples, 196.

Proper names, derivation of, 105.

propose, 112.

Provençal language, 164, 218, 219.

Punic language, 297, 298.

Pushto language — see Afghan.

Q, the letter, derivation of, 465, 466.

queer, 113.

Quippos, Peruvian substitute for writing, 450.

R, the letter, derivation of, 465.

Rabbinic Hebrew, 297.

Race, relation of language to, 14, 160–61, 371–2; value of language as evidence of, 370–76, 381.

Races, different advantage gained from language by, 446–7.

Rask, Professor Rasmus, referred to, 5.

Rate of linguistic change, its variety and the circumstances affecting it, 31–2, 137–9, 148–53.

read, 80.

Reason and instinct, 438–9.

red tape, 125.

Reduplication, in Indo-European verb, 267–8; in Polynesian, 338–9.

Reflectiveness, different degrees of, in the processes of word-making, 40–41, 50–51, 121–4.

Reflexive or middle forms of Indo-European verbs, 268.

reign, 468.

Relational and auxiliary words, 117–20 ; in monosyllabic languages, 335–7.

Relationship, names of, as signs of Indo-European unity, 195; examples, 196.

Relative words, their derivation, 114.

reliable, 40–41.

Renan, M. Ernest, referred to, vii. note, 177 note, 284–6.

reproach, 113.

Rhæto-Romanic language, 189, 218.

right, 113.

Rig-Veda, 226.

Romaic, or Modern Greek, language, 221.

Romanic languages, their origin, 165–8, 189 ; age, literature, etc., 218–19 ; futures of, 118.

romantic, 131.

Roots, monosyllabic, the germs of Indo-European language, 255–66, 279–86; their sufficiency, 257; their division into pronominal and verbal, 258–9,

261; examples, 259; their significance, 259–60, 285; how far absolutely primitive, 261–4; difficulties and objections answered, 256–7, 260–66, 279–86; development of inflective speech from them, 266–77, 286; roots at the basis of all linguistic development, 289, 397; triliteral Semitic roots, 301; fixedness of Scythian roots, 317; roots of Polynesian language, 338; of Egyptian, 342; roots of Chinese and other monosyllabic languages, their words also, 330–32, 334–7; various treatment of roots, in languages of different structure, 360; futility of comparison of roots of different families, 392–4; roots, how originated, 426–34; of what character and office, 423–6; their scantiness at the outset, 434.

rubber, 130.

Russian language, 191, 214; its synthetic character, 281.

Ruthenian language, 214.

-s, as ending, in English, of third person singular present of verbs, 63, 93, 267; of possessive case, 82; of plural, 82.

Sabean language, 299.

Sabellian or Sabine language, 220.

Samaritan language, 297.

Samoyedic branch of Scythian language, 309–10.

Sanskrit language, 150, 192, 225–9; its intrusion into India, 201; its importance to Indo-European philology, 4, 228–9.

Santal language, 327.

Sassanian inscriptions, 223.

Scandinavian group of Germanic languages, 188, 210, 212.

Schlegels, the brothers August Wilhelm and Friedrich von, referred to, 5.

Schleicher, Professor August, quoted or referred to, vi., 47 note, 163 note, 200, 203, 214 note, 272 note, 303 note, 331 note; his system of morphological notation explained, 364–7.

schooner, 38.

Science of language — see Linguistic science.

Scythian or Altaic family of languages, 308–21, 324–28; its branches, their age and literature, and history of the races speaking them, 308–15; uncertainty of the tie connecting them, 315–16, 320–21, 324; characteristic structural features, 316–20.

second, 108–9.

Semitic alphabet, 461–3.

Semitic family of languages, 234, 294–308; its branches, their age and literature, and history of the races speaking them, 294–300; characteristic structural features, 300–306, 360–61; triliteral roots, 301–3; internal flexion, 301, 361; conjugation, 303; declension, 304; syntax, 304; stiffness of meaning and persistence of form in Semitic words, 304–5; asserted connection, with this family, of Egyptian and other African dialects, 306–7, 343; of Indo-European family, 307, 394.

Semivowels, 91.

Servian language, 191, 214.

seven, 196.

Shah-Nameh, Persian epic of Firdusi, 223, 325.

shall and will, 86, 118.

Shelter, analogy between language and, 401–3.

Shemitic family — see Semitic.

Shi-King, Chinese classic, 332.

-ship, 60.

Shoshonee language, 350.

Siamese language, 336.

Sibilants, 91.

Sigismund of Germany, as language-maker, 36.

Signification of words, changes of, 100–123.

Silent letters in English words, 28.

Sinai, inscriptions of, 299.

Sioux language, 350.

Siryanian language, 309.

sister, 387.

Skipetar language — see Albanian.

slave, 131.

Slavic or Slavonic branch of Indo-European languages, 191, 213–15.

Slovakian language, 214.

Slovenian language, 214.

smith, 105.

Smith, 105.

Smithsonian Institution, 353.

Social nature of man, relation of speech to, 403–5, 440–41.

Sonant and surd letters, 91; their exchanges, 92–3.

Sorbian language, 214.

sound, 387.

Sounds, articulate — see Articulate.

South-African family of languages, 344–5.

sovereign, 468.

spake, 29.

Spanish language, 189, 219; German and Arabic elements in, 168.
Spirants, 91; their derivation, 92.
spirit, 112.
splash, 425.
State languages, so called, 363.
Steinthal, Professor H., referred to, vi., 338 note, 367, 448 note, 450 note.
Structure, characteristic, of different families of language, 291-4, 357-69.
Study of language — see Linguistic science.
subject, 112.
Subjunctive mood, origin of, 268; loss of, in English, 86-7.
substantial, 112.
Substantive verb, derivation of, 115; wanting in Semitic, 304.
such, 57.
Suffixes, how produced, 57-64; their universal presence in Indo-European words, 65, 292; primary and secondary, 255.
sun, 103-4.
Suras, language of, 327.
Surd and sonant letters, 91; their exchanges, 92.
sure, 111.
Swabian dialect of Old High-German, 211; of Middle High-German, 163, 212.
Swedish language, 212.
Swift, Dean, caricature of etymological processes by, 389-90.
sycophant, 130.
Syllabic modes of writing, 460-61.
Syllable, nature of, 89.
Symbolism, signs of, in Semitic word-formation, 302 ; in beginnings of speech, 430.
Symbols, forerunners of writing, 449.
sympathy, 112.
Synonymous words, 110.
Syriac language, 294, 297, 298, 306; alphabet, its diffusion, 313, 462.
Syro-Arabian family — see Semitic.

Talmuds, 298.
Tamil language, 326.
Tamulian languages, 326.
Targums, 298.
Tartaric or Tataric family — see Scythian.
Tartar and *Tatar*, 38.
Technical vocabularies, their relation to a language, 19, 23, 156.
telegram, 40.
telegraph, 83, 146.
Telinga or Telugu language, 326.

Tenses, development of Indo-European, 266-70; Semitic, 303; Scythian, 320; modern preterits in Germanic languages, 79-82, 117; English perfects and futures, 117-19; Romanic futures, 118.
Terminology, artificial production of a, 122.
-th, ending of third person singular present in English verbs, 63, 93, 267.
-th, noun suffix, 64.
than, 115.
thank, 111.
that, pronoun, 430.
that, conjunction, 114.
the, 114, 115.
thou, 196.
Thought, relation of language and, 403-21; the two not identical, 405-11; not coterminous, 411; how far thought is carried on in language, 412-13; its processes aided by speech, 417-21; such thought as ours only made possible by expression, 420; insufficiency of language as expression of thought, 20, 109-11, 406-7.
three, 196.
throng, 262.
Tiberius of Rome, as language-maker, 36.
Tibetan language, 337.
Time, peculiar treatment of, in Semitic verb, 303.
to, infinitive sign, 119.
topgallantsails, 72.
Tradition, the means by which a language is kept in existence, 23; its defects, and their consequences, 27-32; causes aiding its strictness, 148-51; tradition of speech and knowledge together, 441-5; its guiding influence on the mind, 445-6.
Triliterality of Semitic roots, 301-3.
Troubadours, songs of, 218.
true, 64, 179.
truth, 64.
Tudas, language of, 327.
Tulu language, 326.
Tungusic branch of Scythian language, 312.
Turanian family, so called, 309; origin and first application of the name, 325.
turkey, 130.
Turkish branch of Scythian language, 191-2; divisions, age, literature, etc., 310-11, 313-14; characteristic structural features, 198, 318-20.
Turkomans, language of, 311.
two, 196.

U, the letter, derivation of, 465.
Ugrian, or Finno-Hungarian, branch of Scythian language, 309, 320, 361; age, literature, etc., 314.
Uigur Turkish language, 311, 313; alphabet, 313, 462.
Ulfilas, Gothic bishop, 213.
Umbrian language, 165, 220.
understand, 113, 133.
Unity of the human race, not demonstrable by evidence of language, 383–94.
Ural-Altaic family — see Scythian.
Urdu language, 224.
Usage, the sole standard of correct speech, 14, 32, 36–40, 128; good and bad usage, 16–17, 22.
Usbeks, language of, 311.

V, the letter, derivation of, 464, 465, 466.
Value of language, 440–47.
Variety of expression for same thought, 407–9.
Variety of human races, not demonstrable by evidence of language, 384–5.
Vater, referred to, 4.
Vedas, Hindu scripture, and their language, 225–7.
Vei language and alphabet, 346.
vend, 262.
Vendidad, geographical notices in, 201 note.
Verbal roots, 259.
Verbs and verbal forms, their development in Indo-European languages, 266–70; Semitic verb, 303; Scythian, 319–20; Polynesian, 338; question whether verbs or nouns are earliest, 423–6.
verity, 178.
viz., 459.
Vocabulary, different extent of, in persons of different age and condition, 18–20; changes of, 25–7; its increase, 25–6, 41, 139; its reduction, 27, 98–100, 139; impregnation with fuller knowledge, 123, 141; enrichment by borrowing, 143–5.
Vocabulary, English, its extent, 18; part of it used by different classes, 18–20; found in Shakspeare and Milton, 23; its changes. 25–7, 140–47.
Vocabulary, primitive Indo-European, attempted restoration of, 205–6.
Voice, as means of expression, 421–3.
Volga, Mongol tribes on, 312.
Volscian language, 220.
Voltaire on etymology, 386.

Vowel and consonant, relation of, 89, 91.
Vowels, changes of value of, 94–5; classification and harmonic sequence of, in Scythian languages, 318; imperfect designation of, in some alphabets, 461–3.

W, the letter, derivation of, 466.
Wallachian language, 189, 218.
was, 115.
Wedgwood, Professor H., referred to, vi. note.
Welsh language, 190, 217–18.
which, 57.
who, relative, 115.
whole, 242.
will and *shall*, 86, 118.
Woguls, language of, 309.
women, 468.
Words, mere signs, not depictions of ideas, 20–22, 32, 70–71, 111; the sole tie between words and ideas a mental association, 14, 32, 409; words posterior to the conceptions they represent, 125–6, 411–12; their value to us dependent on conventional usage, not etymology, 14, 128–9, 132–4, 404, 409; how far we think in or with words, 410–20; word-making a historical process, 126–9; history of words, why studied, 129; linguistic science founded on their study, 54–5; its method, 238–9, 247–8; words made up of elements originally independent, 55–67; their phonetic changes, 69–98; their changes of meaning, 100–121; identity of words and roots in monosyllabic languages, 330–31.
work, 30.
Wotiak language, 309.
Writing, auxiliary and complement of speech, 447: parallelisms between its origin and history and those of speech, 448, 449, 451, 453, 456, 457, 458, 459; desire of communication its primary impulse, 448; not at first connected with and subordinated to spoken language, 449; its forerunners and historical beginnings, 449–50; picture-writing, 450–52; hieroglyphs, 452 seq.; Egyptian writing, 452–5; Chinese, 455–9; cuneiform, 459–60; syllabic, 460–61; Semitic or Phenician, 461–3; Greek and its derivatives, 463 seq.; Latin, 465; English, 466.
wrong, 113.

wrought, 30, 111.

X, the letter, derivation of, 466.

Y, the letter, derivation of, 464, 466.
Yakut language, 310–11.
Yamato, Japanese dialect, 328.
ye, you, 30.
Yenisean language, 355.

Yukagiri language, 330.

Z, the letter, derivation of, 466.
Zend-avesta, 201 note, 222.
Zend language, 150, 222.
Zingian family — see South-African.
Zoroaster, 222.
zounds, 277.
Zulu language, 344–5.

CPSIA information can be obtained at www.ICGtesting.com
Printed in the USA
LVOW06s0839170913

352697LV00001B/51/P